Perl

A Beginner's Guide

Perl
A Beginner's Guide

R. Allen Wyke and
Donald Thomas

Osborne/**McGraw-Hill**

Berkeley New York St. Louis San Francisco
Auckland Bogotá Hamburg London Madrid
Mexico City Milan Montreal New Delhi Panama City
Paris São Paulo Singapore Sydney Tokyo Toronto

Osborne/**McGraw-Hill**
2600 Tenth Street
Berkeley, California 94710
U.S.A.

For information on translations or book distributors outside the U.S.A., or to arrange bulk purchase discounts for sales promotions, premiums, or fund-raisers, please contact Osborne/**McGraw-Hill** at the above address.

Perl: A Beginner's Guide

1234567890 AGM AGM 01987654321

ISBN 0-07-212957-3

Publisher Brandon A. Nordin
Vice President & Associate Publisher Scott Rogers
Acquisitions Editor Rebekah Young
Project Editor Elizabeth Seymour
Acquisitions Coordinator Paulina Pobocha
Technical Editor Brian Jepson
Copy Editor Marcia Baker
Proofreader Stephany Otis
Indexer Karen Arrigoni
Illustrators Lyssa Wald and Michael Mueller
Computer Designers Gary Corrigan and Roberta Steele
Series Design Gary Corrigan
Cover Series Design Gregg Scott
Cover Illustration Kevin Curry

This book was composed with Corel VENTURA™ Publisher.

About the Authors

R. Allen Wyke, Director of Product Technology at Engage, has expert experience in Perl, XML, and JavaScript. He is the co-author of several computer and Internet-related books, including The Perl 5 Programmer's Reference and Pure JavaScript. Wyke has also penned columns and articles for SunWorld and ITworld.com publications.

Donald B. Thomas is a software design engineer at Engage Technologies. He works extensively with Perl, WML, XML, Java, and JavaScript.

Contents at a Glance

Contents

Introduction

Welcome to *Perl: A Beginner's Guide*! First, we want you to know how excited we are that you've given us the opportunity to show, teach, and expose you to the Perl programming language. Without beginners, there would be no intermediate or advanced programmers. You are the next generation that will carry the Perl language well into the twenty-first century and, hopefully, teach future generations what you've learned.

Perl has had quite a history, and those who program in the language are almost cult-like in their following. This is a close community that reaches out to spread the word about Perl—a community waiting with open arms to welcome you as a beginner and help nurture you through your evolution. Enough about Perl programmers for now, though. Let's introduce the book.

What we tried to do here is not only teach you the Perl language and programming techniques, but also help you learn how to operate within the Perl community. We want you to become an evangelist for Perl. We want you to tell your fellow students, coworkers, or friends who operate in the computer world about Perl and how wonderful it is. We want you to move from a beginner, through the intermediate stages, and on to become an advanced programmer. Perl is a great language, and we want this book to be your first step in understanding how to program in it.

Who Should Read This Book?

Well, for starters, if the title didn't give it away, this book is for beginners. But there are different kinds of beginners, so we'll clarify.

Perl: A Beginner's Guide is a book both for those beginning to program in the Perl language and those who are beginning to program in any language. So many beginner books today lose sight of the basic concepts and semantics that go along with programming, and our aim was not to do this. We want to build and strengthen your programming skills as you learn the language. Our approach is similar to that of learning grammar and spelling of the English (or whatever your language may have been) language in grade school. The grammar and spelling are underlying characteristics and requirements across all languages, but this book teaches you those in the Perl language.

Your next question might be, "Well, I learned how to do some programming in a previous life and I don't want to learn those underlying skills again. Is this book still for me?" In one word—absolutely. True, you might read through some sections faster than a first-time programmer, but most sections have Perl at the heart of their topics. And, like any language, just because an idea is present doesn't mean it's implemented the same way in different languages. In this book, we try to show you the Perl way so, if you are aware of other methods, the book can help clarify this for you.

If you aren't a beginning programmer or a beginning Perl programmer, then you may have been exposed to Perl to some degree. Is this book also for you? Again, the answer is absolutely. When we first learned Perl, we thought we knew it all just because we could open files, look for occurrences of words or strings, and write the output back to a browser or another file. Well, there's much more to Perl than that, and we touch on all these topics.

Finally, what if you have been programming in Perl quite a bit or you are an advanced programmer? Is this book for you? If you fall into one of these categories, you may need to choose another book. If you want to pick up in-depth details on the language in a short period of time for a project, this isn't the book for you. If you are still reading at this point, then we assume you bought the book and you want to read it. For you who have made it this far, let's take a few minutes to discuss what we plan to cover during our time together.

Organization of the Modules

This book is in two primary sections with 13 chapters, or "modules," as we call them. The first section gets you up and running with the Perl language. It gives you a list history and some operating environment information, and it discusses many of the basic concepts that need to be covered so you understand both Perl and programming in general.

The second section of the book builds on the first by applying what has been learned to specific tasks in Perl. This section guides you through manipulating files and directories, to building Web application programs and connecting to databases. We end the section with a module that touches on some advanced Perl topics.

Now, let's take a closer look at what makes up each section.

Part 1: Getting Started

The first section of the book focuses on getting you started with the Perl programming language. Within this section are five modules: Module 1, "Introduction to Perl," introduces you to the Perl language, provides some history, gives you information on the environments in which it works, and leads you through installing it. Module 2, "Scalar Data and Operators," teaches you about the data types in Perl and how you can use the various operators to accomplish your decision-making tasks.

Module 3, "Control Structures," is the first chapter that applies some of what you have learned. It exposes you to conditional and control statements, and shows you how to handle nested loops. Module 4, "Arrays, Lists, and Hashes," shows you different methods of storing data. Module 5, "Program Flow and Subroutines," concludes the section by looking at how you should organize your programs and shows you how to use subroutines.

Part 2: Applying Your Knowledge

The second section of the book puts you right to work. Module 6, "Working with Files and Directories," teaches you about opening file and directory streams, and how to read and write from them. Module 7, "Regular Expressions," covers the topic of pattern matching, which many argue is the single strongest point within Perl.

Module 8, "Packages and Modules," not only shows you how to use Perl package libraries (if you don't know what we're talking about, don't worry!), but also how to build them. Module 9, "Interacting with Databases Using the Perl DBI," shows you how to connect to databases for all your data repository access needs. And Module 10, "Writing CGI Programs," ends the focus on doing specific things in Perl by showing you how to build CGI programs to use when you create your Web sites.

Module 11, "System Functions," takes a slightly different objective by addressing the topic of system functions in the Perl language. We discuss the different system functions and how they can be run from the commandline or within the Perl environment. Module 12, "Error Messages and Debugging," takes you through the jungle of debugging code and problems.

The final module, Module 13, "Advanced Features and Concepts," is where you can have some fun. You've basically finished the book at this point and this module discusses object-oriented programming, PerlScript, and the Perl/Tk for creating GUI applications. All interesting stuff.

Writing Conventions

Before you start flipping pages and learning about Perl, we want to discuss the writing conventions used in this book. We want you to know what you can expect from each of the modules. Special elements are contained in the *Beginner's Guide* series, a series specifically designed to teach beginners about a particular topic. The elements are as follows:

- **Goals** Each module starts with a list of four or five goals. These goals give you insight into what you can accomplish by reading the module.
- **Ask the Expert** Within each of the modules, you find this section, which consists of questions and answers to help you understand some of the more complex topics of the Perl language.
- **1-Minute Drill** Ahhhhh, drills! The 1-Minute Drills, which are also within each of the modules, are quick and to-the-point questions that test you on something you just read.

- **Notes and Hints** These give you a bit more information or advice on a topic. Within each module, you can find Notes and Hints that are interlaced within the paragraphs to give you a heads-up on problem areas or a URL for an online resource.
- **Projects** Because many of us learn better through examples, each module will contain projects. Some of these projects will take you through a specific task and some will have you writing code – both positioned to teach you, through examples. If we provided code in these Projects, you can also access it from www.osborne.com to save you some time typing.
- **Mastery Check** Each of the modules ends with a Master Check. This is a quiz of five to ten questions to test what you have just read in the module. This gives you the chance to make sure you learned all the important points we focused on and that you met the previously defined goals of the module.

In addition to the structural components of the book, you also see other conventions used to alert you to new terms or syntax keywords. To help you understand what each of these mean, read the following list:

- **New Terms and Commands** New terms and actual system commands are in italics. For example, when using a new term, we might say, "In Perl, these libraries are called *packages*," where packages is a new term. When we refer to something you are suppose to type, look for boldface, which may look like, " . . . type **perl -v** at the command line to . . . ".
- **Perl Keywords** Whenever we use Courier New as the font on a set of characters within the body of a paragraph, this means the characters make up a Perl keyword. For instance, we may say, ". . . to use the `chomp()` function, you simply need to . . ."
- **User Entered Placeholder** If there's a place where we need to show, for instance, that a function takes an arbitrary argument, this appears in boldface, and `Courier New` font AND bold. This is to show A) we're talking about actual Perl code, and B) you should replace the part in boldface with whatever value is appropriate. So, for instance, we might say, " . . . it must be accessed using the `$_[`**`index`**`]` format. . . ." In this example, you would put the appropriate value in place of **index**.

- **STRONG Emphasis** If there's a case where we want to emphasis something strongly, we use all caps. For example, we might say, ". . . you MUST document. . . "
- **User Actions** This refers to things such as selecting an item from a menu. In these instances, we again use boldface to signify what you're selecting. An example might be, "To launch the Run dialog box, click the **Start** button and select the **Run** menu item."
- **Module and Section References** We came up with the following scheme from referencing other modules and sections within those modules. We give the module number followed by the name of the module in quotation marks. If we need to refer to a specific section in that module, we also enclose the name of that section in quotes. For example, " . . . look in Module 13, "Advanced Features and Concepts" under the section "Object-Oriented Programming" for more information on. . . ."

That's it! Now you should be ready to pick up this book and fully understand, not only the information in it, but also how the book is written. Good luck, and we'll see you at the end of the book!

R. Allen Wyke
Donald B. Thomas

Part 1

Getting Started

Module 1

Introduction to Perl

The Goals of This Module

- ✓ Learn where Perl came from and where it is going
- Understand how to install Perl and how it works
- Practice good programming techniques within the Perl language
- Create your first Perl script and see it run

Welcome to *Perl: A Beginner's Guide.* Your purchase of this book shows your desire and dedication to learn one of the most widely used programming languages around today. Long before Java or JavaScript invaded the Internet and surrounding scenes, and even before the Web was born, Perl had a strong hold in its community. From automating UNIX administration tasks, to performing the routine parsing of files, Perl has been used as a true utility language.

Note

For the purpose of Perl, when UNIX is referred to, the reference is generic, to all flavors, including UNIX-compatible operating systems such as Linux. If the system has a noticeable difference that needs to be pointed out, then this is done.

Today, Perl, which means *Practical Extraction and Reporting Language,* is used in many new and creative ways, in addition to the good old reasons. *Common Gateway Interface* (CGI), file processing, Microsoft Windows scripting, *graphical user interfaces* (GUI), database access, you name it—Perl can do it. And, in addition to being a versatile and useful language, Perl is relatively easy to learn.

Note

When we speak of the Windows platform here, we are referring to the Windows 95, Windows 98, Windows Millennium edition (Me), Windows NT, and Windows 2000 editions (this is abbreviated 95/98/Me/NT/2000). If you want to run Perl on the Windows 3.*x* platform, then you must run a version that is compatible with MS-DOS.

True, some complex angles exist to Perl and some concepts may be difficult to understand, but you can ease into those. The purpose of this book is to start you on the path toward becoming an accomplished Perl programmer, **not** to scare you off with hard-to-understand terminology and "system talk." Do note, though, that becoming a Perl programmer is more than just scripting some code—it is a perspective on how to solve everyday problems, tackle cumbersome issues, and live the good life with an easy, yet powerful, programming language.

So enough talk, let's get started! In this first module, you learn a bit of background and the foundation for the experience you will gather while you read this book. You learn some history on the language and some good programming techniques. You even start and complete your first Perl script! The objective is simple: to introduce you to the language in an easy to understand, and nonthreatening manner.

Note

Perl programs are commonly called *scripts,* so the terms "programs" and "scripts" are used interchangeably in this book. Treat them as the same.

The History

As mentioned in the opening paragraphs, Perl is one of the older programming languages when it comes to those commonly discussed for Web uses. Its origin dates back to 1987 and, since then, Perl has seen four more major versions, and one semimajor release. Today, Perl boasts one of the largest groups of programmers and you find the loyalty within the tight group of users matches that of Linux, OS/2, and the Mac OS.

Because of its rich history, you should know some Perl background. So, in this first section of the book, you learn about the early days of Perl, and then move into version 4, next learn about the advances version 5 added, and then learn about the latest and greatest version of the language: Perl 5.6.

The Beginning

Larry Wall, the author of the language, first released Perl to the usenet group comp.sources on October 18, 1987. This new language, which was distributed free of charge by Mr. Wall, was derived from the C programming language and was further influenced by languages such as BASIC, awk, sed, and the UNIX shell. Perl took the best of all these worlds and wrapped them into a single, functional language.

People, with little or no programming experience, were able to pick it up quickly and start programming with Perl. In addition to its ease of learning, Perl was simply a useful language. From the beginning, Perl had an unbelievable capability to manipulate text, files, and system processes. This free, easy, and useful approach allowed the Perl language to catch on quickly.

Today, Perl is maintained by a core group of volunteers (the "Perl Porters") and programmers around the world. Like Linux, Mozilla, sendmail, or any other open source effort, Perl has tapped the world as its development team, and leverages the knowledge of many to provide us with the best possible language for our work.

Up to Perl 4

After Perl 1.0 came Perl 2.0, which was released on June 5, 1988. By this time, the number of Perl programmers had grown, as did the use of the language. Many different types of programmers were using Perl for everyday tasks and individuals within major corporations started promoting the language.

A year and a half passed before the world saw Perl 3.0, which was released October 18, 1989, some two years after 1.0 hit the wire. With this release, Perl was first distributed under the GNU *General Public License* (GPL) version 1.0, which allows for the distribution of free software. By this time Perl had taken off.

Thousands of programmers were using it and the Web, which was in its infant stage, really gave Perl a boost. Perl had been widely used by UNIX administrators, but was quickly becoming the standard for writing CGI scripts for processing form data sent on the Internet. CGI is covered in Module 10, so it won't be discussed in detail here but, do note, it was a significant module in the history of Perl.

Then, in March of 1991, Perl 4.0 was released under the GPL as well as the new Perl Artistic License. This is the version of the language with which many Perl programmers started. Perl was now a fairly mature language that had a robust set of functionality, although it did suffer from some performance problems.

Tip

For more information on the GNU Licenses see their Web site at http://www.gnu.org. There you can read information on the GNU GPL.

Perl 4 was the last version seen for three-and-a-half years as the language underwent a complete rewrite. This doesn't mean progress wasn't made during those years, though—in fact, this was the time Perl began to reach out and be noticed.

In January 1992 Matthias Neeracher released the first version of Perl for the Macintosh (MacPerl 4.0.2). By the end of the year, MacPerl was up to version 4.0.5, which included support for *Data Base Management* (*DBM*) and sockets. 1993 saw continued work on MacPerl, and the final version of the core Perl 4 language, Perl 4.036. The final version of MacPerl, 4.1.8, which implemented Perl 4.036, soon followed.

Hint

Don't let the differences in versions here confuse you. This is discussed more in a few pages in the section titled "Platform Support."

Introducing Perl 5

By this time, the Perl community was ready for a new version of the language. Ports were popping up all over the place, database access was available, and additional prebuilt scripts were abundant. However, it was time for a new version of the language.

In October 1994 Perl 5 was released. This version had many enhancements and took the language to the next level. Perl 5 was the first release that pushed this once-simple scripting language beyond simple administrative tasks and into a more powerful spotlight. Here are some of the enhancements that were added:

- Complete rewrite of the interpreter to increase speed, efficiency, and functionality.
- Support for modules, which lets programmers develop their own "libraries" that could be included into scripts by others.
- Object-oriented features, which allowed for the construction of true objects, and paved the way for concepts such as inheritance, encapsulation, and polymorphism (don't worry if these terms scare you; they are discussed more in Module 13).
- Increased diagnostics and warnings generated for coding techniques.

During the Perl 5 era, the release of Perl for Win32 was also seen—the Microsoft Windows port of Perl. This port, which was funded by Microsoft for inclusion in its Windows NT Resource Kit, was developed by Hip Communications. Dick Hardt, the person at Hip who is widely known as the driving force behind getting Perl for Win32 started, went on to start ActiveWare Internet Corporation and ActiveState Tool Corporation. Since then, Perl for Win32 has followed Hardt, where it is now maintained, free-of-charge to the public, by ActiveState.

What 5.6 Brings to the Table

You are now up to the present, where in March 2000, Perl 5.6 was released to the world. Besides a new syntax for versioning and declaring subroutine attributes, Perl 5.6 adds a lot of little features that programmers have been asking for that weren't in previous editions. This includes, but isn't limited to, the following:

Note

Wondering what happened to Perl 5.5? Well, 5.5 was the beta version of 5.6. So, you are correct—no 5.5 was released as a final version.

- Unicode and UTF-8 support
- 64-bit support
- Files larger than 2GB now supported
- And even more diagnostics

For those of you who may have some programming experience already, you might also be interested in these higher-level enhancements:

- Lexically scoped warning categories
- The open( ) function has had an argument added
- pack( ) function enhancements

Hint

Once you install Perl 5.6, which you do later in this module, you can refer to the perldelta document, which contains differences between versions, for more information on these items.

Now that's enough history; let's move on to supported platforms. You probably are ready to start writing code and this will take you a step closer.

Note

At press time for this book, Larry Wall had just announced Perl 6.0, which will be a complete rewrite. Check http://www.perl.com for information.

1-Minute Drill

- **Who invented the Perl programming language?**
- **What does Perl stand for?**

Platform Support

The number of supported platforms is one reason Perl caught on so well. Even though Perl was originally designed on and for UNIX systems, it wasn't long before support for other popular platforms followed. Some of the ports were one-offs that took the source code and made it work on a particular operating system. Others took the functionality beyond the distribution and added features specific to a system. All in all, however, Perl has maintained a fairly consistent set of functionality across these systems and, even though differences exist, in many cases, a script on one system can run on another.

- **Larry Wall**
- **Actually stands for "Practical Extraction and Reporting Language," but if you hang around long enough in the Perl world, you may also see it referred to as the "Pathologically Eclectic Rubbish Lister."**

Before you learn about the supported platforms, we want to give you a better description of how the language is developed. Earlier in the module, Macintosh and Windows versions were discussed, and you saw that the versioning across these systems differed. The best guide is to think of Perl as having a "standard distribution," which is the most up-to-date source code that's considered stable. Supported platforms, such as on Mac OS and Windows, are implementations, or prebuilt binaries, of this distribution and sometimes have their own versioning system. This is often done because those ports have added features that are specific to the operating system.

Note

To help clarify what's discussed in this book, we always try to include the official distribution version when speaking of these other ports and other versioning schemas.

In talking about ports for Perl, we are going to separate out what we call the "Big Three," which refer to the Windows, UNIX, and the Mac OS versions of the language. We have also included a separate section that contains a list and information for other platforms that have been ported. For a current list of ports, you can always check http://www.perl.com CPAN-local/ports, which has a comprehensive guide of what is out and available for you.

Windows

Originally, two versions of Perl existed for the Windows 32-bit platform. One was the Perl for Win32 from ActiveState, which was mentioned earlier. And then, starting with Perl 5.004, the standard distribution of Perl included support for the Windows 32-bit platform. These two have many similarities because much of the standard distribution was based on ActiveState's work; however, there were some differences. Since then, however, these code bases have been merged and the result is ActivePerl, which is maintained by ActiveState.

The versioning of ActivePerl now usually has the same versioning as the standard distribution, but they currently also reference a "build" versioning system. The first version of ActivePerl, for instance, which

Platform	Notes
AIX	Starting with 4.3.3, Perl 5 ships standard with AIX
BSD/OS	Perl started shipping with BSD/OS as of version 4.1
Cygwin	5.005_03 is the current version you can download, but the platform is supported in the core Perl distribution
Debian	The distribution for this platform is maintained by Darren Stalder, however, ActiveState makes a package of ActivePerl that can be installed on a Debian system. 5.005_03 since Debian 2.2 and 5.004_04 since 2.1
DEC OSF/1	See Tru64
Digital UNIX	See Tru64
HP-UX	Supported in the Perl source distribution
IRIX	Perl 5.004_04 shipped with IRIX 6.5
Mac OS X	Standard component starting with the Developer Previews. Mac OS X 1.0 Server had Perl 5.005_3
NonStop-UX	This is really old, so you may want to try compiling from the Perl source distribution
OpenBSD	Perl shipped with OpenBSD 2.5 and 2.7 will ship with Perl 5.6.0
OpenLinux	Support contained within standard distribution
Red Hat	The distribution for this system is maintained by Red Hat, however, a distribution is available from ActiveState. 5.005_03 has been included since Red Hat 6.0
ReliantUNIX	You have to download this, but 5.003 shipped with SINIX 5.43. Also consider compiling the distribution
SINIX	See ReliantUNIX
Slackware	The Perl distribution has shipped since Slackware 2.5
Sun/Solaris	Support contained within standard distribution, but binaries are available from ActiveState and www.sunfreeware.com
SuSE	The Perl distribution has shipped since SuSE 6.0
Tru64	Starting with Tru64 5.0, Perl 5 ships with the OS. Formerly known as Digital UNIX, formerly known as DEC OSF/1

Table 1-1 **Flavors of UNIX That Can Run Perl**

supported Perl 5.6, was ActivePerl 5.6 Build 612. A day later, the good people at ActiveState found a minor error had been missed in the documentation and decided to build 613. It's all Perl 5.6 from your point of view, which is the focus of this book.

UNIX

UNIX was the platform that started it all. In fact, as you learn the Perl language, you can see UNIX characteristics and commands embedded deep within the language. This isn't a bad thing though, because if UNIX excels at anything, it's what can be accomplished with a simple shell script or commandline access. Table 1-1, on the preceding page, has a list of some of the supported UNIX flavors on which you can run Perl.

Mac OS

The current Macintosh version of Perl is one of the most interesting ports that you are going to hear about. As many of you out there that have used a Mac know, this particular platform is usually not thought of as an administrative type of operating system. Also, it has its own built-in scripting language called AppleScript that has an unbelievable amount of power, which begs the question, "why Perl?"

As previously mentioned, Perl programmers are a tight-knit group and having the capability to control systems and run scripts on about any platform is a powerful thing—so why not Mac? The Mac OS can also run a Web server, so the need certainly exists to build CGI scripts for those instances as well. And, if you are using a Macintosh and reading this book, then you already have a reason—just because.

Like the Windows platform, the Mac implementation of Perl has its own sort of versioning system. MacPerl didn't support every release of the standard distribution, so to model the versioning system of this Mac port after it wouldn't have been a wise choice. This is why you see MacPerl 4.1.8 implemented Perl 4.036, and the current release, MacPerl 5.2.0r4, supports Perl 5.004_04.

Others

Obviously, we don't want to discuss every single platform Perl can run on in this book. Sure, many different characteristics and items should be understood before programming on systems other than the Big Three, but this isn't something a beginner needs to worry about.

As good practice, and in case you are working on a system not previously discussed, however, we have included Table 1-2, which contains a list of common Perl ports. In doing so, we have also listed the current version and included any notes that could be relevant to your programming efforts on these systems.

Tip

To see a current version of this list, visit http://www.perl.com/CPAN-local/ports. Also expect all of these will be at 5.6.0 soon, or maybe even by the time you read this book.

Things You Need to Know

Before we start programming, you need to know a few things about the Perl language. The idea here is not to tell you everything about how the interpreter works or how it interacts with system calls—this is a beginner's book and you should walk away with a beginner's knowledge. You should also have an idea of what happens in the background and what you have to do to get up-and-running with Perl on your system. The focus here is on getting you started with Perl.

How It Works

First and foremost, you should understand Perl is an interpreted language, not a compiled one like C or C++. What this means is Perl programs are not compiled into binary (1s and 0s) before you can run them. In fact, you, as the programmer, don't compile Perl programs at all—you simply create a text file with your Perl code.

Perl programs are fed to an interpreter, which, ultimately, converts your code in byte code (which is done before it's run), and then runs it. By comparison, if you take a C program, you have to compile, or build, the program before you can even run it. And this building is specific to the operating system on which you want the application to run. So, if you want a program to run on Windows 2000, Mac OS 9, and Red Hat Linux 6.2, then you must compile it on each of these systems. Perl, on the other

Platform	Perl Version	Notes
Amiga	5.6.0	Starting with Perl 5.005, support for this platform has been included in the Perl source distribution
AS/400	5.005_02	
BeOS	5.6.0	Starting with Perl 5.005, support for this platform has been included in the Perl source distribution. However, BeOS 5 shipped with Perl 5.005_3
DOS	5.6.0	Supported in the Perl source distribution
EPOC/Psion	5.6.0	Supported in the Perl source distribution
LynxOS	5.6.0	Starting with Perl 5.005, support has been included in the standard Perl distribution
Mac OS	5.004_04	MacPerl 5.2.0r4 is the current version. The MacPerl maintainers are currently working on Perl 5.005 implementation
MPE/iX	5.6.0	Starting with Perl 5.005, support for this platform has been included in the distribution
NonStop	5.001m	This is really old, so you may want to try compiling from the Perl source distribution
OS/2	5.6.0	Supported in the Perl source distribution
OS390	5.6.0	Starting with Perl 5.005_02, support for this platform has been included in the Perl source distribution; however, 5.6.0 doesn't work on this platform according to some
PowerMAX	5.6.0	Starting with Perl 5.005, support for this platform has been included in the distribution
QNX	5.6.0	Support contained within standard distribution
Tandem	5.001m	This is really old, so you may want to try compiling from the Perl source distribution
VMS	5.6.0	Starting with Perl 5.005, support for this platform has been included in the Perl source distribution
VOS	5.6.0	Starting with Perl 5.005_03, support for this platform has been included in the Perl source distribution
Windows 95/98/ Me/NT/2000	5.6.0	Starting with Perl 5.005, support for this platform has been included in the Perl source distribution

Table 1-2 **List of Some of the Perl Ports and Their Current Versions**

hand, would simply let you run the same script on each system. True, your script may have to approach some of the tasks differently on each system (see Module 11 for more information), but you needn't compile.

Installing Perl

Perl is a free language, so having a version installed on your system is no more complicated than finding it and going through the installation process. Since many of you may have never installed Perl on a machine or may not have it, as the first project we wanted to step you through the installation process.

Project 1-1: Installing Perl

In this project, the objective is simple: to step through the installation process of the Perl interpreter. If you already have Perl on your system, this is a good chance to run through the steps again or to upgrade to 5.6 if you have an older version.

> **Hint**
>
> Want to know what version of Perl you have? We don't want to give away too much at this point, but if you know how to call the Perl interpreter, you can pass it the -v option to check the version. Here are some quick instructions on how that's done:
>
> **UNIX and Windows:** Assuming the Perl interpreter is in your path, simply type **perl –v** at a command line.
>
> **Macintosh:** Even though you could create a script with only the line "#!/usr/bin/perl -v" and run it, the easiest way is for you to start MacPerl, and then select About MacPerl... from the Apple menu. This displays a dialog box that contains the version (MacPerl version) and patchlevel (source distribution level).

Step-by-Step

Because installers do change, your instructions may vary slightly from what you read here. If the instructions vary in your case, be sure to read the INSTALL and/or README files for accurate instructions.

Note

Although binary distributions of Perl are available for the various flavors of UNIX and Linux, they won't be discussed here, but you will learn the basics of the building process for these systems. If you are a Linux user and you have a package manager, like RPM for Red Hat or DEB for Debian Linux, then you should use that application to install Perl. Because Perl is such an integral part of these and other flavors of Linux, you should be very careful about installing a new version over the one that came with your system.

Note

If you don't have administrator rights on your machine, you may not have the proper permissions to install Perl. You can try, but a chance exists that restrictions, such as account space, have been imposed. If you are unable to install, but still want to go through the process, talk with your system administrator or even load Linux on a home computer you may already have.

For UNIX:

1. Download the standard distribution source code from http://www.perl.com/pub/language/info/software.html. If this link is broken, start back at the main page (http://www.perl.com) and follow the links to software or download. The file you should be downloading will be named something like stable.tar.gz.
2. Unzip the file using the command **gzip -d stable.tar.gz**. This leaves a file called stable.tar. If you don't have the gzip program on your machine, you can obtain a copy at http://www.gnu.org.

Hint

Not sure if you have a copy of gzip on your machine? Type **find / -name gzip -print** at a command prompt to search all directories that you have access to for this program.

3. Next, untar the file using the command **tar -xvf stable.tar.** This leaves you with a directory called perl-5.6.0. If you are installing a newer version of Perl than 5.6.0, then your directory might have a different name. In either case, the contents of this directory look something like Figure 1-1.

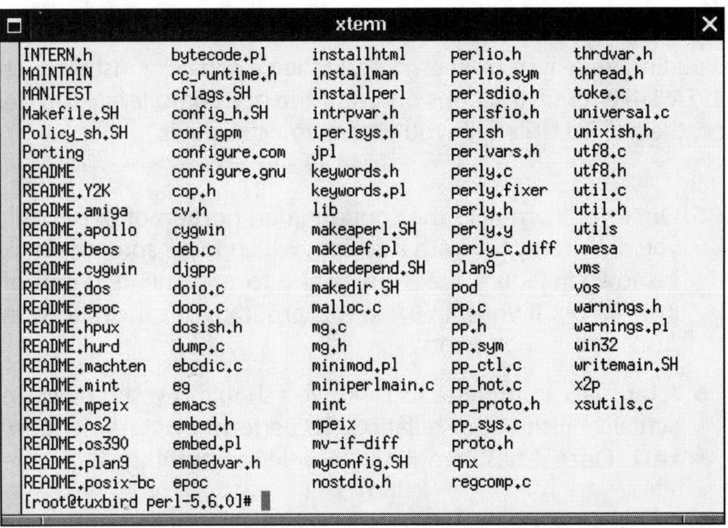

xterm
INTERN.h bytecode.pl installhtml perlio.h thrdvar.h
MAINTAIN cc_runtime.h installman perlio.sym thread.h
MANIFEST cflags.SH installperl perlsdio.h toke.c
Makefile.SH config_h.SH intrpvar.h perlsfio.h universal.c
Policy_sh.SH configpm iperlsys.h perlsh unixish.h
Porting configure.com jpl perlvars.h utf8.c
README configure.gnu keywords.h perly.c utf8.h
README.Y2K cop.h keywords.pl perly.fixer util.c
README.amiga cv.h lib perly.h util.h
README.apollo cygwin makeaperl.SH perly.y utils
README.beos deb.c makedef.pl perly_c.diff vmesa
README.cygwin djgpp makedepend.SH plan9 vms
README.dos doio.c makedir.SH pod vos
README.epoc doop.c malloc.c pp.c warnings.h
README.hpux dosish.h mg.c pp.h warnings.pl
README.hurd dump.c mg.h pp.sym win32
README.machten ebcdic.c minimod.pl pp_ctl.c writemain.SH
README.mint eg miniperlmain.c pp_hot.c x2p
README.mpeix emacs mint pp_proto.h xsutils.c
README.os2 embed.h mpeix pp_sys.c
README.os390 embed.pl mv-if-diff proto.h
README.plan9 embedvar.h myconfig.SH qnx
README.posix-bc epoc nostdio.h regcomp.c
[root@tuxbird perl-5.6.0]#

Figure 1-1 **Contents of your directory after extracting the Perl distribution**

4. The next step involves configuring the build process. Because the number of options for this process is too great to outline in detail here (this could literally be 100 pages), we will simply point you in the right direction.

   A. First, you need to look at the INSTALL file for detailed installation instructions. The actual process you need to read about is referred to as the configuration process.

   B. In addition to this file, you should check to see if a README file exists for your specific operating system. These files are named README.* where "*" is the name of the system (for example, README.beos).

   C. Depending on the options you want to use, you type some variation of sh Configure -*options*, where *options* reflect the configuration options you determined accurate from reading the README files.

   D. Next, depending on how you perform the installation and what system you are on, you go through a process of answering from a few to many questions about how you want to build the Perl interpreter.

Tip

If you find your system doesn't have the cc compiler installed, check the INSTALL file for instructions on using the gcc compiler. If you don't have gcc, the INSTALL file tells you where you can get it.

5. Once you complete the configuration portion of the installation, you are prompted with a screen, which looks something like what is shown in Figure 1-2. Type **make** to start the next part of the installation. If you can't find this program, it's most likely in your /usr/local/bin directory.
6. After make completes its tasks, you should test the build before you actually finish the installation. To perform this task, type **make test**. Once it has completed, you see something like Figure 1-3.

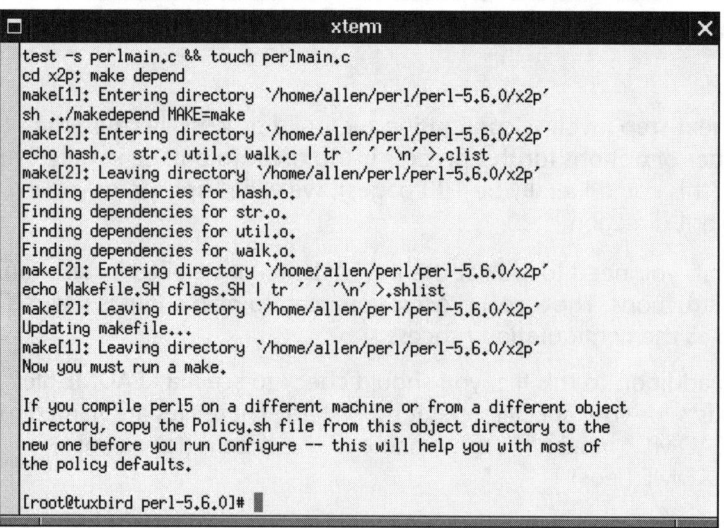

Figure 1-2 **Once you complete the configuration process, you should see this screen**

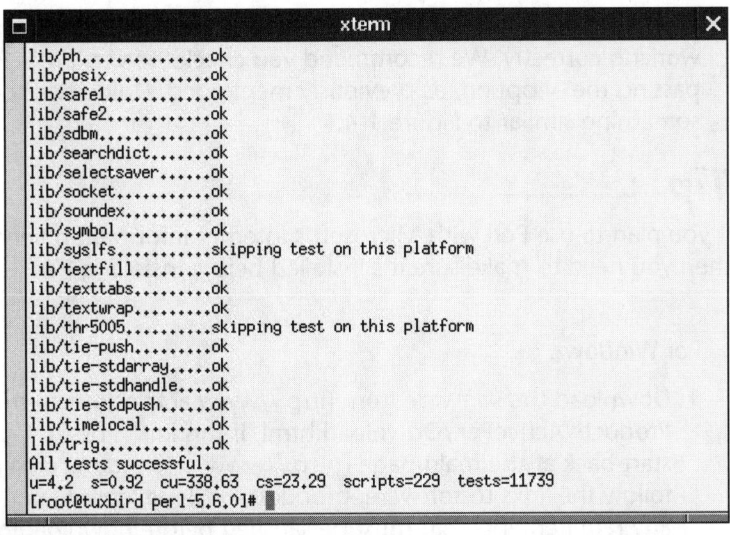

Figure 1-3 **Results of running make test**

Note

If the make test fails, we suggest checking the news groups for others who've had similar problems. If that doesn't work, then you may want to submit a bug report (see the section "Reporting Problems" in the INSTALL document).

7. Now you're at the final steps of the process, which will complete the installation. To finish, type **make install**. This process, which can take several minutes to complete, may ask you a few questions, but they should be simple and you should be able to accept the defaults. When it's done, you should see Installation complete written to your screen.

Now you're ready to run Perl! Double-check that everything is working correctly. We recommend you check the version of Perl by passing the -v option, as previously mentioned. Doing so should return something similar to Figure 1-4.

Tip

If you plan to use Perl with Microsoft's Internet Information Server (IIS), then you need to make sure it's installed before installing Perl.

For Windows:

1. Download the software from http://www.activestate.com/Products/ActivePerl/Download.html. If this link is broken, start back at the main page (http://www.activestate.com) and follow the links to software, products, or download. Please read any requirements that must be satisfied before downloading.

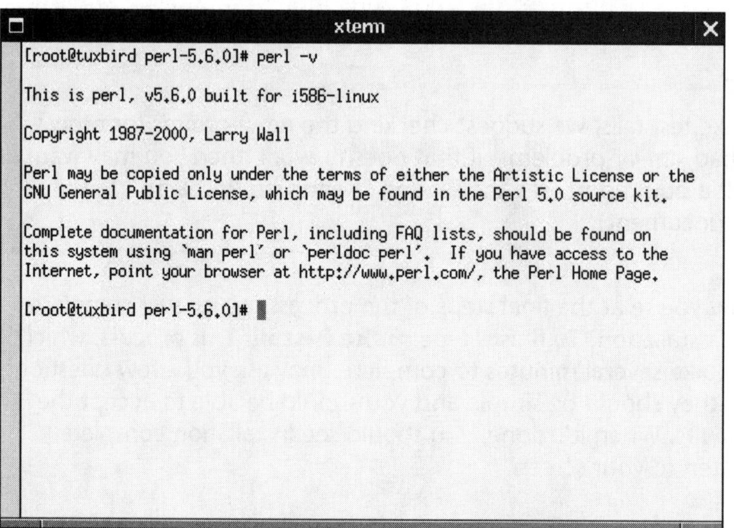

Figure 1-4 **The Setup Options dialog box lets you select configuration options for ActivePerl**

2. Once downloaded, double-click the file to launch the installer. You should see the ActivePerl Setup dialog box appear, as shown in Figure 1-5. Click Next.

Tip

If you want to, you can download the source code (same location as given in the UNIX installation steps) and compile it for your Windows platform. However, those instructions and requirements are beyond the scope of this book.

3. Select the option to accept the license agreement, and then click Next.
4. The next screen, as shown in Figure 1-6, enables you to specify which components you want installed. Click Next here. We recommend you leave this at the default of all options unless you have a good reason, such as lack of hard disk space, not to do so.

Note

If you see components here you aren't sure about, don't worry. They are discussed shortly.

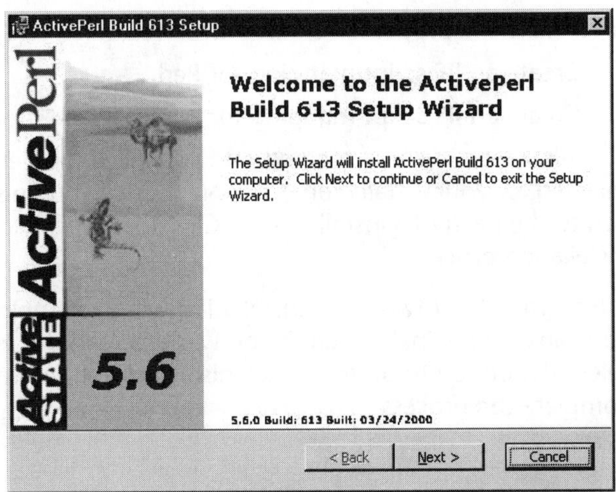

Figure 1-5 Testing your installation on the command line

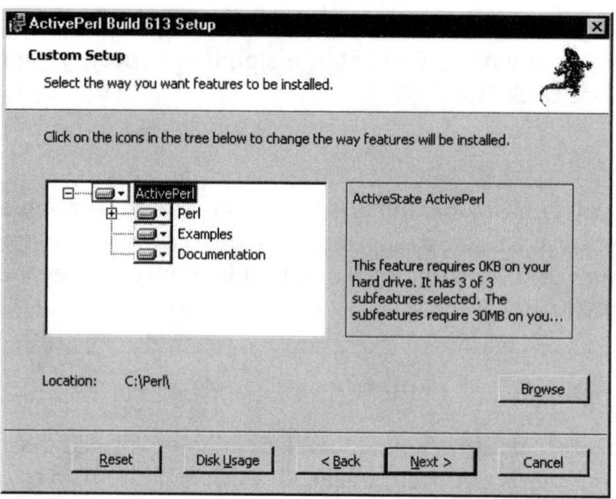

Figure 1-6 **The Custom Setup dialog box enables you to select the ActivePerl components to install**

5. The Setup Options dialog box enables you to select which setup options you want to configure. These options, shown in Figure 1-7, let you do the following:
   - Add the Perl binary to your PATH environment variable
   - Create the proper file extension association
   - Create an IIS script mapping for Perl
   - Create an IIS script mapping for Perl ISAPI

   For this screen, we also recommend you leave the default of all selected for your installation. Click Next once you finish. This takes you to the Ready To Install screen. Click Install now to start the installation process.

6. After a minute or two, your installation will be complete, and then you can see the final screen. If you want to read the release notes, select the option to do so. Click Finish to close the installer and complete the process.

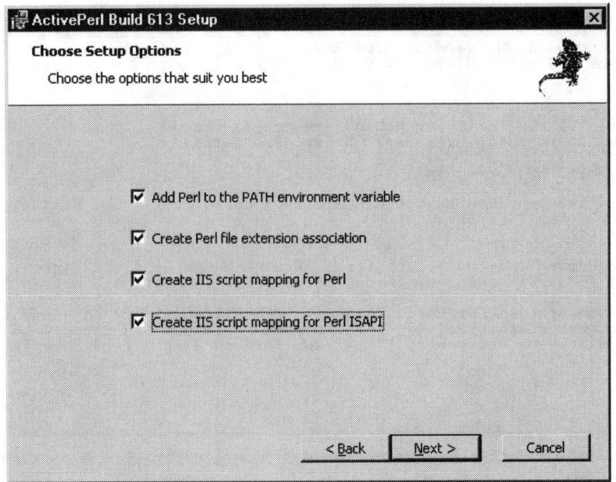

Figure 1-7 MacPerl installation options window

Like within the UNIX environment, if you want to verify Perl is installed and your PATH was set up correctly, start a command prompt by selecting Start, and then the Run menu option and type **cmd** (Windows 95/98/Me users, type **command**). Once the prompt window is launched, type **perl –v**. This tells the Perl interpreter to output the version. You should see something like Figure 1-8.

Note

Mac OS X users can follow the directions under UNIX to install Perl 5.6. Check the INSTALL file after unzipping and untaring for any special Mac OS X instructions.

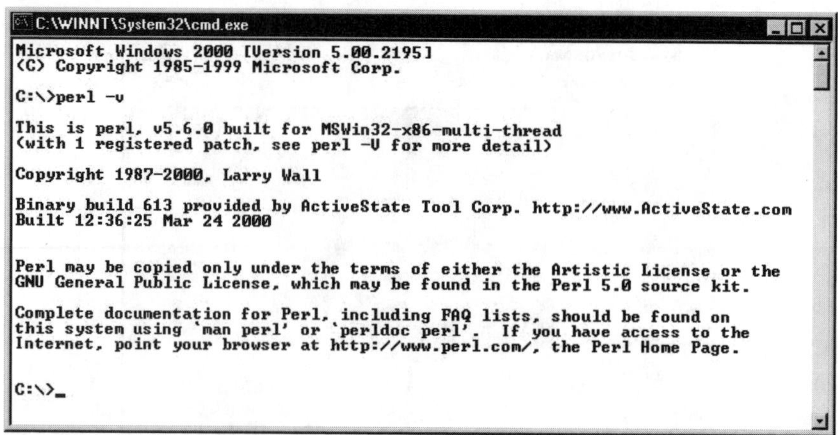

Figure 1-8 MacPerl folder after installation

For Mac OS (pre-Mac OS X):

1. Follow one of the links on http://www.macperl.com/depts/getmp.html to download the software, which is in MacBinary format (.bin extension). If this link is broken, start back at the main page (http://www.macperl.com) and follow the links to software or download. Assuming you use a browser to download MacPerl, the file should uncompress and leave you with the installation program. This program will be named something like "Mac_Perl_520r4_appl". If the file didn't decompress after downloading, you can drop it on an application, such as StuffIt Expander, to prepare it. If you don't have this application, you can download it from http://www.aladdinsys.com.
2. Now double-click the install file to launch the installer. This presents you with the README screen. Click Continue.
3. The next screen provides a few options. It enables you to
   - Select the Easy Install or a Custom Install
   - Select the disk on which you want to install the application
   - Select the folder in which you want to install if you click the pull-down menu beside the disk's name (as shown in Figure 1-9)

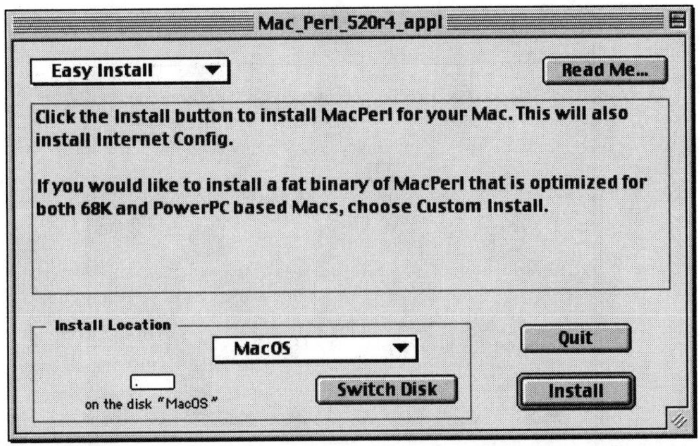

Figure 1-9 Check the version of Perl after the installation

We recommend you simply leave these options set to the default unless you need to change disk or folder locations. Once you're ready, click the Continue button to start the installation.

4. After about 30 seconds, the installation will finish and you can click the Quit button in the dialog box.

After the installation, a directory, which looks like Figure 1-10, is contained on your system. This folder has all the files you need to run Perl programs on the Mac and some additional resources.

Like most other Mac programs, MacPerl has preference settings. If you double-click the MacPerl application in the folder, shown in Figure 1-10, and select Preferences from the Edit menu, then you see the dialog box shown in Figure 1-11.

From this dialog box, you have the capability to do the following:

- **Libraries** This section enables you to add or remove paths to your library modules. We discuss modules in Module 8.
- **Environment** This section enables you to set environment variables for scripts you run on MacPerl. These simulate the environment variables available on UNIX and Windows platforms.

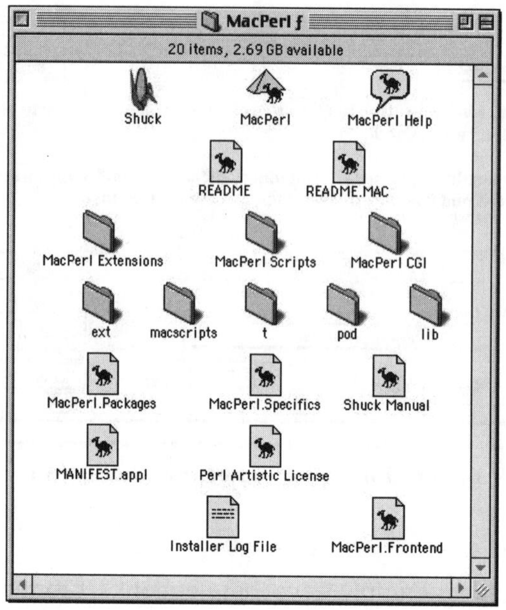

Figure 1-10 MacPerl preferences window

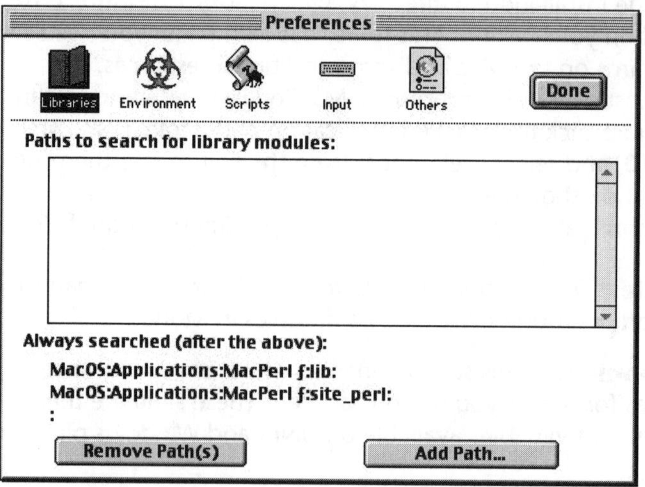

Figure 1-11 Opening screen of ActivePerl 5.6 (a.k.a. Perl 5.6.0) installer

- **Scripts** This section lets you select how you want scripts handled if opened from the Finder, including double-clicking scripts within a folder. This can either be set to Edit or Run. You can also tell MacPerl whether to check for the #! in your scripts, which designates the path to your Perl interpreter and any interpreter options you want to pass. Personally, we like to select this option because it is the first step for making sure our scripts run in all environments (UNIX, Windows, and so forth).
- **Input** This section gives you the option to allow, or not to allow, inline input.
- **Others** This section lets you access other preferences for other Mac OS applications and functions, such as Internet Config.

Notes About the Platforms

Now that you have Perl installed on your system, you're ready to learn about your distribution. Because every operating system and environment is different, it's impossible for Perl to behave and act exactly the same way across all the platforms. Because of this, you should take the time to be exposed to some of the limitations and/or advantages your platform has to offer.

UNIX

The UNIX variations themselves are not that limiting. Nearly anything you can do within the UNIX environment, you can simulate, control, or report on in Perl. This means you have commands like kill or grep that can be used, and you can obtain UNIX-like information from within your scripts. One key thing to remember is directory paths contain / as the directory separator character.

Note

For more information on the various UNIX flavors of Perl, go to the Perl Language Page at http://www.perl.com.

Windows

In addition to the built-in functions of Perl, you should be aware of some enhancements in ActivePerl. The ActivePerl distribution comes with more than just the Perl interpreter, which can be confusing to many people. As you probably saw in the install, it also comes with the following:

- **Perl Package Manager (PPM)** A tool that enables you to manage your Perl extensions and modules easily.
- **Perl for ISAPI** A Microsoft IIS filter that enhances the performance of Perl running in your Web environment.
- **PerlScript** A scripting engine, like JScript or VBScript, which can be used to create scripts that run within the Internet Explorer browser or against the Windows Script Host and for use with Active Server Pages.

In addition to these components, the actual Perl implementation has enhancements specific to the Windows operating system. With this version of Perl, you can do everything from work with the Windows Registry to generate Window's events to the Event Viewer. Unlike UNIX which uses the forward slash, `/`, to separate directory paths, Windows uses a backslash (`\`).

Tip

For more information on ActivePerl and other ActiveState offerings, check out http://www.activestate.com.

Mac OS

Like ActivePerl, MacPerl has some features specific to the Mac platform. This includes additions, as well as features and functions that couldn't be implemented. Many of the UNIX-like system functions, like fork, kill, and exec, are simply not implemented in MacPerl—the operating system has no concept of these functions. Others like `time`, `open`, and `exit`

Hint

The Mac OS breaks away from the use of slashes for separating its folders and, instead, uses the colon, :. So, if your built-in disk was named MyMac and you wanted to reference a folder named Perl Programs within that disk, you would do so like this: MyMac:Perl Programs.

are implemented, but not in the same manner. For a more detailed list of differences between the standard distribution and MacPerl, check out http://www.macperl.com/depts/MacPerlFAQ.html#differences.

Note

As many of you know, the next generation of the Mac OS is right around the corner. In fact, by the time you get this book, Mac OS X (pronounced *ten*), which will ship with Perl 5.6, should be available. This new operating system is based on some of the technology from NeXT (started by Apple founder and current CEO Steve Jobs) and has UNIX-like capabilities. Because of this, we expect to see MacPerl fade away in favor of the standard distribution source code Mac OS X users will be able to compile like all the UNIX users.

Where to Get Help

Once you have installed the interpreter, you're ready to get started in your Perl programming endeavors. But before you do so, we want to point you to some documentation in case you need any help. The first bit of help comes with the Perl interpreter and is commonly referred to as *manpages,* a term that reflects Perl's UNIX roots.

Distribution Documentation

Within UNIX, you can access the introductory page of this documentation simply by typing **man perl**. Once opened, you not only see information about Perl, you also see the names of other manpages, such as perldelta, perlfaq, and perlfunc, which are available. You can access these pages in the same manner as the introductory page by typing **man** before the name of the page.

For Windows, the ActivePerl documentation is stored in the \html subdirectory of the installation (something like c:\perl\html). Once inside this directory, simply load the index.html page in your favorite browser. Because ActivePerl ships with other Perl components specific to the Windows environment, you can see information that is additional to the standard Perl language.

Within the Mac OS environment, the Perl documentation is located in the pod subdirectory of the MacPerl folder (this should be in something like *<install_disk>*:MacPerl *f*:pod, where *<install_disk>* is the name of the disk on which you installed MacPerl). MacPerl contains a program called "Shuck," which is used to read this documentation. You can use this either by dropping a .pod file on Shuck or simply double-clicking the file. You can also access much of this information from the Help menu, which also links to online resources, of MacPerl.

Note

POD is the acronym for Plain Old Documentation.

Online Resources

In addition to the documentation shipped with Perl, we highly recommend you also check out some online resources. Perl is a language that has thrived online and continues to grow because of the efforts of contributors who are linked by the Web. Three types of resources are online, which we recommend you look into and they are contained in Tables 1-3, 1-4, and 1-5.

Hint

Check out www.perl.com's reference page at http://www.perl.com/reference for more resources.

Where	Description
http://www.activestate.com	You can find information here on the Windows port of Perl called ActivePerl
http://www.macperl.com	You can find information here on the Mac OS port of Perl called MacPerl
http://www.perl.com	You can find anything from documentation, software, and archives to articles. This is handy and should be in every Perl programmer's bookmark list
http://www.perl.org	This is basically a front door to Perl in the online world. From here, you can find links to other sites, news, resources, and lists of *frequently asked questions* (*FAQs*)
http://www.perldoc.com	A new site with a wealth of documentation on Perl and Perl libraries
http://www.pm.org	This is the Perl Mongers pages, which is basically a virtual community of Perl programmers around the world. Here, you can find links to local organizations that promote the user of Perl and may be in your area. This is a user group online

Table 1-3 Browser-Accessible Web Resources

Where	Description
comp.lang.perl.*	The main usenet, or news group, Perl communication is under. By using the * symbol, we mean, in addition to the resources listed in this table, you may want to check more available resources on topics before you throw in the towel on a difficult problem
comp.lang.perl.announce	News group that contains Perl-related announcements, such as new releases
comp.lang.perl.misc	Unmoderated discussion of Perl
comp.lang.perl.moderated	Moderated discussion of Perl
comp.lang.perl.modules	Devoted to the discussion of the many Perl modules available across the Web today. Modules are discussed further in Module 8
comp.lang.perl.tk	Discussions on using the Perl/Tk, which is a "tool kit" for creating graphical interfaces in Perl. This capability is discussed in Module 13

Table 1-4 Usenet Groups That Discuss Perl

Where	Description
Perl-UNIX-Users	General discussions around using Perl in the UNIX environment. You can subscribe to this list at http://listserv.activestate.com/ mailman/listinfo/ perl-unix-users
Perl-Win32-Admin	Discussion on how to use ActivePerl to perform Windows administration tasks. You can subscribe to this list at http://listserv.activestate.com/mailman/listinfo/ perl-win32-admin
Perl-Win32-Announce	Listserv that contains Perl-related announcements, such as new releases. You can subscribe to this list by sending e-mail to listmanager@activestate.com with SUBSCRIBE Perl-Win32-Announce in the body of the e-mail
Perl-Win32-Porters	Discussion on porting and development issues around ActivePerl. You can subscribe to this list by sending e-mail to listmanager@activestate.com with SUBSCRIBE Perl-Win32-Porters in the body of the e-mail
Perl-Win32-Users	General discussions around ActivePerl. You can subscribe to this list by sending e-mail to listmanager@activestate.com with SUBSCRIBE Perl-Win32-Users in the body of the e-mail
Perl-XML	Discussion on using Perl to work with XML documents. You can subscribe to this at http://listserv.activestate.com/ mailman/ listinfo/perl-xml

Table 1-5 **Popular E-mail Listserv's That Discuss Perl**

Note

If you want to search old news postings, try going to http:// www. deja.com/usenet. From there, you can search for answers before posting a new question.

Creating a Perl Program

Creating a Perl program is a task you should approach correctly. Sure, you can simply open a text file, type in some lines of code, and run it, but is this always the best way? If you need something short, sweet, and quick, then this could be fine, but if you are writing a long, in-depth script, which you want to use in the future or you'll be passing off to another person or group, you should follow some basic guidelines.

- Plan the flow of your script by what functions you want it to perform.
- Organize the script so you can reuse parts, if needed.
- Document, document, document (as our former boss Kerry said).

Getting Started

The first thing we do when writing a script is to take a template we have created and save it under the script name of our current project. Because we use a template, all the scripts we write have a consistent look and feel to them—this is true no matter who's looking at it. In a Perl script, you need to understand a few things before you start and before you create a template.

Comments

The first thing you should understand is the syntax for a comment. A *comment* is nothing more than text in your code, which isn't supposed to be interpreted as code. This text is often used to add information or other descriptive text about your code or sections of it.

Unlike Java, JavaScript, C/C++, or other C-flavored programming languages, Perl uses the number sign, # (referred to as *pound* or *sharp*), to designate a comment. When one of these is used, it means the text starting after the # until the end of the line is a comment. Perl has no multiline comment market, so you needn't be concerned about it running too far. Here's an example of a comment to give you a better idea:

```
# My comments go here
```

The First Line

The next thing you should know about writing a Perl program is that many of the platforms, including flavors of UNIX, require the first line to start with a #! and the path to the Perl interpreter. Implementations on the Mac and Windows platforms, as well as some others, don't require this line; however, because run-time options can be passed to the Perl interpreter on this line, they can be used. In these instances, the interpreters usually ignore the path and only look at the options.

For instance, if you want to run your script in Warning mode and the Perl interpreter was in /usr/bin, then you would have the following first line:

```
#!/usr/bin/perl -w
```

See how easy this is? And this works on most other platforms, even if your platform does not need the path. Because the Perl interpreter can accept many different options, a list of them is included in Table 1-6. Don't worry if some of the terminology is a bit complex here—as a beginner, you won't use many of these. If you're interested in a more in-depth description, check the perlrun manpage. Table 1-7 lists debugger options.

Creating a Template

Because you want your script to include information, such as who wrote it, when it was written, what it does, and what version it is, the template you want to use should provide room to fill in this information. In addition, if you are creating any subroutines in the script, you'll also want to provide what is passed in, what is returned, and a description of the function.

Option	**Description**
-0[*digits*]	Specifies the input record separator as an octal number
-a	Turns on Autosplit mode when used with a -n option or a p option
-C	Allows for the use of native wide character APIs
-c	Tells the interpreter to check the syntax of the script without executing it
-d	Runs the script in the Perl debugger
-D:*module*	Runs the program under the control of another module
-D*letters*	Enables you to specify debugging flags. See Table 1-7 for a list of the flags
-D*numbers*	Enables you to specify debugging flags. See Table 1-7 for a list of the flags
-e *commandline*	Can be used to enter one line of a Perl program
-F*pattern*	Specifies a pattern to split on if an a option is also used
-h	Prints a summary of the options
-i[*extension*]	Tells the interpreter that files processed by the <> construct should be edited in place
-I[*directory*]	Places the directories passed in the search path of modules
-l[*octnum*]	Enables automatic line-ending processing

Table 1-6 **Perl Interpreter Options**

Option	Description
-m[*module*]	Executes use `module()` before the program
-M[*module*]	Executes use `module()` before the program, but you can add extra code in quotes after the module name
-n	Tells the interpreter to assume a loop over your program, which makes it iterate over filename arguments like sed -n or awk
-p	Tells the interpreter to assume a loop over your program, which makes it iterate over filename arguments like sed
-P	Runs your program through a C preprocessor before compilation
-s	Enables some switch parsing for switches on the command line
-S	Makes Perl use the PATH environment variable to search for the program
-T	Forces "taint" checks to be turned on for testing
-u	This deprecated option tells Perl to create a core file after compiling our program
-U	Allows the interpreter to do unsafe operations, such as the unlinking of directories
-v	Prints the exact Perl version
-V	Prints summary of major Perl configuration values
-V:*name*	Prints to STDOUT the value of the *name*d configuration variable
-w	Prints warnings
-W	Enables all warnings
-X	Disables all warnings
-x *directory*	Tells the interpreter the Perl program is embedded in a larger chunk of unrelated text, such as an e-mail

Table 1-6 Perl Interpreter Options *(continued)*

Number	Letter	Description
1	p	Tokenizing and parsing
2	s	Stack snapshots
4	l	Context (loop) stack processing
8	t	Trace
16	o	Method of overloading resolution
32	c	String/numeric conversions
64	P	Print preprocessor command
128	m	Memory allocation
256	f	Format processing
512	r	Regular expression parsing and execution

Table 1-7 Debugger Options

Number	Letter	Description
1024	x	Syntax tree dump
2048	u	Tainting checks
4096	L	Memory leaks (to work, it must have -DLEAKTEST when Perl is compiled)
8192	H	Hash dump—usurps values()
16384	X	Scratchpad allocation
32768	D	Cleaning up
65536	S	Thread synchronization

Table 1-7 **Debugger Options** ***(continued)***

The following is what we use as our template and this is a good starting place for you.

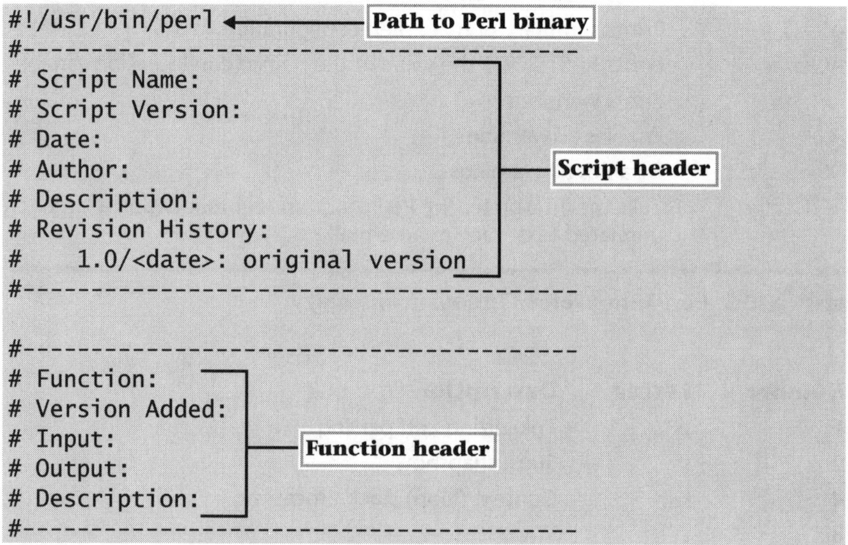

```
#!/usr/bin/perl
#----------------------------------------
# Script Name:
# Script Version:
# Date:
# Author:
# Description:
# Revision History:
#    1.0/<date>: original version
#----------------------------------------

#----------------------------------------
# Function:
# Version Added:
# Input:
# Output:
# Description:
#----------------------------------------
```


Now that you have a template and some basic Perl understanding, you can start programming!

A Hello Script

The first program you'll complete is probably the first program 90 percent of the Perl programmers today also completed. This is the old faithful Hello, World! program. The idea is simple—to have the program output text that says Hello, World!

In this program, you are introduced to a built-in Perl function called `print`, which sends output to a specific location. In this program, the location is *standard output* (*STDOUT*), or in simple terms, your screen.

To get started, we are going to take our template and fill in our information, such as name, version, date, author, and description. Once you have that, save the file as Hello.pl. Because this is a simple program, only one Perl programming line is in it—print `"Hello, World\n"`.

> **Hint**
>
> Want to know more about the `"print ()"` function? Check out the perlfunc manpage that comes with your Perl distribution.

Don't worry about the `\n` right now because the next module covers it and others like it. Just understand that `\n` represents a newline character and causes the cursor to put your command prompt on the next line when you run the program. If you want to see the difference for yourself, try it with and without it.

```
#!/usr/bin/perl
#----------------------------------------
# Script Name: Hello.pl
# Script Version: 1.0
# Date: 10.01.2000
# Author: R. Allen Wyke
# Description: Prints "Hello, World!" to the user's screen.
# Revision History:
#    1.0: original version
#----------------------------------------

print "Hello, World!\n";
```

Using the print function to send output to your screen

Script information

Note

UNIX users need to change the file permissions on the file to make it an executable. A quick-and-easy way to do this is to type **chmod 755 Hello.pl**. If you want more information on chmod, type **man chmod**.

Now, to run the program, you type one of the following commands:

- **UNIX** ./Hello.pl
- **Windows** perl Hello.pl
- **Mac OS** Drop the Hello.pl site on to the MacPerl icon, and then select **Run Hello.pl** from the **Script** menu.

When you run the program on the Windows platform, you should see the same results as shown in Illustration 1. For comparison, we also included a capture of the results from MacPerl (see Illustration 2), and Perl on our Linux machine running Red Hat 6.0 (see Illustration 3).

Illustration 1

Illustration 2

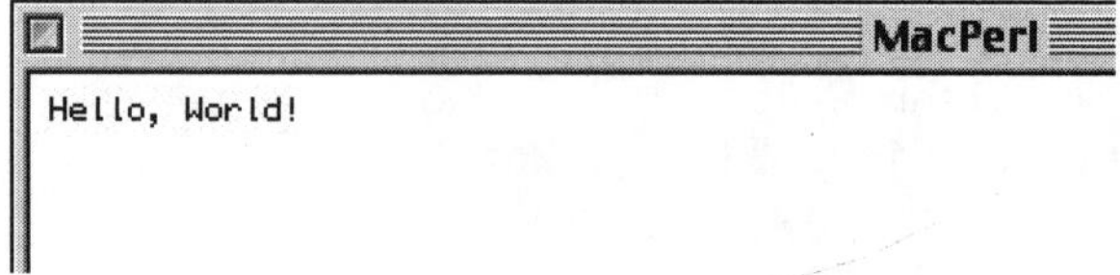

Illustration 3

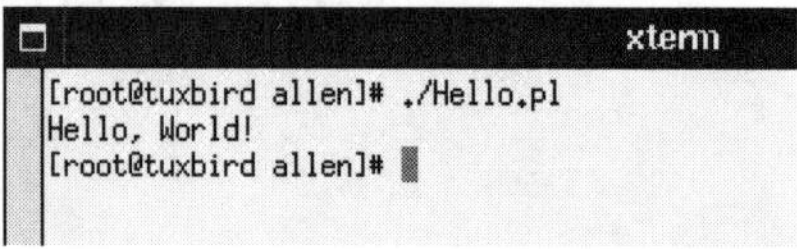

Note

If you programmed in another language, you might have noticed we didn't use parentheses () with the "`print ()`" function. In Perl you can use parentheses or not—the choice is yours.

Going a Bit Further

So, how was the experience of writing your first successful Perl programming? Satisfying, but too simple and not too exciting, you say? Well, before we end this module, let's add a little excitement to make it more interesting. Because the following modules are used to introduce you further to the language, we are limiting what we do here so you don't become confused. What we will do, however, is change the script to prompt for your name, prepare your response, and then return another result to your screen.

In this script, we use a new function called `chomp ()`, which is a simple function that removes a trailing newline character at the end of a string. When you accept input from the command line, the return that's pressed by the user is also stored in the string. Using chomp, we can remove that extra newline character and focus only on the alphanumeric data entered.

Note

Perl also has a function called chomp (), which removes the last character of a string. Unlike chomp (), chomp () removes any character, no matter what it is, whereas chomp () only removes the character if it's a newline character. When you only need to remove a trailing newline character, you should always use chomp () because it's safer.

Before we chop off the newline character, we need to get the data from the user. The way to do this is to print some text to the screen asking for the user's name, and then read what the user types into a variable. This information, which is read in through *standard input* (*STDIN*), can then easily have the chomp function applied to it. Because this information is in a variable, it's also easy to reuse that variable in our second print statement to output what the user entered.

```
#!/usr/bin/perl
#-----------------------------------------
# Script Name: Hello.pl
# Script Version: 2.0
# Date: 10.01.2000
# Author: R. Allen Wyke
# Description: Prompts user for name, strips of newline character
# and prints "Hello <name>!" screen where name = the text entered.
# Revision History:
#     1.0: original version
#     2.0: added prompt for user's name and returned text based on it.
#-----------------------------------------

# ask user for name
print "What is your name? ";
$input = <STDIN>;

# remove newline character
chomp($input);

# print results to page
print "Hello $input!\n";
```

Hint

Notice we could use $input within the quotes of the print function. If we had used tick marks (single quotes), this wouldn't have been possible—it would have literally sent "$input" to the screen.

And that's it! We have just expanded our program to take input directly from the user. The illustration below shows what this looks like after execution. Again, we included the results on MacPerl in the illustration on the next page because it's the only system we are talking about with no real command line.

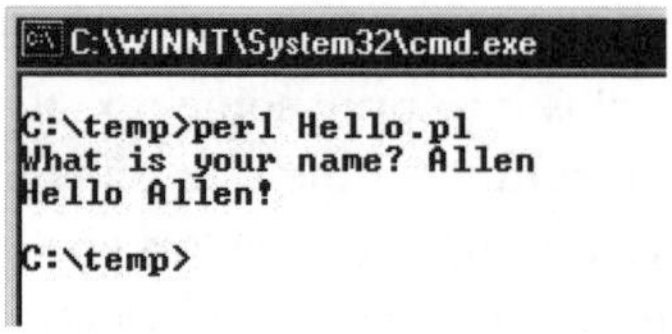

```
C:\WINNT\System32\cmd.exe

C:\temp>perl Hello.pl
What is your name? Allen
Hello Allen!

C:\temp>
```

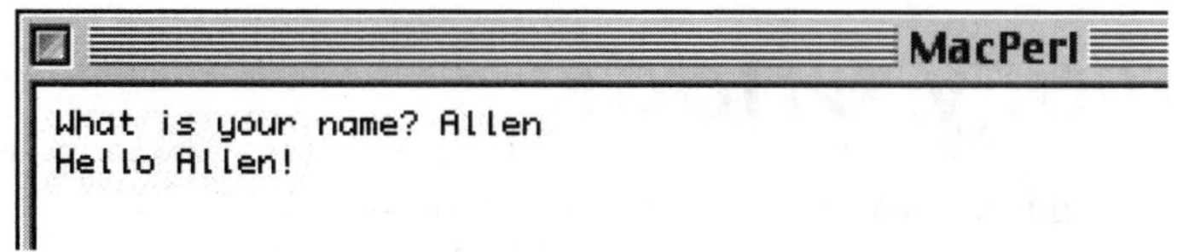

As you can see, the program simply prompted the user for his name, read this information into a variable, removed the trailing return character, and printed the results to the screen.

1-Minute Drill

- **Using the first Hello.pl script you wrote, remove the newline, \n, in the print statement and see what happens to the output.**
- **Using the second Hello.pl version, use single quotes instead of double quotes for both print statements and see what happens.**

Moving On

In this module, we covered a lot of important ground. Some of you may have wanted more examples and code, but that comes with the next module. Understanding the history of Perl, how to install it, and some basics to get you started is important. Again, Perl is more than just a scripting and programming language—it is a powerful tool in your tool belt. Understanding its roots, where to get it, and how it works can benefit you in the long run.

- **Doesn't give you a new line after "Hello, World!"**
- **First print statement works as before, but second one prints "Hello $input!\n" to the screen**

Mastery Check

1. What should the first line of your Perl script include?

   A. #!

   B. Path to your interpreter

   C. Interpreter run-time options

   D. All of the above

2. Which of the following is a valid Perl comment?

   A. /*comment*/

   B. //comment

   C. #comment

   D. ‘comment

3. If you need to find information about Perl, where would you go?

   A. http://www.perl.com

   B. http://www.perl.org

   C. comp.lang.perl

   D. All of the above

4. What does CPAN stand for? (You need to do a little research online here.)

   A. Coding Perl in All Nations

   B. Comprehensive Perl Archive Network

   C. Cooperating with Perl Around Networks

   D. Coding Perl And Networking

Module 2

Scalar Data

The Goals of This Module

- Learn about the various data types used in Perl
- Understand how to assign scalar data to variables
- Learn about the different types of scalar operators
- Understand how type conversions work in Perl

Now that you have a brief introduction in the history of Perl, let's get right into learning how to program in it. All programs are written for a reason. Your program could be used to perform calculations, build a Web page, or search through a file for a certain word. Either way, you are attempting to solve a problem and, most likely, that problem revolves around data manipulation if you are using Perl.

Scalar data is the most basic type of data Perl is used to manipulate. The term *scalar data* refers to a single data type that encompasses numbers and strings but, for this module, we make a separation between the two. In this module, you learn about the different data types and are introduced to the concept of assigning various types to variables. You learn about the operators present in Perl that can be used on this data and, finally, you also learn how Perl handles type conversions between different data types. To get started, let's look at the different data types.

Data Types

Data types can be separated into two different categories. First, are numbers like 62, 6.2e10, or 7FF. Second, are character strings like "hello". To start this module, we discuss numbers and, once you have learned how they are handled, we move on to discuss strings.

Numbers

Numbers, from a users' standpoint, commonly come in two different forms. The first type of number is an *integer,* which refers to a whole number. A whole number is basically a number with no decimal point, like 62 or -1992. These whole numbers are represented as base 10 digits. If you want to include decimal points, these are the second kind of numbers, which are called *floating-point* numbers. Floating-point numbers look like 62.2 or -1.992e20. Two other special types of numbers discussed in this section are octal and hexadecimal numbers. *Octal* numbers are represented with base 8 digits and *hexadecimal* numbers with base 16 digits.

Unlike most other programming languages, integers and floating-point numbers are interchangeable in Perl simply because the language doesn't support integers. An integer mode can be enabled if you must use integers for some special reason. This special mode must be enabled by the user if she needs it. To learn more about the integer mode and how it functions, look at the integer section of the root libraries documentation included with Perl. All numbers, even though you entered the numbers as integers, are converted to floating-point numbers. This simplifies programming because you never have to worry about mixing integers and floating-point numbers in performing calculations.

Note

Don't worry because you won't have true integer values. Almost any type of calculation you can perform can function properly with a floating-point number.

Now that you know about integer and floating-point numbers, let's look at exactly what number formats Perl can handle.

What Is Accepted	**Examples**
Numbers entered as integers	5, 3050
Numbers entered as floating-points	5.22, .083
Negative signs on the left-hand side of any number	-5, -.083
Numbers with the *e* notation	5e20, -1.24e12
Negative signs on the *e* notations power of 10 value	5e-20, -1.24e-12
Hexadecimal numbers	0x55ff
Octal numbers	0435

The *e* notation is the "power of 10" indicator. The number 4e20 reads "4 times 10 to the 20th power." Two of the number formats given in the previous table may be new to you. These two are hexadecimal and octal numbers.

Octal numbers are specified with a leading 0. The example given, 0435, is an octal number simply because its first digit is a 0. With this in mind, always remember you should never start a base 10 value with the number 0 because it will be interpreted as an octal in your script. Octal numbers range from 0 to 7, as you can see in the following table. To give you a better understanding, let's look at how the octal numbers match up with the normal decimal numbers to which you are more accustomed.

Decimal Number	Octal Representation
0	0
1	1
2	2
3	3
4	4
5	5
6	6
7	7
8	10
9	11
10	12
11	13
12	14
13	15
14	16
15	17
16	20

The other number format you might not be familiar with are the hexadecimal numbers, which range from 0 to 9 and *A* to *F,* and are signified in Perl by having "0*x*" in front of the actual number. Again, let's compare the hexadecimal numbers to the decimal numbers to give you a better idea of how they relate.

Decimal Number	Hexadecimal Representation
0	0
1	1
2	2
3	3
4	4
5	5
6	6

Decimal Number	Hexadecimal Representation
7	7
8	8
9	9
10	A
11	B
12	C
13	D
14	E
15	F
16	10

You're probably wondering why anyone would use octal or hexadecimal numbers in their programs because these numbering systems seem confusing. The reason is these types of numbers make it easy to access the memory locations of a computer. Memory is addressed in binary numbers. *Binary* numbers are of the base 2, which means they can only have two different values—0 or 1. In comparison, octal numbers are of the base 8, and hexadecimal numbers are of the base 16. Because the bases for these numbers are multiples of 2, it's easier for you to represent a memory location using them.

Note

Binary numbers are discussed in more detail in the operators section of this module.

1-Minute Drill

- **What are the different types of numbers Perl accepts?**
- **With what digit should you never start a base 10 integer value?**

That pretty much covers numerical data types in Perl, so let's move on to strings.

- **Integers, floating-point numbers, octal numbers, and hexadecimal numbers**
- **An integer value can never begin with the 0 digit**

Strings

As you've already learned, a string is simply a sequence of characters. A string can be made up of any combination of characters from the entire 256 character set that's available to you. This means a string can contain digits, symbols, and alphabetical letters. In Perl, strings can contain anywhere from zero characters all the way up to however many characters it takes to fill your available memory. These characteristics make strings much more flexible in Perl than in most other programming languages.

Strings come in two different forms: single-quoted strings and double-quoted strings. Each of these two types has different programming characteristics. Let's look at the two types of strings in more detail and discuss what makes them different from each other.

Single-Quoted Strings

A *single-quoted string* in Perl is a sequence of letters, digits, or symbols enclosed in single quotes. All the characters inside the single quotes make up the string. Within these strings, the single quote and the backslash have special meanings. There are rules to follow when the single-quote character needs to be part of the string itself. If you require the string to contain a single quote, you must put a backslash before it. If you don't use the backslash, your single quote is interpreted as the end of the string and everything after it is lost. If you need to escape the backslash, you must add an additional backslash to it. Let's look at some examples.

Example	**Explanation**
'Hello World'	This is a string of 11 characters. The space between Hello and World does count as a character in the string.
'Hello World'	This is a string of 11 characters. The return (newline) character does count as a character in the string.
''	This is a string of 0 characters. This is referred to as the **null string** in Perl.
'Hello World\Planet'	This is a string of 18 characters. The backslash is part of the string and it reads exactly as it appears between the single quotes.
'Hello \'World\''	This is a string of 13 characters. It reads Hello 'World'. This is an example of having to use the backslash character to add single quotes to a single-quoted string.
''Hello' World'	This is a string of 0 characters (the null string) because we didn't use the backslash to add the single quotes around Hello.

Example	Explanation
'Hello World\\'	This is a string of 12 characters. It reads Hello World\. This is an example of having to use an extra backslash to escape the backslash function. If we hadn't added the extra backslash, the '\' would have been seen as a single quote and the string wouldn't have terminated until another single quote was reached.

Now that you understand single-quoted strings and how to enter them, let's talk about double-quoted strings.

Double-Quoted Strings

A double-quoted string is similar to a single-quoted string because it is made up of a sequence of characters. In a single-quoted string, however, the backslash has no other special use than to add a single quote or a backslash to the string. In a double-quoted string, the backslash enables you to execute different functions inside the string itself. If you want to have a backslash as part of your string now, it won't be a problem. All you have to do is add an extra backslash in front of another backslash and it shows up as a normal character. If you need a double quote inside your double-quoted string, all you have to do is add a backslash in front of the double quote. Let's look at some examples to make this more clear.

Example	Explanation
"Hello World"	This is a string of 11 characters.
"Hello 'World'"	This is a string of 13 characters and it reads Hello 'World'. Notice that inside the double-quoted string, you don't have to add the backslash in front of the single quote to have it be a part of the string.
"Hello World\today"	This is a string of 16 characters and it reads Hello World <tab>oday. The \t is the representation for tab. This is an example of what happens if you try to add a backslash to a double-quoted string without adding an extra backslash in front of it.
"Hello World\\today"	This is a string of 17 characters and it reads Hello World\today.
"Hello \"World\""	This is a string of 13 characters and it reads Hello "World"

As you saw in one of the previous examples, the backslash character can be used to specify different escape sequences inside a double-quoted string *Escape sequences* are sequences of characters set aside by the language that performs certain functions. Here's a list of all the escape sequences you can use inside a double-quoted string.

Representation	Result
\a	Bell (otherwise known as "beep")
\b	Backspace
\c	Enables you to execute any control character by placing the character just after \c. For example, if you want to execute the Ctrl D function from your program, enter \cD inside your double-quoted string
\e	Escape
\f	Form-feed
\l	Make only the next letter lowercase
\n	This is the newline character (most often used)
\r	Carriage return
\t	Tab (most often used)
\u	Make only the next letter uppercase
\x	Enables you to enter hex numbers
\v	Vertical tab
\\	Backslash
\"	Double Quote
\	Enables you to enter octal numbers
\L	Make all the letters lowercase until you see \E
\U	Make all the letters uppercase until you see \E
\Q	Add a backslash-quote to all the nonalphanumerics until you see \E
\E	This terminates any \L, \U, or \Q that you started

You'll probably only use a few of these in your double-quoted strings when you begin programming in Perl. The tab and the newline escape sequences are the ones most often used. Here are some examples to make this a little more clear.

Example	Explanation
"Hello World\n"	This is a string of 11 characters and it reads Hello World, followed by a newline
"Hello\tWorld"	This is also a string of 11 characters. It reads just as it appears, but Hello and World now have a tab between them
"H\Uello World\E"	This is also a string a 11 characters and it reads HELLO WORLD

Double-quoted strings have another additional feature that single-quoted strings don't support. Inside a double-quoted string, you can add a variable and the value of that variable will be displayed instead of the variable name. This process is called *variable interpolation.* Here's a simple example of how variable interpolation functions in a program.

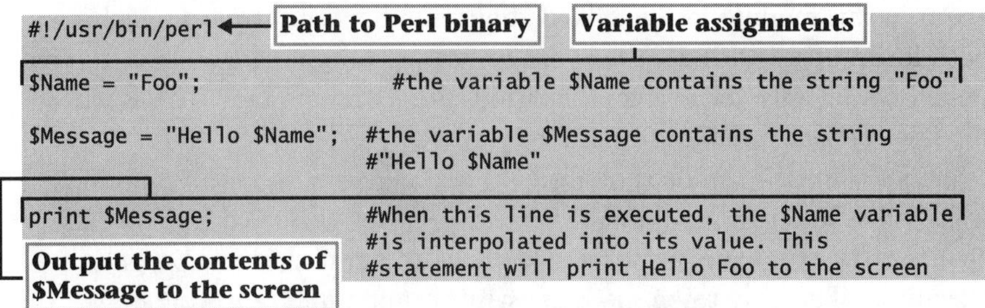

#!/usr/bin/perl
Path to Perl binary
Variable assignments
$Name = "Foo"; #the variable $Name contains the string "Foo"
$Message = "Hello $Name"; #the variable $Message contains the string #"Hello $Name"
print $Message; #When this line is executed, the $Name variable #is interpolated into its value. This #statement will print Hello Foo to the screen
Output the contents of $Message to the screen

The following illustration displays the screen output generated by the variable interpolation example.

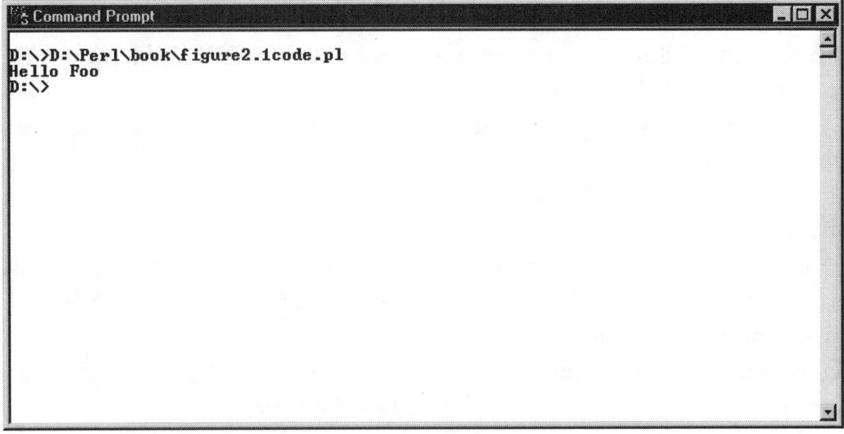

1-Minute Drill

- **What features do double-quoted strings have that single-quoted strings don't support?**
- **What are the two most-often used escape sequences in double-quoted strings?**

- **Escape sequences and variable interpolation**
- **\n (newline), and \t (tab)**

Variables are something we haven't covered yet, so let's discuss them next.

Variable Assignments

So far in this module, we've talked about numbers and strings, which are both forms of scalar data. When you're writing programs, you have to save some of your scalar data values for various programming uses. This is where the use of scalar variables comes into play.

A *scalar variable* can be thought of as a storage bin. You can put one scalar value into the bin and take it out whenever you need it. You can change what you have in the storage bin at any time during a program's execution. The only thing that's constant throughout your program's execution is the name you give your variable.

Naming Scalar Variables

You need to follow certain rules when you create scalar variable names in Perl.

You have to begin your scalar variable name with the '$' character. This character is only used for declaring scalar variables. In a future module, we introduce you to a different kind of variable. With this in mind, remember the dollar sign character is only used for scalars.

The '$' character must be followed by at least one letter. Scalar variable names cannot begin with a numeric character. Perl is a case-sensitive programming language. The variable $a is different from the variable $A. Once you have the '$' and one letter, you can then add up to 255 digits, letters, and underscores to complete your scalar variable name.

Now you know the rules to follow when naming scalar variables, so let's look at some examples.

```
# These are examples of legal scalar variable names:

$a1             #This is a perfectly legal variable name

$A1             #This is also legal but it is a different variable than the
#first because Perl is case-sensitive
```

```
$abcd1234       #This is legal but the name would not be very helpful in
#determining what it contains

$time_of_day    #This is valid and helpful to you as a programmer because
#you will know what it contains just from the name
```


Now let's look at some invalid scalar variable names. This should help you get a better idea of what you can and cannot use for names when you begin writing your programs in Perl.

```
#These are examples of invalid scalar variable names:

$               #invalid because it does not begin with at least one letter

Time_of_day               #invalid because it does not begin with the '$'
#character

$1_employee            #invalid because it does not begin with a letter

$time.eastern    #invalid because a variable name can only contain letters,
#numbers, and underscores

$wake_up!        #invalid again because a variable name can only contain
#letters, numbers, and underscores
```

Assigning Values to Scalar Variables

Now that you know the rules to follow when creating scalar variable names, you need to learn how to assign values to them. In the Perl programming language, a set of tasks can be executed by specifying different operators. Operators are covered in detail later in this module. For now, let's narrow down our discussion about operators to only one, the assignment operator. When you enter the *assignment operator* into a Perl program, it appears as the equals "=" character. This assignment operator takes whatever is on its right side and assigns it to the variable on its left side. Let's look at some examples to make this a little more clear.

```
#These are examples of how the assignment operator functions

$a=5;                          #$a now contains the scalar value of 5

$state="North Carolina";#$state contains the scalar string North Carolina
#(including the space in between North and Carolina)

$b=12;                           #$b is assigned the value 12

$a=$b;       #$a is assigned to whatever $b contains
```

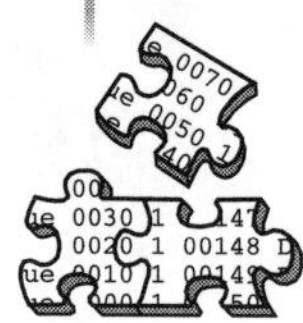

Project 2-1: Saving Data to Scalar Variables

Write a program that can save your name and your age into separate scalar variables.

What Operators Do

So far you know what types of scalar data are valid in Perl. We covered how to create valid variable names and assign scalar values to them. Now you need to know how to do something with the data you've stored. This leads into the topic of operators.

An *operator* is simply defined as an operation that takes one or more values, performs some sort of calculation, and yields a new result. Now, going back to math class, the values on which the operator "operates" are called the *operands*. The result is referred to as the *result* (of course).

The operators we cover in this module are specifically for numbers and strings. Perl expects to see numbers OR strings when using any of these operators.

Note

If you are using an operator and you give it a number and a string, you still get a result. This result will probably be impacted by some sort of type conversion. Type conversions are covered in more detail in the last section of this module.

Common Operators

The first set of common operators we cover is for numbers. Once we discuss them and give you some examples of how each of them functions, we move on to talk about operators for strings.

The most common operators for numbers are the same ones you've been using all your life. Perl provides you with the addition, subtraction, multiplication, and division operators. The following table illustrates how each operator is represented.

Operator	Description
+	Addition
-	Subtraction
*	Multiplication
/	Division

Now let's look at some examples of these operators in use.

Calculation	Result
1 + 2	The result is 3
1.2 + 2.3	The result is 3.5
2.3 – 1.2	The result is 1.1
3 * 5	The result is 15
3 * 5.5	The result is 16.5; remember all numbers in Perl are floating-point numbers
9 / 3	The result is 3
9 / 2	The result is 4.5
9/.001	The result is 9000

As you can see from the previous table, these operators perform exactly as you would expect. Now, let's look at how these operators can be used to manipulate scalar variable values. This ties in the use of the numeric operators we just talked about and the assignment operator we covered in the previous section of this module. Here's an example program to demonstrate.

Variable assignments

```
#!/usr/bin/perl

$x = 5;             #here we are assigning a value to a scalar variable

$y = 15.5;          #same here

$z = .05;           #same here
```

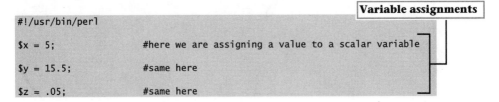

```
$a = $x + $y;          #we are adding the contents of $x and $y and

                       #assigning the result to $a

print "a equals $a\n"; #output the contents of $a

$b = $z + 5;           #here we are adding 5 to the contents of $z and
#assigning the result to $b

print "b equals $b\n"; #output the contents of $b

$c = $x / $z;          #divide $x by $z and assign the result to $c

print "c equals $c\n"; #output the contents of $c

$d = $x * $y;          #multiply $x and $y and assign the result to $d

print "d equals $d\n"; #output the contents of $d

$x = $x + 2.5;         #add 2.5 to the contents of $x and assign $x its new
#value

print "x equals $x\n"; #output the contents of $x
```

Examples of the basic operators in use with screen outputs

The following illustration shows the screen output generated by the basic mathematical operators example.

```
Command Prompt

D:\>D:\Perl\book\figure2.2code.pl
a equals 20.5
b equals 5.05
c equals 100
d equals 77.5
x equals 7.5

D:\>_
```

In addition to the standard operators just covered, Perl also supports a few additional operators that may come in handy when you begin writing programs. The first one we discuss is the modulus operator.

The *modulus operator* is represented as the percent "%" character in Perl. This operator can be used on two numbers at the same time. The first step in computing a modulus result in Perl is to take whatever numbers have been entered and convert them to integers. Once this has been done, a normal division of the two numbers takes place. The result of this division is thrown out and the remainder is saved. This remainder is the result for a modulus calculation. For example:

Modulus Calculation	Result
10 % 1	10 divided by 1 is 10 with no remainder, so the result is 0
10.2 % 2.1	First the two numbers are converted to integer values. Then 10 is divided by 2, which is 5 with no remainder, so the result is again 0
10.3 % 3.4	Again, the numbers are converted to integers, and then the division takes place. 10 divided by 3 is 3 with a remainder of 1, so the result is 1
10 % 4	10 divided by 4 is 2 with a remainder of 2, so the result is 2
10 % 5	No remainder here, so the result is 0
10 % 6	Result is 4
10 % 7	Result is 3
10 % 8	Result is 2
10 % 9	Result is 1
10 % 10	Result is 0

Another operator Perl supports is the exponentiation operator. The *exponentiation operator* is represented as two asterisks "* *" characters. With the exponentiation operator, it's possible to give a number an exponent value. Here are some examples.

Exponentiation Calculation	Result
3 ** 3	This is 3 (the base number) to the third power or 3*3*3, which yields 27
3 ** 4	This is 3 to the fourth power or 3*3*3*3, which yields 81
5 ** 2.5	This yields 55.90

This operator is a good example of how powerful this programming language is. Most other mainstream programming languages don't have an exponentiation operator. Let's go to a programming example that uses the modulus and exponentiation operators, so you can see how they work in a real program.

Variable assignments

```
#!/usr/bin/perl
$x = 5;               #here we are assigning a value to a scalar variable
$y = 15.5;            #same here
$z = .05;             #same here
$a = $x % 2;          #the modulus of 5 divided by 2
print "a equals $a\n"; #output the contents of $a
$b = $y % 2.3;        #the modulus of 15.5 divided by 2.3
print "b equals $b\n"; #output the contents of $b
$c = $x ** $y;        #5 to the 15.5
print "c equals $c\n"; #output the contents of $c
$d = $x ** 3;         #5 to the third power
print "d equals $d\n"; #output the contents of $d
```

Examples of the modulus and exponentiation operators in use with screen outputs

The following illustration is the screen output for the modulus and exponentiation programming example.

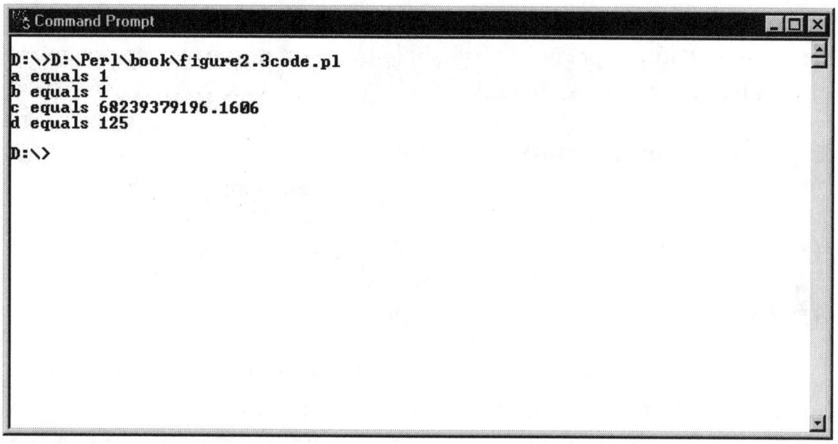

```
Command Prompt

D:\>D:\Perl\book\figure2.3code.pl
a equals 1
b equals 1
c equals 68239379196.1606
d equals 125

D:\>
```

Note

When you're using the exponentiation operator, you should never use a large number as your exponent. An exponent of 1,000,000 or more with any base number is usually too large to store. Also, you should never use a negative base number with a floating-point exponent. This yields an imaginary number, which Perl won't understand. Either case will result in a fatal error.

Another set of operators can prove useful throughout your programming adventures: the comparison operators. *Comparison operators* are often used in decision making. For example, the if structure in Perl depends on the outcome of a comparison. If the comparison evaluates to be true, then the if structure executes. If the comparison evaluates to be false, then it is skipped. Let's look at how the comparison operators are represented in Perl.

Operator	Description
<	Less than
>	Greater than
==	Equal to (not equals)
<=	Less than or equal to
>=	Greater than or equal to
!=	Not equal to
<=>	Comparison (more on this one in the following table)

Note

The if structure is covered in detail in Module 3.

Now that you've been introduced to the comparison operators for numbers, here are some examples of them in use to give you a better idea of how they work.

Example Statements	Evaluates To
$a < 5	True if $a is less than 5, false if it's not
$a > 5	True if $a is greater than 5, false if it's not
$a == 5	True if $a is equal to 5, false if it's not
$a <= 5	True if $a is less than or equal to 5, false if it's not
$a >= 5	True if $a is greater than or equal to 5, false if it's not

Example Statements	Evaluates To
$a != 5	True if $a is not equal to 5, false if it's
$a <=> 5	1 If $a is greater than 5 -1 If $a is less than 5 0 If $a is equal to 5

Now you need to learn how true and false are represented in Perl. True is a nonzero value. In the previous example of the if structure, if the evaluation returns a nonzero value, then it is true and the structure will execute. False is represented as a 0. If the evaluation for the same if structure were to return a 0, then the structure wouldn't be executed.

Let's look at a programming example to clarify the use of numeric comparison operators and what they return.

Variable assignments

```
#!/usr/bin/perl
$x = 5;                  #here we are assigning a value to a scalar variable
$y = 15.5;               #same here
$z = .05;                #same here
$a = $x < 6;             #is $x less than 6
print "a equals $a\n"; #output the contents of $a
$b = $x > 6;             #is $x greater than 6
print "b equals $b\n"; #output the contents of $b
$c = $x <= 5;            #is $x less than or equal to 5
print "c equals $c\n"; #output the contents of $c
$d = $x >= 5;            #is $x greater than or equal to 5
print "d equals $d\n"; #output the contents of $d
$e = $x == 5;            #is $x equal to 5
print "e equals $e\n"; #output the contents of $e
$f = $x != 5;            #is $x not equal to 5
print "f equals $f\n"; #output the contents of $f
$g = $x <=> 6;           #how does the value of #x compare to 6
print "g equals $g\n"; #output the contents of $g
```

Examples of the number comparison operators in use with screen outputs

The screen output for the numeric comparison operators programming example is displayed in the following illustration.

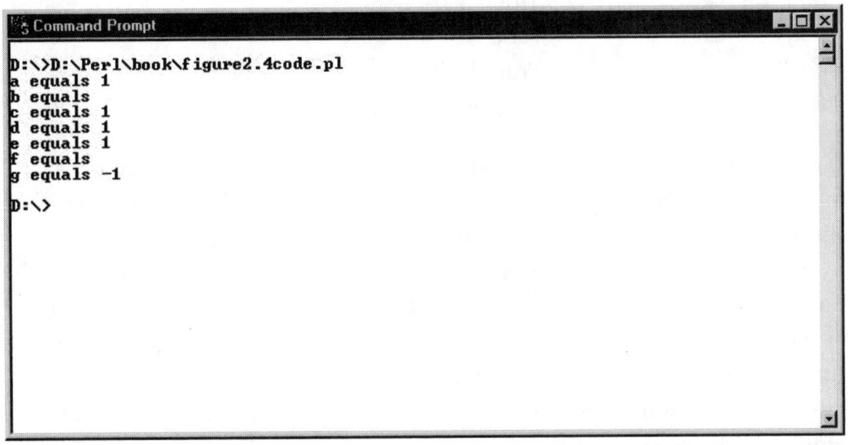

```
Command Prompt
D:\>D:\Perl\book\figure2.4code.pl
a equals 1
b equals
c equals 1
d equals 1
e equals 1
f equals
g equals -1

D:\>
```

Now that you know about the common operators for numbers, it's time to move on and cover operators for strings. As you may recall, a string can contain any of the 256 characters available to you. This means a string could be all numbers. A string of numbers and a number should be treated differently, and Perl does just that.

The following table shows the comparison operators, along with a description for each one.

Operator	Description
lt	Less than
gt	Greater than
le	Less than or equal to
ge	Greater than or equal to
eq	Equal to
ne	Not equal to
cmp	Comparison

Now let's see some examples of these operators in use.

Example Statements	Evaluates To
"dog" lt "cat"	False because the ASCII value *d* is greater than the ASCII value *c*
"345" gt "62"	False because the ASCII value of 3 is less than the ASCII value of 6

Example Statements	Evaluates To
"dog" le "cat"	False
"dog" ge "cat"	True
"dog" eq "cat"	False
"dog" ne "cat"	True
"dog" cmp "cat"	1 because the first value is greater

As you can see from the previous table, the comparison operators function the same for strings as they do for numbers. The cmp operator also carries the same rules for evaluation that it did for numbers.

One thing you should have noticed about the previous examples is how the strings containing numbers were treaded differently than normal numbers. Because they are treated differently, you need to make sure you are using the correct operator when you perform calculations. If you use the le operator where you meant to use the <= operator, you probably won't get the correct results.

Note

Perl does perform type conversions for you when you mix operators with strings and numbers. The last section of this module covers this topic in more detail.

Here's another programming example to clarify the use of string comparison operators and what they return.

Variable assignments

```
#!/usr/bin/perl
$x = "dog";              #here we are assigning a value to a scalar variable
$y = "cat";              #same here
$z = "foo";              #same here
$a = $x lt $y;           #is $x less than $y
print "a equals $a\n";   #output the contents of $a
$b = $x gt $y;           #is $x greater than $y
print "b equals $b\n";   #output the contents of $b
```

Examples of the string comparison operators in use with screen outputs

```
$c = $x le $y;          #is $x less than or equal to $y
print "c equals $c\n";  #output the contents of $c
$d = $x ge $y;          #is $x greater than or equal to $y
print "d equals $d\n";  #output the contents of $d
$e = $x eq $y;          #is $x equal to $y
print "e equals $e\n";  #output the contents of $e
$f = $x ne $y;          #is $x not equal to $y
print "f equals $f\n";  #output the contents of $f
$g = $x cmp $y;         #compare $x and $y
print "g equals $g\n";  #output the contents of $g
$h = "560" lt "1200";   #is the string 560 less than the string 1200
print "h equals $h\n";  #output the contents of $h
```

Examples of the string comparison operators in use with screen outputs

The following illustration is the screen output for the string comparison operators programming example.

```
Command Prompt

D:\>D:\Perl\book\figure2.5code.pl
a equals
b equals 1
c equals
d equals 1
e equals
f equals 1
g equals 1
h equals

D:\>
```

We have now covered the common operators you'll use in Perl programming for strings and numbers. We need to address a few more operators, however, which brings us to the next section of this module.

More Complex Operators and Functions

Perl provides you with an additional set of operators that are meant to save you time over using the traditional operators we talked about in the previous section. These additional operators can also be separated into the categories of numbers and strings. First, let's look at the additional operators for numbers.

The *binary assignment operator* is a short-hand way of representing a calculation and an assignment. For example, from the previous section, if you wanted to add some number to a variable and set the result equal to that variable, your code would look something like:

```
$x = $x + 10;
```

Using the binary assignment operator, you can accomplish the same task with:

```
$x += 10;
```

Binary assignment operators exist for addition, subtraction, multiplication, division, and exponentiation. Here are some examples to show each of these operators in use and how they compare to their equivalent standard statements.

With Binary Assignment Operator	Same as Saying
$x +=2	$x = $x + 2
$x -= 2	$x = $x - 2
$x /= 5	$x = $x / 5
$x *= 5	$x = $x * 5
$x **=4	$x = $x ** 4

Let's go to a programming example to demonstrate that using the binary assignment operators and the basic operators yields the same results.

Variable assignments

```
#!/usr/bin/perl
$x = 12;                    #here we are assigning a value to a scalar variable
$y = 3;                    #same here
$z = 2;                     #same here
```

Addition using the basic addition operator

Addition with the addition binary assignment operator

```
$x1 = $x + 10;          #add 10 to $x and set the result equal to $x1
$x += 10;               #add 10 to $x and set the result equal to $x
$a = $x == $x1;         #compare $x and $x1 for equality
print "a equals $a\n";  #output the contents of $a
$y1 = $y * 3;           #multiply the contents of $y by 3 and set the
                        #result equal to $y1
$y *= 3;                #multiply the contents of $y by 3 and set the
                        #result equal to $y
$b = $y == $y1;         #compare $y and $y1 for equality
print "b equals $b\n";  #output the contents of $b
```

An equality comparison to ensure the same result was obtained

Output the true (nonzero) or false(zero) value of the comparison to the screen

Another example using the multiplication binary assignment operator

The following illustration shows the screen output for the binary assignment operators programming example.

```
Command Prompt
D:\>D:\Perl\book\figure2.6code.pl
a equals 1
b equals 1

D:\>
```

In this programming example, the values $a and $b represent the outcome of the equality operators evaluation. The values compared were equal, so the statement was true. Remember, in Perl, true is represented as a nonzero value, or in this example, 1.

We should cover a few more operators for numbers: the autoincrement and autodecrement operators. These operators are an even shorter version of the += and -= binary assignment operators. The *autoincrement operator* is represented by two plus '++' characters, side by side. The *autodecrement operator* is represented by two minus '--' characters, side by side. Here's a programming example to show how they function.

Variable assignments

```
#!/usr/bin/perl

$x = 12;                 #here we are assigning a value to a scalar variable

$y = 3;                  #same here

$z = 2;                  #same here

++$x;                    #increment the value of $x by one and save the new
#value back into $x

print "x equals $x\n";   #output the contents of $x

$a = ++$y;               #increment the value of $y by one, save the new
#value back into $y, and set that new value equal to $a also

print "y equals $y\n";   #output the contents of $y

print "a equals $a\n";   #output the contents of $a also

$b = $z++;               #set the contents of $z equal to $b, increment the
#value of $z by one and save the new value back into $z

print "z equals $z\n";   #output the contents of $z

print "b equals $b\n";   #output the contents of $b

-$x;                    #decrement the value of $x by one and save the new
#value back into $x

print "x equals $x\n";   #output the contents of $x
```

The screen output for the autoincrement and autodecrement programming example is displayed in the following illustration.

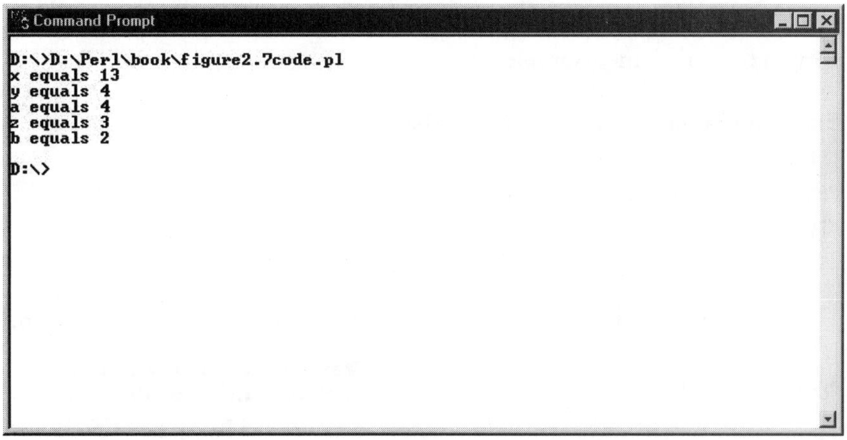

```
D:\>D:\Perl\book\figure2.7code.pl
x equals 13
y equals 4
a equals 4
z equals 3
b equals 2

D:\>
```

In the previous example, note that it DOES matter where these operators appear. For example, consider the following assignment from the program:

```
$a = ++$y;
```

This piece of code will increment the value of $y by one before anything is assigned to $a. In this case, both $a and $y contain the same values after the assignment executes. Now consider this assignment:

```
$b = $z++;
```

Here $b gets the contents of $z, and then the value of $z is incremented by one. The value of $b is one less than the value of $z when this assignment executes.

Now that the more complex operators for numbers have been covered, let's discuss the more complex operators for strings.

The concatenation operator is the first of the more complex operators we discuss. The *concatenation operator* is represented by the period "."

character. It takes two strings and combines them to form a new, longer string. Here are some examples.

Example Statement	Evaluates to
"Hello" . "World"	HelloWorld
"Hello" . " " . "World"	Hello World
"Hello" . "\n" . "World"	Hello World

Now let's look at a programming example to see this operator in action.

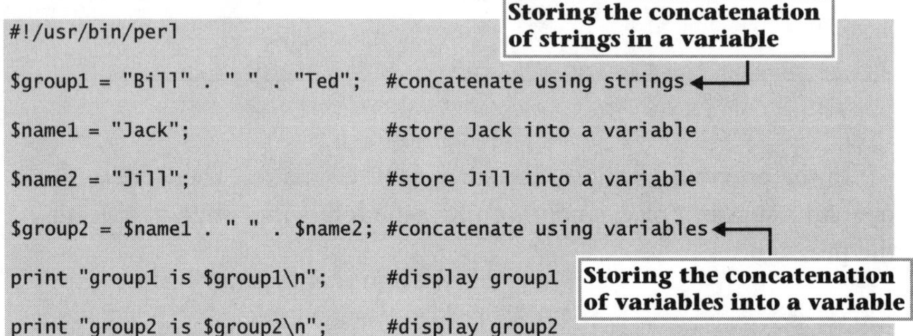

```
#!/usr/bin/perl

$group1 = "Bill" . " " . "Ted";  #concatenate using strings

$name1 = "Jack";                 #store Jack into a variable

$name2 = "Jill";                 #store Jill into a variable

$group2 = $name1 . " " . $name2; #concatenate using variables

print "group1 is $group1\n";     #display group1

print "group2 is $group2\n";     #display group2
```

Storing the concatenation of strings in a variable
Storing the concatenation of variables into a variable

The following illustration shows the screen output for the concatenation programming example.

```
Command Prompt

D:\>D:\Perl\book\figure2.8code.pl
group1 is Bill Ted
group2 is Jack Jill

D:\>
```

Another string operator available to you is the *string repetition operator,* which is represented by the lowercase *x* character. It accepts a string on its left side and a number on its right side. The number tells the operator how many times to repeat the string. The line of code

```
$name = "Bill" x 5;
```

stores the string "BillBillBillBillBill" in the $name variable.

Earlier in this module, during our discussion on double-quoted strings, you learned several "backslash" operators can be used within a string to change its format. A subset of these operators can be used outside of a double-quoted string to get the same result. Let's look at the new functions and see how they compare to those you've already learned about.

New Function	Backslash Operator	Result
lc	\L	All letters in the string are converted to lowercase
lcfirst	\l	Only the first letter in the string is converted to lowercase
uc	\U	All letters in the string are converted to uppercase
ucfirst	\u	Only the first letter in the string is converted to uppercase

Now let's look at a coding example of these new functions in use.

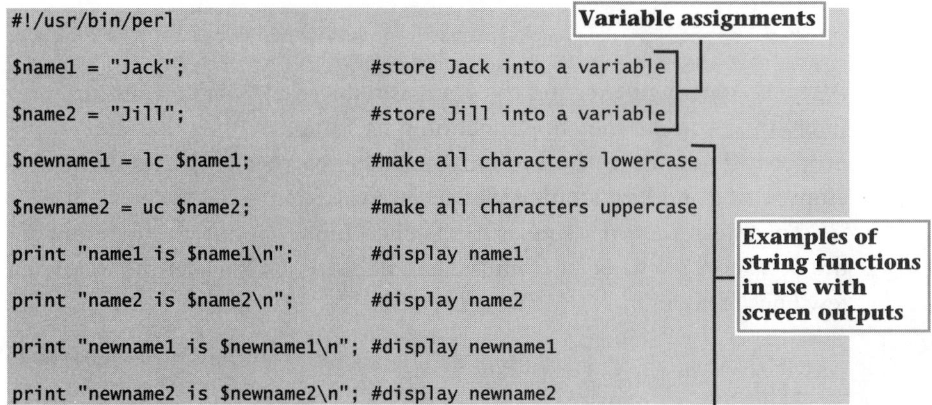

```
#!/usr/bin/perl
$name1 = "Jack";                  #store Jack into a variable
$name2 = "Jill";                  #store Jill into a variable
$newname1 = lc $name1;            #make all characters lowercase
$newname2 = uc $name2;            #make all characters uppercase
print "name1 is $name1\n";        #display name1
print "name2 is $name2\n";        #display name2
print "newname1 is $newname1\n";  #display newname1
print "newname2 is $newname2\n";  #display newname2
```

Variable assignments
Examples of string functions in use with screen outputs

The following illustration is the screen output for the string functions programming example.

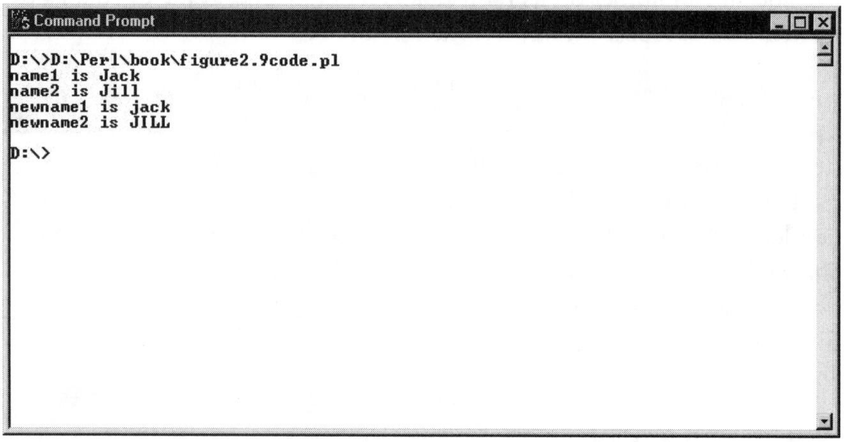

```
Command Prompt
D:\>D:\Perl\book\figure2.9code.pl
name1 is Jack
name2 is Jill
newname1 is jack
newname2 is JILL

D:\>
```

The last two string functions covered here are closely related: the chop and chomp functions. The *chop function* drops the last character of a string. If you consider the following line of code

```
$state = "North Carolina\n";
```

Then you can chop the last character, in this case \n, off the string by saying:

```
chop $state;
```

After this statement executes the string is reduced to "North Carolina". Every time you use the chop function on a string, another character is dropped. If you try to chop an empty string, you're left with the same empty string and Perl won't generate an error.

The *chomp function* is similar to the chop function, but it only removes the newline '\n' character from the end of a string. Consider the following few lines of code

```
$state = "North Carolina\n";

chomp $state;
```

Now $state contains the string "North Carolina". If we use the chomp operator on $state again, it still contains "North Carolina".

2

Note

When you are storing user input strings for use in your programs, they are saved with the newline character at the end. If you want to delete the newline character, but you want to make sure you don't delete any other characters in the string, use the chomp function. Even if a newline character is not at the end of the user input, you are still safe using this function.

The logical operators provided in Perl work for both strings and numbers. These operators look for zero and non-zero values in determining their output. Let's look at the logical operators and what they do.

Logical Operator	Description
||	Logical or
&&	Logical and
!	Logical not

The following is an example program that demonstrates these operators in use.

Variable assignments

```
#!/usr/bin/perl

$x = 10;

$y = 0;

$a = $x || $y;              #if the contents of either $x

                            #or $y are nonzero then this will

                            #evaluate to true

print "a equals $a\n";
```

Logical OR comparison

Logical AND comparison

```
$b = $$x && $y;             #if $x and $y are both nonzero
                            #then this will evaluate to true
print "b equals $b\n";
$c = ! $x;                  #not $x will be false
print "c equals $c\n";
$d = ! $y;                  #not $y will the true
print "d equals $d\n";
```

The logical NOT operator inverts any nonzero value to zero and vise versa

The following illustration displays the screen output for the logical operators programming example.

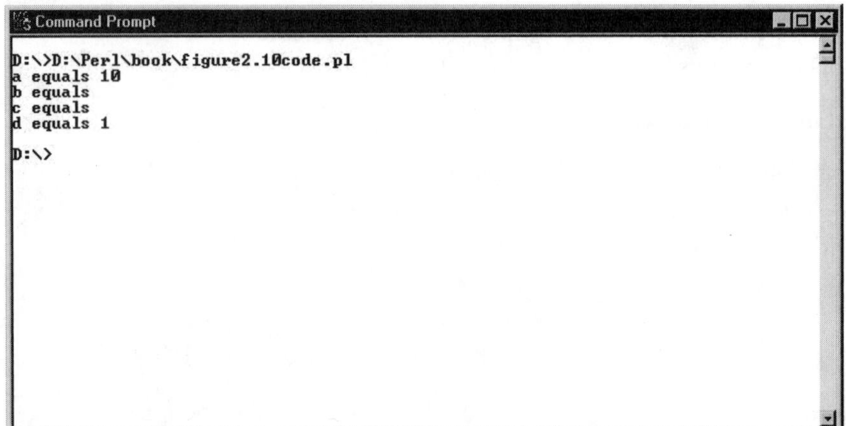

Note

The value for $a from the previous example was 10. Because the expression evaluated to true, you might have been expecting the value of $a to be 1. Remember, any nonzero value returned from this type of operation represents a true response.

Bit-Manipulation Operators

Perl provides you with the capability to manipulate the bits of integers through the use of bit-manipulation operators. These *bit-manipulation operators* first convert floating-point numbers to integers. Then they convert the integer to its binary representation. Once they have the number in its binary form, any of the following operations can be performed.

Bit-Manipulation Operator	Description
&	Bitwise and
|	Bitwise or
^	Bitwise exclusive or
~	Bitwise not
<<, >>	Left shift and right shift

To understand how these operators work, here's a truth table of all the logical comparators.

X value	Y value	Z value	and	or	exclusive or	not
1	1	1	true	true	false	000
1	1	0	false	true	false	001
1	0	1	false	true	false	010
1	0	0	false	true	true	011

Now, using this truth table, you can figure out how the bit-manipulation operators compute their results. Here's a simple example to make this more clear.

The integer number 3 is 011 in binary notation. The integer number 7 is 0111 in binary notation. When Perl is performing a bitwise "and", here is what it does:

```
0011   #this is 3 in binary notation
0111   #this is 7 in binary notation
----------------------------------------------------------------
0011   #"and" is true when both values are true, so you wind up with 0011,
       which is 3.
```

The previous example in a program would look like this:

```
$a = 3 & 7;        #the result of this operation would be 3
```

The *left* and *right shift operators* manipulate the bits of an integer by shifting them a specified number of times to the right or to the left. Here's an example of how this works.

```
$a = 7 >> 1  # this will shift the binary representation of
#7 one bit to the right.
```

From the previous example, 7 is 0111 in binary form. Shifting the bits one space to the right leaves us with 0011. In our example, $a is equal to 3. The left shift operator functions the same, except it shifts the bits to the left.

Note

The new bits that are shifted into a binary number are always 0, no matter which shift operator you use.

Operator Precedence

Operator precedence is an important topic to cover before you begin writing programs that need to perform calculations. *Operator precedence* refers to the order in which operators are executed when performing a calculation. You probably remember from math class that multiplication and division come before addition and subtraction in the order of operations. You'll be happy to know Perl follows these same rules of precedence.

Another term to be familiar with when talking about operator precedence is *associativity,* which refers to the order in which two or more operators of the same precedence level are executed.

The following table contains all the operators starting with the highest precedence level. The table also contains the associativity properties of each group of operators.

Operator	Description	Associativity
->	Dereference operator or method call	Left-to-right
++, —	Autoincrement and autodecrement	Not applicable
**	Exponentiation operator	Right-to-left

Operator	**Description**	**Associativity**
-, +, \, !, ~	Operators with one operand Signed numbers	Right-to-left
=~, !~	Matching operators	Left-to-right
*, /, %, x	Multiplication, division, modulus, string replicate	Left-to-right
+, -, .	Plus, minus, concatenate	Left-to-right
<<, >>	Shifting operators	Left-to-right
chomp, chop, uc, etc.	Named unary functions	Not applicable
<, <=, >, >=, lt, gt, le, ge	Inequality comparison operators	Not applicable
==, !=, <=>, eq, ne, cmp	Equality comparison operators	Not applicable
&	Bitwise "and"	Left-to-right
|, ^	Bitwise "or" and "exclusive or"	Left-to-right
&&	Logical "and"	Left-to-right
||	Logical "or"	Left-to-right
.., ...	Non-inclusive and inclusive range	Not applicable
?:	If-then-else	Right-to-left
=, +=, -=, *=, etc.	Binary assignment operators	Right-to-left
,	comma	Left-to-right
not	Logical not	Right-to-left
and	Logical and	Left-to-right
or, xor	Logical or and xor	Left-to-right

Note

You can force any operation to take place first by placing parentheses "()" around it.

Now that you have this table as a reference, here are some examples of how this works.

Calculation	**How Perl Sees It**
2*3+10	6+10 or 16
2*3*10	6*10 or 60
2*10/5	20/5 or 4
2**2*5+10	4*5+10 or 20+10 or 30

Now let's perform the same calculations with a Perl program for completeness.

```
#!/usr/bin/perl

$a = 2 * 3 + 10;      <-- Multiplication before division

print "a equals $a\n";

$b = 2 * 3 * 10;      <-- Multiplication moves from left to right

print "b equals $b\n";

$c = 2 * 10 / 5;      <-- Associative rules apply here also

print "c equals $c\n";

$d = 2 ** 2 * 5 + 10; <-- Exponentiation comes before multiplication

print "d equals $d\n";
```

Exponentiation comes before multiplication: eighth line
The following illustration shows the screen output for the operator precedence programming example.

```
Command Prompt
D:\>D:\Perl\book\figure2.11code.pl
a equals 16
b equals 60
c equals 4
d equals 30

D:\>
```

Project 2-2: Working with Operators

Starting with the program from Project 2-1, add the code necessary to calculate the number of hours you have been alive according to your age. Also output your name and newly calculated hours of life to the screen on separate lines.

Type Conversion

In this module, we discussed two different data types: numbers and strings. Both of these types are stored in the same kind of variable. Because either data type can be stored in the same kind of variable, at one time or another, you'll probably mix data types by mistake. This isn't a major problem, as it would be in most programming languages.

A type conversion takes place when you try to use a number with a string operator or visa versa. For example, if you pass a string containing "12cats" to a numeric operator, the 'cats' portion of the string is dropped and the integer value 12 is used for the calculation. Perl removes any leading white spaces and any trailing nonnumeric characters when performing type conversions from strings to numbers. If you pass a number (for example, 145) to a string operator, the number is converted to a string. A good example of how this might happen is if you want to make a "less than" comparison on two different numbers and you use the 'lt' operator instead of the '<' operator. Your numbers are now compared according to their ASCII values. The string "3" is greater than the string "290" because the ASCII value of 3 is greater than the ASCII value of 2. You can see this would cause a problem in calculations if you were expecting an integer comparison.

Mastery Check

1. What do hexadecimal numbers begin with?

A. #

B. 0

C. Hex

D. 0x

Mastery Check

2. Which of the following is an octal number?

   A. 0x4325

   B. 8888

   C. 0563

   D. Oct86

3. How long can a string be?

   A. 256 characters

   B. 255 characters

   C. As many characters as memory will allow

   D. None of the above

4. What kind of string supports variable interpolation?

   A. Single-quoted string

   B. Double-quoted string

   C. All of the above

   D. None of the above

5. Which of the following is a valid scalar variable name?

   A. $Time.1

   B. $time1

   C. $1time

   D. All of the above

6. Given $x = 3 * 4 + 6 / 12 – 2, select the order in which these operators execute.

   A. /, *, –, +

   B. *, +, /, -

   C. *, /, –, +

   D. *, /, +, -

Module 3

Control Structures

The Goals of This Module

- Introduce you to the various types of conditional statements available
- Cover some control statements that can be used inside loops
- Introduce you to the concept of nested loops

So far, you have learned about the various data types in Perl, as well as how variable assignments and operators are used. Now it's time to learn about control structures and how they are used in programs. These structures are used in most of the programs you write simply because they give you some control over how your programs execute. This module begins by looking at the most basic piece of any control structure, the block statement, and then moves on to cover the rest of the conditional statements. Once you complete this section, we introduce you to some control statements you can use inside loops and, finally, we cover the concept of nested loops and how they function.

Conditional Statements

Conditional statements are used in programming languages when a decision needs to be made before a section of code is executed. You might need to make sure a counter has reached a certain number before executing code or you may want to check the contents of a variable to make sure the value is what you thought it should be. Before we cover the different conditional statements in detail, we need to discuss the basic building block of any conditional structure, the statement block.

Statement blocks

A *statement block* is a sequence of executable statements that are grouped together with curly braces. *Curly braces* are the '{' and '}' characters. A statement block in a program looks like this:

```
{
$a = 12;
$a += 5;
print "a equals $a\n";
}
```

Here's another example of a statement block with the curly braces located differently.

```
{$a = 12;
$a += 5;
print "a equals $a\n";}
```

Note

The previous statement blocks are identical in functionality even though the curly braces are in different locations. You can put the curly braces anywhere you want as long as they are before and after the lines of code you want to encompass in the statement block.

The lines of code in a statement block are always guaranteed to be executed, so they can be referred to as *unconditional statements*. An empty statement block is accepted in Perl, but it probably won't be helpful to you.

Now that you understand what statement blocks are and how they function, let's get right into learning about the different types of conditional statements.

The if-then-else Conditional Statement

The *if-then-else* conditional statement takes an expression and evaluates it for a true/false value. If the evaluation of the expression yields a true value, the statement block for the then portion of the statement is executed. If the evaluation of the expression returns false, the else statement block is executed. Here's the syntax for the if-then-else conditional statement.

```
if (expression)
{
'then' statement block
}
else
{
'else' statement block
}
```

Leaving the else portion of this statement off is perfectly legal if you don't need it. Here's the syntax for an if-then statement without an else.

```
if (expression)
{
'then' statement block
}
```

Note

No syntactical changes are between an if-then-else statement and an if-then statement, other than the else portion that includes its statement block was removed.

Now that you know the syntax for the if-then-else statement, let's look at a short program containing one.

```
#!/usr/bin/perl
$a = 20;
if ($a = 15){
print "a is equal to 15.\n";
}
else {
print "a is not equal to 15.\n";
}
```

This program prints "a is equal to 15" if the if expression evaluates to true; otherwise, it prints "a is not equal to 15."

Having an else statement block without first having an if statement block is illegal in Perl. If you're only concerned about the cases when the expression evaluates to false, you can use the unless conditional statement to avoid having an if-then-else statement. The syntax for the unless conditional statement is as follows.

```
unless (expression)
{
'unless' statement block
}
else
{
'else' statement block
}
```

The unless conditional statement evaluates the expression for a true/false value and, as long as that value is false, the unless statement block is executed. When the expression evaluates to true, the else statement block is executed. The else portion of this statement can be dropped, just as we discussed earlier with the if-then-else example.

Note

The unless conditional statement is most useful when you only care about the cases when the expression evaluates to false. If you run into a case where you need to use an unless conditional statement, you probably won't need to add an else statement. Using an else with an unless is basically an if-then-else statement in reverse order, which doesn't buy you anything.

Yet another option you have when using the if-then-else conditional statement is the capability to add elsif statements, if necessary. The syntax for an if-then-else conditional statement containing elsif statements is as follows.

```
if (expression)
{
'then' statement block
}
elsif (expression)
{
'elsif' statement block
}
else
{
'else' statement block
}
```

Elsif statements are used when you have more than one expression to evaluate to select the correct statement block to execute. As with the plain if-then-else statement, when any section of the control structure is executed, the rest of it is ignored. You can have as many elsif statements in an if-then-else control structure as you need.

Note

Notice the elsif statement isn't spelled "elseif."

Now that we've covered all the options for the if-then-else conditional statement, let's look at a few programming examples to see this statement in use.

```
#!/usr/bin/perl
$a = 15;          # scalar variable assignment
if ($a < 25) {         # conditional if statement
print "a is less than 25";
}
else  {            # conditional else statement
print "a is greater than or equal to 25";
}
```

Path to Perl binary

The expression $a < 25 evaluates to true

This statement block is executed

The else conditional statement along with its statement block are both skipped

The following illustration shows the screen output for the if-then-else programming example.

```
Command Prompt
D:\>D:\Perl\book\figure3.1code.pl
a is less than 25
D:\>
```

The previous example should give you a good idea of how an if-then-else conditional statement works. Here's a coding example of an unless conditional statement.

```
#!/usr/bin/perl
$a = 15;      # scalar variable assignment
unless ($a > 25) {  # unless conditional statement
print "a is still less than 25";
}
```

Notice our expression changed from the previous example

This expression evaluates to false, which executes the unless statement block

3

The following illustration is the screen output for the unless programming example.

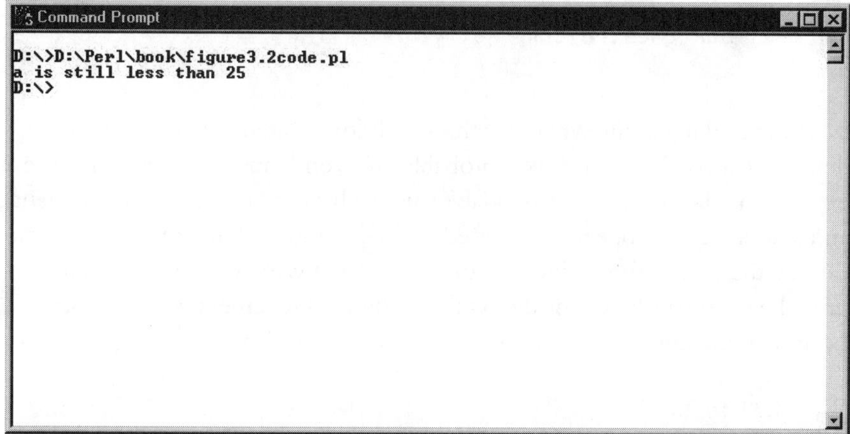

Now you should have a good understanding of the if-then-else conditional statement, as well as all the options you have to choose from when using it. Let's move on to another conditional statement you will probably use a lot, the while statement.

1-Minute Drill

- **List all the available parts of an if-then-else conditional statement.**
- **If you only care about the else case of an if-then-else conditional statement, what conditional statement should you use instead?**

- **If statement, elsif statement, statement blocks, and the else statement**
- **The unless conditional statement**

The while Conditional Statement

The *while* conditional statement is a useful one because it enables you to repeat a statement block as many times as you need. The while statement works just like an if-then-else conditional statement in that you specify an expression for a true/false evaluation. The one main difference, however, is it continues to execute the statement block as long as the expression is true. Here's the syntax for a while conditional statement.

```
While (expression)
{
'while' statement block
}
```

After looking at the syntax for this conditional statement and trying to determine a good use for it, you probably are wondering how and when the expression will ever evaluate to a false value. This is where the autoincrement and autodecrement operators covered in the last module come in handy. You can use these operators to increase or decrease the value of a number each time the statement block for the while conditional statement is executed. Look at a programming example to make this more clear.

```
#!/usr/bin/perl
$a = 15;                #scalar variable assignment
while ($a < 25){        #while conditional statement
print "$a is still less than 25 \n";
$a++;                   #autoincrement operator
}
```

The statement block executes as long as $a is less than 25

This autoincrement operator increases the value of $a by one each time the statement block is executed

The screen output for the while programming example is shown in the following illustration.

```
D:\>D:\Perl\book\figure3.3code.pl
15 is still less than 25
16 is still less than 25
17 is still less than 25
18 is still less than 25
19 is still less than 25
20 is still less than 25
21 is still less than 25
22 is still less than 25
23 is still less than 25
24 is still less than 25

D:\>
```

A while statement can easily be designed to be an infinite loop. For instance, in the previous example, if we'd left the autoincrement statement out of the statement block, we would have had an infinite loop. The value of $a would have always been less than 25. Infinite loops are useful in programming in many ways. Probably the best example is if you set up a program to run inside an infinite while loop, which constantly checks for some sort of system error. This error would cause the loop to terminate, which would immediately let you know some sort of error must have occurred.

The statement block of the while conditional statement can be executed an infinite number of times, as we just discussed, but it's perfectly legal for the statement block to never be executed. If the expression evaluates to false on the first iteration, the whole statement is skipped.

Now that we've covered the while statement, let's discuss another similar conditional statement.

1-Minute Drill

- **What is the main functional difference between the if-then-else and while conditional statements?**
- **Which operators that you've learned about are most often used inside a while loop?**

The until Conditional Statement

The *until* conditional statement is the opposite of the while statement. The until statement block only executes as long as the expression evaluates to false. Here's the syntax for the until conditional statement.

```
until (expression)
{
'until' statement block
}
```

Now let's look at a programming example of the until conditional statement in use to give you a better idea of how it functions.

```
#!/usr/bin/perl
$a = 15;     # scalar variable assignment
until ($a > 25){     # the until conditional statement
print "The value of a is $a \n";
$a++;     #autoincrement operator
}
```

The statement block executes until $a is greater than 25

This autoincrement operator increases the value of $a by one each time the statement block is executed

---

- **if-then-else statements cannot create loops, where while statements are designed to do just that**
- **The autoincrement and autodecrement operators**

The following illustration is the screen output for the until programming example.

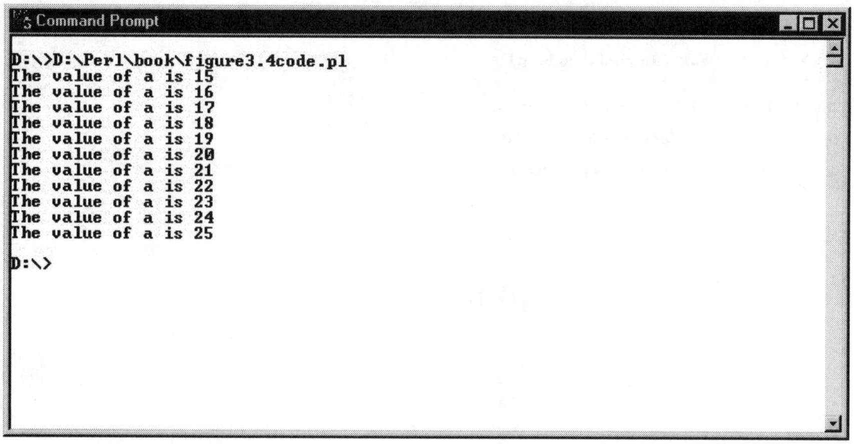

```
Command Prompt
D:\>D:\Perl\book\figure3.4code.pl
The value of a is 15
The value of a is 16
The value of a is 17
The value of a is 18
The value of a is 19
The value of a is 20
The value of a is 21
The value of a is 22
The value of a is 23
The value of a is 24
The value of a is 25

D:\>
```

Note

In the previous while statement programming example, the statement block was executed ten times. Now, using the until statement and reversing the expression, the statement block was executed 11 times. Remember this when you're writing code because even though it seems these two examples should yield the same results, they don't.

Here's another programming example that uses user input along with the until conditional statement.

```
#!/usr/bin/perl
print "what is 2 + 2\n";  # user question
$a = <STDIN>;    # store input from user
until ($a == 4){    # until conditional statement
print "You know that is not right, try again \n";
$a = <STDIN>;    # input from user again
}
print "yes, that should have been easier for you";
```

Present the user with a question

This line reads in whatever the user enters and stores it in to $a

This statement block will be executed until $a is equal to 4

The execution of this statement is not completed until the user presses the return key

This line will execute when the until expression is true and the statement block is skipped

The following illustration displays the screen output for the until programming example with user input.

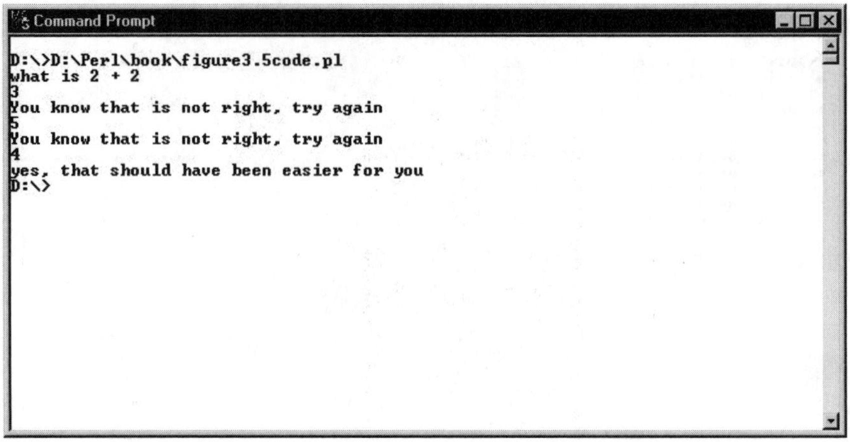

```
Command Prompt
D:\>D:\Perl\book\figure3.5code.pl
what is 2 + 2
3
You know that is not right, try again
5
You know that is not right, try again
4
yes, that should have been easier for you
D:\>
```

The previous programming example demonstrates how an until statement can be used to control the execution of a program. The program continues to prompt the user for the correct answer until she enters the right one.

The next conditional statement uses the while and until statements just discussed, but in a different order.

The do while-until Conditional Statement

In the previous two sections of this module, we discussed that when using the while or until conditional statements, it was possible for their statement blocks never to be executed. If the expression evaluated to false when true was expected, the whole statement was skipped. In some cases, you may require the statement block to be executed at least one time. Perl enables you to do this by using the *do while-until* conditional statement. Let's look at the syntax for the do while statement and, remember, the do until statement has the same syntax with until substituted for while.

```
do
{
'do' statement block
} while (expression)
```

The do while-until conditional statement enables you to execute the statement block at least one time, no matter what the expression evaluates to. Here's a programming example to demonstrate this.

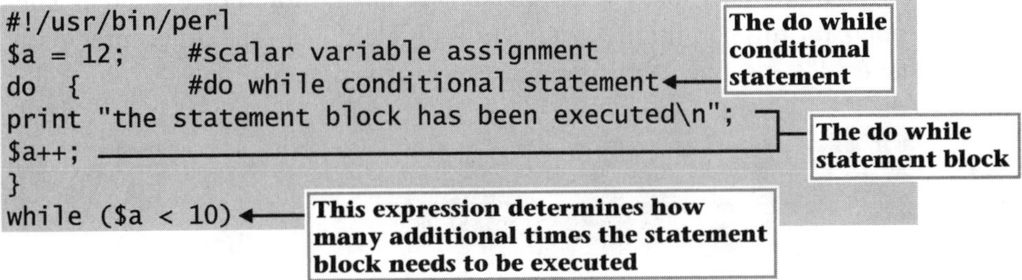

#!/usr/bin/perl
$a = 12;   #scalar variable assignment
do {   #do while conditional statement
print "the statement block has been executed\n";
$a++;
}
while ($a < 10)
The do while conditional statement
The do while statement block
This expression determines how many additional times the statement block needs to be executed

See the following illustration for the screen output for the do while programming example.

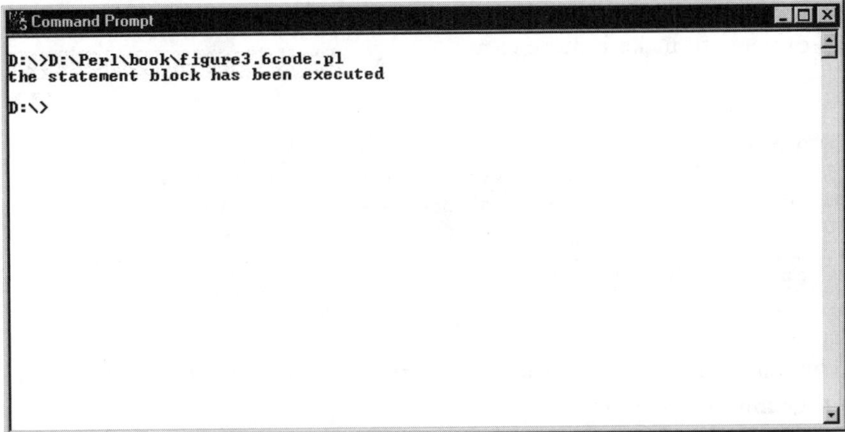

As you can see in the illustration, the statement block was executed one time even though the while expression could never be true. If we were to substitute the while statement with the until statement, we would get an infinite loop. The statement block would execute until $a is less than 10, which could never happen.

Now that you've been introduced to the do while-until control statement, let's move on to the for conditional statement.

The for Conditional Statement

The *for* statement is widely used by programmers in all languages. The reason for this is the *for* statement provides you with a shorthand method of specifying how many times a statement block should be executed. The syntax for this conditional statement is different from the others previously covered. Let's look at it and discuss each part in detail.

```
for (statement; conditional expression; iterator statement)
{
'for' statement block
}
```

Notice from the syntax on the first line that the for statement has three parts. The first line given here reads "for statement until conditional expression; iterator statement." Most of the time, the expressions in your for statement contain a range of numbers and this range of numbers determines how many times the statement block gets executed. Here's an example to make it more clear.

```
#!/usr/bin/perl
for ($a=1; $a < 10; $a++){ #the for conditional statement
print "the statement block has been executed $a times \n";
}
```

This gives you a range from one to nine

The following illustration shows the screen output generated from the for programming example.

```
Command Prompt
D:\>D:\Perl\book\figure3.7code.pl
the statment block has been executed 1 times
the statment block has been executed 2 times
the statment block has been executed 3 times
the statment block has been executed 4 times
the statment block has been executed 5 times
the statment block has been executed 6 times
the statment block has been executed 7 times
the statment block has been executed 8 times
the statment block has been executed 9 times

D:\>
```

The for statement from the previous example reads "for $a equals 1 to $a less than 10, increment $a." The value of $a is one the first time the for statement executes. Before the statement block is executed, the value of $a is incremented by one so, after the block executes, the new value of $a can be evaluated to ensure it's still less than ten. Each time the evaluation is true, $a is again incremented by one and the statement block gets executed. In this example, the statement block was executed nine times.

1-Minute Drill

- **From the previous programming example, what was the final value of $a?**
- **How many times would the statement block have been executed if expression 2 had been $a <= 10 and what would the final value of $a have been?**

- **10**
- **10, 11**

Project 3-1: Creating a Counting Loop

Write a program that creates a counting loop just like the one in the previous programming example without using the for conditional statement. You may use any of the other conditional statements you learned in this module. The program should display the number of times the statement block has been executed, along with the final value of the counter variable you use.

If you're using the for conditional statement and you need the statement, conditional expression, iterator statement, or any combination of the three components to contain more than one statement, you can use a comma "," to separate them. Here's a programming example that demonstrates this.

```
#!/usr/bin/perl
for ($a = 1; $a < 10; $a++, print "the value of a is now $a \n"){
print "the statement block has been executed $a times \n";
}
```

Notice the iterator portion of the for conditional statement contains two statements separated by a comma

The print statement will be executed along with the autoincrement operator

The following illustration is the screen output generated from the for programming example using commas.

```
Command Prompt
D:\>D:\Perl\book\figure3.8code.pl
the statment block has been executed 1 times
the value of a is now 2
the statment block has been executed 2 times
the value of a is now 3
the statment block has been executed 3 times
the value of a is now 4
the statment block has been executed 4 times
the value of a is now 5
the statment block has been executed 5 times
the value of a is now 6
the statment block has been executed 6 times
the value of a is now 7
the statment block has been executed 7 times
the value of a is now 8
the statment block has been executed 8 times
the value of a is now 9
the statment block has been executed 9 times
the value of a is now 10

D:\>
```

This programming example keeps track of how many times the statement block executes, as well as the value $a contains throughout execution. Now that the for conditional statement has been covered in detail, let's move on to discuss the last two conditional statements.

The foreach Conditional Statement

The *foreach* conditional statement can be used to iterate through an array variable's contents. This enables you to specify different ranges for a loop to iterate over, rather than only being able to specify a start and end point.

Note

The array variable is a topic we haven't covered yet. For now, think of the array variable as containing a list of numbers or strings all associated together. These pieces of scalar data are referred to as *elements* of the array. This topic is covered in detail in the next module of this book.

Let's look at the syntax for the foreach conditional statement before discussing it in detail.

```
foreach scalar variable (array variable)
{
'foreach' statement block
}
```

The scalar variable in the foreach statement will be set equal to the current element being used from the array. Note, once the foreach statement has completed execution, the scalar variable is reset to equal the value it was before the statement began execution. A variable that's only valid in certain sections of a program is said to have a *scope* in those sections. Because the scalar variable has a scope inside the foreach loop only, the value it's assigned inside of the loop isn't valid outside of the loop. This sounds a little confusing so here's a programming example to make this easier to grasp.

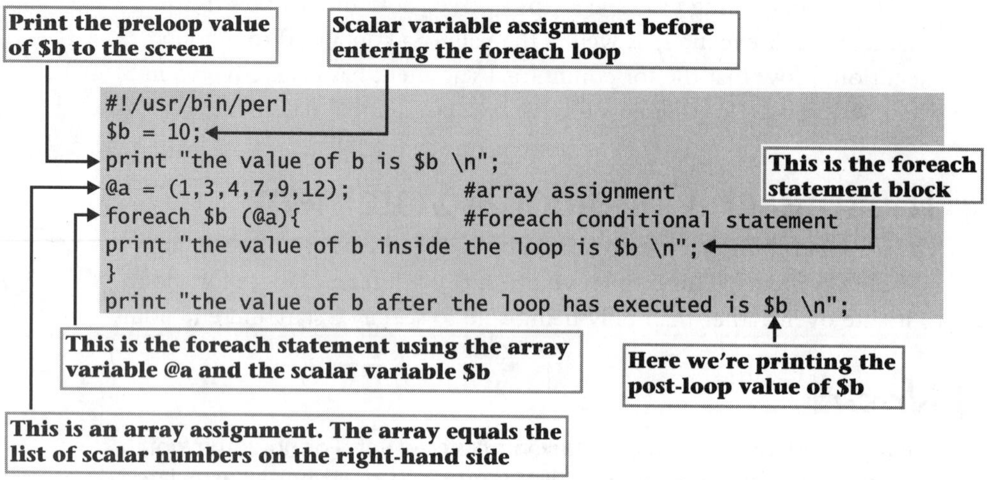
Print the preloop value of $b to the screen
Scalar variable assignment before entering the foreach loop
#!/usr/bin/perl
$b = 10;
print "the value of b is $b \n";
@a = (1,3,4,7,9,12); #array assignment
foreach $b (@a){ #foreach conditional statement
print "the value of b inside the loop is $b \n";
}
print "the value of b after the loop has executed is $b \n";
This is the foreach statement block
This is the foreach statement using the array variable @a and the scalar variable $b
Here we're printing the post-loop value of $b
This is an array assignment. The array equals the list of scalar numbers on the right-hand side

The following illustration displays the screen output for the foreach programming example.

```
Command Prompt
D:\>D:\Perl\book\figure3.9code.pl
the value of b before entering the loop is 10
the value of b inside the loop is 1
the value of b inside the loop is 3
the value of b inside the loop is 4
the value of b inside the loop is 7
the value of b inside the loop is 9
the value of b inside the loop is 12
the value of b after the loop has executed is 10

D:\>
```

You should notice that the value of $b before entering the loop and after exiting the loop remains the same, even though it's assigned different values inside the foreach loop. Again, this is because the values that $b are assigned inside the loop are out of scope outside the loop.

To make the foreach statement a little simpler, you can choose to use the implied $_ scalar variable. The syntax of the foreach statement using this variable is as follows.

```
foreach (array variable)
{
'foreach' statement block
}
```

Inside the statement block, you can use the print statement to see what the array element's value is. Here's another programming example and, remember, we're using the implied $_ scalar variable.

```
#!/usr/bin/perl
@a = (1,3,4,7,9,12);
foreach (@a){
print;
print "\n";
}
```

Array assignment

The foreach conditional statement using the implied $_ scalar variable

This prints the contents of the $_ variable

See the screen output for the foreach programming example using the implied scalar variable in the following illustration.

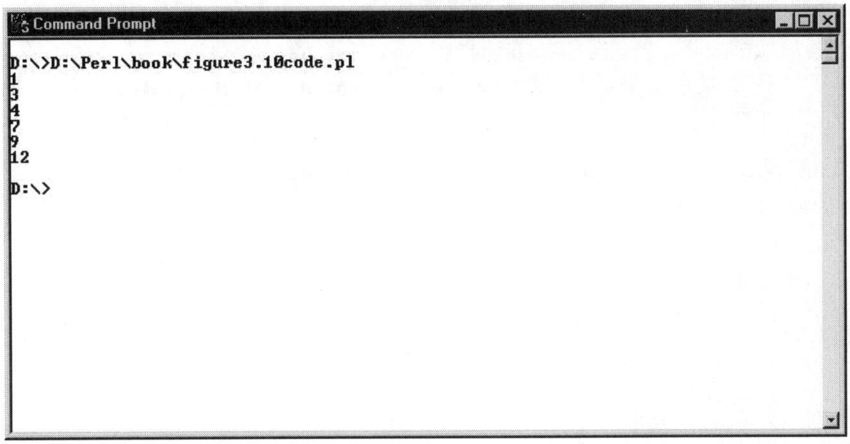

```
Command Prompt
D:\>D:\Perl\book\figure3.10code.pl
1
3
4
7
9
12

D:\>
```

Because we are using the implied $_ scalar variable, Perl automatically knows you are referring to that variable when you don't give the print statement any arguments. This is only a shorthand way to use a foreach statement and save you time when programming.

The last conditional statement we cover uses most of the statements you learned in this module and reapplies them in a simpler form.

The Single Line Conditional Statements

The *single line* conditional statements can be used when you don't need multiple statements inside a statement block. If you're only concerned about one statement, this structure can save you time when programming. Here's the syntax for these statements.

```
any Perl statement (space) if, while, until, or unless (space) expression
```

And here are a few single line conditional statements being used in a program.

```
#!/usr/bin/perl
$a = 15;
$b = 10;
$a++ if ($b < 20);
print "a equals $a \n";
print "a was incremented by one \n" if ($a == 16);
$b++ while ($b < 20);
print "b was incremented until it reached 20 \n" if ($b == 20);
$a– until ($a == 2);
print $a;
```

This is an if single line conditional statement

$b is incremented as long as it is less than 20

$a is decremented until it equals 2

The following illustration displays the screen output for the single line conditional statements programming example.

```
Command Prompt
D:\>D:\Perl\book\figure3.11code.pl
a equals 16
a was incremented by one
b was incremented until it reached 20
2
D:\>
```


As you can see from the previous programming example, single line conditional statements can save you some typing over implementing full conditional structures.

Now that you've been introduced to all the conditional statements in Perl, let's move on to the next section of this module and discuss some control statements that can be used inside program loops.

Control Statements

Perl provides you with three different control statements that can be used inside a loop to override its normal behavior. These statements are fairly straightforward, so let's get right into discussing them.

The next Control Statement

The *next* control statement can be used inside a loop to skip the rest of the block during an iteration and continue until a normal loop termination occurs. The syntax for the next statement is as follows.

```
next;
```

Here's a programming example that uses a while loop and the next control statement.

```
#!/usr/bin/perl
$a = 15;
while ($a < 25) {
$a++;
next if ($a == 20);
print "$a is still less than 25 \n";
}
print "exiting";
```

This is a basic while loop like we covered in the previous section

When $a equals 20, the print statement is skipped and the loop jumps to its next iteration

The following illustration shows the screen output for the next control statement programming example.

```
Command Prompt
D:\>D:\Perl\book\figure3.12code.pl
16 is still less than 25
17 is still less than 25
18 is still less than 25
19 is still less than 25
21 is still less than 25
22 is still less than 25
23 is still less than 25
24 is still less than 25
25 is still less than 25
exiting
D:\>
```

Looking at the illustration, you can see the print statement for the $a = 20 loop iteration was skipped and the loop continued executing until its normal termination.

Note

In the previous programming example, we used an if single line conditional statement with the next control statement to specify when it should be executed. If we had used only the next control statement by itself, the print statement inside the statement block would have been skipped on every loop iteration.

The previous programming example should give you a good idea of how the next control statement functions. Now let's move on to cover another control statement that can be used inside a program loop.

The last Control Statement

The *last* control statement is similar to the next control statement we just covered, except it terminates the loop upon execution. The syntax for the last statement is simply:

```
last;
```

Here's a programming example to demonstrate how the last control statement functions.

```
#!/usr/bin/perl
$a = 15;
while ($a < 25) {
$a++;
last if ($a == 20);
print "$a is still less than 25 \n";
}
print "exiting";
```

Again, we are using a basic while loop

When $a equals 20, the last statement is executed, which terminates the rest of the loop

The following illustration shows the screen output for the last control statement programming example.

```
D:\>D:\Perl\book\figure3.13code.pl
16 is still less than 25
17 is still less than 25
18 is still less than 25
19 is still less than 25
exiting
D:\>
```

The screen capture of this program's execution shows the while loop being terminated when $a = 20. The last statement overrides the remaining portion of the loop. We need to cover one more control statement now.

Note

Just as we did with the *next* programming example, we used an if single line conditional statement to determine when the *last* control statement should be executed. If we had only used the *last* control statement by itself, $a would have been incremented one time and the program would have terminated.

The redo Control Statement

The *redo* control statement repeats an iteration of a loop. The syntax for this control statement is as follows.

```
redo;
```

Here's another programming example to show this control statement in action.

```
#!/usr/bin/perl
$a = 15;
while ($a < 25)
$a++;
print "$a is still less than 25 \n";
redo if ($a == 25);
}
print "exiting";
```

Again, we're using a basic while loop

When $a equals 25, the loop should terminate, but the redo statement is executed, which forces the loop to execute one more time

The following illustration shows the screen output for the redo control statement programming example.

```
Command Prompt

D:\>D:\Perl\book\figure3.14code.pl
16 is still less than 25
17 is still less than 25
18 is still less than 25
19 is still less than 25
20 is still less than 25
21 is still less than 25
22 is still less than 25
23 is still less than 25
24 is still less than 25
25 is still less than 25
26 is still less than 25
exiting
D:\>
```

Notice in the illustration, the next-to-last line of output says 26 is still less than 25. This happened because the loop was executed one extra time with the redo statement.

Note

Using the redo statement without a conditional statement in this program would create an infinite counting loop.

The control statements available to you have now been covered. The last section of this module introduces you to the concept of nested loops.

1-Minute Drill

- **Which control statement should you use if you want to override any expression evaluation and exit a loop?**
- **Do the statements following a control statement in a statement block get executed when the control statement is executed?**

Nested Loops

The concept of *nested loops* is fairly straightforward and easy to grasp. Perl enables you to nest any conditional statement inside another conditional statement's statement block. You can nest as many conditional statements as you want, but be careful not to confuse yourself with too many. It's much easier to try to separate loops and keep them as simple as possible when writing programs.

The best way to grasp the idea of nested loops is to look at some programming examples. First, here's an example that contains nested while loops.

```
#!/usr/bin/perl
$a = 1;
while ($a < 5){          <-- This is the first while statement
$a++;
print "$a \n";
$b = 1;
     while ($b < 5){     <-- This is the nested while statement
     $c = $a * $b;
     print "times $b is $c \n";
     $b++;
     }
}
```

The screen output for the while nested loop programming example is shown in the following illustration.

- **The last control statement should be used in this case**
- **No, when a control statement is executed, anything that comes after it in sequential order is skipped**

```
Command Prompt
D:\>D:\Perl\book\figure3.15code.pl
2
times 1 is 2
times 2 is 4
times 3 is 6
times 4 is 8
3
times 1 is 3
times 2 is 6
times 3 is 9
times 4 is 12
4
times 1 is 4
times 2 is 8
times 3 is 12
times 4 is 16
5
times 1 is 5
times 2 is 10
times 3 is 15
times 4 is 20

D:\>
```

In the previous programming example, the second while statement completes all the iterations of its loop for every time the first while statement completes one iteration. Here's another programming example that contains a mixture of nested if and while loops.

```
#!/usr/bin/perl
$a = 1;
while ($a < 5){
$a++;
print "multiplying $a \n";
$b = 1;
    while ($b < 5) {
        if ($b == 2 || $b == 4){
        print "$b is one of my favorite numbers.\n";
        }
    $c = $a * $b;
    print "times $b is $c \n";
    $b++;
        if ($b == 5) {
        print "\n";
        }       }
}
```

This is the first while statement

This while statement is nested under the first while statement

This if statement checks to see if the value of $b is 2 or 4

These if statements are nested inside the nested while loop

The following illustration is the screen output for the nested loop programming example containing if and while statements.

```
D:\>D:\Perl\book\figure3.16code.pl
multiplying 2
times 1 is 2
2 is one of my favorite numbers.
times 2 is 4
times 3 is 6
4 is one of my favorite numbers.
times 4 is 8

multiplying 3
times 1 is 3
2 is one of my favorite numbers.
times 2 is 6
times 3 is 9
4 is one of my favorite numbers.
times 4 is 12

multiplying 4
times 1 is 4
2 is one of my favorite numbers.
times 2 is 8
times 3 is 12
4 is one of my favorite numbers.
times 4 is 16

multiplying 5
times 1 is 5
2 is one of my favorite numbers.
times 2 is 10
times 3 is 15
4 is one of my favorite numbers.
times 4 is 20

D:\>
```

As you can see from the previous example, the more nested loops and statements you have, the more confusing it is to follow. A good idea is to tab or space over for each level that a particular loop or statement is nested. If you don't follow this practice, you might spend extra time trying to figure out where you are missing a curly brace to close off a statement block. We recommend you consult the perlstyle manpage for the standard formatting guidelines to follow.

Project 3-2: Counting and Displaying Odd Numbers

Building on Project 3-1 in this module, write a program using any of the conditional or control statements you've learned so far that count and display the odd numbers from one to twenty-one without using an array or specifying the odd numbers as arguments.

1. Which conditional statement executes a statement block as long as the specified expression is true?

   A. while

   B. do while

   C. until

   D. Both A and B

2. How many expressions is a for statement required to have?

   A. 1

   B. 2

   C. 3

   D. None

3. What makes do while and while statements unique?

   A. Nothing, they are identical

   B. Do while statements always execute the statement block once

   C. While statements always execute the statement block once

   D. None of the above

4. How many levels of control statements can be nested in Perl?

   A. 3

   B. It depends on the type of conditional statements used

   C. An unlimited amount

   D. Both B and C

Mastery Check

5. Which of the following is a valid use of a control statement?

   A. next;

   B. next for ($variable < 10);

   C. redo until ($variable == 25);

   D. All of the above

6. Which of the following groups of conditional statements can be used with a single line conditional statement?

   A. If, while, until, and unless

   B. If, for, unless, and until

   C. Foreach, for, until, and unless

   D. None of the above

Module 4

Lists, Arrays, and Hashes

The Goals of This Module

- Introduce you to lists
- Cover array objects
- Introduce you to hashes

This module covers three important data structures you'll probably use a lot when you are writing programs. These three structures are lists, arrays, and hashes. The basic building block for each of these structures is something you're already familiar with: scalar data. You learned all about scalar data in Module 2 of this book. Now we're going to build on your knowledge of scalar data by discussing lists. Once we complete this section, we move on to tell you about arrays and their many programming uses. We conclude this module with a discussion on hashes. When you complete this module, you'll be familiar with most of the basic building blocks of any program so, with this in mind, let's get right into our discussion on lists.

Lists

A *list* is best defined as a group of ordered scalar data; it's a sequence of scalar values enclosed in parentheses. The following is a simple example of what a list looks like.

```
(1,2,3,6,9,12)
```

This is a list containing six separate scalar values. Because a list is made up of scalar values, it can contain numbers and strings. Here's an example of a list that contains both numbers and strings:

```
(1,2,"hello",3.6,"again",6,10,"world")
```

This list contains eight separate scalar values. A list can contain as many scalar values as your memory allows. Lists can also contain scalar variables. These variables are interpolated into their value, just as they are in double-quoted strings. Here's an example:

```
(1,2,"Hello",$name,6,10)
```

This list contains six scalar values. The actual list will contain the contents of the variable $name. If the contents of the scalar variable $name is "Ben," the list will contain:

```
1,2,Hello,Ben,6,10
```

A scalar variable can be used as a value in a list, as in the previous example, and it can also be used inside a string that is part of a list. The variable inside a string is also subject to interpolation. Here's an example to demonstrate this:

```
(6.2,"Hello $name", 3,10)
```

Assuming $name = Ben, this list contains four scalar values, 6.2, the string "Hello Ben," 3, and 10. A list needn't contain any scalar values to be created. This type of list is referred to as an *empty list,* and it appears as follows:


```
()
```

Lists can also contain expressions as part of their contents. For example, you could create the following list and it would be perfectly legal:

```
(4 + 7 , $value1 * $value2 , "Hello", 10)
```

This list contains the following four scalar values: 11, the result of the expression's evaluation, Hello, and 10.

Let's say you want to create a list that contains a range of numbers in numerical order. You can always create the list by entering each number in the correct order or you can use the operator Perl has set aside for you to create that same list with much less effort. This operator is called the *list range operator* and it appears as two periods ".." side by side. Let's look at a few examples of this operator in use:

```
(1 .. 10)
```

This is a list containing ten scalar values starting with 1 and incrementing by 1 until it reaches 10. The list would appear as follows:

```
(1,2,3,4,5,6,7,8,9,10)
```

You can also use the list range operator to specify the range for a certain section of a list, for example:

```
(1,3,4,7,9..13,15)
```

This list contains the following ten scalar values:

```
(1,3,4,7,9,10,11,12,13,15)
```

If you specify a list using this operator, and you give it the same start and end values, you'll be left with a list containing one scalar value. For example:

```
(5 .. 5)
```

This list contains 5 as its only scalar value. If you give the operator a starting number greater in value than the ending number, you are left with the empty list.

So far, the examples we provided of this operator in use have all dealt with whole numbers; however, its uses aren't limited to whole numbers. Using this operator with decimal numbers is also perfectly legal. Here's an example list containing decimal numbers that uses the list range operator:

```
(2.5 .. 7.5)
```

This list contains the following six scalar values:

```
(2.5,3.5,4.5,5.5,6.5,7.5)
```

Building on the previous example, if you specify the start number to be 2.5 and the end number to be 7.9, when the list range operator reaches 7.5, it determines if it is less than 7.9; it is, so the operator checks the next increment, which is 8.5. The operator determines that 8.5 is greater than 7.9, so the last scalar value in the list is 7.5. Here's an example using different numbers to demonstrate this behavior further. Consider the following list:

```
(-5.5 .. 3.8)
```

This list contains the following values when the list range operator is executed:

```
(-5.5, -4.5, -3.5, -2.5, -1.5, -0.5, 1.5, 2.5, 3.5)
```

In addition to accepting integer and decimal numbers, the list range operator also accepts letters. If you want to create a list that contains all the letters in the alphabet, use the following list:

```
(a .. z)
```

This list contains all the letters in the alphabet. You can also mix numbers and letters in the same list using the list range operator. For example:

```
(a .. z, 1 .. 10)
```


This list contains all the letters in the alphabet followed by the numbers one through ten.

The list range operator also takes scalar variables as arguments when creating a list. Using variables to set the start and end values of a list gives you some flexibility if you need a list to be different sizes, depending on the situation. Let's assume you have two scalar variables that contain numeric user input ($user1 and $user2) and you want your list boundaries to be set using these variables. Using the list range operator, the list would be entered as follows:

```
($user1 .. $user2)
```

The number of scalar values the previous list contains will always change according to the values the scalar variables contain.

1-Minute Drill

- **What is the maximum size of a list?**
- **Name all the different components that can be used to create a list.**

- **The maximum size of a list is limited by the amount of memory you have available**
- **Scalar data, scalar variables, and expressions**

Now that we've covered lists in detail, you're probably wondering what to do with them. This is where our next topic in this module comes into play. Let's go to the next section and learn about the array variable and all its uses.

Arrays

An *array variable* is much like a scalar variable in that it's created to store data. The difference is the array variable is designed to store a list, whereas a scalar variable is used to store singular scalar data. The array variable is signified by beginning with the @ character. The naming rules for array variables are the same as for scalar variable names. These rules were covered in Module 2 of this book. After the @ symbol, the name must begin with a letter, and then any combination of letters, numbers, or underscores may follow. If you're writing a program and are using array and scalar variables, these variables can be named the same, simply because the first character designations ($ versus @) are different. Having a scalar variable named $HT and @HT in the same program is legal. The first thing you should learn before you proceed is how to create an array containing scalar values.

Putting Items In

The process of creating an array is simple. The following piece of code creates an array containing ten values:

```
@numbers = (1 .. 10);
```

This line of code creates the array, @numbers, which contains the numbers one through ten. The previous line of code is called an *array assignment*. Each of the numbers contained in the array is referred to as an *element* of that array. You can print the contents of an array to the screen using the same print command we've been using. The following piece of code:

```
print @numbers;
```

prints "12345678910" to the screen. Whenever you print the contents of an array using only its name, as we did in the previous example, you don't get spaces between the different elements. This could cause some confusion, depending on the contents of the array. If you want to print the contents of an array with spaces in between the elements, you have to make the array part of a string. For example, if you wanted to print the contents of the @numbers array with spaces in between the elements, the line of code would look like:

```
print "@numbers";
```

This print statement prints "1 2 3 4 5 6 7 8 9 10" to the screen. This format is much easier to read, and it helps distinguish the elements from one another.

Now that you've been introduced to the array variable, we need to cover a few more list options.

A list can contain an array as one of its elements. The contents of that array become pieces of scalar data in the list. Here's a programming example to demonstrate this behavior:

```
#!/usr/bin/perl
@list1 = (5,7,9);                    #an array containing 3 elements
print "List 1 contains @list1 \n";
@list2 = (1,3,@list1,11,13,15,17);   #an array containing 9 elements
print "List 2 contains @list2 \n";
```

Path to Perl binary

A list containing an array as one of its elements

The output of the previous programming example can be seen in the following illustration.

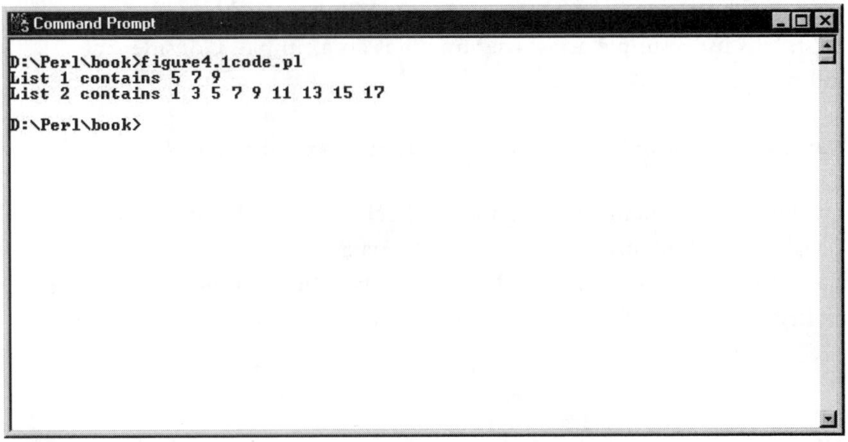

```
Command Prompt
D:\Perl\book>figure4.1code.pl
List 1 contains 5 7 9
List 2 contains 1 3 5 7 9 11 13 15 17

D:\Perl\book>
```

As you can see from the screen output, the values of @list1 become part of @list2.

Another option you have is the capability to set one array variable equal to another array variable. Here's a short example to demonstrate this:

```
#!/usr/bin/perl
@list1 = (4 .. 12);
print "List 1 contains @list1 \n";
@list2 = @list1;   # <-- @list2 contains the contents of @list1
print "List 2 contains @list2 \n";
```

The output of the previous programming example can be seen in the following illustration.

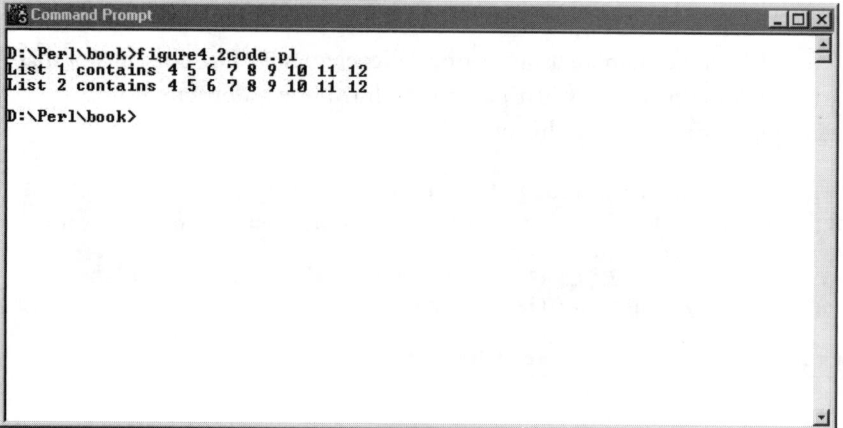

Command Prompt
D:\Perl\book>figure4.2code.pl
List 1 contains 4 5 6 7 8 9 10 11 12
List 2 contains 4 5 6 7 8 9 10 11 12
D:\Perl\book>

You have seen how to assign scalar values to arrays and now we're going to show you how to assign values to scalar variables from arrays. First, let's use a simple array assignment as an example. Consider the following:

```
@array = ($scalar1, $scalar2, $scalar3, $scalar4);
```

This array contains four elements. Each of these elements is a scalar variable that contains some sort of scalar data. When this line of code is executed, the array variable, @array, receives the contents of $scalar1 as its first element, $scalar2 as its second element, and so on. If you want to use this array's contents to assign values to scalar variables, you would write the following piece of code:

```
($scalar1, $scalar2) = @array;
```

This line of code assigns the first element of @array equal to $scalar1 and the second element equal to $scalar2. If you have more scalar variables than the array has elements, all the extra scalar variables will be undefined. Here's a short programming example to demonstrate this:

```
#!/usr/bin/perl
@array1 = (1, 2, 3, 4);
print "The contents of the array are @array1 \n";
($scalar1, $scalar2, $scalar3, $scalar4, $scalar5) = @array1;
print "Scalar1 equals $scalar1\n";
print "Scalar2 equals $scalar2\n";
print "Scalar3 equals $scalar3\n";
print "Scalar4 equals $scalar4\n";
print "Scalar5 equals $scalar5\n";
```

Array assignment

These scalar variables are assigned values from the array in the order they appear in the list

The output of the previous programming example can be seen in the following illustration.

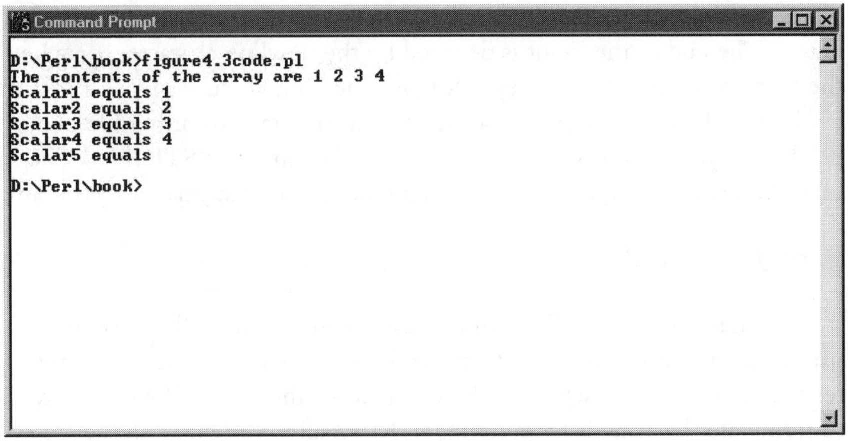

```
Command Prompt
D:\Perl\book>figure4.3code.pl
The contents of the array are 1 2 3 4
Scalar1 equals 1
Scalar2 equals 2
Scalar3 equals 3
Scalar4 equals 4
Scalar5 equals

D:\Perl\book>
```

Notice only four elements are in the array and there are five scalar variables. The fifth scalar variable is automatically set to null with no warnings.

If you're creating an array that contains several strings, Perl provides a shorthand method called the *quote word* function, which you can use. This function enables you to assign strings to an array without using commas. Let's look at a few examples. This is how you would normally create an array containing several strings:

```
@array1 = ( Bill, Ted, Jack, Jill );
```

Using the quote word function, you can simplify this line of code to the following:

```
@array1 = qw( Bill Ted Jack Jill );
```

The last method of array creation we cover uses the standard input file. We used this concept in some of the examples in the previous module, but let's discuss it again here. The standard input file is denoted in a program by '<STDIN>'. Whenever you use this special designation, Perl takes a line of input from the command line. The following is a simple example of how <STDIN> can be used to capture user input:

```
Print "Please enter your name. \n";
$name = <STDIN>;
```

In this example, the scalar variable $name contains whatever the user enters. The end of the input is denoted by the newline character, or when the user presses the Return key. Now for the array discussion.

Perl enables you to read an array in from the standard input file. To do this, all you must do is set an array variable equal to <STDIN>. The following is an example of how this statement would appear in a program:

```
@array1 = <STDIN>;
```

You need to know a few things before you try this. When you're using standard input to populate an array, the newline character doesn't terminate the array, it separates the elements of the array. The only way to terminate the array is by entering CTRL+Z after you enter all the elements of the array.

The next programming example demonstrates this new concept:

Note

Depending on what platform you are using, the termination sequence may be different. For UNIX, the termination sequence is CTRL+D and, for Windows, it's CTRL+Z or F6.

```
#!/usr/bin/perl
print "Please enter all of the elements of the array followed by CTRL-C \n";
@array1 = <STDIN>;
print "The elements of the array are \n @array1";
```

Array assignment

The output of the previous programming example can be seen in the following illustration.

```
Command Prompt

D:\Perl\book>figure4.4code.pl
Please enter all of the elements of the array followed by CTRL-C
Jack
Jill
5
10
Bill
Ted
The elements of the array are
 Jack
 Jill
 5
 10
 Bill
 Ted

D:\Perl\book>^C
```

1-Minute Drill

- **What is an array designed to contain?**
- **What character signifies the variable is, indeed, an array variable?**

- **Lists**
- **The @ character**

Now you should have a good understanding of what a list can contain and how to assign lists to array variables. Keeping what you have learned in mind, let's move on to the next section and discuss how to use the data stored in an array.

Accessing Array Elements

Once you create a list and store it in an array variable, you must be able to access the stored information. Each element of an array has its own *subscript* or placeholder. These unique numbers are used as keys to retrieve information from the array. Perl uses a standard subscript system, which begins with the digit 0 and increments by one until the end of the array is reached. Consider the following array:

```
@array1 = (2, 4, 6, 8, 10, 12);
```

This array contains six elements. The subscript of the first element '2' is 0, the subscript for the next element '4' is 1, and so on. The subscripts are used along with the square braces '[' and ']' to retrieve or manipulate the elements of the array. The syntax for the statement is as follows:

```
$array[0] = 5;
```

This line of code accesses the first element of an array named '@array' and replaces that element, regardless of its value, with the digit 5.

Note

The $ character is used whenever you are accessing singular data. The $ character and the array name should always be used when you're accessing elements of an array.

Now, here's a programming example that demonstrates a few different array element interactions:

```
#!/usr/bin/perl
@array1 = (2,4,6,8,10,12);
$element1 = $array1[0];
$element2 = $array1[1];
$element3 = $array1[2];
$element6 = $array1[5]
```

The array @array1 is declared
The first, second, third, and last elements of the array are assigned to scalar variables

```
print "Element 1 equals $element1 \n";
print "Element 2 equals $element2 \n";
print "Element 3 equals $element3 \n";
print "Element 6 equals $element6 \n";
$array1[0] = 14;
$element1 = $array1[0];
print "The first element is now equal to $element1 \n";
```

The contents of the scalar variables containing the array elements are printed to the screen

The new value is reassigned to $element1

The first element of the array is assigned a new value of 14

4

The output of the previous programming example can be seen in the following illustration.

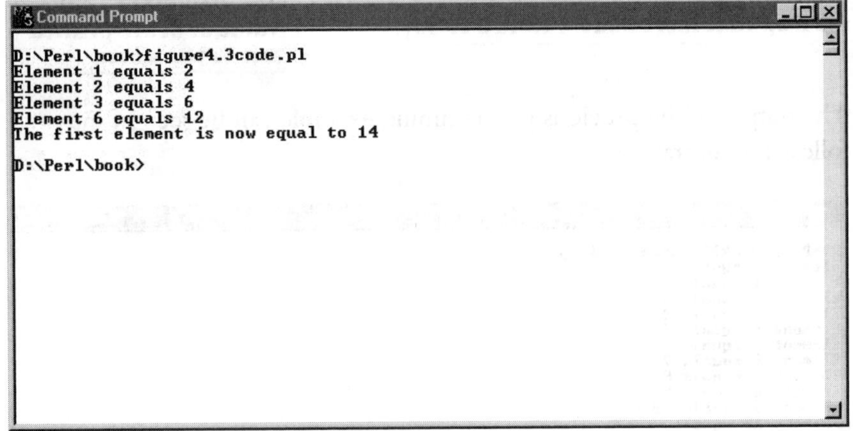
Command Prompt
D:\Perl\book>figure4.3code.pl
Element 1 equals 2
Element 2 equals 4
Element 3 equals 6
Element 6 equals 12
The first element is now equal to 14
D:\Perl\book>

You can manipulate the elements of an array in several other ways. You can use the autoincrement and autodecrement operators, as well as the binary assignment operators. Here are a few examples:

```
@array = (1,2,3,4,5,6,7,8,9,10);
$array[1]++;        #This will add 1 to the second element of the array
$array[2]--;        #This will subtract one from the third element
$array[3] += 5;     #This will add 5 to the fourth element
```

Note

Don't forget the subscripts of the elements in this array are off by one because the first element's subscript is 0. The last element of an array is always n-1, where *n* is the number of elements.

The subscript value used when manipulating array data needn't be an integer as we used in the previous programming example. It can be specified as a scalar variable so you can access different elements of an array using the same line of code. Here's a programming example that uses a for loop and a scalar variable to index an array:

```
#!/usr/bin/perl
@array = (1 .. 10);
for ($i = 0; $i <= 10; $i++) {
    $element = $array[$i];
    print "Element $i equals $element \n";
}
```

The array assignment

The scalar variable $i is used to index the array

The for loop that increments i from 0 to 10

The elements and the value of $i are printed out to the screen

The output of the previous programming example can be seen in the following illustration.

Command Prompt

```
D:\Perl\book>figure4.6code.pl
Element 0 equals 1
Element 1 equals 2
Element 2 equals 3
Element 3 equals 4
Element 4 equals 5
Element 5 equals 6
Element 6 equals 7
Element 7 equals 8
Element 8 equals 9
Element 9 equals 10
Element 10 equals

D:\Perl\book>
```

Note

For the last value of $i, the contents of the variable $element are null. This happened because we indexed the array one element too far. Remember, whenever you do this, your scalar variable will always be set to null.

Project 4-1: Working with Arrays

Write a program using the tools you've learned so far that will print all the elements of any given array. Assume you don't know how many elements the array contains, even though you will know.

When you are accessing elements of an array and setting the values equal to scalar variables, you have to make sure you're accessing elements that actually exist. If you try to access an element that doesn't exist, your scalar variable will be set equal to null by default.

If you're accessing elements of an array to change their values, you need to double-check to make sure you change the right elements. If you try to change an element that doesn't exist, a new element in that position is created automatically. Here's an example to demonstrate this. Consider the following array:

```
@array1 = ( 2, 4, 6, 8);
```

This array contains four elements. If you want to change the last element of the array to 10, and you use 4 as your subscript instead of 3, a new element '10' will be added on to the end of the @array1 array. Another example is, if you use the subscript 6 on the original @array1 when you try to change the value of an element, three new elements will be created automatically. Elements five and six will be created with null as their value and element seven will be created with the value you specified.

An important thing to do when you write programs using data from other sources is the capability to determine the length of an array. You can do this in several ways. Probably the easiest and least confusing is as follows:

```
@array = (1,3,5,7,9,11,13,15,17,19);
```

This array contains ten elements. We chose to use the odd numbers, so the element numbers and their values wouldn't be easy to mix up. To determine the length of the array, you can use the following line of code:

```
$length = @array;
```

After this statement executes, the scalar variable $length will contain the number of elements contained in the array. For this example, $length would contain ten.

Another method of determining the length of an array is to use the following statement:

```
$index = $#array;
```

In this line of code, the scalar variable on the left can be given any name. The name following the '$#' characters must be the same name as that of the array. For this example, $index would contain nine.

Note

This method of determining the length of an array gives you the index of the last element of an array. Remember, the first index of an array is 0, so if you use this $# method to get a length, you must add 1 to what you get. If you forget to do this, your length will always be off by 1.

Now that you've been introduced to these two new methods, here's a programming example that incorporates them both, so you can see them being used:

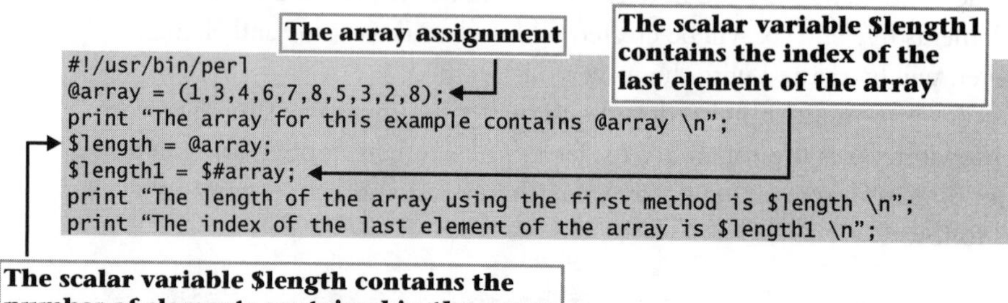
The array assignment
The scalar variable $length1 contains the index of the last element of the array
The scalar variable $length contains the number of elements contained in the array

```
#!/usr/bin/perl
@array = (1,3,4,6,7,8,5,3,2,8);
print "The array for this example contains @array \n";
$length = @array;
$length1 = $#array;
print "The length of the array using the first method is $length \n";
print "The index of the last element of the array is $length1 \n";
```

The output of the previous programming example can be seen in the following illustration.

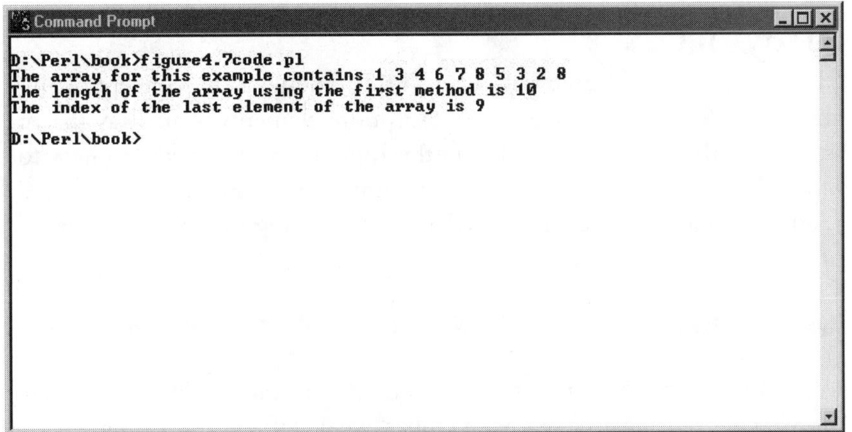

Command Prompt
D:\Perl\book>figure4.7code.pl
The array for this example contains 1 3 4 6 7 8 5 3 2 8
The length of the array using the first method is 10
The index of the last element of the array is 9
D:\Perl\book>

1-Minute Drill

- **What is the first index digit of any newly created array?**
- **What happens if you try to access elements of an array that don't exist? Are warnings generated?**
- **When accessing single elements of any array, what character must you use in front of the array name? Why?**
- **What happens if you try to change a nonexistent element in an existing array?**

Project 4-2: More Work with Arrays

Now that you know how to determine the length of an array, the first project for this module should be much easier for you to program. You can first determine the array length using either of the methods we just covered, and then use that length as the upper limit for a 'for' loop that will increment through the array one element at a time. Take a few moments and go back to your Project 4-1 and recode it to incorporate the exact length of any given array determined by either of the methods you just learned.

- **0**
- **The action returns null, if warnings are enabled, it does generate a warning**
- **$, because you are accessing singular (or scalar) data**
- **A new element is created and all the elements between the last original element and the new element are populated with null**

Array Slices

The next topic we're going to cover in this module is the concept of an array slice. An *array slice* refers to two or more elements of an array that are accessed at the same time. Earlier in this module, we showed you how to access the elements of an array, one at a time. Given an array name like @array, you access an element of that array by using the following line of code:

```
$value = $array[0];
```

In this case, the $ character is used in front of the array name because only one element is being accessed. Remember, we said if you are accessing singular data, you always use the $ character. Now that we're talking about an array slice, you are accessing more than one element, so you no longer have to use the $ character in front of the array name. Here's a programming example to demonstrate the use of the array slice concept:

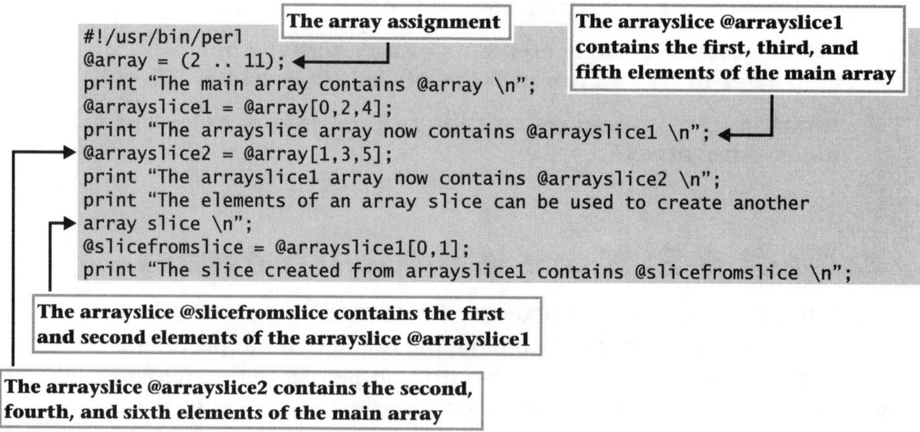

```
#!/usr/bin/perl
@array = (2 .. 11);
print "The main array contains @array \n";
@arrayslice1 = @array[0,2,4];
print "The arrayslice array now contains @arrayslice1 \n";
@arrayslice2 = @array[1,3,5];
print "The arrayslice1 array now contains @arrayslice2 \n";
print "The elements of an array slice can be used to create another
array slice \n";
@slicefromslice = @arrayslice1[0,1];
print "The slice created from arrayslice1 contains @slicefromslice \n";
```

The array assignment
The arrayslice @arrayslice1 contains the first, third, and fifth elements of the main array
The arrayslice @slicefromslice contains the first and second elements of the arrayslice @arrayslice1
The arrayslice @arrayslice2 contains the second, fourth, and sixth elements of the main array

The output of the previous programming example can be seen in the following illustration.

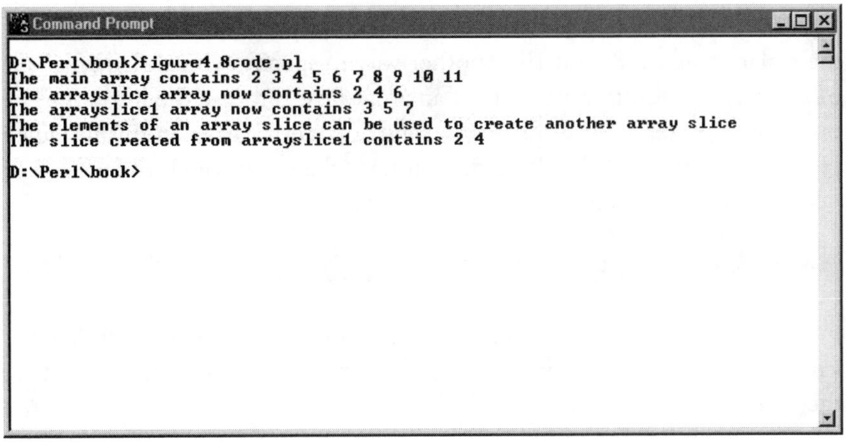

```
D:\Perl\book>figure4.8code.pl
The main array contains 2 3 4 5 6 7 8 9 10 11
The arrayslice array now contains 2 4 6
The arrayslice1 array now contains 3 5 7
The elements of an array slice can be used to create another array slice
The slice created from arrayslice1 contains 2 4

D:\Perl\book>
```


From this programming example, you can see that array slices are threaded, just as full arrays are. Array slices are usually derived from full arrays, but they also can be derived from other array slices. You'll find using array slices comes in handy when you're dealing with data in array format.

When you're using an array slice, you have a few options for specifying its elements. The first option you have is to specify the elements by entering the index numbers, just as we did in the previous example. Let's look at another example of this before we move on. Consider the following array:

```
@array = (2,4,6,8,10,12);
```

If you want an array slice of this array containing the first, fourth, and fifth elements of the array, you would use the following line of code:

```
@arrayslice = @array[0,3,4];
```

Note

If you want the array slice you are creating to contain the last element of the array, you can use the index of negative one. Using a negative index will count back from the end of the array. An index of negative two would give you the next to the last element of the array.

After this line of code has executed, the array @arrayslice will contain the scalar values 2, 8, and 10. Another way to specify which elements of an array are going to be parts of an array slice is to use the list range operator. You learned about the list range operator earlier in this module. Here are a few lines of code to demonstrate the use of the list range operator. First, consider the following array:

```
@array = (1,2,3,4,5,6,7,8,9,10,11,12);
```

This array contains 12 elements. If you want to assign an array slice the values contained in the third through the seventh elements, you would use the following line of code:

```
@arrayslice = @array[2 .. 6];
```

This is the same as saying:

```
@arrayslice = @array[2,3,4,5,6];
```

After this statement has executed, your array slice will contain the scalar values 3 through 7, in that order.

Note

Remember, the elements of an array are always indexed beginning with the 0 digit. If you specify a range beginning with the digit 1, you miss the first element of the array from which you are getting data.

Another way to specify which elements of an array are contained in an array slice is to use scalar variables. These variables can be used to specify each element of an array or they can be used as one or both of the boundaries for the list range operator. Consider the following array:

```
@array = (1,2,3,4,5,6,7,8,9,10);
```

This array contains ten elements (indexed from 0 to 9). If you want to create an array slice from this array using scalar variables, you could use any of the following lines of code. Assume any of the scalar variables used contain digits:

```
@arrayslice = @array[$index1, $index2, $index3];
@arrayslice = @array[2 .. $index1];
@arrayslice = @array[$index1 .. $index2];
```

With any of the three previous methods for specifying elements of an array slice if you specify an index of an element that doesn't exist, that element will be set to null in your array slice.

Here's a programming example to demonstrate each of the previous methods we just discussed:


```
#!/usr/bin/perl
$index1 = 14;
$index2 = 18;
$index3 = 20;
@array = (1 .. 20);
print "The array from which all slices will be created contains @array \n\n";
@arrayslice1 = @array[0,2,3];
print "Arrayslice1 contains @arrayslice1 \n\n";
@arrayslice2 = @array[4 .. 10];
print “Arrayslice2 contains @arrayslice2 \n\n";
@arrayslice3 = @array[11 .. $index1];
print “Arrayslice3 contains @arrayslice3 \n\n";
@arrayslice4 = @array[$index2 .. $index3];
print “Arrayslice4 contains @arrayslice4 \n\n";
```

The main array is assigned 20 elements

@arrayslice1 contains elements 1, 3, and 4 from the main array

@arrayslice2 contains elements 5 through 11 from the main array

@arrayslice3 contains elements 12 through 15 from the main array

@arrayslice4 contains elements 19 through 21 from the main array

The output of the previous programming example can be seen in the following illustration.

```
Command Prompt

D:\Perl\book>figure4.9code.pl
The array from which all slices will be created contains 1 2 3 4 5 6 7 8 9 10 11
 12 13 14 15 16 17 18 19 20

Arrayslice1 contains 1 3 4

Arrayslice2 contains 5 6 7 8 9 10 11

Arrayslice3 contains 12 13 14 15

Arrayslice4 contains 19 20


D:\Perl\book>
```

Note

The last slice we created in the previous programming example, @arrayslice4, does contain three elements, but the last element was set to null because 21 elements weren't in the main array.

Now that we've covered how to use array slices to create new arrays, we need to move on and talk about how to assign values to array slices. You can assign values to array slices, just as you can assign values to regular arrays. When you assign values to an array slice, you use the slice notation on the left side of the programming statement. Consider the following array:

```
@array = (1 .. 10);
```

You can use an array slice to reassign new values to this array. The following is an example line of code that would reassign new values to the fifth, eighth, and third elements of this array:

```
@array[4,7,2] = (21,22,23);
```

Note

Notice the indexes used in an array slice can be in any order.

Scalar variables and the list range operator can also be used to specify the elements of the array slice here. The following lines of code are perfectly legal:

```
@array[$index1, $index2] = (10,20);
@array[$index1 .. $index2] = (10,20);
```

Remember, if you specify more elements than values, the extra elements will be assigned to null. If you specify more values than elements, the extra values are ignored. Here's a programming example that demonstrates the use of array slices to assign values:

```
#!/usr/bin/perl
@array = qw(bill ted jack jill foo bar);
print "The original array contains the names @array \n";
@array[2 .. 4] = ( 10, 20, 30, 40, 50 );
print "The array now contains @array \n";
@array[0 .. 5] = ( fred );
print "The array now contains @array \n";
@array1[0 .. 3] = (1 .. 4);
print "The new array contains @array1 \n";
```

The main array is assigned six elements

Elements 3, 4, and 5 are assigned to 10, 20, and 30, respectively

This is only an example showing an array needn't exist to use an array slice. This line of code creates a new array containing four elements

All the elements of the array are to be assigned new values, but there is only one value so the array is reduced to that one value. All the other elements of the array are assigned to null

The output of the previous programming example can be seen in the following illustration.

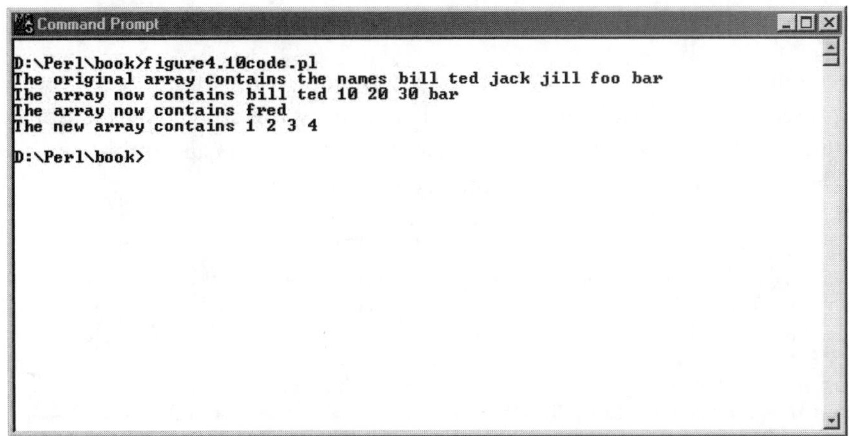

Command Prompt
D:\Perl\book>figure4.10code.pl
The original array contains the names bill ted jack jill foo bar
The array now contains bill ted 10 20 30 bar
The array now contains fred
The new array contains 1 2 3 4
D:\Perl\book>

Now that we've covered arrays and array slices, we need to talk about how to distinguish them from scalar variables when they're used inside double-quoted strings. By now, you know any variable name inside a double-quoted string will be interpolated to its value when executed. What you don't know is how to distinguish between the two, so you can have both scalar and array variables interpolated correctly. Consider the following few lines of code before this discussion begins:

```
@array = (this, is, not, the, right, variable);
$array = "hello";
```

Given these two lines of code, we need to discuss how to have each of these variables inside a double-quoted string. If you want the scalar variable $array to be part of a double-quoted string, it's fairly straightforward. The following line of code takes care of that for you:

```
print "$array world \n";
```

When this line of code executes, the screen output will be "hello world." Now, what if you want to have the scalar variable $array and a number enclosed in square braces inside the same double quote? Consider the following line of code:

```
print "$array[2] world \n";
```

This isn't correct because the Perl interpreter will see the square braces and replace the variable with the third element of the array. The solution to the problem is to override the square braces and you can do this in several ways. Here's a programming example to demonstrate:

```
#!/usr/bin/perl
@array = qw(this is not the right variable);
print "The test array contains --> @array \n";
$array = "Hello";
print "The scalar value contains $array \n";
print "$array world \n";        #prints the scalar value
print "$array[2] world \n";     #prints the array value
print "$array\[2] world \n";    #prints the scalar value and [2]
print "$array"."[2] world \n"; #same here
print "${array}[2] world \n";   #same here
```

The test array is created

The test scalar value is created

The scalar value and "[2]" are again part of the string because the curly braces separate the scalar variable from the square braces

The scalar value and "[2]" are part of the string because the backslash overrides the left square brace

Again, the scalar value and "[2]" are part of the string because we used two separate strings and joined them with the concatenate operator

The scalar value is interpolated inside the string

The array value is interpolated inside the string

The output of the previous programming example can be seen in the following illustration.

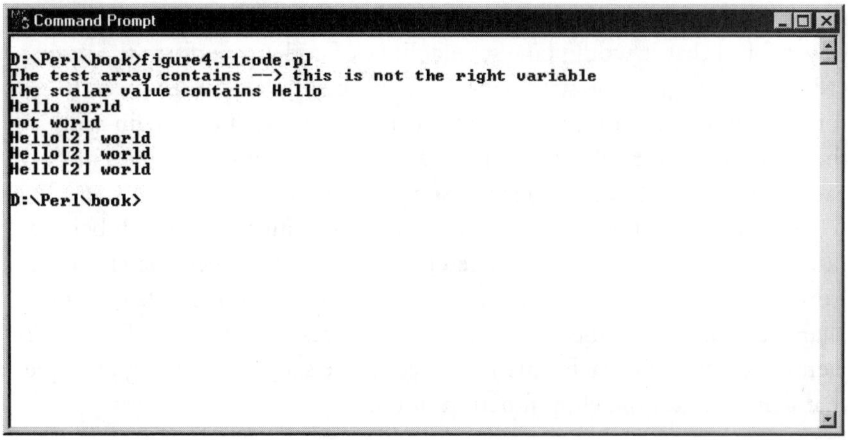

```
D:\Perl\book>figure4.11code.pl
The test array contains --> this is not the right variable
The scalar value contains Hello
Hello world
not world
Hello[2] world
Hello[2] world
Hello[2] world

D:\Perl\book>
```

The previous programming example demonstrates each of the three ways to override the square braces inside double-quoted strings. This only comes in handy for you if you require a number or other variable name to be inside of the square braces inside of a double-quoted string.

1-Minute Drill

- **How does an array slice differ from a normal array?**
- **Can an array slice be used to create a new array?**
- **Can an array slice be used to add new elements to an existing array?**
- **What happens if you specify more values for a slice than you do elements? Are errors or warning generated?**

This pretty much sums up all you need to know about array slices. That said, it's time to move on to the next section of this module, where we discuss the various library functions available for use on arrays.

- **An array slice contains a copy of a partial existing array**
- **Yes**
- **Yes**
- **The extra values are thrown out. No, unless you use the -w option that tells the interpreter you want all warnings generated**

Array Functions

Perl provides you with several different array functions to make manipulating data inside arrays easier. Some of these functions are powerful in that it would take several lines of code to perform the same task they do in just one statement. You've already been introduced to some of these functions, but not in the array context. Let's begin with the functions you're already familiar with. We give you examples of how each of them works through some short programs.

The first array function we discuss is the *chop* function, which behaves just as it does for scalar values. The chop function removes one character from the end of a specified string each time it is called, regardless of the character. For arrays, the chop function removes one character from every element of the array each time it's called. Here's a programming example that demonstrates the chop function in use:

The original array is created

```
#!/usr/bin/perl
@array = ("This\n" , "array\n" , "will\n" , "never\n", "be\n" , "the\n" ,
"same\n");
print "The original array contains --> @array \n";
chop(@array);
print "After one chop the array contains --> @array \n";
chop(@array);
print "After two chops the array contains --> @array \n";
chop(@array);
chop(@array);
print "After four chops the array contains --> @array \n";
```

Each time a chop is executed, one character is removed

The output of the previous programming example can be seen in the following illustration.

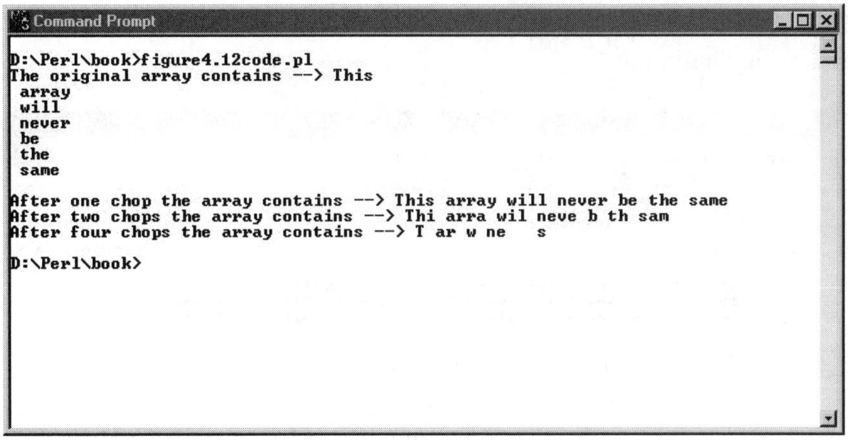

```
D:\Perl\book>figure4.12code.pl
The original array contains --> This
 array
 will
 never
 be
 the
 same

After one chop the array contains --> This array will never be the same
After two chops the array contains --> Thi arra wil neve b th sam
After four chops the array contains --> T ar w ne   s

D:\Perl\book>
```

As you can see from the previous example, one character was removed from each element of the array each time the chop function was executed.

Note

Notice from the previous example, the final array still contains seven elements, two of which contain null. The reason for this is because after all four chops are executed, the seventh element of the array is not null. If the seventh element had been the same length element or shorter than the sixth element, the array would have been reduced to only four elements.

The next function we need to cover is the *chomp* function, which acts a lot like the chop function we just covered, except it only removes the newline character from the end of an element. This function should always be used if the sole purpose in the beginning is only to remove the newline character. Here's a quick programming example that shows the chomp function in use:

```
#!/usr/bin/perl
@array = ("This\n" , "array\n" , "will\n" , "be\n" , "the\n" , "same\n");
print "The original array contains --> @array \n";
chomp(@array);
print "After one chomp the array contains --> @array \n";
chomp(@array);
print "After two chomps the array contains --> @array \n";
chomp(@array);
chomp(@array);
print "After four chomps the array still contains --> @array \n";
```

The original array is created

Each time a chomp is executed, only the newline character can be removed

The output of the previous programming example can be seen in the following illustration.

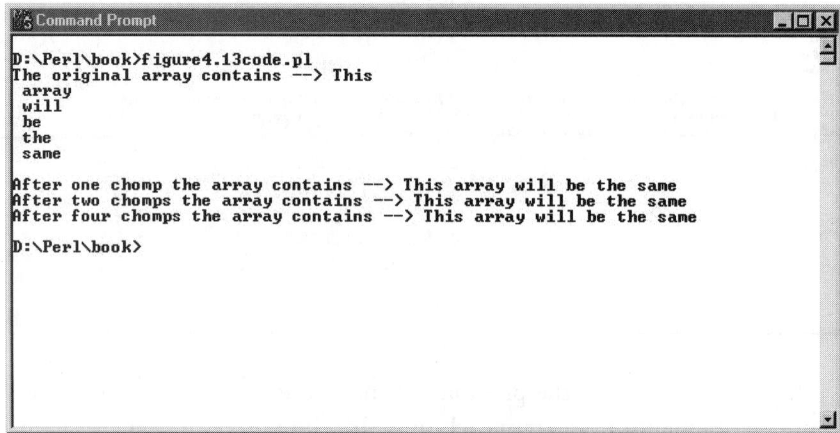
Command Prompt
D:\Perl\book>figure4.13code.pl
The original array contains --> This
array
will
be
the
same
After one chomp the array contains --> This array will be the same
After two chomps the array contains --> This array will be the same
After four chomps the array contains --> This array will be the same
D:\Perl\book>

From the previous example, you can see the chomp function will only remove the newline character, no matter how many times it's called on the same array.

Note

Remember always to use the chomp function instead of the chop function to get rid of the newline character. This character will always be present at the end of each piece of user input you take in. Using this function ensures you never remove any important data by accident.

The next array functions we cover are the push and pop functions. In discussing these functions, we may introduce a few new concepts, so we'll be sure to cover everything in detail. The *push* and *pop* functions are helpful when an array is set up to be used as a stack. You can think of a stack as a *first in, last out* (*FILO*) model. The first element you push into the stack will be the last element you can pop off the stack. By the same token, the last element you push into the stack will be the first element you pop off the stack. The push and pop functions always operate on the right-hand side of a list.

Stacks are often used to keep track of information throughout the run time of programs. The best way to understand how these functions operate is to look at a programming example of them in use. Consider the following program that uses both the push and the pop functions:

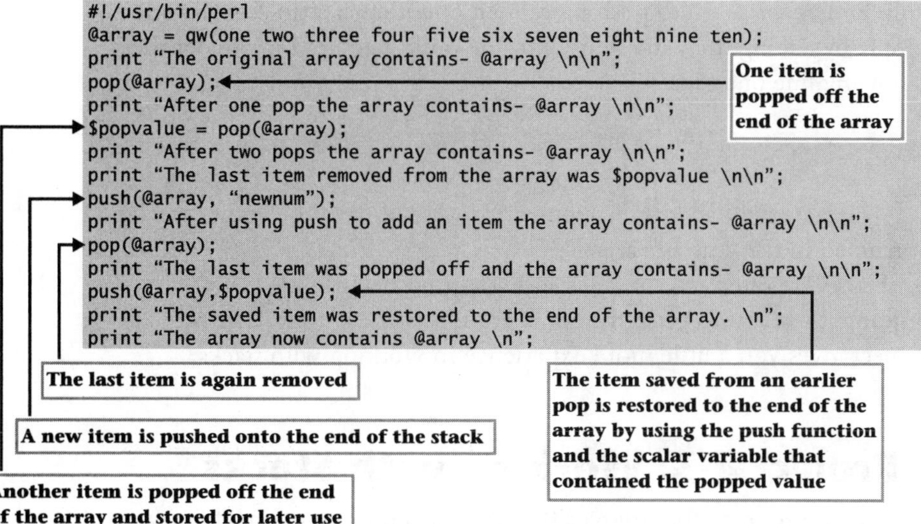

```
#!/usr/bin/perl
@array = qw(one two three four five six seven eight nine ten);
print “The original array contains- @array \n\n”;
pop(@array);
print “After one pop the array contains- @array \n\n”;
$popvalue = pop(@array);
print “After two pops the array contains- @array \n\n”;
print “The last item removed from the array was $popvalue \n\n”;
push(@array, “newnum”);
print “After using push to add an item the array contains- @array \n\n”;
pop(@array);
print “The last item was popped off and the array contains- @array \n\n”;
push(@array,$popvalue);
print “The saved item was restored to the end of the array. \n”;
print “The array now contains @array \n”;
```

One item is popped off the end of the array
The last item is again removed
A new item is pushed onto the end of the stack
Another item is popped off the end of the array and stored for later use
The item saved from an earlier pop is restored to the end of the array by using the push function and the scalar variable that contained the popped value

The output of the previous programming example can be seen in the following illustration.

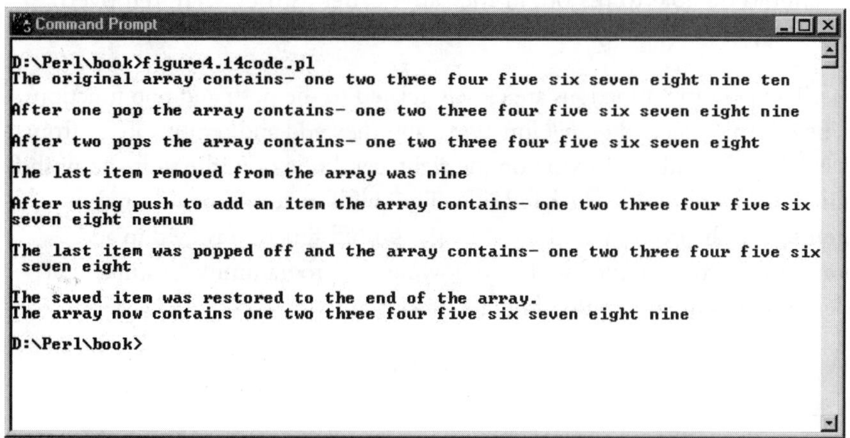

```
Command Prompt
D:\Perl\book>figure4.14code.pl
The original array contains- one two three four five six seven eight nine ten

After one pop the array contains- one two three four five six seven eight nine

After two pops the array contains- one two three four five six seven eight

The last item removed from the array was nine

After using push to add an item the array contains- one two three four five six
seven eight newnum

The last item was popped off and the array contains- one two three four five six
 seven eight

The saved item was restored to the end of the array.
The array now contains one two three four five six seven eight nine

D:\Perl\book>
```

The previous programming example should give you a good idea of how a stack works, as well as how to use the push and pop functions. The pop function returns undef if it tries to pop the last element from an empty stack. This won't generate an error or warning, but if you try to save the popped value in this case, your scalar variable will be set equal to null. Perl enables you to push more than one item at a time onto a stack simply by adding the extra items into the push statement. Consider the following line of code:

```
push (@array, 1, 2, 3);
```

This statement adds three elements, 1, 2, and 3, to the end of the list contained in the @array variable.

Stacks are often talked about and used in programming, so it's important for you to grasp the concept of how they work. The next project gives you a little more experience in working with stacks.

Project 4-3: Working with Stacks

Write a program that mimics the push and pop functionality on an array without using the push and pop functions. You can use any other function or concept you have learned up to this point in the book. Your program should save all the removed items and you should be able to restore in the same order as they were removed. Multiple stacks may be necessary.

The next two functions are closely related to the push and pop functions. They are the *shift* and *unshift* functions, and they add and remove items from a list. But, instead of working on the right-hand side of it, the shift and unshift functions work on the left-hand side. The shift function is used to remove items from the front of the list, while the unshift function is used to add items to the front of the list. The following is a programming example that demonstrates the use of the shift and unshift functions:

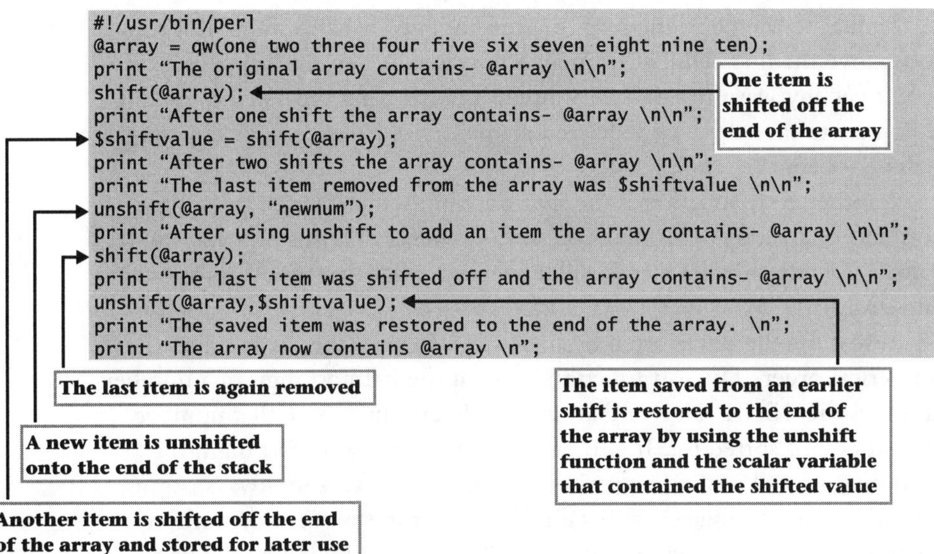
```
#!/usr/bin/perl
@array = qw(one two three four five six seven eight nine ten);
print "The original array contains- @array \n\n";
shift(@array);
print "After one shift the array contains- @array \n\n";
$shiftvalue = shift(@array);
print "After two shifts the array contains- @array \n\n";
print "The last item removed from the array was $shiftvalue \n\n";
unshift(@array, "newnum");
print "After using unshift to add an item the array contains- @array \n\n";
shift(@array);
print "The last item was shifted off and the array contains- @array \n\n";
unshift(@array,$shiftvalue);
print "The saved item was restored to the end of the array. \n";
print "The array now contains @array \n";
```
One item is shifted off the end of the array
The last item is again removed
The item saved from an earlier shift is restored to the end of the array by using the unshift function and the scalar variable that contained the shifted value
A new item is unshifted onto the end of the stack
Another item is shifted off the end of the array and stored for later use

The output of the previous programming example can be seen in the following illustration.

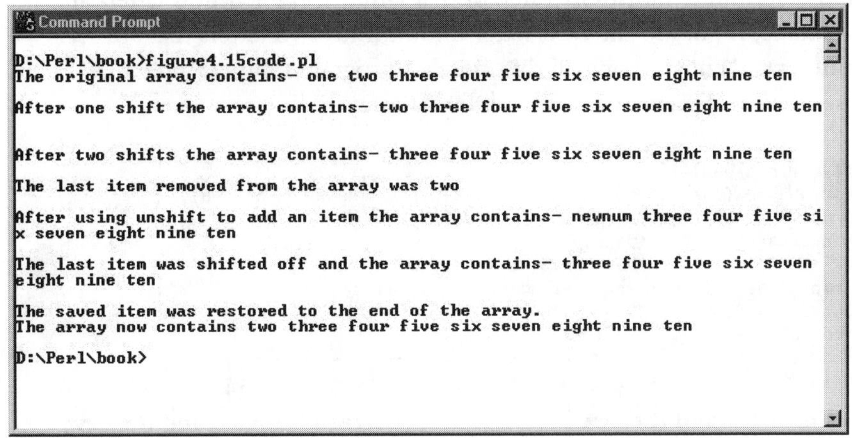
Command Prompt
D:\Perl\book>figure4.15code.pl
The original array contains- one two three four five six seven eight nine ten
After one shift the array contains- two three four five six seven eight nine ten
After two shifts the array contains- three four five six seven eight nine ten
The last item removed from the array was two
After using unshift to add an item the array contains- newnum three four five si
x seven eight nine ten
The last item was shifted off and the array contains- three four five six seven
eight nine ten
The saved item was restored to the end of the array.
The array now contains two three four five six seven eight nine ten
D:\Perl\book>

4

Similar to the pop function, the shift function returns undef if it tries to remove the first element from an empty list. When this happens, you won't get any warnings or errors, unless you're using the –w option, but if you try to save the newly deleted element, your scalar variable contents will be set equal to null.

Another array function is the *sort* function, which is used to sort the contents of an array. This function sorts elements in terms of their ASCII values. To refresh your memory, let's review what that means for numbers and strings.

When numbers are sorted by their ASCII value, they aren't placed in numerical order. The sort function looks at the leftmost digit of a number and uses the ASCII value of that digit to determine where that number should be in a sorted list. If two numbers have the same first digit, the next digit is used in the comparison. Remember, that sort always begins with the leftmost digit. As an example, if you run the sort function on an array that contains two numbers—300 and 8—300 will be the first element in the new array because the ASCII value of 3 is less than the ASCII value of 8.

Sort follows the same rules for strings. It looks at the leftmost letter and determines the ASCII value of that letter. If the leftmost letters are the same, it goes to the next letter until it finds two letters that are different. Remembering all this, here's a programming example that uses the sort function on a few different arrays:

```
#!/usr/bin/perl
@array = qw(one two three four five six seven eight nine ten);
print "The original array contains @array \n\n";
@sortedarray = sort(@array);
print "The sorted array contains @sortedarray \n\n";
print "The original array still contains @array \n\n";
@array1 = (500, 9, 2000, -11000, 25, -27);print "The original array1
 contains @array1 \n\n";
@sortedarray1 = sort(@array1);
print "The sorted array1 contains @sortedarray1 \n\n";
```

@array is sorted and the new array is stored in @sortedarray

@array1 is sorted and the new array is stored in @sortedarray1

The output of the previous programming example can be seen in the following illustration.

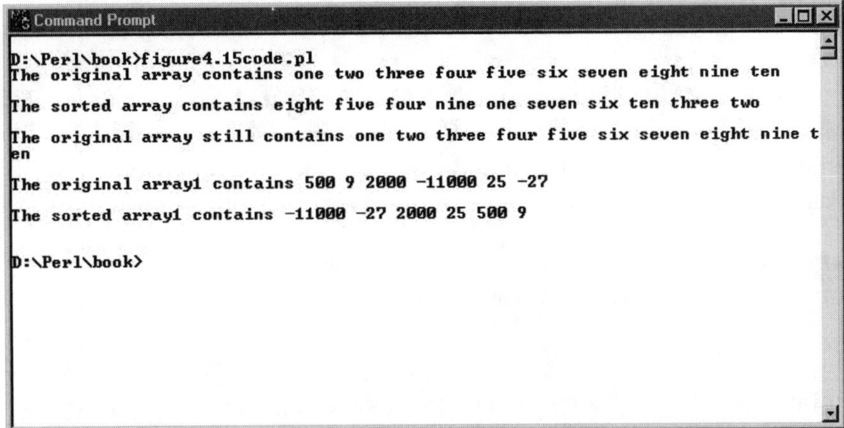
Command Prompt
D:\Perl\book>figure4.15code.pl
The original array contains one two three four five six seven eight nine ten
The sorted array contains eight five four nine one seven six ten three two
The original array still contains one two three four five six seven eight nine t
en
The original array1 contains 500 9 2000 -11000 25 -27
The sorted array1 contains -11000 -27 2000 25 500 9
D:\Perl\book>

Note

What's important to note here is the original array's order was NOT altered. Because of this, you must always store the sorted list into a new array variable if you will need to use it for anything.

This example should give you a good idea of how the sort function works. You should have noticed the negative signs on the two integers moved them to the first and second positions in the sorted list. This is because the ASCII values for the negative numbers are less than those for the positive numbers. The sort function is most helpful when you need to sort data in alphabetical order. When you need to sort data in numerical order, you have to add an argument to the sort statement. Here's an example line of code that demonstrates how to sort numerically:

```
@sorted = sort {$a <=> $b} @array;
```

This line of code will sort the contents of @array into ascending order and store the newly created array into the @sorted array variable. If you want to sort numerically in descending order, switch the $a and $b variables, so you have {$b <=> $a} as part of the statement.

Once you've sorted any list, you may not like the ascending order; that's easy to change with the next function we cover. Let's move on and introduce it.

The *reverse* function does exactly what it says—it reverses the order of a list. This function doesn't use ASCII values or any fancy algorithm, it simply places the last items first and vise versa. Here's a programming example that demonstrates the use of the reverse function:

```
#!/usr/bin/perl
@array = qw(one two three four five six seven eight nine ten);
rint "The original array contains @array \n\n";
@reversearray = reverse(@array);
print "The reversed array contains @reversearray \n\n";
print "The original array still contains @array \n\n";
@array1 = (500, 9, 2000, -11000, 25, -27);
print "The original array1 contains @array1 \n\n";
@reversearray1 = reverse(@array1);
print "The reversed array1 contains @reversearray1 \n\n";
```

@array is reversed and the new array is stored in @reversearray

@array1 is reversed and the new array is stored in @reversearray1

The output of the previous programming example can be seen in the following illustration.

```
Command Prompt
D:\Perl\book>figure4.16code.pl
The original array contains one two three four five six seven eight nine ten

The reversed array contains ten nine eight seven six five four three two one

The original array still contains one two three four five six seven eight nine t
en

The original array1 contains 500 9 2000 -11000 25 -27

The reversed array1 contains -27 25 -11000 2000 9 500


D:\Perl\book>
```

Note

Again, it's important to note the reverse function doesn't change the original array. If the reversed array needs to be used for anything, it must be stored in another array variable.

The previous example should give you a good idea how the reverse function works. It can be used on any list, no matter what it contains. The last two functions we cover deal with conversions between scalar strings and lists. These functions are important because they enable you to transform input data into whatever form you might need.

The first of these two functions is the *join* function, which is primarily used to "join" the elements of an array into a scalar string. Let's look at the syntax for this statement first, and then we'll discuss it in more detail.

```
$string = join ("separator", @array);
```

This function takes an array as one of its arguments. This array is to be joined into a scalar string and the elements of the array are to be separated by a specified "separator" in that string. If you want the string to contain spaces between each element, you simply put a " " for the separator field. You can make the separator anything you like. Let's look at a programming example of the join function in action.

```
#!/usr/bin/perl
@array = qw(one two three four five);
print "The original array contains @array \n\n";
$string = join ("-@-", sort(@array));
print "The string contains $string \n";
$string = join (":)", @array, twenty);
print "The string contains $string \n";
$string = join ("  ", @array, 12, 15);
print "The string contains $string \n";
$string = join (" MT ", @array);
print "The string contains $string \n";
```

The elements of the array are first sorted, and then they are placed into a scalar string and separated by the "-@-" sequence of characters

A new element is added to the end of the array, and then the elements are placed into the scalar string separated by the ":)" sequence of characters

Two new elements are added and the string is created with spaces as the separator

The output of the previous programming example can be seen in the following illustration.

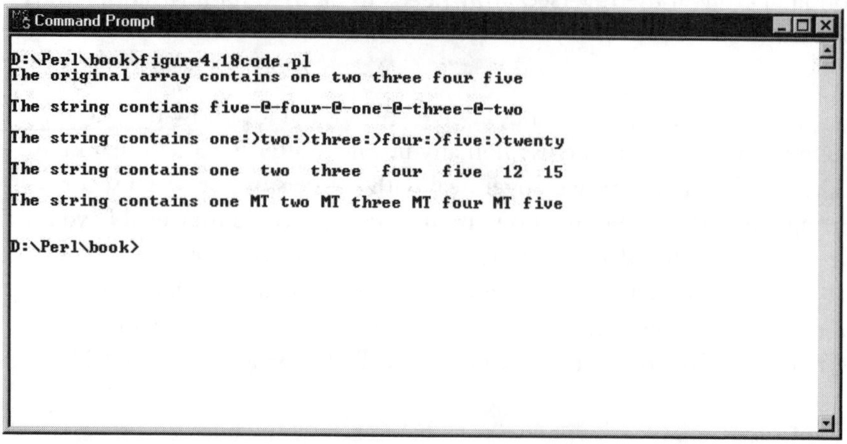

```
D:\Perl\book>figure4.18code.pl
The original array contains one two three four five

The string contians five-@-four-@-one-@-three-@-two

The string contains one:>two:>three:>four:>five:>twenty

The string contains one  two  three  four  five  12  15

The string contains one MT two MT three MT four MT five

D:\Perl\book>
```

This programming example demonstrates the use of the join function along with other array functions we covered in this section. Now, let's move on to the last function in this section.

The *split* function is used to "split" a string into a list, so it can be stored in an array variable. Basically, it does the opposite of the join function. With these two functions, you can put data in whatever format you need. The syntax for the split function is as follows.

```
@array = split("separator", $string);
```

Here the array variable on the left side of the statement will contain the newly created array. The separator is what the function is going to search for. When it finds the separator anywhere in the string, it creates a new element in the array. Every time the separator is found and something is after it, a new element is created in the array. Here's a programming example that uses the split function to create arrays from strings:

```
#!/usr/bin/perl
$string = "one two three four five";
print "The original string contains $string \n\n";
```

```
@array = split (" ", $string);
print "The array contains @array \n\n";
$string = "Bill - Ted - Jack - Jill";
@array = split (" ", $string);
print "The array contains @array \n\n";
@array = split (" - ", $string);
print "The array contains @array \n\n";
```

An array is created from the given string that contains elements made up of whatever is separated by empty spaces in that string

Another array is created from the same string, but its elements are separated by the character sequence ' - ' in that string

The output of the previous programming example can be seen in the following illustration.

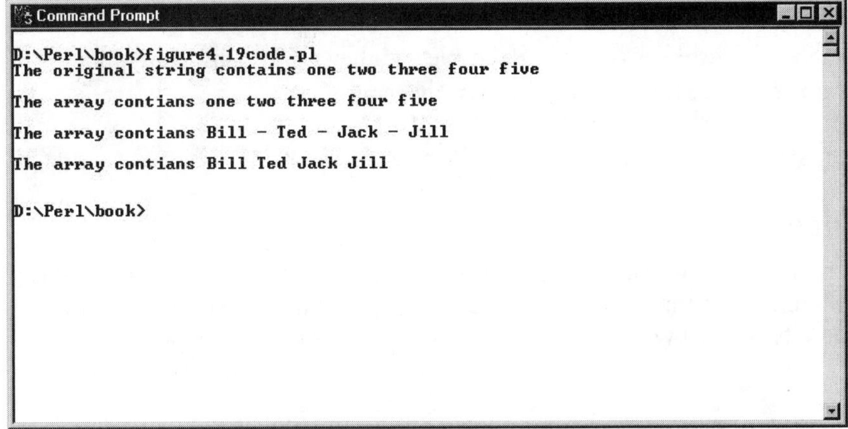

Command Prompt
D:\Perl\book>figure4.19code.pl
The original string contains one two three four five
The array contians one two three four five
The array contians Bill - Ted - Jack - Jill
The array contians Bill Ted Jack Jill
D:\Perl\book>

1-Minute Drill

- **Which array functions are used to manipulate the right side of an array?**
- **Which array functions are used to manipulate the left side of an array?**
- **What function can be used to create a list from a scalar string?**

- **Push and pop**
- **Shift and unshift**
- **Split**

This concludes our discussion of arrays. Now we move to the next section of this module and talk about a specialized form of an array.

Hashes

A *hash* is another type of variable that you can use to store scalar data. The naming conventions for the hash are the same as for the array and scalar variables except the hash variable name begins with the percent '%' sign. Hashes are similar to arrays in that they store lists of information, but they have one major difference. The elements of a hash aren't indexed the same as elements stored in an array variable. For arrays, the first element has an index of 0, the second element has an index of 1, and so on. Each of the elements contained in a hash has what are called *keys,* which are used as the index. These keys are user definable and they can be almost anything you like. Here's the syntax for the hash variable:

```
%hash = (key, element, key, element);
```

Note

A hash is signified by the percent '%' character. Because this character is different from that of an array or a scalar, you may have one of each of these types—all with the same name—and they won't overlap.

When you create a hash, you need to follow this syntax by pairing keys and elements together, and always with the keys first.

Note

If you mix up the order in which the keys and values are entered when creating a hash, you won't get any errors, but you will have a list that is keyed with the wrong strings and contains the wrong values.

Once you create a hash, you can access its elements by using the following syntax:

```
$hash{$key}
```

The previous line of code retrieves one element from the hash that corresponds to the key position. In addition to being able to retrieve elements, you can also add new elements by using the following syntax.

```
$hash{$key} = $value;
```

The previous line of code creates a new element in an existing hash and it also creates a new hash containing one element if it doesn't already exist. Here's a simple programming example that demonstrates how to create hashes several different ways:

A hash is created containing four elements

The value stored in the *a* key's position is set equal to the scalar variable $value

```
#!/usr/bin/perl
%hash1 = ( a, 1, b, 2, c, 3, d, 4);
$value = $hash1{a};
print "The value stored under the a key is $value \n\n";
$value1 = $hash1{c};
print "The value stored under the c key is $value1 \n\n";
$hash1{e} = 5;
$value2 = $hash1{e};
print "The value stored under the newly created e key is $value2 \n\n";
$hash2{f} = 6;
$value3 = $hash2{f};
print "The value stored in the new hash under the f key is $value3 \n\n";
```

A new element is added to the existing hash under the *e* key

A new hash is created that contains one element stored under the *f* key

The output of the previous programming example can be seen in the following illustration.

```
Command Prompt
D:\Perl\book>figure4.20code.pl
The value stored under the a key is 1

The value stored under the c key is 3

The value stored under the newly created e key is 5

The value stored in the new hash under the f key is 6

the contents of %hash1 are e 5 a 1 b 2 c 3 d 4

D:\Perl\book>
```

You may have noticed from the previous example that we didn't print all the contents of the first hash at one time. You can't just put the hash variable name inside double quotes and have it interpolate into its contents. If you want to see all the contents of a hash, it's easily done by setting the hash equal to an array and printing the array. The following lines of code print to the screen the keys and values of the %hash1 variable used in the previous programming example:

```
@array = %hash1;
print "The keys and elements stored in %hash1 are @array \n";
```

Note

The order of the elements won't necessarily be correct when you set a hash equal to an array variable. Remember this if you have to do so. Also, the hash name '%hash1' is printed as part of the string because it isn't considered a variable name inside double quotes.

Now that you've seen how to create and store values in hashes, you need to learn several hash functions that should come in handy. The first function we discuss is the *keys* function, which can be used to select all the keys in a hash and store them in an array variable. Once you have the list of keys stored, you can navigate through the hash much easier. The following is the syntax for the keys function:

```
keys(%hash);
```

If you want to store the list of keys in an array variable, you can use the following line of code:

```
@array = keys(%hash);
```

Now that you've been introduced to the keys function, here's a programming example that demonstrates some of its many uses:

This is a loop that counts through the entire hash and prints all its keys and values

A hash is created containing four elements

All the keys in the hash are stored in the array variable @array1

```
#!/usr/bin/perl
%hash1 = ( a, 1, b, 2, c, 3, d, 4);
@array1 = keys(%hash1);
print "The keys in the hash variable are @array1 \n";
foreach $key (keys(%hash1)) {
print "The current key is $key \n";
print "The corresponding value is $hash1{$key} \n";
}
if (%hash1) {
print "The Hash contains at least one element \n";
}
else {
print "The Hash is empty \n";}
```

This if-then-else structure determines if the hash is empty or not

The output of the previous programming example can be seen in the following illustration.

```
Command Prompt

D:\Perl\book>figure4.21code.pl
The keys in the hash variable are a b c d
The current key is a
The corresponding value is 1
The current key is b
The corresponding value is 2
The current key is c
The corresponding value is 3
The current key is d
The corresponding value is 4
The Hash contains at least one element

D:\Perl\book>
```

The next function we cover is closely related to the keys function. Instead of returning the keys of a hash, the *values* function returns the values of it. The following is the syntax for the values function:

```
values(%hash);
```

If you want to store the list of values in an array variable, you can use the following line of code:

```
@array = values(%hash);
```

Even though you can use this function to get the values from a hash, it probably won't be that useful to you because you won't get a list of the corresponding keys. The keys are a fundamental piece of a hash and they alone are what makes a hash so useful. If you don't know what keys go along with the elements and you can get away with it, you probably should use an array instead of a hash. The following programming example demonstrates the values function being used:

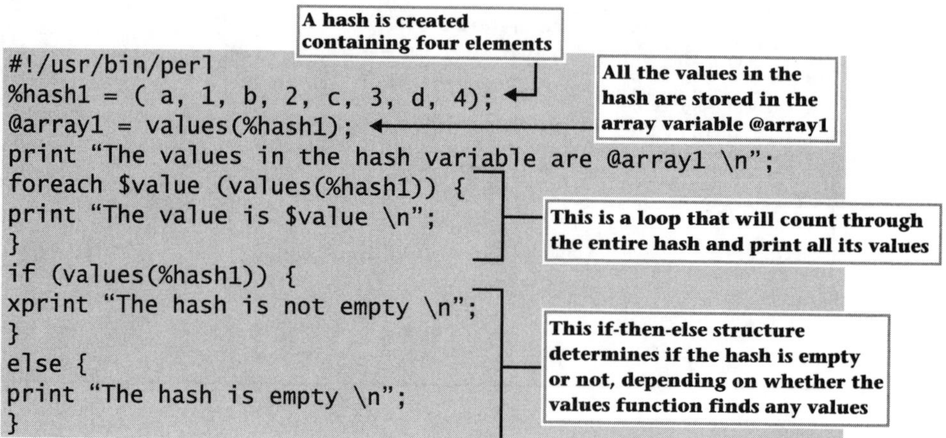
A hash is created containing four elements
All the values in the hash are stored in the array variable @array1
This is a loop that will count through the entire hash and print all its values
This if-then-else structure determines if the hash is empty or not, depending on whether the values function finds any values

```
#!/usr/bin/perl
%hash1 = ( a, 1, b, 2, c, 3, d, 4);
@array1 = values(%hash1);
print "The values in the hash variable are @array1 \n";
foreach $value (values(%hash1)) {
print "The value is $value \n";
}
if (values(%hash1)) {
xprint "The hash is not empty \n";
}
else {
print "The hash is empty \n";
}
```

The output of the previous programming example can be seen in the following illustration.

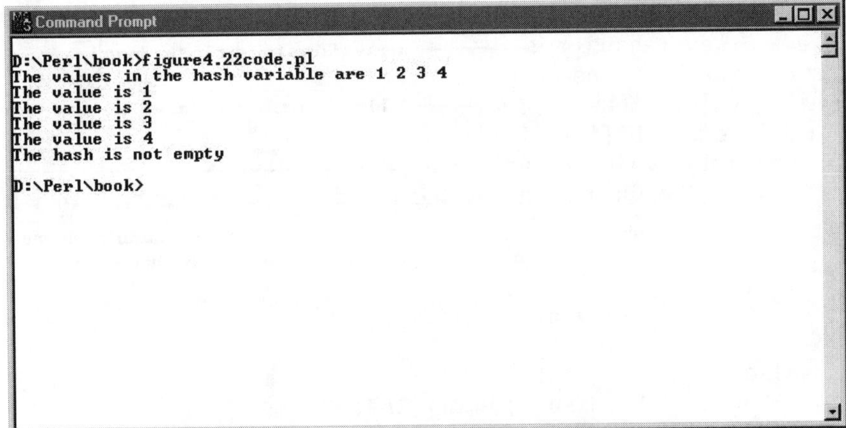

Command Prompt
D:\Perl\book>figure4.22code.pl
The values in the hash variable are 1 2 3 4
The value is 1
The value is 2
The value is 3
The value is 4
The hash is not empty
D:\Perl\book>

The next function we cover is the *delete* function for hashes, which should come in handy at this point because you know how to create and add elements to a hash, but you don't know how to remove items. The syntax for the delete function is as follows:

```
delete $hash{$key};
```

This function deletes two items at a time and the items for deletion are selected by their corresponding key. The two items here refer to the key and the element stored under that key. Here's a quick programming example that shows the delete hash function in use:

The counter is initialized to zero
A hash is created containing four elements
The keys are stored in the array @keys for use in the loop
While the hash contains at least one value
Increment the counter
Store the remaining elements of the hash in @array1
This if-then-else structure determines if the hash is empty or not, depending on whether the values function finds any values
Delete an element of the hash that corresponds to the current key

```
#!/usr/bin/perl
%hash1 = ( a, 1, b, 2, c, 3, d, 4);
$i = 0;
@keys = keys(%hash1);
print "the keys are @keys \n";
while (values(%hash1)){
   delete $hash1{$keys[$i]};
   @array1 = values(%hash1);
   print "The values in the hash variable are @array1 \n";
   $i++;

   if (values(%hash1)) {
      print "The hash is not empty \n";
   }
   else {
      print "The hash is empty \n";
   }
}
```

The output of the previous programming example can be seen in the following illustration.

```
Command Prompt
D:\Perl\book>figure4.23code.pl
the keys are
The values in the hash variable are 2 3 4
The hash is not empty
The values in the hash variable are 3 4
The hash is not empty
The values in the hash variable are 4
The hash is not empty
The values in the hash variable are
The hash is empty

D:\Perl\book>
```

The previous programming example was designed to give you an idea of how all these hash functions can work together in one program. Take some time to look back over the material and make sure you understand it all before moving on to the last function we cover for hashes.

You can think of the *each* hash function as a shortcut to get all the values and keys from a hash. Instead of having to store all the keys first, and then iterate through them one at a time to get all the values, the each function retrieves key/value pairs, beginning at the front of the hash and incrementing automatically each time it's called until it reaches the end of the hash. The syntax for this function is as follows:

```
each(%hash);
```

Here's a programming example that prints all the keys and elements of a hash using the each function:

```
#!/usr/bin/perl
%hash1 = ( a, 1, b, 2, c, 3, d, 4);
while (@values = each(%hash1)){
  print "The key/value pair is @values \n";
  }
```

A hash is created containing four elements

The key/value pair is stored in the array @values, one pair at a time, until the end of the hash is reached

Print the current key/value pair

The output of the previous programming example can be seen in the following illustration.

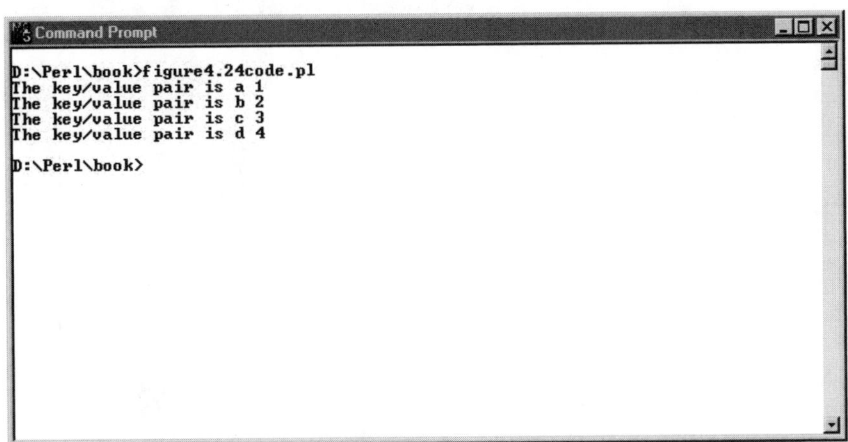

Command Prompt
D:\Perl\book>figure4.24code.pl
The key/value pair is a 1
The key/value pair is b 2
The key/value pair is c 3
The key/value pair is d 4

D:\Perl\book>

By comparing the last two programming examples, you can see how much time and effort the each hash function can save you. This function is so useful because it iterates itself without having to add any additional code. Using the each function is always the fastest and most accurate way to determine the contents of a hash.

1-Minute Drill

- **What is the main difference between a hash and an array?**
- **What character signifies the variable is, indeed, a hash variable?**
- **Are hash variables interpolated inside a double-quoted string?**

- **A hash uses user defined keys as its index**
- **The % character**
- **No**

Mastery Check

1. Which of the following is a valid list?

A. (1, 3, 4, 7, 9)

B. (Hello, $value + $value1, 2, 3)

C. (These, are , letters, a .. z)

D. All of the above

2. What forms of data can be used with the list range operator?

A. strings

B. numbers

C. scalar variables

D. Both A and B

3. Which of the following is a valid array assignment?

A. @array = {1, 2, 3, 4, 5, 6};

B. $array[1] = 12;

C. @array = [1 .. 10];.

D. All of the above

4. What array function can be used to remove the last character from all the elements of an array?

A. chop

B. chomp

C. Neither A nor B

D. Both A and B

Mastery Check

5. What array functions mimic the behavior of a stack?

   A. Push and pop

   B. Shift and unshift

   C. Both A and B

   D. Neither A nor B

6. What does an array slice use to determine the elements it will contain?

   A. The array length

   B. The array index numbers

   C. The element order

   D. None of the above

7. Which of the following are valid hash key names?

   A. a

   B. 25

   C. $value

   D. All of the above

8. What hash function can be used to access all the elements of a hash?

   A. values

   B. each

   C. keys

   D. All of the above

Module 5

Program Flow and Subroutines

The Goals of This Module

- Learn how to organize your programs into reusable code segments
- Understand the concepts of subroutines in Perl
- Start passing in arguments and returning data
- Get a grasp on the levels of private data within a subroutine

Program flow and subroutines are a way to help you break your code into segments. By doing so, you often can better organize your programs by functionality, rather than absolute flow. Additionally this gives you the capability to create sections or functionality to reuse, rather than to rewrite. From a programmer's perspective, this is a good thing, which reduces extra code.

Drawing an analogy from the real world is easy. For instance, reusable code is like having a bucket. Generally speaking, the bucket can be used for many different tasks, such as carrying water, dirt, or miscellaneous items. The bucket can also be used on different occasions, such as to wash the car on Monday or to carry rocks on Tuesday. The bucket becomes something you use for different things at different times, but an underlying commonality is between them—it's still a bucket and the tasks that revolve around it demonstrate the capability the bucket has.

Code segments and the desire for their reuse are no different. You want to create segments that are disconnected enough from your program to reuse elsewhere and flexible enough to use for different types of tasks. A fine line exists between flexibility and reusability, so be careful. A too-flexible segment might contain too much code or offer too little functionality. As a programmer, you have to determine where that line falls. If you find it takes you more time to try to break up your code logically, then you probably are breaking it up too small or with too much functionality.

In this module, we step you through program flow in Perl and how to use subroutines to create reusable code. We might even help you find that fine line through this education process and our examples. Ultimately, this module gives you the capability and knowledge to draw your own lines and successfully create reusable code segments in your programs.

Organization Basics

Overall program organization is the capability to create logical and functional segments in your programs. This isn't a new concept to the programming world, in fact, nearly all programming languages have this capability in one form or another. Some are more advanced than others and some have other segment-enabling functionality that gives even more flexibility. No matter what language you use, though, you should have at least some of the following tools at your disposal:

- **Functions** These are reusable sections of code usually at the beginning or the end of your program (depending on the language). These sections are often created because you want to perform a certain operation more than once. In Perl, these functions are called *subroutines* and they're the focus of this module.
- **Libraries** These are external files that contain multiple functions and/or properties often related in topic or functionality. For instance, you may have a "math" library that has addition, subtraction, multiplication, and division functions contained within it. Storing these often-used functions in their own library enables you to organize your code better and to reuse it in other programs later. In Perl, these libraries are called *packages,* which are files by the same name. Packages can contain groups of related modules that are designed to be exportable and reusable. This topic, although introduced here, is discussed in more detail in Module 8, "Packages and Modules."
- **Objects** These are reusable items that take on certain characteristics and potentially perform tasks or other functionality. In programming terms, *objects* have properties (characteristics) and methods (functionality) that can operate on those properties. In your code, you create an instance of an object and that instance now has all the properties and methods of the class definition. Objects are a big topic in Perl, which is covered in Module 13, "Advanced Features and Concepts" under the section "Object-Oriented Programming."

To give you a more visual look at how this fits together, we included the following illustration. As the drawing shows, we have a program that contains two object instances, an object definition, and two functions. The two object instances are created from object definitions in an external library the program imports. One of the functions is also pulled from the external library.

Note

When you look at this drawing, remember it's meant to represent how external elements can be included in your programs. This doesn't mean, however, a library must include both objects and functions—it could easily include only one type.

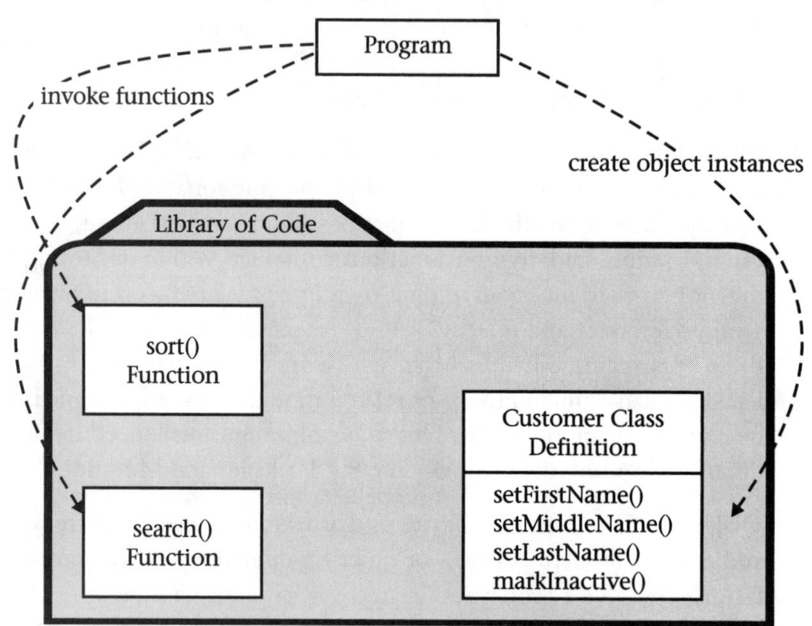

Now that you have an idea of what makes up programs, let's dive deeper into the why's and how's of program organization. From this point on, we use the Perl terminology for "functions," which are subroutines, and "libraries," which are packages. We wanted to introduce these topics under the more common (across other programming languages) terminology, but now we need to focus on the way they are used in Perl. Let's get on to the good stuff.

Why You Should Organize

Although reasons to organize seem fairly obvious to many people, it's a topic worth discussing. Let's face it—if it were that obvious, why do most of us admit we aren't well organized? Reasons other than code reuse warrant organization. We want to arm you with the information necessary to make good decisions on when and when not to organize, specifically with subroutines.

The first and foremost reason to organize is to be able to find, debug, add, or delete easily, not only from a Perl script, but also from your entire repository of programs. As a programmer, one of the hardest things to do is edit an unorganized or undocumented piece of code. You could spend days trying to find the right place in the code to make your changes, which results in lost time. By organizing your code in some fashion, whether it's logical or functional, you can quickly find the areas on which you need to focus.

Okay, Define Logical and Functional!

So far, we mentioned logical and functional program flow two or three times in this module. We wanted to give you some time to absorb the difference before we clarified it. But enough waiting, let's settle this.

When we talk about *logical program* flow, we are referring to the flow the program goes through when it solves a task. For instance, when you get up in the morning, you may take a shower, get dressed, eat breakfast, and then go to work. A program designed logically would follow that same process, regardless of any common ground between steps, like opening doors or walking. So, for instance, following this type of approach you would declare variables—instead of at the top—and subroutines—instead of at the bottom—*as needed*.

A *functional* flow is more of one where you group like-functions together. For instance, at the end of your program, you would put all of your subroutines, organized by similar functionality. Walking, opening, and driving subroutines might be next to each other, while talking and other forms of communicating might follow.

A true program should fall somewhere in the middle of these two approaches. You would generally declare global variables at the same place, and subroutines should appear one after the other. In the main body of the program, however, your code should flow in a more logical sense. This creates somewhat human-readable code, which can help you in the long run—especially when debugging.

In Your Code

From a coding standpoint, you can do several things for organization. These are simple requirements yet, if they're followed, they can drastically increase the readability and editability of your programs. These requirements are grouped into the following areas:

- **Comments** We can't stress this one enough—you MUST document your code with good and detailed comments. We touched on this concept in Module 1, so refer to that module if you want some pointers on how this is done technically and how it should be done from a programming perspective.

  Good comment:

  ```
  # Calculate a cost-of-living adjustment and
  # raise the employee's salary by that amount:
  $salary += $salary * $col_percentage;
  ```

  Bad comment:

  ```
  # Increment salary by salary times col_percentage:
  $salary += $salary * $col_percentage;
  ```

- **Subroutines** If you have anything that must be performed multiple times in your or other programs, you should create subroutines. For instance, if you need to adjust the case of all users' input, then you might want to create a subroutine that automatically performs this task with a single call. Placing this sort of code in a subroutine enables you to reuse it in your script, as well as in other scripts that need the same functionality.

- **Modules and Packages** Subroutines and properties with a common theme, which are designed to be both exportable and reusable, are called *modules*. These modules are stored in *packages,* which are library files of the same name. This enables you to include these subroutines and properties contained in variables, into any and all programs where they're needed.

- **Segments** If you organize your code in segments, whether they are functional or logical, then it makes for an easy time when you debug your scripts. For instance, if you have several subroutines that format text output, then you should put these subroutines near to each other. In addition, try to declare global variables or any other global elements in a common location, so you can easily find and change them if needed.

Your Program Repository

Organization from a repository standpoint is also important. If nothing else, you should keep similar programs in organized directories. This enables you and anyone else using your programs to find the program or package needed quickly. Yes, programs like `grep` do quickly search through directories and files for specific keywords, but this isn't quick when you have tons of programs. And who wants to learn every possible option you need to run the exact `grep` command your request demands? Here's a quick example.

Programs, for instance, that deal with accepting form submissions on the Web could be kept in a www directory. You might even go one step further, depending on the number of programs you have, by adding directory levels. If one set of forms is related to shopping on your site, then you might have it in a `www/shopping` directory. If another set collects user data, then you could store those in a `www/userdata` directory. Whatever level or breakdown you deem necessary is better than no organization at all. But, remember, good, descriptive directory names in local locations can ease your retrieval of programs.

Note

In the directory examples just mentioned, we used a forward slash ("/") to represent a directory, which is the method used on UNIX systems. For Windows systems, you should use a backslash ("\"), although Perl commonly accepts forward slashes. For Mac OS systems, use the colon (":") to signify a change in folders.

As you can see, organization is important when programming. Without organization, chaos can ensue and managing your scripts will be difficult to impossible. With that chaos comes many late nights and headaches. Perl provides several methods for organization and, with good programming practices, you can use them to your advantage.

Ask the Expert

Question: Maintaining my programs and packages in directories sounds like a good idea, but I need to organize a LOT of files—more than I want to create directories for. Is there a better way to organize these files?

Answer: Yes. Several applications out there enable you to create "trees" of code. So, for instance, you might create a Web site tree and, within that tree, you might have a "branch" for your forms, another branch for personalized pages, and so forth. These applications also enable you to control access to programs for editing and version control. The process is rather simple: if you need to make a change to a program, you can check out the script, which blocks all others from using it, and then check the script in again. Microsoft has a product called *Visual SourceSafe* (http://msdn.microsoft.com/ssafe) and an Open Source product called *Concurrent Versions System (CVS)* can also be used. You can get more information on CVS from http://www.cyclic.com. Other products are also available, but these are two of the most popular.

That's enough preaching on organization for now. Let's move into how you can actually create code segments in your programs.

Creating Code Segments

Creating code segments isn't a complex task if you think about how your program is going to be structured. It does, however, involve some preliminary planning on your part and the ability to adapt your decisions if you find other changes are necessary once you start programming. Being a good programmer is not only knowing how to program in a particular language, but also how well your planning and programming style measures.

Before you start, you should decide what the functional parts of your script are and how they should flow logically. This involves the grouping of functionality, potentially reusable, into process parts, followed by the consideration of the logical flow of your program. In other words, you can reuse stuff, put it in subroutines, put all common components in common locations (that is, subroutines at the bottom, global variable declarations at the top), and write the main body of your code so it flows in a way that makes sense. This is best explained with an example, so let's step through one.

Say we're creating a script that can open a text file, count the number of lines, and then write the number to a separate file. Several steps are involved in accomplishing this task, but they can be summed into the following:

1. Opening the input file for reading
2. Opening the output file for writing
3. Count the number of lines of the input file
4. Writing the result to the output file
5. Close the input and output file

The first thing we need to do is open both an input—Step 1—and an output—Step 2—file. This is done using the Perl `open()` function. This function takes a *filehandle,* which is a string used by your code to refer to the opened file and the name of the file it is to open. In addition, we want to see if the file successfully opened, so we include a little error checking. The code we use to accomplish these first two steps is

```
# open our input and output files
open(INFILE, "input.txt") or die "Error (input): $!";
open(OUTFILE, ">output.txt") or die "Error (output): $!";
```

Note

We won't go into any detail on the `open()` function in this module because it's covered in Module 6, "Working with Files and Directories." Just notice that `INFILE` and `OUTFILE` are the filehandles, and the > before the `output.txt` reference means the file was opened for write access. `$!` contains the error message if an error occurs.

The next thing we need to do is count the number of lines in the `input.txt` file. To do this, we define a variable, `$counter`, to hold the currently running count, and we use a while loop to iterate through the file. The following is the code we use:

```
# declare a variable to hold the count
$counter = 0;

# iterate through the file one line at a time
# and increase the counter on each pass.
while(<INFILE>){
  $counter++;
}
```

After we count the number of lines, we want to print that value to the `output.txt` file. As in the past, we use the `print()` function to perform this task. Because we are printing to a specific file, we pass an additional argument that tells the `print()` function to print to the `OUTFILE` filehandle. This looks like the following:

```
# print the value of the counter to the OUTPUT file
print OUTFILE "The file contained $counter lines";
```

The final step in this short program is to close the files we opened for processing. This includes both the input and output files. To do this, we use the `close()` function, which simply takes the filehandle as an argument to close the file.

```
# close the files
close OUTFILE;
close INFILE;
```

That does it! Our program is complete. All we have to do now is put it all together in one file. We included one here so you can see how we suggest you organize it. As you can see, we used our normal header,

Hint

If you want to try this at home, all you need is to have Perl installed and working and a file named `input.txt` with some lines of text in the same directory as the program. Once the program finishes running, you can open the `output.txt` file it creates to see the results.

opened both files, declared variables, iterated through the file, wrote the results, and closed the files. Functional, as well as logical, flow occurs by having the opening and closing of files together.

```
#!/usr/bin/perl -w
#----------------------------------------
# Script Name: num-lines.pl
# Script Version: 1.0
# Date: 10.16.2000
# Author: R. Allen Wyke
# Description: opens a file, counts the number of lines
#    in it, and writes that number to a second file.
# Revision History:
#    1.0/<10.16.2000>: original version
#----------------------------------------

# open our input and output files
open(INFILE, "input.txt") or die "Error (input): $!";
open(OUTFILE, ">output.txt") or die "Error (output): $!";

# declare a variable to hold the count
$counter = 0;

# iterate through the file one line at a time
# and increase the counter on each pass.
while(<INFILE>){
  $counter++;
}

# print the value of the counter to the OUTPUT file
print OUTFILE "The file contained $counter lines";

# close the files
close OUTFILE;
close INFILE;
```

Until this point, we've taken a hard look at program flow and organization. You learned what elements and functionality are available in Perl to help a programmer with organization, and we introduced you to the process of using these. Now, it's time to dive deeper into the actual elements and how they work. Specifically, it's time to look at subroutines.

5

1-Minute Drill

- **What is one method of organizing your code into segments? (Hint: although you could answer this in several ways, the answer we're looking for is what is the focus of this module?)**
- **What can external code segments be stored in within the Perl language?**

Hint

Want more information on "Perl Style?" Check out the perlstyle manpage.

Subroutines

As previously discussed, a subroutine is Perl's method of creating functions. These functions enable you to do everything from passing in arguments and modifying values to returning data. In this section of the module, we look into subroutines and how they work. We discuss how they are prepared, how arguments are passed, and how to return data properly.

Declaring

The declaration of subroutines within the Perl language is done using the `sub` language keyword. Following this keyword is a name identifier, which is used to call the subroutine when needed. When you name your subroutines, avoid giving them the same name as an existing reserved word, unless you plan to override them (more on that later). Doing so can

---

- **Using subroutines. You could also say keeping your programs in descriptive directory structures. Also, you can say that using logical and functional flow is a method of organizing your code into segments.**
- **They are stored in packages and grouped in modules if you use Perl terms, but they can also be called libraries.**

result in the wrong functions being called, which can prove challenging when you debug.

Tip

Throughout this section, you'll hear us refer to a caller regarding subroutines. By *caller,* we mean what actually called the subroutine. Was it another subroutine or another function? Maybe it was just called in the main body of your program? In any case, the caller of the subroutine is what receives the return data and is responsible for passing on that information if any further processing is needed.

In addition to this naming guideline, also note that naming a subroutine in all capital letters is a loosely held convention for internal Perl subroutines, so don't use all capital letters for subroutines you write. These subroutines tell the Perl interpreter to call the module indirectly (usually because of some triggered event). See the section on "Predefined Subroutines" later in this module for more information. Now that you know about these two instances, let's look at what you should be doing with subroutines.

The basic syntax is as follows, where *NAME* references the name you want to call the subroutine and *code* is the code you want to execute when the subroutine is called.

```
sub NAME{
  code;
}
```

Unlike many programming languages, subroutines don't explicitly list, in the definition, any parameters that may be passed. Instead, as you see later in this module, arguments are stored in an array that's accessible to the subroutine when called. In addition, you must use the `local()` and `my()` functions, also discussed later, to store and work with values local to the routine.

Not all subroutines have arguments passed. Some only need to perform a specific task, such as provide an entry in a log file, at a specific instance—a task that is somewhat independent of the program calling it.

For instance, if you want to define a subroutine, called &myAddress, that displayed your address to the user's screen, you could use the following:

```
sub myAddress{
  print "Pat Doe\n";
  print "123 Somestreet Dr.\n";
  print "Anytown, USA\n";
}
```

Now that we've defined this subroutine, all you must do to call it is enter &myAddress in your program. This calls the subroutine and causes the output to be sent to the user's screen. This looks like the following:

```
# call the &myAddress subroutine
&myAddress;
```

Note

As mentioned before, Perl is flexible (or lenient, depending on how you look at it) when it comes to syntax, so variations occur, like not including the & before the name of the subroutine, with this syntax. For instance, using & without passing any arguments makes the current @_ visible to the called subroutine. If you want more information, check out the perlsub manpage.

address.pl

Project 5-1: Using Our Subroutine

Here's a project you should be able to complete quickly. Take the subroutine and its call we just defined and turn it into a complete program that you can run on your system.

Now that you've been introduced to subroutines and what they are used for, let's look more closely at them. The real power of subroutines is not only reusing them, but their capability to accept data through arguments and return data for continued processing.

Arguments

Arguments represent parameters that can be passed to a subroutine for processing. Here are the technical details. When arguments are passed to a Perl subroutine, they are stored in a `@_` local array and can be accessed using the `$_[`***`index`***`]` format. So, if you want to grab the first argument for processing, you would access it from `$_[0]`. A second argument, if passed, can be accessed from `$_[1]`, and so on. Remember, arrays are zero-based, so the first element in an array is in the 0 position.

Note

The values in the `@_` array are actually aliases to the arguments. If the value of an argument changes outside of the subroutine, so does the value of the argument to the subroutine.

We bet your first question is, "What happens if only two arguments are passed and I try to retrieve a third one?" Well, as you've seen in the language, Perl is forgiving. If you try to retrieve an argument position that doesn't exist, you simply get a null or undefined value, not something unexpected. Also, if the argument passed is an array a or hash element that doesn't exist when the subroutine was called, it's only created if it's modified or the reference is taken.

To test this, here's a little example. As in past examples, the first thing to do is decide what the program should accomplish. For this example, we'll keep it simple and create a program that does the following:

- Prompts the user for two different strings.
- Outputs the result of concatenating the two strings together.

First, we take the script template and insert all the header information about our program. Next, we write the code that prompts the user for two strings. For simplicity, we separate these into two separate prompts, rather than one. As you learned in Module 1, "Introduction to Perl," you use the `chomp()` function to remove the trailing newline character before you concatenate the strings (because this program captures the trailing newline when the user presses the ENTER or RETURN key). Up to this point, we have the following:

Our normal program header

```
#!/usr/bin/perl -w
#-----------------------------------------
# Script Name: sub-ex.pl
# Script Version: 1.0
# Date: 10.16.2000
# Author: R. Allen Wyke
# Description: This script takes two strings, passes them to a
#    subroutine, and prints out the result of concatenating them.
# Revision History:
#    1.0/<10.16.00>: original version
#-----------------------------------------

# prompt user for two strings. Remove newline and
# store into variables
print "\nEnter the first string: ";
chomp($first = <STDIN>);
print "\nEnter the second string: ";
chomp($second = <STDIN>);
```

Prompting for and process the first string

Prompting for and process the second string

In the script, we elected to store the first string in a variable named `$first` and the second string in a variable called `$second`. We also removed the newline character in the process. This part of the example provides us with the data we need to process, so let's define our subroutine.

Like the header of the program, we want to use the template to create some comments about the subroutine. We want to describe what it does, what version of the program it was added in, what is passed in, and what is returned. As for the subroutine itself, which we call `&combine`, we can retrieve the arguments being passed, concatenate them, and print them to the user's screen all in one line. This yields the following:

Subroutine header

```
#-----------------------------------------
# Subroutine: combine
# Version Added: 1.0
# Input: 2 strings
# Output: prints results to screen
# Description: concatenates the two strings passed in,
#   and prints the results to the user's screen.
#-----------------------------------------

sub combine{
  print "\nThe combined strings are: " . $_[0] . $_[1] . "\n";
}
```

Actual processing on one line

`sub` declaration using the name `combine`

This section, in conjunction with the first section, gives us the real meat of our program, at least from a functionality standpoint. Now that the user is prompted for input, that input is processed, and the subroutine is defined, there's only one last thing to do. We must call the subroutine for execution. As previously mentioned, we simply specify the name of the subroutine we are calling. Because we're passing arguments, though, we must give the arguments within the parentheses following the call.

```
&combine($first,$second);
```

If we put all this together, we have the complete program (we called `sub-ex.pl`), which is included here. If you want to see the results of running it on a Linux machine, look at the illustration on the next page.


```
#!/usr/bin/perl -w
#----------------------------------------
# Script Name: sub-ex.pl
# Script Version: 1.0
# Date: 10.16.2000
# Author: R. Allen Wyke
# Description: This script takes two strings, passes them to a
#    subroutine, and prints out the result of concatenating them.
# Revision History:
#    1.0/<10.16.00>: original version
#----------------------------------------

# prompt user for two strings. Remove newline and
# store into variables
print "\nEnter the first string: ";
chomp($first = <STDIN>);
print "\nEnter the second string: ";
chomp($second = <STDIN>);

# call subroutine
&combine($first,$second);

#----------------------------------------
# Subroutine: combine
# Version Added: 1.0
# Input: 2 strings
# Output: prints results to screen
# Description: concatenates the two strings passed in,
#   and prints the results to the user's screen.
#----------------------------------------

sub combine{
  print "\nThe combined strings are: "  $_[0] . $_[1] . "\n";
}
```

```
[root@tuxbird allen]# ./Listing05-01.pl

Enter the first string: Base

Enter the second string: ball

The combined strings are: Baseball
[root@tuxbird allen]#
```

Predefined Subroutines

Because we're discussing subroutines, mentioning a few predefined subroutines is important. A bit earlier, we mentioned Perl loosely considered subroutines with all caps names to be core and called by the run-time system itself. Some of the subroutines this statement refers to are in Table 5-1.

Using these subroutines is fairly easy. For instance, say you want to have your program output your name, the program name, the program version, and the date the program was created. This can be done using the `BEGIN` subroutine. Even though this subroutine is generally used when creating packages and modules, we included a quick example to show you how it works.

```
#!/usr/bin/perl -w
#-----------------------------------------
# Script Name: BEGIN.pl
# Script Version: 1.0
# Date: 10.16.2000
# Author: R. Allen Wyke
# Description: A simple script that shows you how to use
#    the BEGIN subroutine.
# Revision History:
#    1.0/<10.16.00>: original version
#-----------------------------------------

# Here is where you put any code you want. For simplicity
# sake, we will just print out a line of text.
print "Hello, World!";

#-----------------------------------------
# Subroutine: BEGIN
# Version Added: 1.0
# Input: none
```

```
# Output: program header
# Description: built-in subroutine that simply prints out
#    some program header information. This routine is called
#    every time the program is executed.
#-----------------------------------------

sub BEGIN{
  print "\n\n------------------------\n";
  print "R. Allen Wyke\n";
  print "BEGIN.pl\n";
  print "Version 1.0\n";
  print "10.16.2000\n";
  print "------------------------\n\n";
}
```

5

The output of running this short program is shown in the following illustration.

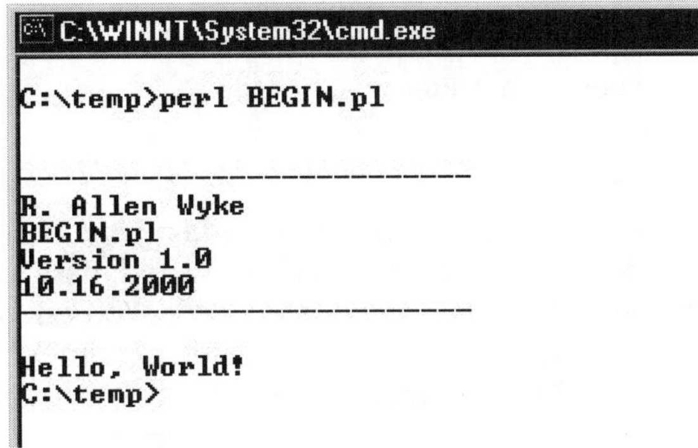

Subroutine	Description
AUTOLOAD	Loads if you make a call to a nonexistent routine. $AUTOLOAD, which holds the name of the incorrectly called routine, is passed to the AUTOLOAD subroutine. In addition to the name of the routine, the information passed to the routine, when applicable, is stored in array @_.
BEGIN	Enables you to specify code to be executed before your regular script is even parsed. See the perlmod documentation page (use **man perlmod** or **perldoc perlmod** at the shell or command prompt) for more details.
END	Enables you to specify code to be executed before your regular script ends, just as the Perl interpreter exits.

Table 5-1 Sample of Some Default Subroutines

my_sub.pl

Project 5-2: Addition Subroutine

Before we go any further, let's make sure you understand the basics of subroutines and passing arguments. Nothing earth-shattering is here, so don't worry. All we want you to do is create a simple subroutine that prompts the user for two digits, and then adds the numbers together. Here are the steps, so you can stay on track.

Step-by-Step

1. Take the script template file we created in the first module and enter all program description information.
2. Write the commands that prompt the user for two digits.
3. Write the subroutine so it can:
   - be passed two digits
   - add them together
   - print the results to the user's screen
4. Put a call to your subroutine.

Note

If you feel especially gifted now, you can try adding in a check for the characters entered by the user. This check would make sure the characters were, in fact, digits, and not alphabetic. You can do this in several ways, but one easy way is to use a little pattern matching. Check out Module 7, "Regular Expressions," for more information.

Returning Data

As you saw in the `sub-ex.pl` example, subroutines do have the capability to send information to a user's screen. However, we may not always want to send information to the screen. In fact, more often than not, you'll use subroutines to return information to your program for further processing.

Returning data in a Perl subroutine can accomplished using the `return` keyword. This word tells the subroutine you want to return a specific value back to the caller. If you don't specify this keyword, the value returned is that of the last expression evaluated. Basically, `return` accomplishes two things: 1) it breaks out of the subroutine; 2) it signifies the data to return.

To see this in action, say you want to create a subroutine that checked to see which of two numbers is greater than the other, and you want to store the greater in another variable. Your code might look like this:

```
#!/usr/bin/perl -w
#----------------------------------------
# Script Name: greater.pl
# Script Version: 1.0
# Date: 10.16.2000
# Author: R. Allen Wyke
# Description: This script takes two numbers and tells
#    you which is greater.
# Revision History:
#    1.0/<10.16.00>: original version
#----------------------------------------

# declare your variables
$first = 5;
$second = 10;

# call the checkGreater() subroutine to see which number
# is greater. Store the returned value in the $greater
# variable.
$greater = checkGreater($first, $second);

# print the results out
print "The first number was $first.\n";
print "The second number was $second.\n";
print "$greater was greater.\n";

#----------------------------------------
# Subroutine: checkGreater
# Version Added: 1.0
# Input: 2 digits
# Output: Returns the greater of the 2 digits
# Description: simple function that returns the greater
#    of the two digits passed.
#----------------------------------------

sub checkGreater{
```

```
  # check to see if the first number is greater
  if($_[0] > $_[1]){
    return $_[0];

  # check to see if the second number is greater
  }elsif($_[1] > $_[0]){
    return $_[1];

  # if neither is greater, they must be equal
  }else{
    return "Neither";
  }
}
```

As you can see in the results of running this program (depicted in the following illustration), the second variable, which contained 10, is the greater number. Returning values from Perl subroutines is a fairly common task, so it is best to learn as much as you can about it.

```
C:\WINNT\System32\cmd.exe

C:\temp>perl greater.pl
The first number was 5.
The second number was 10.
10 was greater.

C:\temp>
```

Ask the Expert

Subroutines include much more than we covered here. Fact is, subroutines have so many intricate details, they can become confusing. Because you are a beginner, we wanted to focus on the basics—defining, passing arguments, and returning data. But, to give you some additional help, here are some questions and answers that might have come up during these exercises.

Question: We've looked at how subroutines can be called within the body of a program, but can it be called in other ways?

Answer: Yes. Subroutines can be loaded from packages, using the `do()`, `require()`, or `use()` functions. You can even use the `eval()` function to define them on the fly.

Question: Earlier in the module, you said I should avoid naming the subroutines the same as other Perl reserved words. I understand why, but what happens if I do?

Answer: You can override these built-in functions, but doing so often results in strange behavior. If you have a good reason, such as trying to emulate a UNIX command on a nonsupporting system, then there's no problem. Things you must know are

- If you've overridden a particular function, but you need to use the default function in a piece of your code instead, precede the call to the function with `CORE::`. For instance, if you have overridden the `chomp()` function, you can refer to the built-in version in your code by using `CORE::chomp`.
- Overridden functions must be defined in a package and imported into your script. If you plan on overriding multiple functions, you should create a single package with all your code. For more information on packages, see Module 8.
- You should avoid including an overridden function in the default `@EXPORT` list of your package. We discuss this list more in Module 8, but the idea is this: when a package is imported in a script, all the subroutines in the `@EXPORT` list are automatically imported and, therefore, override any functions of the same name. This can be a bad thing if someone else is using your package or if you forgot you included a particular function that is overridden. You can place them in the `@EXPORT_OK` list, which puts the power back in your package user's hands.

5

Advanced Topics

At this point, you may feel like you've mastered Perl subroutines and understand some of its peculiarity, but here's a little secret. We've only touched on all the details of subroutines so far in this module. In fact, we haven't touched on many details. Some are because of the different focus of this book, while others are because of their complexity. This is a book for beginners, and going into details on these topics could cook your brain—it still does ours! Don't worry, though, we're going to give you a taste of some of the more useful advanced features now.

Temporary Data with `local()`

The `local()` function enables you to declare variables that are local to a subroutine. This means, in general, these variables are inaccessible outside the subroutine and, if they contain the same name as a global variable, the global variable is unaffected by any manipulation that occurs within the subroutine. An exception does exist, however. If nested subroutines are within the first one (the one with the `local()` declaration), then it, too, has access to the variable. You see this in an example a little later.

So, why would you use the `local()` function? Well, when writing code you may want to create variables that are only seen within a certain scope—you only want part of your program to see and understand that variable. For instance, say you have to use a counter to count the number of times you call a given subroutine or go through a loop in that subroutine. But, you have five different subroutines you want to maintain counts for and they are called at different times. This prevents you from declaring one variable and resetting it within each subroutine, because the previous count would be lost.

One solution would be to define five different variables. This seems like a waste of time and coming up with five different names for the same basic thing doesn't make sense either (this especially doesn't make sense if you have 100 variables!). Using the `local()` function, you can define a variable of the same name, say, `$counter`, within each subroutine without having them overwrite or affect each other. To give you a better understanding, here's an example we've named `local-ex.pl`.

```
#!/usr/bin/perl -w
#----------------------------------------
# Script Name: local-ex.pl
# Script Version: 1.0
# Date: 10.16.2000
# Author: R. Allen Wyke
# Description: This script demonstrates how the local() function
#    works in Perl.
```

```
# Revision History:
#    1.0/<10.16.00>: original version
#---------------------------------------

# create a global variable called counter and assign it to zero
$counter = 0;

# print initial value of counter
print "Global (initial): $counter\n";

# call first subroutine
&firstCount;

# print counter again - its the global one
print "Global (before second sub): " . ++$counter . "\n";

# call second subroutine
&secondCount;

# print counter last time - its the global one
print "Global (last): " . ++$counter . "\n";

#---------------------------------------
# Subroutine: firstCount
# Version Added: 1.0
# Input: none
# Output: prints value of counter, at various stages, to screen
# Description: simple function that increments value of counter,
#    at various stages, and prints their value to the screen.
#    Additionally, it calls a second subroutine to show how the
#    "localized" counter variable is passed on.
#---------------------------------------

sub firstCount{

  # global variable again since local has not been created
  print "Global (inside first sub): " . ++$counter . "\n";

  # create local version, but set equal to 3
  local $counter = 3;

  # now write counter again (it's the local version)
  print "Local (inside first sub - initial): $counter\n";

  # increment counter
  print "Local (inside first sub - incremented): " . ++$counter . "\n";

  # call second subroutine, but pass an argument so it knows
  # that it was called by the first subroutine.
  &secondCount("firstCount");
}
```

```
#--------------------------------------
# Subroutine: secondCount
# Version Added: 1.0
# Input: none
# Output: prints value of counter, at various stages, to screen
# Description: simple function that increments value of counter,
#    at various stages, and prints their value to the screen.
#    Because the first subroutine calls this one, there is an
#    additional check to see if any arguments have been passed.
#    If so, then it changes what is printed to the screen.
#--------------------------------------

sub secondCount{

  # check to see if another subroutine called this one
  if($_[0]){
    print "\n----------YES!! $_[0] called this time----------\n";
  }

  # global variable again since local has not been created
  print "Global??? (inside second sub): " . ++$counter . "\n";

  # create local version, but set equal to 10
  local $counter = 10;

  # now write counter again (it's the local version)
  print "Local (inside second sub): $counter\n";

  # if another subroutine called, let user know it is done
  if($_[0]){
    print "------------Done with $_[0]'s call------------\n\n";
  }
}
```

The first thing we do is create a global variable called `$counter` and assign it a value of 0, which we immediately print. Next, we call our `&firstCount` subroutine and begin to execute it. Within this subroutine, we again print the value of `$counter` but, this time, after incrementing it by 1. Because nothing has been done to this variable at this point, the outputted value is 1. This is where it starts to get fun!

After printing this initial value, which was nothing more than the global variable after being incremented, we localize a version of `$counter`, but this one is set equal to 3. Again, we print the value of `$counter` but, this time, it is 3, the value of the localized version. In the next action, we again print an incremented version of `$counter` to show it's now equal to 4 (the value of the localized `$counter` plus 1).

Just before the subroutine ends, we call `&secondCount`, the second subroutine.

> **Note**
>
> When we call the second subroutine from within the first, we pass it an argument. This is done so we can change the output to show it was called by the first subroutine.

In the second subroutine, we check to see if an argument is passed. If so, we print the value of the argument, along with some dashes, so it shows up easily in the output. The remaining code looks a lot like `&firstCount`. We print an incremented version of the global counter, which is actually the localized counter from `&firstCount`, we declare a `&secondCount` localized version with a new value, and then we print it. Finally, if an argument was passed, we again end the subroutine with the name of the calling subroutine with dashes around it.

Now that the second subroutine has completed, the program jumps back to where it was called in the first subroutine. Seeing nothing is left to do, the program jumps all the way back up to where the first subroutine was called in the main program. Once it has returned, we print another incremented version of `$counter` and find it has a value of 2—where the original `$counter` ended. This is because the last time this global version was updated was in the first part of the call to `&firstCount`, where it equaled 1. Remember, the global counter incremented in the second subroutine was actually the localized version from `&firstCount`.

Next, the script calls the second subroutine again but, this time, it isn't from inside the first subroutine. Because no arguments are passed, it avoids printing the extra lines of text and goes right into printing the value of `++$counter`, which is now 3 and represents the value of the original global counter. Finally, it declares another local version of `$counter`, again assigning it to 10, and then prints its value. Once the subroutine has completed, it jumps back to where it was called for a final print statement to print the value of an incremented global `$counter`, which now equals 4.

What a long explanation! We hope we didn't lose you there. To help you, look at the next illustration to see what was actually written to the screen. If you look at it and trace through the code again, you should be able to follow the example easily.

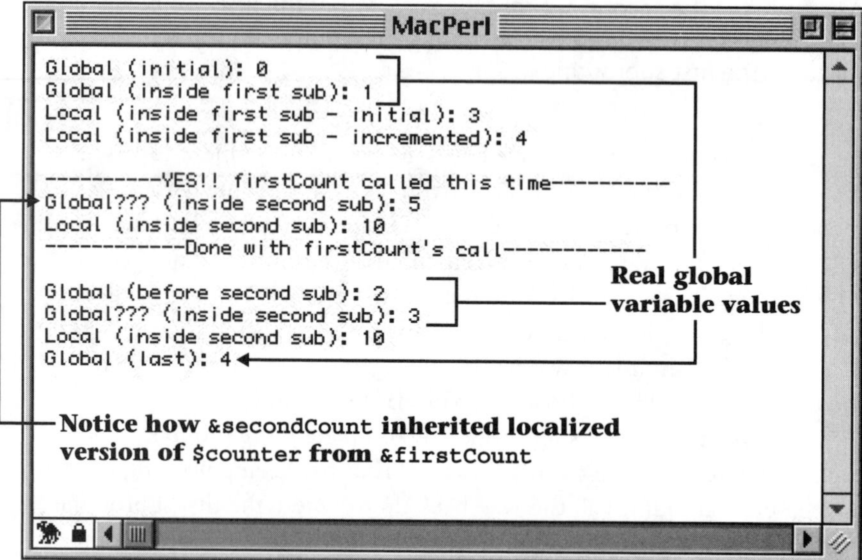
MacPerl
Global (initial): 0
Global (inside first sub): 1
Local (inside first sub - initial): 3
Local (inside first sub - incremented): 4
----------YES!! firstCount called this time----------
Global??? (inside second sub): 5
Local (inside second sub): 10
------------Done with firstCount's call------------
Global (before second sub): 2
Global??? (inside second sub): 3
Local (inside second sub): 10
Global (last): 4
Real global variable values
Notice how &secondCount inherited localized version of $counter from &firstCount

As you can see, the `local()` function can do some interesting things. Do remember, as shown in this example, that subroutines called with a subroutine where `local()` is used inherit the first subroutine's version.

Note

Other intricacies exist with the `local()` function that are beyond the scope of a beginner's book. We recommend you read the perlsub manpage for more information on `local()` and how it can be used.

Private Data with `my()`

Now that we've looked at `local()`, we're going to check out another, similar function called `my()`. Like `local()`, `my()` enables you to specify that a variable contained in a subroutine is only to be used local to that routine. Unlike the `local()` function, however, `my()` doesn't allow nested subroutines to act on the variables—they aren't passed on. Because of this, `my()` is often considered a safer method of declaring variables that are local to a subroutine.

To give you an example, let's take the `local-ex.pl` we just went over, change all the occurrences of using the `local()` function to using `my()` (two places—one in each subroutine), and then save it under a file named `my-ex.pl`. Now run the script.

As you can see in the following illustration, some differences occurred in what the `local-ex.pl` example returned, as seen in the previous illustration (specifically, the lines we began with the word "Global"). If you look, the lines all increment by 1, one after the other. In short, they are all acting on the same global variable, which was the original one defined in the main part of the program. Where we used the `my()` function, a change in value was held, in scope, to that subroutine.

5

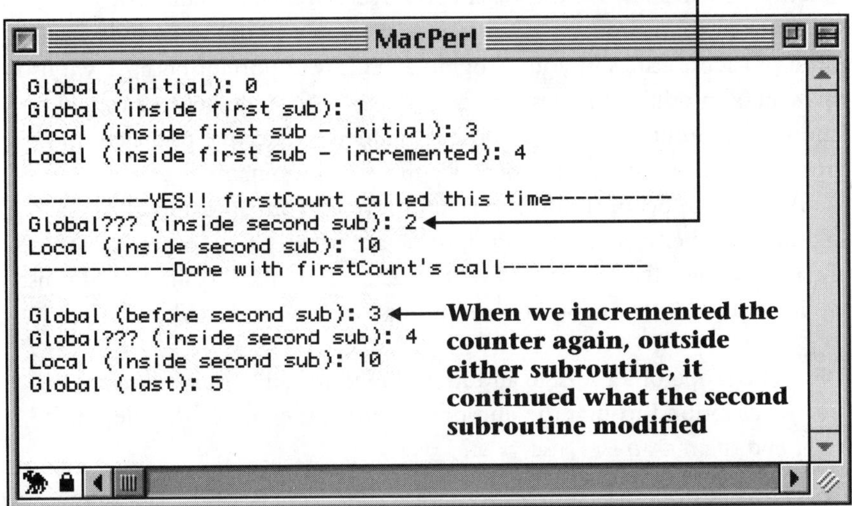
When the second subroutine was called, it incremented the original global counter
MacPerl
Global (initial): 0
Global (inside first sub): 1
Local (inside first sub - initial): 3
Local (inside first sub - incremented): 4
----------YES!! firstCount called this time----------
Global??? (inside second sub): 2
Local (inside second sub): 10
------------Done with firstCount's call------------
Global (before second sub): 3
Global??? (inside second sub): 4
Local (inside second sub): 10
Global (last): 5
When we incremented the counter again, outside either subroutine, it continued what the second subroutine modified

Now you may wonder what `my()` is used for in the real world. Usually the `my()` function is used when creating packages and modules. Unlike `local()`, `my()` provides a safer manner in which variables can be declared and used without *stomping* (that means *overwriting* for you newbies) on other variables that might have been defined elsewhere in the program. Because you may not know who is using your packages and modules, this is important.

As mentioned earlier, we discuss modules in detail in Module 8, so we'll save this discussion for later. At this point, we wanted to introduce you to the method of creating private, with `my()`, and semiprivate, with `local()`, data in subroutines.

1-Minute Drill

- **Why is using `my()` instead of `local()` recommended?**
- **If you have more than one variable passed to the `local()` function, do they have to be put in parentheses?**

Importing Subroutines from Packages

Importing subroutines from other packages is an important piece of functionality in Perl, which Module 8 covers in more detail. However, we do want to introduce you to the syntax you will use to include any imported subroutines in your programs. This is important because we use this syntax in other modules for certain tasks before we get to Module 8. Imported subroutines refer to those contained in external packages, or modules, and are often referenced by their package name.

A few steps occur in importing subroutines from an external package. Like many other functions in Perl, some are trickier than others and there are always one-offs that act differently than "normal." To simplify this list, we included the following bulleted points to get you started.

- The scope of a package and its included modules starts with the declaration through the end of the block, the end of the file, or the end of an `eval()` use.
- You can use the `require()` or `use()` functions to include packages or specific modules in your code. For instance, if you wanted to include a package called `MyPackage`, then you could enter `use MyPackage`.

- **Because this is often safer (no inheritance of values by nested subroutines) and faster**
- **Yes. Even though nearly all Perl's functions enable you either to specify or leave off parentheses, they are required when passing multiple variables to `local()`**

- `require()` specifies the argument, which can be more than just a package (such as the version of Perl), and is absolutely required for the script to run. `use()`, which is similar, acts as a method to import semantics, such as subroutines, into the current script.
- If you want to include a package located in a www directory, then you could use the syntax `use www::MyPackage` where `::` represents a change in directory.
- If you want to include a specific module in the package, you can pass a comma-separated list after the package name. For example, `use www::MyPackage 'mymod', 'yourmod'` would import the symbols, which are variables or subroutines, `mymod` and `yourmod` from the `MyPackage` package, which was located in the `www` directory.

Hint

For more information on `use()` and `require()` check out their entries in the perlfunc manpage.

Moving On

With the conclusion of this module, we laid the basic foundation for your programming experience in Perl. Now you know about the language itself, how it works, and a little of its history. Next, you learned about data types and operators, and then about using control structures. In the last two modules, you learned about more advanced ways to store data, and how to take advantage of subroutines and control program flow.

This section has been your Perl primer, which introduced you to concepts, semantics, and rules you need to know and understand before proceeding. Now it's time to put on your new Perl tool belt, throw on some working clothes, and dig right in to programming in the Perl language. We're about to start applying that newly gained knowledge to get you some experience.

For the rest of this book, we go over using the language to do everything from accessing files and directories, to handling Web requests and using databases. We show you how to take advantage of system calls and regular expressions, as well as how to go over error messages and debug your scripts. In the final module, after you put in your 12-hour day, we separate the passionate from the nonpassionate and dive into advanced Perl topics.

So, enough talk—let's begin the second portion of this book and start applying the knowledge you gained in the first five modules.

Mastery Check

1. What is the statement that signifies you are creating a subroutine?

   A. function

   B. func

   C. subroutine

   D. sub

2. Where should you organize your programming efforts?

   A. In your code

   B. In your program repository

   C. Neither A nor B

   D. Both A and B

3. The `local()` and `my()` functions are used to prevent the exposure of certain variables to the rest of your script. What, where *what* is a common programming term, does this define?

   A. scope

   B. range

   C. ability

Part 2

Applying Your Knowledge

Module 6

Working with Files and Directories

The Goals of This Module

- Discuss how to work with files
- Cover how to manipulate directories

This module covers the topics of how to work with files and directories. In the first section, we discuss how to work with files and go over everything you can do with files using Perl. Then we move on to the next section of the module, which covers how to work with a directory system, how to move around in a directory structure, and how to create and remove directories. Both of the sections introduce you to commands that vary, depending on what operating system you're using. Remember this as you read through this module.

Basic File Manipulation

Working with files using Perl is both simple and straightforward. Some new ideas may be introduced in this module, but don't worry about them. We explain them all in detail. The first thing to do when you work with a file is to open it. Once you open the file, you can make the necessary changes, and then you can close it. These are the basic steps in working with files and the next section covers both these tasks.

Opening and Closing Files

When you are opening a file from a program, you are automatically working with the current directory. The current directory is determined by where you are when you execute the program. If the file you want to open is in your current directory, you only have to give the name of that file. If the file is in another directory, you need to include the path to the file along with the filename. Also, when you open a file, you create a file variable name called a *file handle,* which can be used to select that particular file for other operations you may want to perform on it. Here's the syntax to open a file:

```
open (file handle, filename);
```

In this statement, file handle is the name of the variable you give the file itself. This variable is used whenever you need to call on the file for any future operation, such as closing it. Filename is the name of the file you want to open. If the file is in your current working directory, you only need to provide the name itself. If the open operation was a success, the statement returns true. Because of this, you can use statements, such as the 'if' statement, to determine if the operation was successful. Let's look at a short programming example that will open a file.

Note

Standard practice is to close a file once you finish working with it. In this example, we aren't going to close the file because we haven't covered the close operation yet.

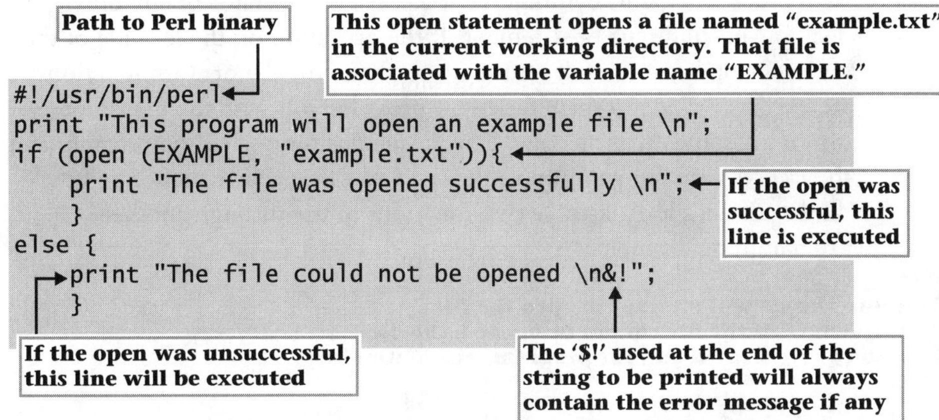

Path to Perl binary
This open statement opens a file named "example.txt" in the current working directory. That file is associated with the variable name "EXAMPLE."
If the open was successful, this line is executed
If the open was unsuccessful, this line will be executed
The '$!' used at the end of the string to be printed will always contain the error message if any

```
#!/usr/bin/perl
print "This program will open an example file \n";
if (open (EXAMPLE, "example.txt")){
    print "The file was opened successfully \n";
    }
else {
    print "The file could not be opened \n&!";
    }
```

The output of the previous programming example, opening a file in the current working directory, is seen in the illustration.

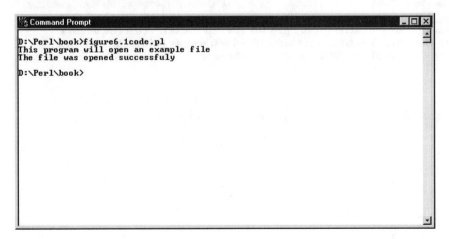

```
Command Prompt
D:\Perl\book>figure6.1code.pl
This program will open an example file
The file was opened successfuly

D:\Perl\book>
```

Note

The file handle for a file can also be a preassigned variable containing the string you want the file handle to be.

From the previous example, you can see the file was opened successfully and the correct statement was executed to let you know.

Before we go any further, we need to introduce you to two functions that can come in handy when you are working with files and directories: the die and warn functions. These functions can be used in conjunction with other statements by using the logical or || operator or any other decision-making type of statement. If the operation on the left side of the logical or operator doesn't return a true value, the die or warn functions are executed. Each of these functions provides you with the option of displaying some error message. The *die function* terminates the program and the *warn function* simply outputs the error message you requested to be displayed. Let's look at these two functions in use through another programming example:

This line of code will attempt to open the file "example.txt." If the file cannot be opened, the die function gets executed and the program terminates.

```
#!/usr/bin/perl
print "This program will open an example file \n";
print "This is an example of the die and warn functions being used with the
|| operator \n";
open (EXAMPLE, "example.txt") || die ("Could not open example.txt \n$!");
open (EXAMPLE1, "nofile.txt") || warn ("Could not open nofile.txt \n$!");
```

This line of code will attempt to open the file "nofile.txt." This file doesn't exist, so the warn function gets executed, which simply prints the specified warning message along with the actual error saved in the $! variable.

The output of the previous programming example, checking for success with the die and warn functions, is seen in this illustration.

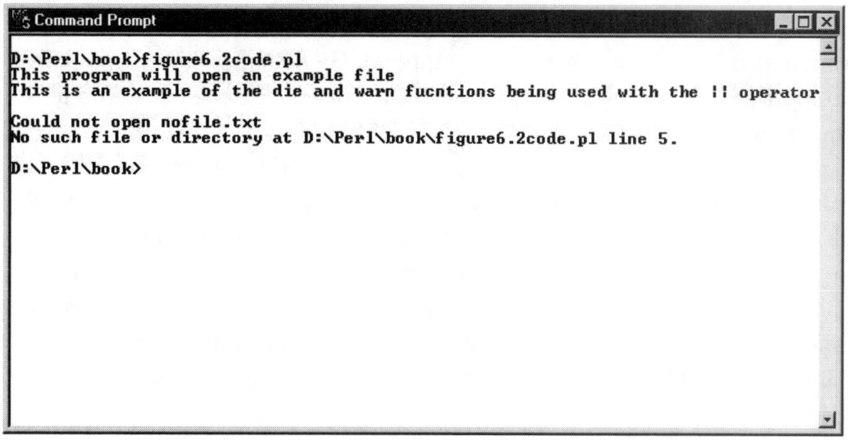

```
D:\Perl\book>figure6.2code.pl
This program will open an example file
This is an example of the die and warn fucntions being used with the || operator

Could not open nofile.txt
No such file or directory at D:\Perl\book\figure6.2code.pl line 5.

D:\Perl\book>
```

Now that you've seen the open function work on files in the current directory, here's an example of an open statement that opens a file in a different directory:

6

```
#!/usr/bin/perl
print "This program will open an example file \n";
open (EXAMPLE, 'd:\Perl\book\test\example.txt') || die ("Could not open
example.txt \n");
```

This line of code will attempt to open the file "example.txt," which resides in a different directory than the current working directory. If the file cannot be opened, the die function gets executed and the program terminates.

Note

Notice in the previous example, we used single quotes to enclose the path and filename. This is because when you use double quotes, the slash (\) is a control character. For UNIX, you can use double quotes without any problems. If you want to use them on a Windows platform, however, you must add a slash to every backslash in the path. The path would look like "D:\\Perl\\book\\test\\example.pl". You can also use the forward slash (/) on a Windows platform, so it would look like "D:/Perl/book/test/example.pl". The decision of which format to use is up to you.

Now that you know how to open a file, you can open them in three different modes: Read, Write, and Append. By default, all files are opened in the *Read* mode, which lets you read the contents of the file without changing it.

The next mode you can open a file in is the *Write* mode, which is dangerous to you, the user. When you open a file in the Write mode, all the current contents of the file are destroyed. The contents you delete are replaced by a write to that file. We show you how to write to a file later in this module. If you want to open a file in Write mode, you need to add one greater than symbol (>) in front of the filename and path if applicable. Here's an open statement that will open a file in Write mode:

```
Open (EXAMPLE, ">D:/Perl/book/test/example.txt");
```

Once the file, example.txt, is opened in Write mode, its contents will be removed and, unless you write anything to the file, it will contain zero bytes. The Write mode is useful when you want to rewrite over the contents of the same file every time.

Another mode you can open a file in is the *Append* mode, which lets you add to the contents of the file without destroying the current contents. When you use the Append mode, you cannot read the existing contents of the file. To open a file in this mode, you have to add two greater than symbols (>>) in front of the filename and path. It would look like this in a program:

```
Open (EXAMPLE, ">>D:\\Perl\\book\\test\\example.txt");
```

The Append mode is useful when you need to add contents to a file without having the need to read the current contents.

If you want to open a file in Read/Write mode and you don't want the contents of the file to be harmed, you can add a plus + and a less than symbol < in front of the filename and path. This character sequence +< signifies the file has been opened in Read/Write mode.

Now that you know how to open a file, you need to learn how to close one. Remember, the file handle is the reference for a file throughout its life in a program. To close a file, you must use this file handle. Here's the syntax for the close statement:

```
close (file handle);
```

This statement is self-explanatory. Once you finish working with the file you have opened, you should always close the file using this statement. The following program is included to give you an example of the close statement being used:

```
#!/usr/bin/perl
print "This program will open an example file \n";
print "This is an example of the die and warn functions being used with the
|| operator \n";
open (EXAMPLE, "example.txt") || die ("Could not open example.txt \n");
close (EXAMPLE);
```

An example of the close statement being used to close the file example.txt

6

This concludes our discussion on opening and closing files. You should feel comfortable executing each of these statements. Now let's move on to the next section and cover some of the things you can do to a file once it's open.

1-Minute Drill

- **What mode should you open a file in if you want to rewrite the contents of the file each time it is opened and what character signifies the use of this mode?**
- **What is always used to reference a file once it has been opened?**

Reading and Writing Files

The previous section of this module taught you how to open and close files. Now that you're comfortable with that information, let's move on to discuss reading and writing to those files. We begin with some of the

---

- **Write mode, >**
- **The filehandle**

easier ways to manipulate files and finish the section with some more advanced concepts.

You know the default mode used when opening a file is the Read mode. This mode lets you read the contents of a file. Along the same lines, the standard input file is STDIN, which means if you don't specify a certain file to read from by using a file handle, user input will serve as the source of information. Just as with STDIN, a file handle can be specified and lines of input from that opened file can be saved into variables in your program. Let's look at a program that will open a file and use the specified file handle to read the first line of information from that file.

Note

Remember, the end of a line is signified by a carriage return.

This line of code will read everything in the file until the first carriage return is encountered and save all the information as a string in the $text variable

```
#!/usr/bin/perl
print "This program will open an example file \n";
open (EXAMPLE, 'd:\Perl\book\test\example.txt') || die ("Could not open
example.txt \n");
$text = <EXAMPLE>;
print "The first line of text read from the file is \n \n $text \n";
```

This line of code simply outputs the contents of the $text variable

The output of the previous programming example, reading information from a file, is displayed in the illustration.

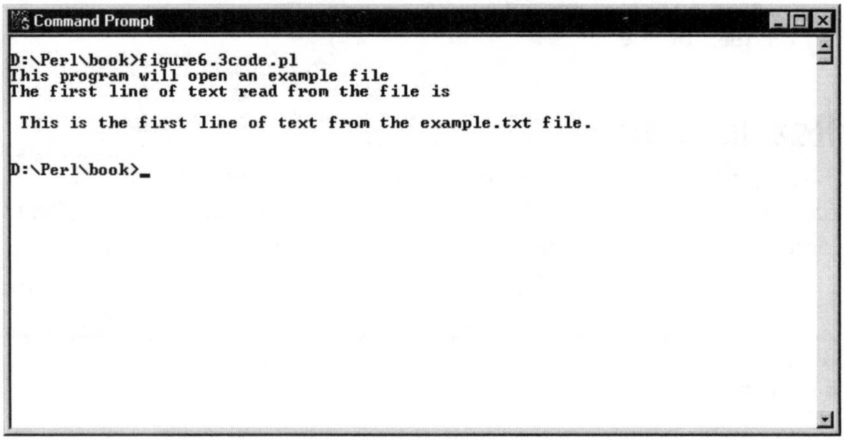

```
Command Prompt

D:\Perl\book>figure6.3code.pl
This program will open an example file
The first line of text read from the file is

 This is the first line of text from the example.txt file.


D:\Perl\book>_
```

The previous example demonstrates how you can read one line of information from a file. If you want to display all the lines of information from a file, you have to place the assignment statement inside a loop that checks to see if there is another line of text to read each time. The following program is an example of one way to read and display an entire file:

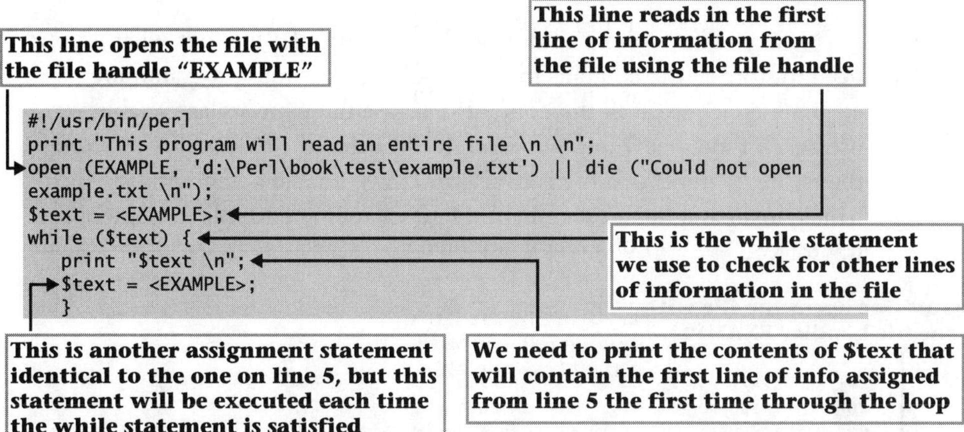
This line opens the file with the file handle "EXAMPLE"
This line reads in the first line of information from the file using the file handle
#!/usr/bin/perl
print "This program will read an entire file \n \n";
open (EXAMPLE, 'd:\Perl\book\test\example.txt') || die ("Could not open example.txt \n");
$text = <EXAMPLE>;
while ($text) {
print "$text \n";
$text = <EXAMPLE>;
}
This is the while statement we use to check for other lines of information in the file
This is another assignment statement identical to the one on line 5, but this statement will be executed each time the while statement is satisfied
We need to print the contents of $text that will contain the first line of info assigned from line 5 the first time through the loop

The following illustration shows the output of the previous programming example, reading and outputting all information from a file.

```
Command Prompt

D:\Perl\book>figure6.4code.pl
This program will read an entire file

The first line from example.txt

The second line from example.txt

The third line from example.txt

D:\Perl\book>
```

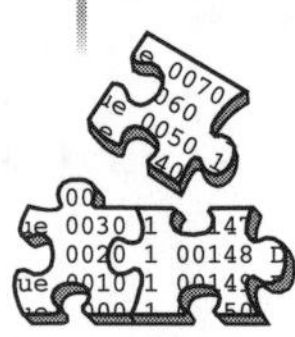

Project 6-1: Reading from Files

Write a program that will read and save all the contents of a file using scalar variables. Once you save all the contents, your program should output an exact copy of the file to the screen all at once before exiting. Don't use an array variable in this program.

Now you know how to display the contents of a file, but what if you need to store all the contents for later use? The previous programming example didn't store all the contents because the same scalar variable was used each time a new line was read in. Probably the easiest way to store the entire contents of a file is to use an array variable along with the file handle in an assignment statement. Here's a coding example to demonstrate this for you.

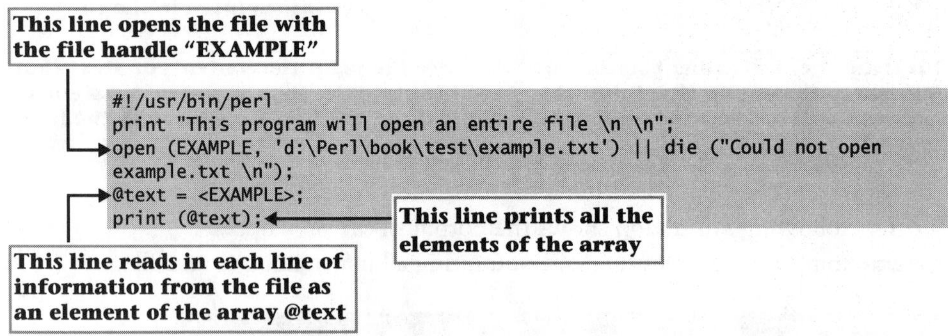
This line opens the file with the file handle "EXAMPLE"
This line prints all the elements of the array
This line reads in each line of information from the file as an element of the array @text

```
#!/usr/bin/perl
print "This program will open an entire file \n \n";
open (EXAMPLE, 'd:\Perl\book\test\example.txt') || die ("Could not open
example.txt \n");
@text = <EXAMPLE>;
print (@text);
```

The output of the previous programming example, storing and outputting all information from a file, is shown in the illustration.

```
Command Prompt
D:\Perl\book>figure6.5code.pl
This program will open an entire file

This is the first line of text from the example.txt file.
This is the second line of text from the file.
This is the third line of text from the file.
D:\Perl\book>
```

The previous example is usually a good way to store the contents of a file when you want the entire file. After you have the file stored in an array, remember that each line of information from the file is a separate element of the array. This can come in handy if you need to search for something in a file because you can search for it one line at a time, or one element at a time. Searching for strings in files is covered in the next module, "Regular Expressions," of this book.

Another way to read information from a file that gives you a little more control is the read function. This function lets you read a certain number of bytes from a file. It lets you store the information in scalar or array variables, and it also lets you specify how many bytes of the information already stored you don't want to overwrite. Look at the syntax for this statement, and then we'll go to a programming example to demonstrate it being used:


```
read (file handle, variable, length, skipbytes);
```

You're already familiar with what the file handle does. The *variable parameter* is what you want to store the information in. The *length field* is where you specify how many bytes of information you want to be read from the file. If you already read some information into a variable and you are using that same variable again in another read statement, you can use the skipbytes field to specify how many bytes of information you don't want to overwrite.

Note

A *byte* of information is one character. If you want to capture the string "Hello World," you must tell the read function to get 11 bytes of information. Remember, the space is also a character.

Let's look at a programming example that demonstrates the use of the read function.

```
#!/usr/bin/perl
print "This program will use the read function to get data from a file \n
\n";

open (EXAMPLE, 'd:\Perl\book\test\example.txt') || die ("Could not open
example.txt \n");
```

This line opens the file with the file handle "EXAMPLE"

```
read (EXAMPLE, $text, 10);
print "$text \n";
read (EXAMPLE, $text, 10, 10);
print "$text \n";
read (EXAMPLE, $text, 2000, 20);
print "$text \n";
```

This read statement writes 10 bytes from the file to that variable

This read statement skips the first 10 previously read bytes and it writes another 10 bytes to the scalar variable

This read statement effectively reads in the rest of the file because it skips the first 20 previously read bytes, and then it attempts to read another 2000 bytes of information

The illustration shows the output of the previous programming example, storing and outputting information using the read function.

```
D:\Perl\book>figure6.6code.pl
This program will use the read function to get data from a file

This is th
This is the first li
This is the first line of text from the example.txt file.
This is the second line of text from the file.
This is the third line of text from the file.

D:\Perl\book>
```

Note

From the previous programming example, you should notice the same scalar variable was used each time read was executed and none of the information that was skipped was overwritten. The read function saves previously read information and when you skip this information, it automatically includes it in the spaces you skipped. If we had included another read statement after the last one, it wouldn't have contained any data because the end of the file had already been reached.

Two other functions are provided for you to use when you are reading from an opened file: seek and tell. The *seek* function can be used to skip forward or backward in an opened file. The syntax for the seek function is as follows:

```
seek (file handle, length, from_where);
```

The length field is used to specify how far to skip in the file. The from_where field is used to determine from where you want to skip. The following table shows the possibilities for this field.

from_where	What It Means
0	Count from the beginning of the file
1	Count from the current position in the file
2	Count from the end of the file

The *tell* function can be used to determine how many bytes you have skipped into a file. The number of bytes is always relative to the beginning of the file when you use this function. The syntax for the function is as follows:

```
tell (file handle);
```

Now that you know the syntax for these statements, here's a programming example to demonstrate the use of each of these functions.

This line opens the file with the file handle "EXAMPLE"

This seek statement jumps 20 bytes from the beginning of the file

```
#!/usr/bin/perl
print "This program will use the read function to get data from a file \n
\n";
open (EXAMPLE, 'd:\Perl\book\test\example.txt') || die ("Could not open
example.txt \n");
seek (EXAMPLE, 20, 0);
$location = tell (EXAMPLE);
print "you have skipped $location bytes ahead in the file \n";
read (EXAMPLE, $text, 10);
print "$text \n";
read (EXAMPLE, $text, 10, 10);
print "$text \n";
$location = tell (EXAMPLE);
print "you are starting at byte $location now \n";
read (EXAMPLE, $text, 2000, 20);
print "$text \n";
```

This line stores the current file location in bytes from the beginning of the file in the scalar variable $location

The rest of the program is the same as the previous example, except that the first 20 bytes of the file were skipped and, therefore, never read

The illustration demonstrates the output of the previous programming example, using the seek and tell functions.

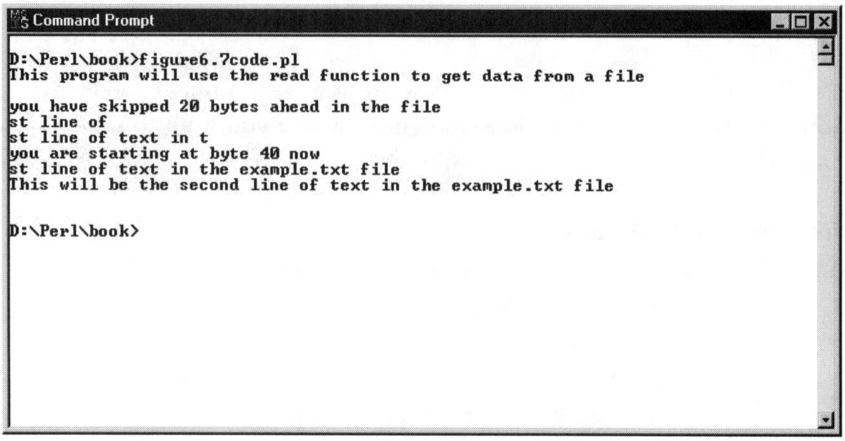

```
Command Prompt
D:\Perl\book>figure6.7code.pl
This program will use the read function to get data from a file

you have skipped 20 bytes ahead in the file
st line of
st line of text in t
you are starting at byte 40 now
st line of text in the example.txt file
This will be the second line of text in the example.txt file


D:\Perl\book>
```

The last function we cover before moving on to discuss writing to files comes in handy for Windows users. The function, *binmode,* lets you read in a binary file. The syntax for this function is as follows:

```
binmode (file handle);
```

Once you use this function with the file handle, you can open any binary file using that file handle.

Now we need to discuss how to write to files once they have been opened. Remember, when you open a file, it is defaulted to read access only. When you need to open a file for write access, you must include the greater than symbol in front of the filename and/or path. The easiest way to write to a file is to use the print statement. Up to this point in the book when you've seen the print statement being used, a file handle hasn't been specified. The reason is, if you don't select a file handle, standard output (STDOUT) is picked for you. STDOUT is the file handle used for printing to the screen. Here's a program that can open a file for write access, write some information to that file, and close the file.

The file "example.txt" is opened for write access, which will delete everything it currently contains

These lines write the first and second lines of text to the file

```
#!/usr/bin/perl
open (EXAMPLE, '>d:\Perl\book\test\example.txt') || die ("Could not open
example.txt \n");
print EXAMPLE "This will be the first line of text in the example.txt file
\n";
print EXAMPLE "This will be the second line of text in the example.txt file
\n";
print "Notice that none of the previous output was sent to the screen \n";
close (EXAMPLE);
open (EXAMPLE, 'd:\Perl\book\test\example.txt') || die ("Could not open
example.txt \n");
print "Now we have opened the file for read access only \n";
read (EXAMPLE, $contents, 2000);
print "The file contains the following \n $contents \n";
close (EXAMPLE);
```

The file is closed so we can reopen it in Read mode

The file is reopened with read access, so the new contents of the file can be printed

6

This illustration shows writing to a file using the print statement, the output of the previous programming example.

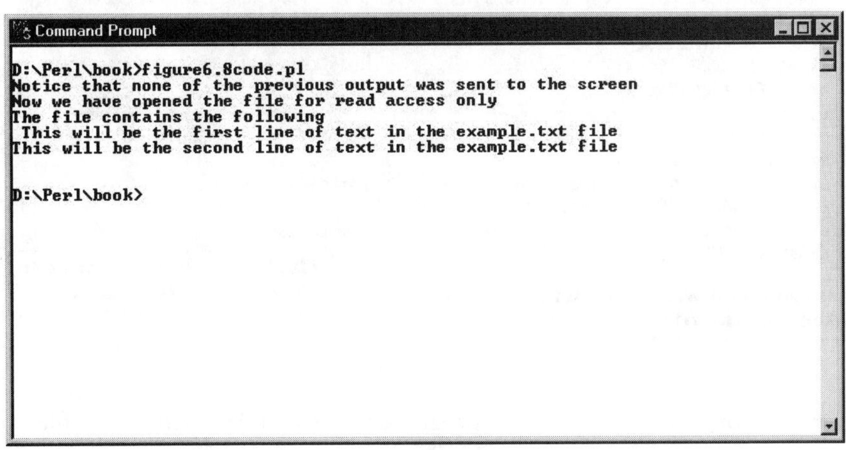
Command Prompt
D:\Perl\book>figure6.8code.pl
Notice that none of the previous output was sent to the screen
Now we have opened the file for read access only
The file contains the following
 This will be the first line of text in the example.txt file
This will be the second line of text in the example.txt file
D:\Perl\book>

In the previous programming example, we opened a file that originally contained some information. However, since we opened it in Write mode, everything was erased. The file we opened now contains only the two lines of text that was written to it.

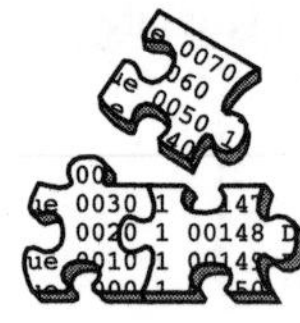

Project 6-2: Creating Files

Building on the previous programming example, write a program that can save the contents of a given file and create a new file in the same directory that contains a copy of the original file's information.

Another way to write to a file is by using STDIN to query the user for information. Here's a program that demonstrates this.

The file "example.txt" is opened for write access, which will delete everything it currently contains

The new information to be stored in the file is taken from STDIN

```
#!/usr/bin/perl
open (EXAMPLE, '>d:\Perl\book\test\example.txt') || die ("Could not open
example.txt \n");
print "Please enter the first line of text you want the file to contain \n";
$text = <STDIN>;
print "Please enter the second line of text you want the file to contain
\n";
$text1 = <STDIN>;
print EXAMPLE "$text";
print EXAMPLE "$text1";
close (EXAMPLE);
open (EXAMPLE, 'd:\Perl\book\test\example.txt') || die ("Could not open
example.txt \n");
print "Now we have opened the file for read access only \n";
read (EXAMPLE, $contents, 2000);
print "The file contains the following \n $contents \n";
close (EXAMPLE);
```

The file is reopened with read access, so the new contents of the file can be printed

The file is closed, so we can reopen it in Read mode

The output of the previous programming example, writing to a file using the print statement and STDIN, is seen in the illustration.

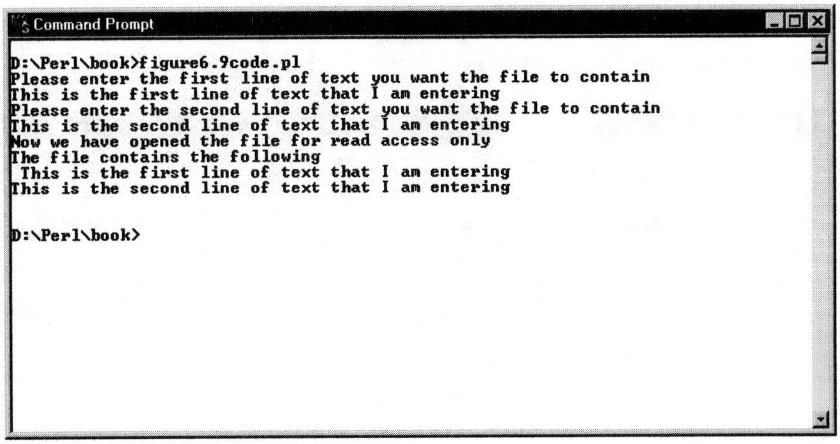

```
D:\Perl\book>figure6.9code.pl
Please enter the first line of text you want the file to contain
This is the first line of text that I am entering
Please enter the second line of text you want the file to contain
This is the second line of text that I am entering
Now we have opened the file for read access only
The file contains the following
 This is the first line of text that I am entering
This is the second line of text that I am entering


D:\Perl\book>
```

6

Yet another way to write to a file is to copy the information from another file into the new file. Several ways exist to do this and, for this example, we use the while structure to copy all the contents from one file to another. The first thing we must do that isn't already done is to create a file that contains the information we want to copy to the new file. We call it "information.txt." Here's an example.

The file "example.txt" is opened for write access, which will delete everything it currently contains

The file "information.txt" is opened for read access

```
#!/usr/bin/perl
open (EXAMPLE, '>d:\Perl\book\test\example.txt') || die ("Could not open
example.txt \n");
open (INFORMATION, 'd:\Perl\book\test\information.txt') || die ("Could not
open information.txt \n");
$copy = <INFORMATION>;
while ($copy) {
    print EXAMPLE ($copy);
    $copy = <INFORMATION>;
}
close (EXAMPLE);
close (INFORMATION);
print "The new file contains : \n";
open (EXAMPLE, 'd:\Perl\book\test\example.txt') || die ("Could not open
example.txt \n");
$contents = <EXAMPLE>;
while ($contents){
    print "$contents \n";
    $contents = <EXAMPLE>;
}
```

This is the while loop that will iterate through each line of the information.txt file

The file is closed, so we can reopen it in Read mode

The file is reopened with read access, so the new contents of the file can be printed

Copying the contents of one file into another, the output of the previous programming example, is shown in this illustration.

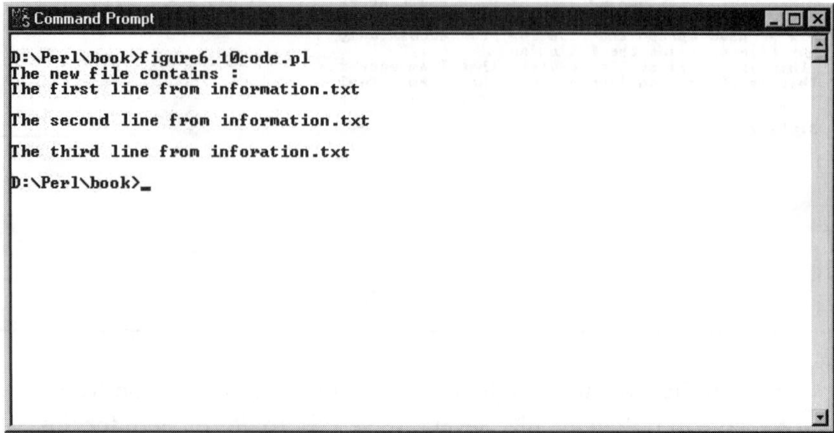

Another way to write to a file is to redirect the standard output to a file. When you do this, any print statement automatically sends the information to the file to which you redirected it. This method saves you the trouble of having to include the file handle in every print statement you have. Here's a programming example to demonstrate this.

This line of code opens the file example.txt under the file handle "EXAMPLE"

```
#!/usr/bin/perl
open (EXAMPLE, 'd:\Perl\book\test\example.txt') || die ("Could not open
example.txt \n");
open (STDOUT, ">output.txt") || die ("Could not open output.txt \n");
$contents = <EXAMPLE>;
while ($contents){
   print "$contents";
   $contents = <EXAMPLE>;
}
close (EXAMPLE);
close (STDOUT);
```

This line of code redirects STDOUT, which represents the standard output file, to the file output.txt

This print statement will send information to the output.txt file because STDOUT was redirected to it

This illustration displays the file created by redirecting standard output to a file.

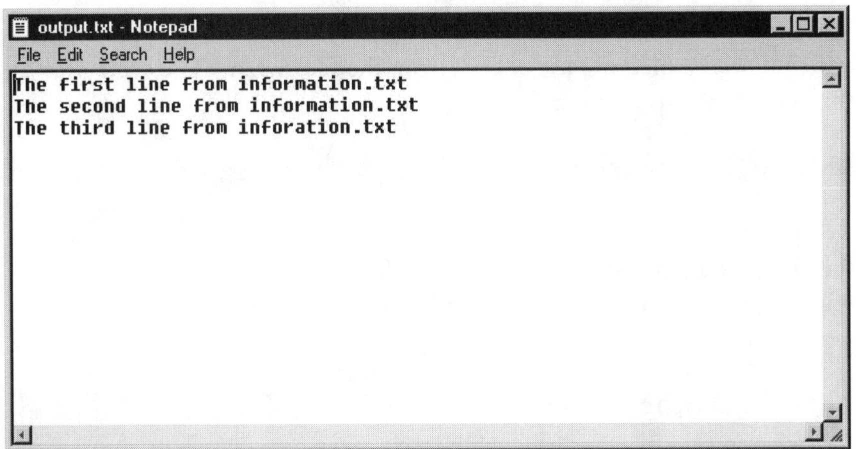

Note

Once you redirect standard output to a file, the rest of the print statements in that program automatically send information to that file unless you specify another file handle to use.

Now that you know how to write to a file, we need to discuss some of the different things you can do to an existing file.

The rename function changes the name of an existing file, as well as moves that file if you specify a different path. The syntax for the rename function is as follows:

```
rename (existing name, new name);
```

This function takes the existing name and the new name as arguments. If the files are renamed successfully, a true value is returned. The following line of code renames a file:

```
rename ("output.txt", "oldout.txt");
```

6

This line of code renames output.txt to oldout.txt. If you want to move the file to another directory in the same file system, you can do so by specifying the complete path and the filename.

Another function you can use on existing files is the *unlink* function, which deletes a file, or a list of files, from the file system. The syntax for this statement is as follows:

```
unlink (filename);
```

Be careful when you use this function because, as previously stated, this function permanently removes a file from your file system. The following line of code removes the file named output.txt from the current working directory.

```
unlink ("output.txt");
```

If you are running on a UNIX platform, you can change the permissions your file has for yourself, your group, and the world by specifying the octal representation of the desired permissions for each of these three groups. Permissions are in the following format:

r w x

The *r* specifies you have read permissions, the *w* represents the write permissions, and the *x* represents the execute permissions. Three sets of "*r w x*" exist for each of the three sections—yourself, your group, and the world—so it looks something like:

r w x r w x r w x

Each group of permissions is represented by a three-digit binary number like 000 or 110. To select the permission you want, you have to specify the corresponding octal number for that particular group. If you want to give everyone—which includes yourself, your group, and the world—permissions to a file, you specify a seven for each group. 0777 would be 111 111 111 in binary and, therefore, every permission for everyone would be turned on. Most of the time, 744 is used because it gives you full permissions for the file and everyone else will only be able to read the file. With that said, here's the syntax for the chmod command:

```
chmod (mode, filename);
```

The mode is where you enter the octal representation for the permissions you want to select for a file. The filename is where you specify the name of that file for which you want to set the new permissions. The following is an example of this function being used:

```
chmod (0744, "output.txt");
```

When this statement is executed, the file output.txt will have *r w x* permission for you, *r* permissions for your UNIX group, and *r* permission for anyone else who has access to your files. To make sure all this is clear, let's look at it mapped out for you.

6

Groups	user	group	world
Octal numbers	7	4	4
Binary numbers	1 1 1	1 0 0	1 0 0
Possible permissions	*r w x*	*r w x*	*r w x*
Selected permissions	*r w x*	*r*	*r*

1-Minute Drill

- **What function can be used to skip ahead in a file before reading any information?**
- **How many bytes of information does this string contain: "How are you today?"**

This concludes our discussion about reading and writing to files. You should feel comfortable working with files using any of the methods discussed. Always remember to open a file in the correct mode, depending

---

- **Seek**
- **18**

on the reason for which you plan to use the file. The next section of this module covers a few ways to obtain the status information for a file.

Obtaining Status Information for a File

The previous two sections of this module introduced you to the various ways you can manipulate files. In this section of the module, we cover the different tools you can use to find out information about files. These tools are sometimes referred to as the *–x file tests* because of the format in which you invoke them. The –x file tests are used along with a file handle to determine a number of different things about the associated file. First, let's look at all the different file test options that are available.

File test operator	What it does
-b	Determines if the given is a block device
-c	Determines if the given is a character device
-d	Determines if the given is a directory
-e	Determines if the given exists
-f	Determines if the given is an ordinary file
-g	Determines if the given has a setgid
-k	Determines if the given has a sticky bit set
-l	Determines if the given is a symbolic link
-o	Determines if the given is owned by the current user
-p	Determines if the given is a named pipe
-r	Determines if the given is a readable
-s	Determines if the given contains any information
-t	Determines if the given represents a terminal
-u	Checks to see if the given has a setuid
-w	Determines if the given is writable
-x	Determines if the given is an executable
-z	Determines if the given is empty
-A	Determines how long it has been since the given was last accessed
-B	Determines if the given is a binary file
-C	Determines how long it has been since a file's inode has been accessed
-M	Determines how long it has been since the given was modified
-O	Determines if the given is owned by the current user. The current user's ID is set at the time of login

File test operator	What it does
-R	Determines if the given is readable by the current user
-S	Determines if the given is a socket
-T	Determines if the given is a text file
-W	Determines if the given is writable by the current user
-X	Determines if the given is executable by the current user

Note

Most of the previous file test options can also be used on directories. We cover directories in the next section of this module.

Now that you've seen all the file test options, here's the syntax for how to use them:


```
-x file
```

-x is where you select which file test option you want to use and *file* is where you specify the filename you want to test. Here's a programming example that shows a few of these file test operators being used.

This line of code checks to see if the file output.txt exists

This line of code finds out how much time has passed since output.txt was modified and it stores the amount (in days) in the scalar variable $last_modified

```
#!/usr/bin/perl
if (-e "output.txt"){
   print "The file really does exist \n";
}
else{
   print "That file does not exist in the current working directory \n";
}
$last_modified = -M "output.txt";
print "It has been $last_modified days since the output.txt file has been
modified \n";
if (-r "output.txt"){
   print "The file is readable \n";
}
else {
   print "The file is not readable \n";
}
if (-z "output.txt"){
   print "The file is empty, you don't want to use an empty file \n";
}
else {
   print "The file does contain some information \n";
}
```

This line checks to see if the file is readable

This line checks to see if the file is empty

The output of the previous programming example, using several of the file test functions on a file, is demonstrated in the illustration.

```
Command Prompt
D:\Perl\book>figure6.12code.pl
The file really does exist
It has been 0.172164351851852 days since the output.txt file has been modified
The file is readable
The file does contain some information

D:\Perl\book>
```

The previous example should give you a good idea of how to use the file test functions to determine whatever you need to know about a file before opening it with a file handle.

1-Minute Drill

- **Which file test option can you use to determine if a file is empty?**
- **What unit of time is returned from any of the time-related file tests?**

The next section of this module covers how to work with the directory system.

Directory Access

This section of the module covers the different functions you can use to manipulate the directory structure. The only use of directories you've seen

---

- **-z**
- **Days**

so far is when you have to specify the complete path to a file. Perl provides several functions that can be used to create directories, change directories, open directories, and so on.

Moving Around

The first function we cover in this section is the *mkdir* function, which is used to create a new directory in the current file system. When you create a new directory using this function, you can also specify what permissions you want the directory to have. Here's the syntax for this statement:

```
mkdir (dirname, mode); ***
```

The *dirname* field in this function contains the name of the newly created directory. The *mode* field is where you specify the permissions, using the octal number system you learned about in the previous section, for the new directory. Like most supplied functions that perform some task, a true is returned if the directory is created successfully.

6

Note

Ensuring functions like mkdir are executed successfully is always a good idea. If an operation, such as creating a directory, fails, you should probably halt the program. The die function is ideal for this.

The following is a simple example that shows a directory being created with some error checking implemented by using an if-then-else statement.

An attempt is made to create a new directory named "newdir"

If the directory is created successfully, this statement will be printed to the screen

```
#!/usr/bin/perl
if (mkdir ("newdir", 0777)){
   print "The directory was created successfully \n";
}
else{
   print "The directory could not be created because of permission or
because a directory with that name already exists \n";
}
```

If the directory cannot be created, this line will be printed to the screen

Note

The mkdir function won't overwrite an existing directory. If the function doesn't create a new directory, it's usually because a directory with the same name already exists or you may not have user permissions to change anything in the current file system.

The term "current working directory" has appeared a few times in this module. A *current working directory* is automatically set as the directory where you execute the program. The current working directory is useful because as long as the files you need to work with are in this directory, you only have to supply the filename to access them. Perl provides a function called *chdir,* which changes this working directory after the program has been initialized. The syntax for this statement is as follows:

```
chdir (dirname);
```

The *dirname* field for this function is where you specify the complete path to the new working directory. The best way to demonstrate this function is with a programming example. The following example searches for a file in the default current working directory, and then we change the working directory and search for the same file again to make sure it's no longer present.

```
#!/usr/bin/perl
if (-e "output.txt"){
   print "The file is present \n";
}
else{
   print "The file does not exist \n";
}
chdir ('d:\perl\book\newdir') || die ("Could not set new working
directory");
if (-e "output.txt"){
   print "The file is present \n";
}
else{
   print "The file does not exist \n";
}
```

We check to see if the file output.txt exists in the default current working directory

We check to ensure the directory has changed by checking for the same filename. This new current working directory was set up as empty.

The current working directory is changed to d:\perl\book\newdir

The next function we cover is the *opendir* function, which lets you open a directory and associate that directory to a directory handle. Once you use this function to open a directory, you can perform other operations on it, such as reading all its contents. The syntax for this function is as follows:

```
opendir (directory handle, directory);
```

The directory handle is the name you associate with the opened directory and the directory field is where you specify which directory to open.

Once you open a directory and complete all your work with it, you must be able to close the directory. To do this, you need to use the *closedir* function. The syntax for this function is as follows:


```
closedir (directory handle);
```

After you open a directory using the opendir function, you can do several things. One of these is to read the contents of the directory using the *readdir* function, which returns the first file or subdirectory in the opened directory. Let's look at the syntax for this function:

```
readdir (directory handle);
```

As previously stated, this function only returns the first file or subdirectory in the opened directory. If you want to read all the contents of a directory, you need to implement some sort of loop that executes the readdir statement while something is there to read.

Project 6-3: Searching for Files

Using the functions you have learned so far, write a program that will take a filename from user input and search for that file in a given directory. You should continue to search for the file until it is located or until there are no other files for which to search.

The next directory functions we cover are the *telldir* and *seekdir* functions, which are used in conjunction with each other and enable you to skip around in a directory list.

Note

When you use the readdir function, it keeps up with its current location in the directory list, so it will know which files and subdirectories it has and hasn't read. If you want to be able to skip around in a directory list instead of having to read the files and subdirectories in order, you can use the telldir and seekdir functions.

The telldir function returns your current location in a directory listing. As you iterate through a directory, you can use this function to see where you are in the listing. The syntax for this function is as follows:

```
telldir (directory handle);
```

If you want to set your starting point in a directory list to somewhere other than the beginning, you must save what the telldir function returns to use with the seekdir function. The following line of code does this for you:

```
$current_location = telldir (directory handle);
```

The seekdir function enables you to set the starting point in a directory listing to anywhere you want. The only catch is the location you use with this function must be returned from the telldir function. Here's the syntax for the seekdir function:

```
seekdir (directory handle, $current_location);
```

Once you've used this function to change your position in a directory listing, you can continue using the readdir function to iterate through the rest of the contents of the directory.

Another function that can be useful when you work with directories is rewinddir, which resets your current directory listing position to the beginning. The syntax for this statement is as follows:

```
rewinddir (directory handle);
```

The last directory function we discuss is the *rmdir* function, and you can probably guess it's used to remove a directory from the current file system. The syntax for this function is as follows:

```
rmdir (directory name);
```

The directory name is the actual name of a directory in the current file system. A directory needn't be open before this function can be used. If the directory you want to remove isn't in the current working directory, however, you must supply the complete path to it.

Note

The rmdir function only removes empty directories.

Mastery Check

1. What does the open function return if a file was opened successfully?

   A. 0

   B. 1

   C. A non-zero value

   D. Both B and C

2. What function can be used to halt the program if a function fails to execute properly?

   A. Warn

   B. Die

   C. Both A and B

   D. None of the above

Mastery Check

3. What is the default mode in which a file is always opened?

   A. read

   B. write

   C. append

   D. read + write

4. What function can be used to move a file?

   A. move

   B. relocate

   C. rename

   D. None of the above

5. What function is used to delete a file from the current file system?

   A. delete

   B. rmfile

   C. unlink

   D. All of the above

6. What function is used to select a new current working directory?

   A. chdir

   B. readdir

   C. telldir

   D. cwddir

Module 7

Regular Expressions

The Goals of This Module

- Examine Regular Expressions
- Cover all the ways to search for them

This module covers everything you need to know about regular expressions. This term may be new to you if you are a beginner, so the first section of this module explains exactly what regular expressions are and covers the built-in comparator functions used with them. Once you've been introduced to them, we move on to the next section of the module, which shows you how to work with them in programs. We introduce you to the various ways to search for them, as well as other tasks that can be performed, such as search and replace. Let's get started.

What Are Regular Expressions?

A *regular expression* is a specification for a group of characters you want to search for in a string. Let's say you are reading in lines from a file and you want to search for the characters SRT in that specific order. The regular expression you would use to search for this sequence is exactly the same sequence of uppercase characters. We get to how to implement the search in a minute but, first, it's important for you to understand the regular expression is what determines the sequence of characters for which you are looking. You have an abundant amount of options when you specify a regular expression. You don't have to specify an exact pattern, like SRT, when you're deciding on what your regular expression should be. As you learn in this module, you can specify small fragments of a complete pattern to search for as well.

Understanding a Pattern

A *pattern* is a certain sequence of characters you may be searching for in a string. The pattern is selected by the user in the form of a regular expression and this pattern is compared to all the contents of the string. The concept of a pattern is simple. It may be a recurring pattern or it may only occur once in ten thousand strings of data.

Before you begin searching for a recurring specific pattern, think about the parts of the pattern that are redundant. This can often help you select one regular expression that can find most or all of the pattern occurrences for which you are searching. For example, if the pattern always begins and ends with the same sequence of characters, but always differs in between, then your regular expression should search for the beginning and the end of the pattern, while ignoring everything in between. Taking a few moments to think about how to break down the pattern in the beginning may save you some programming time when you implement your search.

Built-in Operators

Before we get too far in to this module, we need to discuss two operators you will see often. The *match* operators are used when you are searching through a string for a matching regular expression.

The first one discussed is represented by the equals sign, followed by the tilde character =~. This operator tests a given string of information to see if the specified regular expression is present. If it is present, the statement returns a true, or non-zero, value. If it doesn't find a match for the regular expression, it returns a zero, or false, value.

The other match operator is represented by the exclamation mark, followed by the tilde character !~. This operator tests a given character string for a match to the regular expression and, if it does find a match, it returns a zero, or false, value. If it doesn't find a match, it returns a non-zero, or true value. This operator is the exact opposite of the '=~' operator you just met.

One more thing you need to be familiar with before we move on is how to specify a regular expression. This is done simply by enclosing the pattern you want to search for with forward slash / characters. Let's look at an example of a regular expression, just to make sure everything is clear so far.

```
/SRT/         #This is a regular expression and the pattern is 'SRT'
```

The following is an example of one way you can use the match operator and a regular expression together:

```
$result = $string =~ /SRT/;
```

The previous statement tests the string, $string, for an occurrence of the regular expression, "SRT," and stores the result in the scalar variable $result. Again, if the search finds an occurrence of the pattern in the string, $result will contain a true, non-zero value after the statement executes.

You can use a scalar variable that contains the pattern you are searching for in between the forward slashes if you need to change the pattern depending on different circumstances. The following two lines of code demonstrate this for you:

```
$sequence = "SRT";
$result = $string =~ /$sequence/;
```

The previous two lines of code and the following line of code are equivalent:

```
$result = $string =~ /SRT/;
```

Now that we've covered the basics of regular expressions and pattern matching, we'll go into much more detail about all the options you have at your disposal.

Pattern Matching Syntax

You can specify a regular expression in a variety of different ways. Given the tools Perl provides for this, you should be able to locate any type of pattern in a string of information. Let's move on to the section of this module that covers all the options you have when you specify a regular expression.

Regular Expression Options

As previously stated, you can use an abundance of options in creating a regular expression that will work for you. We begin by covering the easiest options and work our way up to some of the more difficult, but powerful, options Perl has to offer.

Before we discuss the regular expression options, here's a programming example to demonstrate a regular expression being used.

```
#!/usr/bin/perl ←——— Path to Perl binary
$string1 = "This is just a string of information";
print "String 1 contains, $string1 \n";
$string2 = "that we will use to search for a regular expression";
```

```
print "String 2 contains, $string2 \n";
print "We will be searching for the regular expression 'str' \n";
if ($result = $string1 =~ /str/) {
   print "I found str in string1  \n";
}
else {
   print "Sorry, I could not find it in string1 \n";
}
if ($result = $string2 =~ /str/) {
   print "I found str in the string2 \n";
}
else {
   print "Sorry, I could not find it in string2 \n";
}
```

The if statement block is executed if the regular expression "str" is found

The illustration displays the output of the previous programming example, searching through strings for a regular expression.

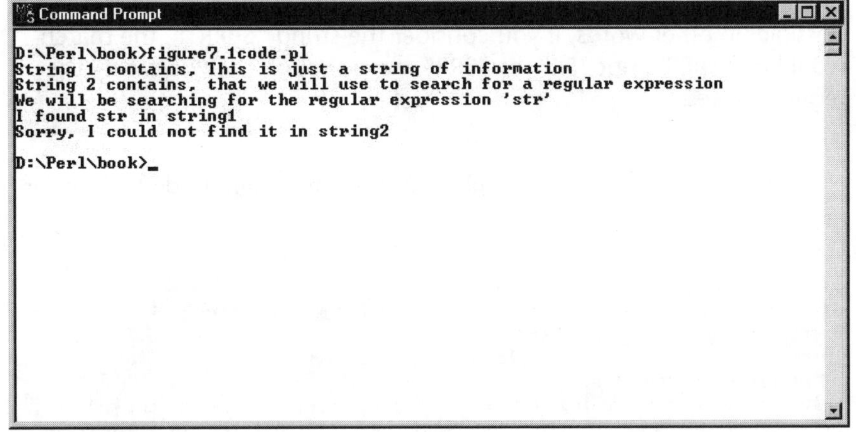
Command Prompt
D:\Perl\book>figure7.1code.pl
String 1 contains, This is just a string of information
String 2 contains, that we will use to search for a regular expression
We will be searching for the regular expression 'str'
I found str in string1
Sorry, I could not find it in string2
D:\Perl\book>_

This programming example should give you a good idea of how a basic regular expression works. The expression "str" was found in string1 as the first three letters of the word "string." Now let's discuss all the options you can use.

The first option we cover is the plus "+" option, which is one of the special characters that can be used inside the forward slashes. *Special characters* are characters that have a special meaning when used as part of a regular expression. The *plus* special character is used to specify that the character preceding it can occur one or more times and still satisfy the regular expression search. Here's an example of this character in use to give you a better idea of how it works. Consider the following statement:

```
$result = $string =~ /SR+/;
```

The regular expression, "/SR+/", will be satisfied by each of the following strings.

```
$string = "SRT";
$string = "SRRT";
$string = "SRRRRRRT";
```

Note

When you use the plus inside a regular expression, the matching sequence of characters always contains as many of the plus characters as possible. In other words, if you consider the string "SRRRT", the match would be "SRRR", not "SR", or "SRR", even though they do satisfy the regular expression.

Here's a programming example that uses a plus sign inside the regular expression.

```
#!/usr/bin/perl
$string1 = "today has been just too much fun for me to handle";
print "String 1 contains, $string1 \n";
$string2 = "I wish everyday could be like today";
print "String 2 contains, $string2 \n";
print "We will be searching for the regular expression 'to+' in string 1 \n";
print "We will be searching for the regular expression 'da+y' in string 2 \n";
if ($result = $string1 =~ /to+/) {
   print "I found 'to+' in string1  \n";
}
else {
   print "Sorry, I could not find it in string1 \n";
}
if ($result = $string2 =~ /da+y/) {
.  print "I found 'da+y' in the string2 \n";
}
else {
   print "Sorry, I could not find it in string2 \n";
}
```

This statement looks for the character sequence "to" with as many o's as possible

This statement looks for the sequence "day" with as many a's as possible

This illustration shows using plus as part of the regular expression.

```
D:\Perl\book>figure7.2code.pl
String 1 contains, today has been just too much fun for me to handle
String 2 contains, I wish everyday could be like today
We will be searching for the regular expression 'to+' in string 1
We will be searching for the regular expression 'da+y' in string 2
I found 'to+' in string1
I found 'da+y' in the string2

D:\Perl\book>
```

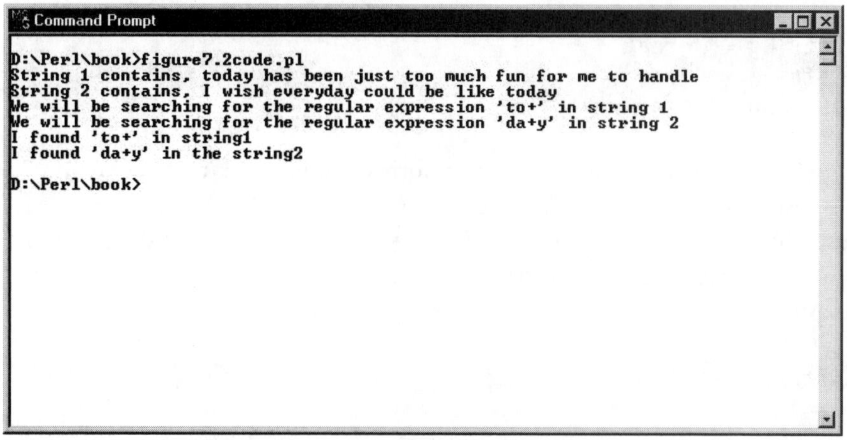

In the previous programming example, the pattern that matches for string1 is the "too" because it meets the requirements of starting with a *t* followed by an *o* and it has the most o's of any other matching sequence. The pattern for string2 is "day" with one or more *a* characters in between the *d* and the *y*. Two occurrences of "day" are in string2, so the closest one to the beginning of the string, the one in "everyday," is the one that matches.

The next special character is the asterisk "*". When this character is used inside the forward slashes, it signifies that zero or more of the previous character can be present to make the match. What this character does is similar to the plus "+" special character, except the asterisks don't require one of the characters to be present. Here's an example of a regular expression that contains the asterisks' special character and a few of the strings that would trigger a match.

```
$string =~ /gr*eat/;
```

The following are a few examples of string that would trigger a match to this regular expression:

```
$string = "great";
$string = "geat";
$string = "grrrrreat";
```

Another special character that performs a similar task to the plus and asterisks special characters is the question mark "?". When this character is used inside the forward slashes, it signifies that zero or one of the previous characters can be present to trigger a match. Here's an example regular expression that uses the question mark special character:

```
$string =~ /too?/;
```

The following are a few examples of some strings that satisfy this regular expression:

```
to
too
today
tool
```

You have just been introduced to three different special characters that enable you to search for one or more, none or more, or none or one selected characters. But what if you want to specify the number of times a character is found? Perl enables you to do this with the curly brace, "{" and "}", characters. Using these braces, you can predetermine how many times a certain character should appear in an expression. Here's an example of how to use these curly braces in a regular expression:

```
$string =~ /gr{3,6}eat/;
```

The following strings all satisfy this regular expression:

```
$string = "grrreat";
$string = "grrrreat";
$string = "grrrrreat";
$string = "grrrrrreat balls of fire";
```

If you need to specify a maximum number of times a character should appear, you can use the following setup:

```
$string =~ /gr{0,5}eat/;
```

This regular expression is satisfied as long as no more than five r's are present in the string. You can also specify a minimum number of occurrences by using the following statement:

```
$string =~ /gr{2,}eat/;
```

This regular expression requires at least 2 r's in the string. Finally, you can specify the exact number of occurrences by using the following setup:

```
$string =~ /gr{2}eat/;
```

This regular expression is satisfied as long as the word "grreat" appears somewhere in the tested string.

The next character we cover is the period ".". When the period is used inside the forward slashes, it signifies that any character, other than the newline character "\n", will match. Here's an example regular expression using a period and some of the strings that it matches:

```
$string =~ /a.t/;
```

All the following strings match this regular expression:

```
$string = "alt";
$string = "act";
$string = "a!t";
$string = "factor";
$string = "author";
```

1-Minute Drill

- **What regular expression would you use to search for a sentence that starts with *T* and ends with e?**
- **After the *T* is located, which occurrence of the character e makes the match if more than one *e* is present in the string?**

- **/T.+e/**
- **The last occurrence of the *e* character in the string**

Building on what you already know, you can use the plus "+" and the period "." special characters to search for any string of characters other than the newline character. This combination of special characters is the simplest solution to the first question in the previous 1-Minute Drill.

The next set of special characters are the right and left square brackets "[" and "]". These brackets are used inside the forward slashes to single out a list of options that will match. An easy way to think about the way these brackets work is to think of an "or" being in between each character inside them. Here's an example regular expression and some of the strings that trigger a match:

```
$string =~ /The year is 200[0123456789]/;
```

Any string that says "The year is," followed by any year between 2000 and 2009, satisfies this regular expression. Here's another example:

```
$string =~ /I am yelling[.!]/;
```

This regular expression can find a match if the sentence, "I am yelling," ends with either a period or an exclamation mark.

Note

The period isn't interpreted as a special character in this regular expression because it's inside the square braces. If the regular expression had been /I am yelling./, the period would have been interpreted as a special character. A match would have still been made because the period specifies that the sentence could end with any character other than the newline character.

The square braces can be used with any combination of characters, such as numbers, symbols, and letters. If you want to specify a range of numbers or letters, there's a shorter way than just typing them all. You can use the dash "-" character to create a range. Instead of typing in [0123456789], you can enter [0-9] and it represents the same sequence of numbers. This also works the same for letters. You can specify every letter of the alphabet by entering [a-z] instead of typing in all the letters. The following is an example regular expression you've already seen, but it has been simplified using the dash special character:

```
$string =~ /The year is 200[0-9]/;
```

This regular expression will be satisfied if the string contains "The year is" and any year from 2000 to 2009.

The special characters we covered so far are the plus, asterisks, question mark, period, and square brace characters. If you want to have one of these characters as part of the regular expression itself, you must use a backslash in front of it. This works the same way as it does for double-quoted strings. If you want to include a backslash as part of the regular expression, you must add another backslash in front of it. Here are a few examples for clarification:

```
$string =~ /hello\?/;
```

Here, the regular expression to be matched is "hello?". If we hadn't used the backslash in front of the question mark, we would have been searching for "hell" with none or one *o* after it. Let's look at another expression:

```
$string =~ /cat\\her/;
```

The regular expression to be matched here is "cat\her".

Note

Make sure when you include the backslash in a regular expression that you include another backslash to "escape" its special meaning. Several escape sequences can be used in regular expressions and they all begin with a single backslash followed by different letters, each of which performs a special task. You won't wind up with what you intended if you forget to include the extra backslash.

Project 7-1: Searching for a Regular Expression in a File

Write a program that will read in all the contents of a file, one line at a time, and for each line that is read in, search for a given regular expression. If the regular expression is found, you should save the string it was found in, so it can be printed out to the screen. You should iterate through every line of the file until the end of the file is reached. As a final step to the program, you should print out the number of times the given regular expression was matched.

So far, all the examples have been matching regular expressions anywhere in a string of data. For instance, if you were searching for the regular expression "eat" in a string, the word "feature" would satisfy your search, even though you might have really been searching for the word "eat." There's a way around this problem when you're working with regular expressions—it's called anchoring patterns.

Anchoring patterns is the idea that you can predetermine exactly where you want the pattern to be for it to match. Four different pattern anchors exist and we start by covering the "\b" pattern anchor.

The *"\b" pattern anchor* tells the regular expression that the given sequence of characters must be on a word boundary. A *word boundary* is basically the beginning or the end of a word. The problem we previously discussed, searching for "eat" in a string, can be solved using the "\b" pattern anchor. Here's an example of how this anchor is used:

```
$string =~ /\beat/;
```

This regular expression will only be satisfied, first, if the pattern is found and, second, if it is found at the beginning of a word. The beginning of a word is a word boundary because it's located at one of the outermost parts of the whole word. The end of a word is also considered a word boundary. Here are a few of the strings that satisfy this regular expression.

```
$string = "eating";
$string = "eat";
$string = "eaten";
$string = "eat@joes";
```

Now let's look at a few strings that will not trigger a match.

```
$string = "feature";
$string = "Eating";
$string = "beat";
```

The string, "feature", does contain "eat", but not at the beginning of the word. The string, "Eating", does contain "Eat" at the beginning of a word but the *E* character is in uppercase and regular expressions are case-sensitive by default.

The following programming example demonstrates the "\b" pattern anchor being used for the beginning of a word:


```
#!/usr/bin/perl
$string1 = "Eating at Joe's is hard to beat";
print "String 1 contains, $string1 \n";
$string2 = "Only eating what you can pay for is always a good idea";
print "String 2 contains, $string2 \n";
print "We are searching for 'eat' at the beginning of a word. \n";
if ($result = $string1 =~ /\beat/) {
   print "I found the string 'eat' in string1  \n";
}
else {
   print "I could not find it in string1 \n";
}
if ($result = $string2 =~ /\beat/) {
   print "I found the string 'eat' in string2  \n";
}
else {
   print "I could not find it in string2 \n";
}
```

These lines of code are searching for the regular expression "eat" at the beginning of a word

The output of the previous programming example, using the "b" patten anchor, is seen in the following illustration.

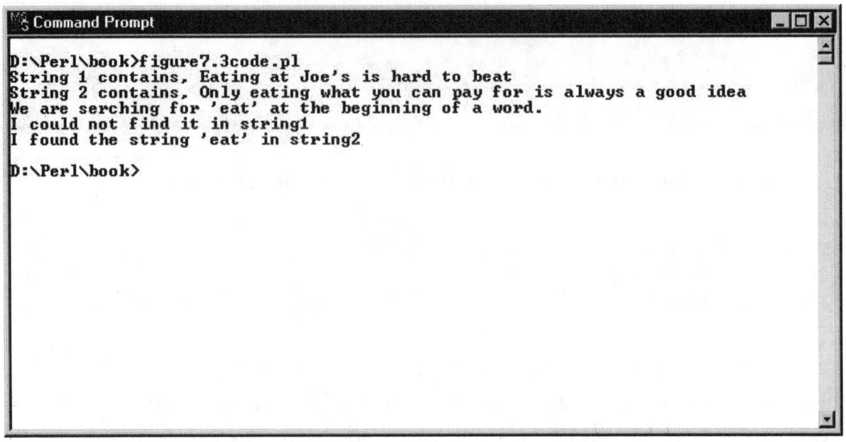

```
D:\Perl\book>figure7.3code.pl
String 1 contains, Eating at Joe's is hard to beat
String 2 contains, Only eating what you can pay for is always a good idea
We are serching for 'eat' at the beginning of a word.
I could not find it in string1
I found the string 'eat' in string2

D:\Perl\book>
```

In the previous programming example, the pattern "eat" wasn't found at the beginning of a word in string1, but it was found in string2.

The "\b" pattern anchor can be used at the end of a sequence, as well as at the beginning. Let's look at an example:

```
$string =~ /eat\b/;
```

This regular expression is only satisfied if the character string "eat" is found at the end of a word. The following is an example of a string that would satisfy this regular expression:

```
$string = "Beat it, get out of here!";
```

If we use the "\b" pattern anchor at the end of the word "eat" instead of at the beginning of the word, we get different results from the previous programming example. Let's compare the results in the next illustration to the previous illustration.

```
#!/usr/bin/perl
$string1 = "Eating at Joe's is hard to beat";
print "String 1 contains, $string1 \n";
$string2 = "Only eating what you can pay for is always a good idea";
print "String 2 contains, $string2 \n";
```

```
print "We are searching for 'eat' at the end of a word. \n";
if ($result = $string1 =~ /eat\b/) {
   print "I found the string 'eat' in string1  \n";
}
else {
   print "I could not find it in string1 \n";
}
if ($result = $string2 =~ /eat\b/) {
   print "I found the string 'eat' in string2  \n";
}
else {
   print "I could not find it in string2 \n";
}
```

These lines of code are searching for the regular expression "eat" at the end of a word

The output of the previous programming example can be seen in the following illustration.

```
Command Prompt
D:\Perl\book>figure7.4code.pl
String 1 contains, Eating at Joe's is hard to beat
String 2 contains, Only eating what you can pay for is always a good idea
We are serching for 'eat' at the end of a word.
I found the string 'eat' in string1
I could not find it in string2

D:\Perl\book>_
```

Notice the results of this programming example differ from those in the previous illustration because we were searching for the string "eat" at the end of a word this time.

In addition to being able to search for a string and the beginning or the end of a word, you can also specify that you want the string to be at the beginning and the end of a word. In other words, you want to search for the exact word. Here's an example:

```
$string =~ /\beat\b/;
```

This regular expression can only be satisfied if the word "eat" is found by itself as part of a string.

Another pattern anchor similar to the one just discussed is the "\B" anchor. This is basically the opposite of the "\b" pattern anchor because it signifies that the string you are searching for must be contained inside a word and not at a word boundary. Consider the following regular expression:

```
$string =~ /\Beat/;
```

The following are a few of the strings that can trigger a match for this regular expression.

```
$string = "meat";
$string = "feature";
```

From this example, you can draw the conclusion that the "\B" pattern anchor simply requires that one or more characters must come before the specified sequence. The following string wouldn't satisfy the regular expression.

```
$string = "eating";
```

This string won't satisfy the regular expression because no characters are before "eat" in the word.

Just like the "\b" pattern anchor, this pattern anchor can be used at the beginning, end, or the beginning and the end of a sequence of characters. Here are a few examples to demonstrate this for you:

```
$string =~ /\Beat\B/;
```

This regular expression requires the string "eat" be an interior portion of a larger word, like "feature." Let's look at one more example:

```
$string =~ /eat\B/;
```

This regular expression requires the string "eat" be followed by at least one character, like in the word "eating," for example.

In addition to being able to specify whether a sequence should be a certain part of a word, you can also do the same for an entire string. The "^" pattern anchor requires the expression you are searching for be at the beginning of a string of information. Let's look at a programming example to demonstrate how this pattern anchor works:

```
#!/usr/bin/perl
$string1 = "if and only if";
print "String 1 contains, $string1 \n";
$string2 = "If and only if";
print "String 2 contains, $string2 \n";
print "We are searching for 'if' at the beginning of a string. \n";
if ($result = $string1 =~ /^if/) {
   print "I found the string 'if' at the beginning of string1  \n";
}
else {
   print "I could not find it in string1 \n";
}
if ($result = $string2 =~ /^if/) {
   print "I found the string 'if' at the beginning of string2  \n";
}
else {
   print "I could not find it in string2 \n";
}
```

These lines of code are searching for the regular expression "if" at the beginning of a string

7

The output of the previous programming example, using the "^" patten anchor, is seen in this illustration.

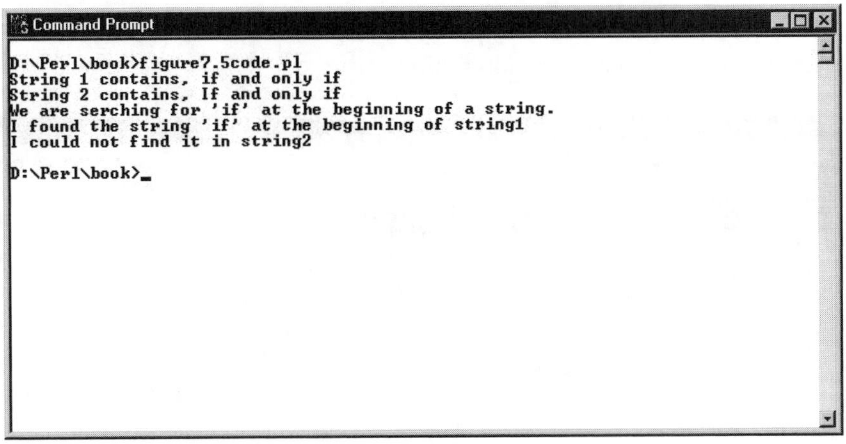

```
Command Prompt

D:\Perl\book>figure7.5code.pl
String 1 contains, if and only if
String 2 contains, If and only if
We are serching for 'if' at the beginning of a string.
I found the string 'if' at the beginning of string1
I could not find it in string2

D:\Perl\book>_
```

In the previous programming example, we specified that we wanted to see "if" at the beginning of the string by putting the "^" character in front of it in the regular expression. You can also specify that the sequence you are looking for be at the end of a string by using the "$" pattern anchor. We demonstrate the use of the "$" pattern anchor using the following programming example:

```
!/usr/bin/perl
$string1 = "if and only if";
print "String 1 contains, $string1 \n";
$string2 = "If and only if.";
print "String 2 contains, $string2 \n";
print "We are searching for 'if' at the end of a string. \n";
if ($result = $string1 =~ /if$/) {
   print "I found the string 'if' at the end of string1  \n";
}
else {
   print "I could not find it in string1 \n";
}
if ($result = $string2 =~ /if$/) {
   print "I found the string 'if' at the end of string2  \n";
}
else {
   print "I could not find it in string2 \n";
}
```

These lines of code are searching for the regular expression "if" at the end of a string

The output of the previous programming example, using the "$" pattern anchor is seen in the illustration.

```
Command Prompt
D:\Perl\book>figure7.6code.pl
String 1 contains, if and only if
String 2 contains, If and only if.
We are serching for 'if' at the end of a string.
I found the string 'if' at the end of string1
I could not find it in string2

D:\Perl\book>
```

Note

From the previous programming example, the pattern "f" wasn't found at the end of the string because we added a period after it. The "^" and "$" pattern anchors require the pattern to be at the very beginning or the very end of a string.

In addition to using these pattern anchors by themselves, you can also use them together for one particular pattern. When you do this, you are effectively saying you want the entire string to match the given pattern exactly. The following is an example regular expression that uses both of these pattern anchors:

```
$string =~ /^Hello$/;
```

The only string that can satisfy this regular expression is "Hello". If any other characters are present, the regular expression cannot find a match.

1-Minute Drill

- **What regular expression would you use to search for the string of characters "go" at the beginning of a word?**
- **What regular expression would you use to ensure the string "go" occurs at the very beginning of a string?**

Earlier in this section, we looked at the square braces and how they can be used to specify different characters that can be valid for a pattern. And we just looked at the "^" pattern anchor and how it can be used to make sure a pattern is found at the absolute beginning of a string. Now we are going to combine these two familiar characters and show you how to select all the characters you don't want to be part of a pattern. This is called *exclusion* and the following is an example of how exclusion works with regular expressions.

```
$string =~ /200[^1-9]/;
```

- **/\bgo/**
- **/^go/**

This regular expression triggers a match as long as the last character isn't one of the numbers from one to nine.

Note

Make sure you don't confuse the "^" exclusion character inside the square braces with the "^" pattern anchor previously discussed. Whenever this character is inside the square braces, it signifies exclusion unless it has been escaped with a backslash.

Perl provides you with a set of character class abbreviations that can be used as a shorthand for different sets of characters. Earlier in this module, you were introduced to the dash "-" character and we showed you how it can be used to save time when designating a range of letters or numbers. These character class abbreviations are an even shorter-hand method of selecting the complete ranges of characters like zero through nine and *a* through *z*. The following table lists each character class abbreviation and what it represents.

Character Class Abbreviation	Represented Character Class	Description
\d	[0-9]	Digits
\D	[^0-9]	No digits
\w	[_a-zA-Z0-9]	Words
\W	[^_a-zA-Z0-9]	No words
\s	[\r\t\n\f]	Spaces
\S	[^ \r\t\n\f]	No spaces

As you can see from the preceding table, these character class abbreviations can be used as a shorthand to represent different groups of characters. They can be used anywhere a normal character is valid in creating a regular expression. The following is a short programming example that demonstrates the use of a few of these abbreviations.

```
#!/usr/bin/perl
$string1 = "The year is 2000 and it is going to be over soon";
print "String 1 contains, $string1 \n";
$string2 = "Next year will be 2001";
print "String 2 contains, $string2 \n";
print "We are searching for four digits followed by a whitespace \n";
```

```
if ($result = $string1 =~ /\d\d\d\d\s/) {
   print "I made a match for string1  \n";
}
else {
   print "I could not find it in string1 \n";
}
if ($result = $string2 =~ /\d\d\d\d\s/) {
   print "I made a match for string2  \n";
}
else {
   print "I could not find it in string2 \n";
}
```

These lines of code are searching for the regular expression that contains four consecutive digits followed by a space

The output of the previous programming example, using the character class abbreviations, is seen in the illustration.

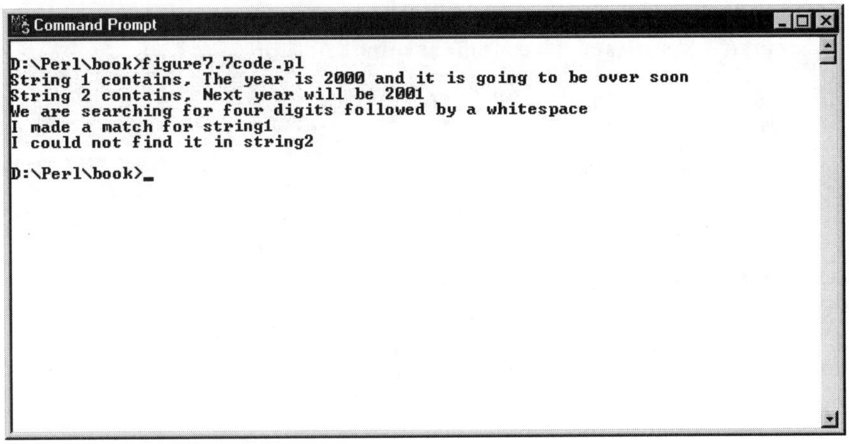

```
Command Prompt

D:\Perl\book>figure7.7code.pl
String 1 contains, The year is 2000 and it is going to be over soon
String 2 contains, Next year will be 2001
We are searching for four digits followed by a whitespace
I made a match for string1
I could not find it in string2

D:\Perl\book>_
```

As you can see from the previous programming example, a match was made for string1, but not for string2, because there wasn't a space after the four consecutive digits.

Earlier in this module, we discussed how to provide a regular expression with a few options to choose from, for example:

```
$string =~ /[Hh]ello [Ww]orld/;
```

This regular expression will be satisfied with "Hello World", "Hello world", "hello World", or "hello world". Here we specified that the first character of each word could be either lowercase or uppercase, but what if you want to give different sequences of characters as options for the regular expression? You can accomplish this by using the pipe "|" special character. This character can be thought of as an "or" for sequences of characters. Here's a programming example to demonstrate the use of the "|"special character.

```
#!/usr/bin/perl
$string1 = "Next year will be 2001";
print "String 1 contains, $string1 \n";
$string2 = "2002 will be here before you know it";
print "String 2 contains, $string2 \n";
print "We are searching for 2000 or 2001 in the string \n";
if ($result = $string1 =~ /2000 | 2001/) {
   print "I made a match for string1  \n";
}
else {
   print "I could not find it in string1 \n";
}
if ($result = $string2 =~ /2000 | 2001/) {
   print "I made a match for string2  \n";
}
else {
   print "I could not find it in string2 \n";
}
```

These lines of code are searching for the regular expression that contains either 2000 or 2001

The output of the previous programming example, using the "|" is seen in this illustration.

```
Command Prompt
D:\Perl\book>figure7.8code.pl
String 1 contains, Next year will be 2001
String 2 contains, 2002 will be here before you know it
We are searching for four 2000 or 2001 in the string
I made a match for string1
I could not find it in string2

D:\Perl\book>_
```

From the previous example, you can see the regular expression was satisfied as long as the string contained either "2000" or "2001".

Another useful tool that Perl provides when working with regular expressions is the capability to save portions of a regular expression. Once the pieces have been saved, they can be reused or the actual pattern that triggers a match can be saved into a scalar variable. The parenthesis symbols "(" and ")" are used to designate which sections of a regular expression are to be saved.

Once you save a portion of a regular expression, you can do two things with it. You can reuse the same pattern over again as part of the same regular expression, which saves you from having to type the pattern repeatedly, or you can actually save the string that triggered the match for the selected portion of the expression. Here's how to reuse a pattern, or patterns first.

Before we talk about reusing patterns, look at the following example that demonstrates the use of the parenthesis symbols in a regular expression:


```
$string =~ /([a-z]+)([-])[a-z]+[-][a-z]+/;
```

For this example, we put the parentheses around the first and second parts of the regular expression, which says find as many letters from *a* to *z* as you can until you see a dash. Even though we put the parentheses around the first and second parts of the expression, we didn't demonstrate their special functionality. Now, let's look at a simplified expression that uses the power of parentheses. The following regular expression uses what was matched in the parentheses over again as part of the expression for which to search.

```
$string =~ /([a-z]+)([-])\1\2\1/;
```

Notice we used a backslash character and either a one or a two as part of the regular expression this time. When you put parentheses around portions of a regular expression, you are effectively saving the matched text and each section is automatically given a number that starts with one moving from left to right. This means the first match we saved is associated with one, and the second match is associated with two. If you want to reuse a saved match, you can simply use a backslash character, followed by the reference number of the pattern you want to reuse.

Now look at a programming example that demonstrates this new concept for you.

```
#!/usr/bin/perl
$string1 = "this-is-an-example-string-that-should-trigger-a-match";
print "String 1 contains, $string1 \n";
$string2 = "This will fail";
print "String 2 contains, $string2 \n";
if ($result = $string1 =~ /([a-z]+)(-)\1\2/) {
   print "I found the pattern in string1  \n";
}
else {
   print "I could not find it in string1 \n";
}
if ($result = $string2 =~ /([a-z]+)([-])\1\2/) {
   print "I found the pattern in string2  \n";
}
else {
   print "I could not find it in string2 \n";
}
```

These lines of code are reusing the saved patterns by adding a backslash and the number

The illustration shows the output of the previous programming example, reusing saved matches.

```
Command Prompt

D:\Perl\book>figure7.9code.pl
String 1 contains, this-is-an-example-string-that-should-trigger-a-match
String 2 contains, This will fail
I found the pattern in string1
I could not find it in string2

D:\Perl\book>
```

From the previous programming example, the string "is-is-" is what triggered the match to the regular expression. This is because we reused the first and second matches as part of the regular expression for which to search.

Note

You can only recall saved matches inside the same regular expression. Once you search for a new regular expression, the matches you saved are no longer valid.

In addition to being able to reuse a match in the same regular expression, you can actually store the portion of the string that matched that particular pattern into a scalar variable. The built-in scalar variables follow the same numbering system as the reusable patterns. The first pattern, from the left, that's enclosed in parentheses is assigned the scalar variable $1, and so on. Using this technique, you can actually see what part of a string triggers a match. Another built-in scalar variable that can come in handy is the "$&" variable, which always contains the last pattern that was matched. Here's a programming example to demonstrate this for you.

These lines of code are using the built-in scalar variables to save the portion of the string that actually triggered the match

```
#!/usr/bin/perl
$string1 = "this-is-an-example-string-that-should-trigger-a-match";
print "String 1 contains, $string1 \n";
$string2 = "This-will-also-trigger-a-match";
print "String 2 contains, $string2 \n";
if ($result = $string1 =~ /([a-z]+)-([a-z]+)/) {
   $firstword = $1;
   $secondword = $2;
   print "I found the pattern '$firstword - $secondword' in  string1 \n";
}
else {
   print "I could not find it in string1 \n";
}
if ($result = $string2 =~ /([a-z]+)-([a-z]+)/) {
   $firstword = $1;
   $secondword = $2;
   print "I found the pattern '$firstword - $secondword' in string2  \n";
}
else {
   print "I could not find it in string2 \n";
}
```

These lines of code specify the first and third portions of the regular expression are to be saved

The illustration displays the output of the previous programming example, saving the patterns that triggered a match.

```
D:\Perl\book>figure7.10code.pl
String 1 contains, this-is-an-example-string-that-should-trigger-a-match
String 2 contains, This-will-also-trigger-a-match
I found the pattern 'this - is' in  string1
I found the pattern 'his - will' in string2

D:\Perl\book>_
```

Notice that output of the previous programming example actually shows what triggered the match for each string. You should also notice that the first character of string2 wasn't included in the matched sequence because regular expressions are case-sensitive.

Note

In the previous example, notice we immediately saved the contents of the built-in scalar variables into normal scalar variables. This is to ensure that the data wouldn't be lost. If you need to save the contents of one of the built-in scalar variables, you should always save it to another scalar variable.

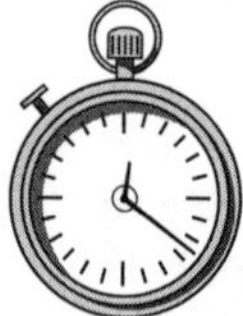

1-Minute Drill

- **What characters are used to save a certain portion of a regular expression?**
- **Once a pattern is saved, how do you reuse the pattern in the regular expression?**
- **What special variable always contains the value that was last matched?**

- **()**
- **Use the backslash character "\" followed by the number—starting with one from the left—of the grouping**
- **$&**

Now that you've been introduced to most of the special characters that can be used inside the forward slashes, this is a good time to talk about their order of precedence. Just like with the mathematical operators, the special characters and sequences that can be used with regular expressions have an order of precedence. This turns out to be important when you are using more than one of these special characters or sequences in the same regular expression. The following list shows the order of precedence for these special characters and sequences, starting with the highest level of precedence at the top.

```
+ * ? { }
^ $ \b \B
|
```

Up until now in this module, you've learned how to specify almost any regular expression imaginable. Now that you have all those tools under your belt, we need to cover more options, but these are options that determine how a pattern is matched, instead of what kind of pattern to match.

We just discussed how regular expressions are case-sensitive, but there's an option to turn off case sensitivity. To ignore the case of letters, you have to add an *i* after the last forward slash of the regular expression. Here's an example regular expression to clarify where the *i* needs to go.

```
$string =~ /gibson/i;
```

This regular expression matches "Gibson" or "GIBSON" or any other combination of uppercase or lowercase letters that make up the word. Remember the last programming example we did when the first character of string2 was thrown out? Now let's look at it again, using the ignore case option and see what happens.

```
#!/usr/bin/perl
$string1 = "this-is-an-example-string-that-should-trigger-a-match";
print "String 1 contains, $string1 \n";
$string2 = "This-will-also-trigger-a-match";
print "String 2 contains, $string2 \n";
```

7

```
if ($result = $string1 =~ /([a-z]+)-([a-z]+)/i) {
   $firstword = $1;
   $secondword = $2;
   print "I found the pattern '$firstword - $secondword' in  string1 \n";
}
else {
   print "I could not find it in string1 \n";
}
if ($result = $string2 =~ /([a-z]+)-([a-z]+)/i) {
   $firstword = $1;
   $secondword = $2;
   print "I found the pattern '$firstword - $secondword' in string2  \n";
}
else {
   print "I could not find it in string2 \n";
}
```

These lines of code are using the built-in scalar variables to save the portion of the string that actually triggered the match

These lines of code specify that the first and third portions of the regular expression are to be saved and the case of any of the letters should be ignored

This illustration displays the output of the previous programming example, making a regular expression ignore the case of letters.

```
Command Prompt
D:\Perl\book>figure7.11code.pl
String 1 contains, this-is-an-example-string-that-should-trigger-a-match
String 2 contains, This-will-also-trigger-a-match
I found the pattern 'this - is' in  string1
I found the pattern 'This - will' in string2

D:\Perl\book>_
```

Notice the *T* is now included in the string that triggered the first match.

Another option you can use when searching for a regular expression is the *g* option, which specifies a string should be searched as many times as a matching pattern can be found. The *g* option is specified in the same location as the *i* option just discussed. Even though the *g* option specifies a string should be searched as many times as there are matches, this won't happen unless the regular expression is set equal to scalar an array variable or the statement is executed inside a loop. Here's an example that executes the regular expression statement inside a loop until no more matches are found.

```
#!/usr/bin/perl
$string1 = "This is an example string that will trigger several matches";
print "String 1 contains, $string1 \n";
while ($string1 =~ /[a-z]+/gi){
   print "A match was made with $& \n";
}
```

This while statement block executes as long as there is a match in string1

This line uses the built-in scalar variable $&, which always contains the string that triggered the most recent match

The output of the previous programming example, searching for all possible matches in a string, is seen in the following illustration.

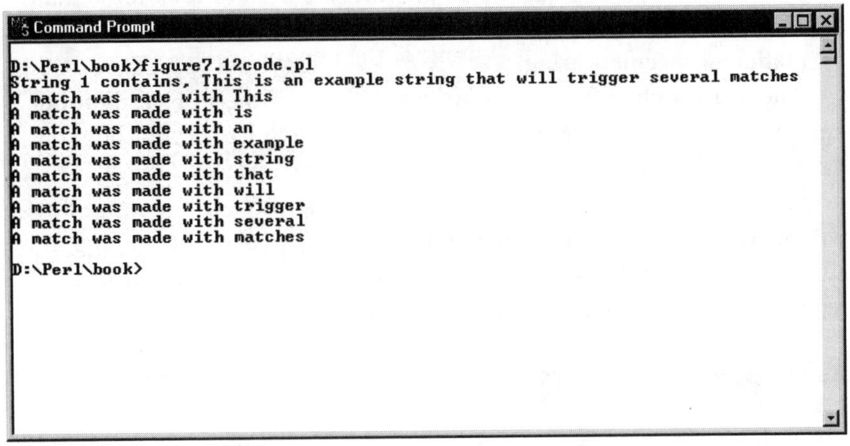

```
Command Prompt
D:\Perl\book>figure7.12code.pl
String 1 contains, This is an example string that will trigger several matches
A match was made with This
A match was made with is
A match was made with an
A match was made with example
A match was made with string
A match was made with that
A match was made with will
A match was made with trigger
A match was made with several
A match was made with matches

D:\Perl\book>
```

The same results can also be obtained by using an array variable in the following manner.

```
#!/usr/bin/perl
$string1 = "This is an example string that will trigger several matches";
@results = $string1 =~ /[a-z]+/gi;
print "@results \n";
```

The last matching option we cover isn't that useful, but we discuss it anyway to be complete. It's the *o* option, which is specified in the same place as the other matching options we covered. The *o* option is used to specify the pattern that is to be matched—the regular expression—can only be evaluated once. What does this mean for you? It means if you're using a scalar variable to contain the regular expression, and the expression is to be evaluated more than one time, the expression is locked in after the first time the expression is searched for. Even if the regular expression is set to change after each iteration, the *o* option won't allow it to change. As we said, this option isn't very useful, but knowing it's there is nice, in case you need it. We covered most of the regular expression options you need in writing Perl programs. Now, let's discuss the available search and replace options.

Search and Replace

The search and replace options Perl provides are used to look for certain patterns, just like a normal regular expression, and to replace those patterns by a different specified string.

The first search and replace option we discuss is the *s* or substitution option. To enable the ***substitution*** option for any regular expression, you have to add an *s* before the first forward slash that surrounds the expression. In addition to adding the *s,* you must also add the string that will be used to replace the matching pattern. This replacement string must also be enclosed by forward slashes. The following is an example of a regular expression statement with the substitution option enabled:

```
$string =~ s/dogs/cats/;
```

In this statement, the regular expression being searched for is "dogs" and whenever this string is found, it will be replaced with the string "cats." Let's look at a programming example that demonstrates the substitution option in use.

```
#!/usr/bin/perl
$string1 = "this-is-an-example-string-that-should-trigger-a-match";
print "String 1 contains, $string1 \n";
$string2 = "This-will-also-trigger-a-match";
print "String 2 contains, $string2 \n";
```

```
if ($result = $string1 =~ s/should/better/) {
   print "I found the pattern in  string1 \n";
   print "String1 now contains $string1 \n";
}
else {
   print "I could not find it in string1 \n";
}
if ($result = $string2 =~ s/trigger/make/) {
   print "I found the pattern in string2  \n";
   print "String2 now contains $string2 \n";
}
else {
   print "I could not find it in string2 \n";
}
```

These statements search and replace patterns in a string

The actual contents of string1 and string2 are permanently changed

The output of the previous programming example, searching and replacing patterns in a string, is seen in the illustration.

```
Command Prompt

D:\Perl\book>figure7.13code.pl
String 1 contains, this-is-an-example-string-that-should-trigger-a-match
String 2 contains, This-will-also-trigger-a-match
I found the pattern in  string1
String1 now contains this-is-an-example-string-that-better-trigger-a-match
I found the pattern in string2
String2 now contains This-will-also-make-a-match

D:\Perl\book>
```

The substitution option also has a set of options that can be selected to change its behavior. You can specify a string should be searched as many times as there are pattern matches with each match triggering a replacement. This option is selected by adding a *g* after the last forward slash of a regular expression. Here's a programming example that uses this option along with the substitution option.

```
#!/usr/bin/perl
$string1 = "The one, the only, the greatest";
print "String 1 contains, $string1 \n";
while ($string1 =~ s/the/big/g) {
   print "I found the pattern in  string1 \n";
   print "String1 now contains $string1 \n";
}
```

This while statement will be executed as many times as there are matches for the regular expression "the"

Each time the pattern "the" is found, it will be replaced with "big"

The illustration displays the output of the previous programming example, searching and replacing all matching patterns in a string.

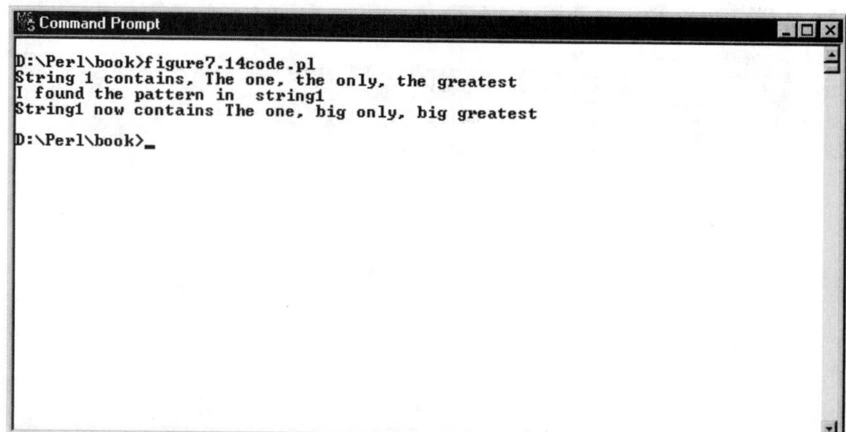
Command Prompt
D:\Perl\book>figure7.14code.pl
String 1 contains, The one, the only, the greatest
I found the pattern in string1
String1 now contains The one, big only, big greatest
D:\Perl\book>_

Note

Notice the first "The" wasn't replaced with "big" because of case sensitivity.

Another option you can use with substitution is the ignore case option, which is selected by adding an *i* after the last forward slash of a regular expression. Here's an example.

```
#!/usr/bin/perl
$string1 = "The one, the only, the greatest";
print "String 1 contains, $string1 \n";
while ($string1 =~ s/the/big/gi) {
   print "I found the pattern in  string1 \n";
   print "String1 now contains $string1 \n";
}
```

This while statement will be executed as many times as there are matches for the regular expression "the"

Each time the pattern, "the" in uppercase, lowercase, or a combination of both is found, it will be replaced with "big"

This illustration displays searching and replacing all matching patterns in a string with case sensitivity deactivated.

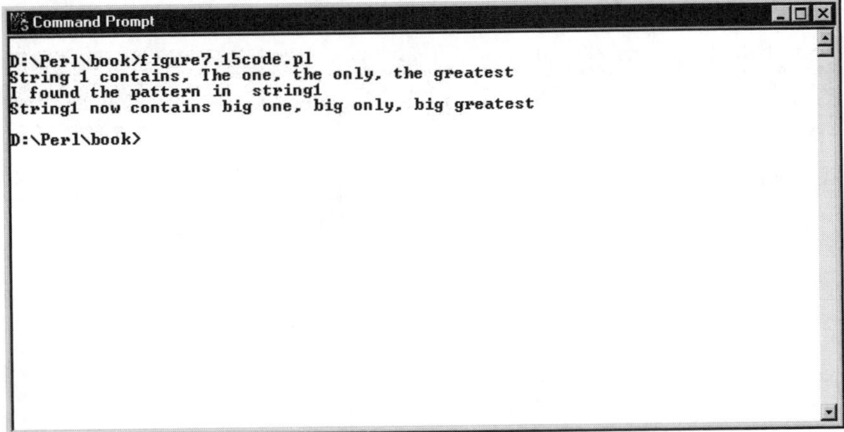
Command Prompt
D:\Perl\book>figure7.15code.pl
String 1 contains, The one, the only, the greatest
I found the pattern in string1
String1 now contains big one, big only, big greatest
D:\Perl\book>

Yet another option you can use along with the substitution option is called the expression option. The *expression* option is turned on by adding an *e* after the last forward slash of a regular expression and it tells the interpreter to treat the replacement string as an expression. Remember, an expression is something like 9 * 9 or $string x 3. Here's an example without the expression option turned on.

```
#!/usr/bin/perl
$string1 = "The one, the only, the greatest";
print "String 1 contains, $string1 \n";
while ($string1 =~ s/the/9 * 9/g) {
   print "I found the pattern in  string1 \n";
   print "String1 now contains $string1 \n";
}
```

This while statement will be executed as many times as there are matches for the regular expression "the"

Each time the pattern "the" is found, it will be replaced with "9 * 9"

The output of the previous programming example, searching and replacing all matching patterns in a string, is seen in this illustration.

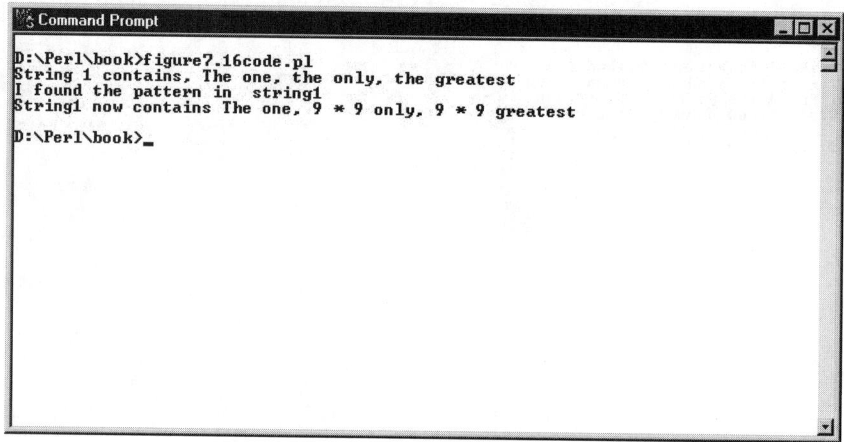
Command Prompt
D:\Perl\book>figure7.16code.pl
String 1 contains, The one, the only, the greatest
I found the pattern in string1
String1 now contains The one, 9 * 9 only, 9 * 9 greatest
D:\Perl\book>_

Now let's look at the same program with the expressions option turned on. You should notice the different output between these two programs.

```
#!/usr/bin/perl
$string1 = "The one, the only, the greatest";
print "String 1 contains, $string1 \n";
while ($string1 =~ s/the/9 * 9/ge) {
   print "I found the pattern in  string1 \n";
   print "String1 now contains $string1 \n";
}
```

This while statement will be executed as many times as there are matches for the regular expression "the"

Each time the pattern "the" is found, it will be replaced with "81", which is what the expression 9 * 9 evaluates to

This illustration shows searching and replacing all matching patterns in a string with the expressions option enabled.

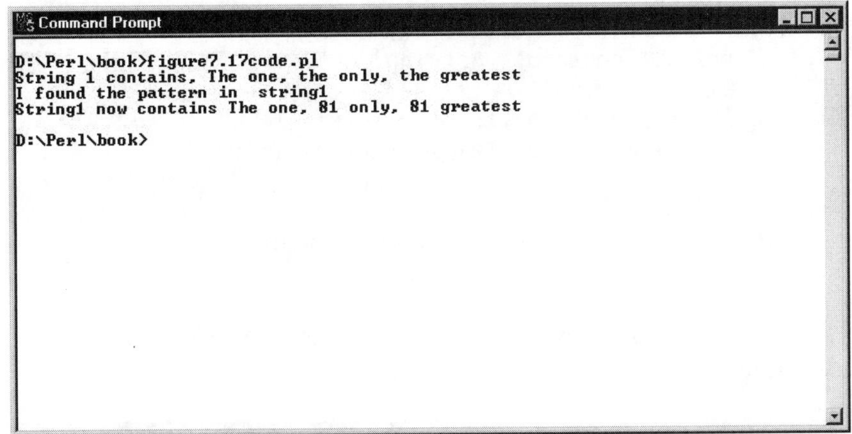
Command Prompt
D:\Perl\book>figure7.17code.pl
String 1 contains, The one, the only, the greatest
I found the pattern in string1
String1 now contains The one, 81 only, 81 greatest
D:\Perl\book>

1-Minute Drill

- **How can the substitution option be used to delete a match?**
- **What option is used along with the substitution option to replace all matches in a string?**

- **If you don't specify anything for the replacement string, the matching string will be deleted**
- ***g***

The last option we cover in this section is called the *translation* option, which is closely related to the substitution option we just discussed, except it replaces on a per character basis. When the substitution option found a match, it replaced the match with any specified string and the replacement string didn't have to be the same size as the search string. With the translation option, you must be a little more careful about what you select as your replacement string. Also, unlike the substitution option, the translation option searches through an entire string without having to activate an additional option. The translation option is enabled by adding a "tr" before the first forward slash of a regular expression. Let's look at an example, and then explain how this option works.

```
#!/usr/bin/perl
$string1 = "today is the best day of all";
print "String 1 contains, $string1 \n";
if ($result = $string1 =~ tr/thed/abc/) {
   print "I found the pattern in  string1 \n";
   print "String1 now contains $string1 \n";
}
else {
   print "I could not make a match in string1 \n";
}
```

The regular expression "thed" is searched for one character at a time

The output of the previous programming example, using the translation option, is seen in the illustration.

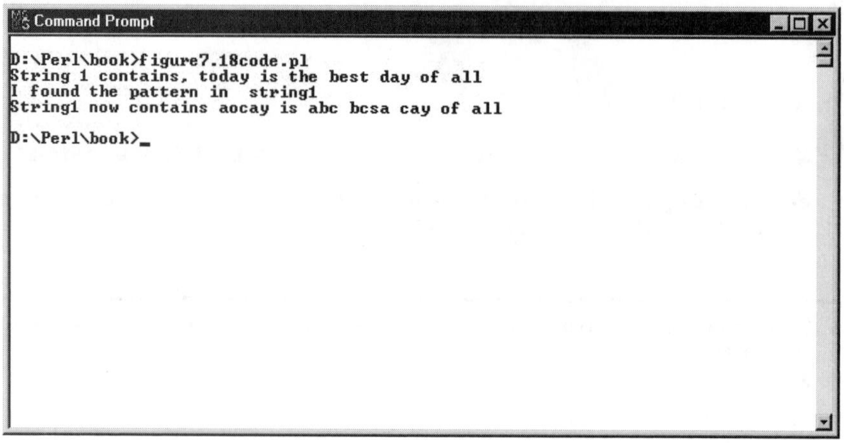

```
Command Prompt
D:\Perl\book>figure7.18code.pl
String 1 contains, today is the best day of all
I found the pattern in  string1
String1 now contains aocay is abc bcsa cay of all

D:\Perl\book>_
```

Now let's discuss what's happening here. The regular expression we're searching for is "thed". Unlike what you're used to, it's really only searching for one character at a time. The character sequence "thed" isn't present in the tested string, but a match is made anyway because at least one of the characters that make up "thed" is present in the string. Looking back at the code, every *t* that's found in the string will be replaced with *a*. Every *h* will be replaced with *b* and every *e* will be replaced with *c*. The character *d* doesn't have a matching replacement character, so the last replacement character in the string, which is *c*, will be used to replace it.

A few options can be used along with the translation option. The first one we cover is the *c* option, which specifies that everything except for the selected characters are to be translated. This option is enabled by adding the *c* character after the last forward slash of a regular expression. The following is an example of a regular expression statement with this option enabled.

```
$string1 =~ tr/0-9/\t/c;
```


The previous statement replaces any character that isn't a digit between zero and nine with a tab. Here's a programming example that demonstrates this option in use.

```
#!/usr/bin/perl
$string1 = "There are 3 options associated with the translation option";
print "Before the translation occurs the string contains, \n '$string1' \n";
$string1 =~ tr/a-z/\t/c;
print "After the translation the string contains,  $string1 \n";
```

This statement will replace any character other than a-z with a tab

Translating a string with the *'c'* option is seen in the following illustration.

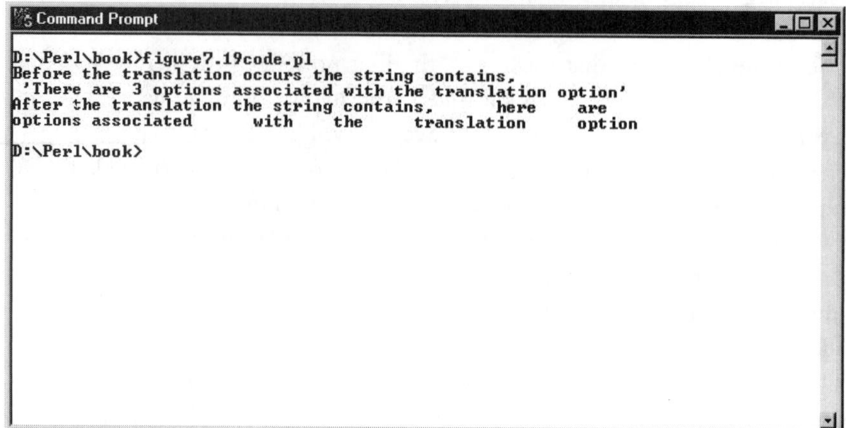

Note

You should notice that in the previous programming example, the regular expression was case-sensitive. You cannot use the *i* ignore case option with the translator option. If you want to make the regular expression ignore the case of letters, you must specify both ranges of letters. You can use "[A-Z][a-z]" to take care of this.

The next option that can be used along with the translation option is the *d* or delete option. The *delete* option is specified in the same place as the *c* option and it deletes all the specified characters in a string. Here's an example that uses the *d* option.

```
#!/usr/bin/perl
$string1 = "There are 3 options associated with the translation option";
print "Before the translation occurs the string contains,\n '$string1' \n";
$string1 =~ tr/a-z //d;
print "After the translation the string contains,  $string1 \n";
```

This statement will delete every letter between a-z and all spaces

Nothing was specified for the replacement string, so a true deletion will occur

The illustration shows the output of the previous programming example, translating a string with the *'d'* option.

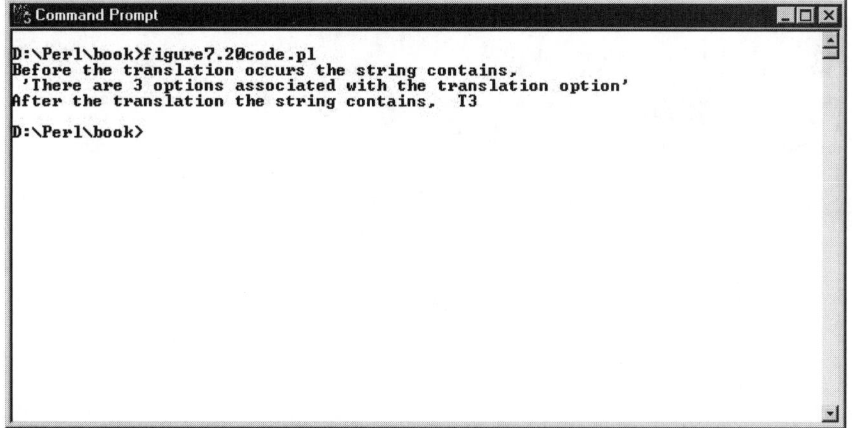

Note

In the previous program, notice we didn't specify a replacement string and, because of this, all the characters to be deleted won't be replaced with anything. After the translation for the string has occurred, it will only contain the characters that weren't specified for deletion.

The last option we discuss for use with the translation option is the *s* or *squeeze* option, which only includes one replacement character for every group of matching characters to be replaced. The best way to describe what the *s* option does is to look at an example. But, first, here's an example that doesn't have the *s* option enabled.

```
#!/usr/bin/perl
string1 = "There are 3 options associated with the translation option";
print "Before the translation occurs the string contains,\n '$string1' \n";
$string1 =~ tr/a-z/9/;
print "After the translation the string contains,  $string1 \n";
```

This statement will replace every letter between a-z with a 9

The output of the previous programming example, translating a string, is seen in this illustration.

```
D:\Perl\book>figure7.21code.pl
Before the translation occurs the string contains,
 'There are 3 options associated with the translation option'
After the translation the string contains,  T9999 999 3 9999999 9999999999 9999
999 9999999999 999999

D:\Perl\book>_
```

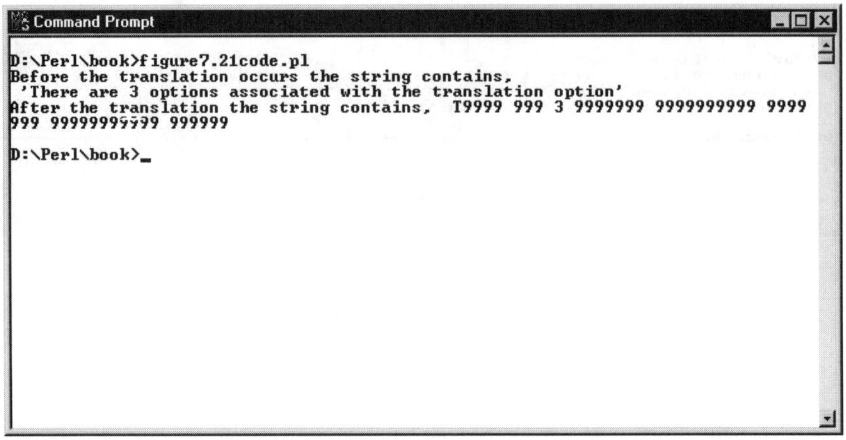

Notice every lowercase letter that was found was replaced with a 9. Now let's look at the same program, which has the *s* option enabled.

```
#!/usr/bin/perl
$string1 = "There are 3 options associated with the translation option";
print "Before the translation occurs the string contains,\n '$string1' \n";
$string1 =~ tr/a-z/9/s;
print "After the translation the string contains,  $string1 \n";
```

This statement will replace every string, or group, of letters with a 9

Translating a string with the *'s'* option is seen in this illustration.

```
D:\Perl\book>figure7.22code.pl
Before the translation occurs the string contains,
 'There are 3 options associated with the translation option'
After the translation the string contains,  T9 9 3 9 9 9 9 9 9

D:\Perl\book>
```

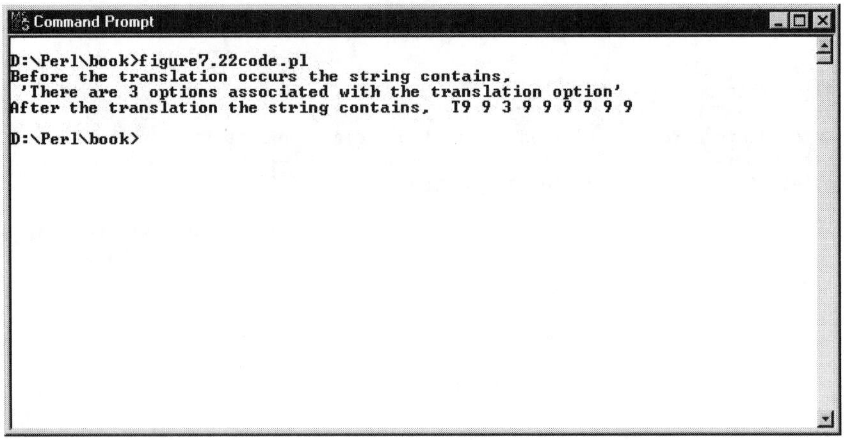

Notice that instead of replacing every letter encountered with a 9, only the strings of matching characters or, in this case of words, are replaced. This option can also be used in conjunction with the *c* option to perform the inverse of the example we just saw.

Project 7-2: Writing a find/replace Application

Write a program that mimics the action of the find/replace option available on most word processors. You should first select the file you want to work with by entering the total path to the file as user input. Once the file is specified, ask for a search item and a replace item to be entered from the command line. Once you have these two pieces of information, you should perform your search for the regular expression through the file and whenever you make a match, perform the replacement. After each replacement is made, you should prompt the user to see if he or she wants to continue. When the end of the file is reached, you should notify the user that the find/replace is complete and print the number of replacements made out to the screen.

This concludes our discussion on searching and replacing strings. Look at the Mastery Check for this module to make sure you understand most of the important topics covered.

1. What character or characters are used to indicate a regular expression?

A. ( )

B. { }

C. backslash

D. forward slash

Mastery Check

2. Which of the following strings will match this regular expression /AV+/?

   A. AV

   B. AVV

   C. Both A and B

   D. None of the above

3. What special character is used to make sure a pattern matches at the very beginning of a string?

   A. $

   B. ^

   C. \b

   D. None of the above

4. Which character class abbreviation is used to represent all digits?

   A. \D

   B. \d

   C. \w

   D. None of the above

5. What special character can be used to give an optional pattern to match in a regular expression?

   A. %

   B. ~

   C. ^

   D. |

6. What option should you use if you are attempting to search and replace a certain string?

   A. *s* or substitute

   B. "tr" or translate

   C. Both A and B

   D. None of the above

Module 8

Packages and Modules

The Goals of This Module

- Acquaint yourself with Perl packages and how they work
- Understand what a module is
- Start using packages and modules
- Begin building your own packages

In Module 5, "Program Flow and Subroutines," we first introduced you to the concept of packages and modules. At that time, we were still deep in the beginning stages of Perl, so we decided to delay a more in-depth discussion on that topic until later in the book. Well, that time is now.

In this module, we discuss Perl packages and Perl modules, which we refer to globally as *libraries*. As we discussed in previous modules, having a good programming style, which includes everything from well-documented code to organization, is extremely important if you want to succeed as a programmer. Libraries help you from the organization standpoint because they enable you to bundle groups of related functions into a library. This can help you in several ways.

First, this enables you to organize your code properly into functional pieces. A library, for instance, may have a group of functionally similar subroutines in it for use in other programs. This lets you *import* those subroutines as needed in not only one program, but in as many programs as you choose.

Besides organization, libraries enable you to share code easily with other programmers. In fact, we use prebuilt Perl libraries later in this book to create *Common Gateway Interface* (*CGI*) scripts and programs that access a database. What the authors of these libraries and modules have done is to build and organize a group of subroutines together, so others can easily import and use them—this is in the same manner you would organize your own code.

Although we touched on both the concepts and the definition of libraries in previous modules, now we take you through an in-depth discussion. To ensure that we cover everything necessary for a beginner, this module is grouped into four sections, which are as follows:

1. What is a package?
2. What is a module?
3. How do they work?
4. How can you build your own?

As you can see, the idea is to introduce you to both packages and modules, and then tell you how they work. The final part of the module steps you through creating your own simple example. We know you want to get started, so let's go!

Definitions

Understanding what something is supposed to be is the first step. Because packages and modules may not be self-explanatory, we first discuss the definition of a package and a module.

What Is a Package?

A *package* is a set of Perl functions grouped into a single file. This file, also called a *library* and ending in a .pl (and sometimes a .pm) extension, is referred to by its filename within your code. A package declares an alternative namespace for the variables and/or subroutines within it. The idea of this is to avoid variables from overwriting, or stomping on, each other.

Think of a *namespace* as being a parallel channel in your code. Because a namespace doesn't overlap the currently running channel (remember, it's parallel) variables can have the same name, but no chance of being interpreted as the other. This is essentially what a package is.

Now you may say you want to use a variable from one namespace in another namespace, but don't worry—you can do that. This is done by simply prefixing the variable with the package name and having a double colon to separate the two, as in the following:

```
$package::variable
```

Note

If you look through old Perl code, you may notice the use of a single colon to separate the package name and the variable. This was the syntax for older versions of Perl, but it has been deprecated, although it does still (currently) work.

So, for instance, if you want to include a package named `mypackage.pl`, then you simply have the following line in your program:

```
require "mypackage.pl";
```

As you might imagine, now that you've begun to understand the Perl way of thinking, this isn't the only way to include a package in your code. You also might be wondering what the word "require" means. Before we go any further, let's talk about the ways to include packages in your scripts and what each method means.

What Is a Module?

In short, a *module* isn't much more than a package. The only real difference is a module is designed to be reusable. This is accomplished by allowing some or all of a module's variables and subroutines to be *exported* into other packages, although it isn't necessary to export anything for a library to be a module. This is an easy concept to understand, but it can be a challenging one to implement correctly in your code. Because of this, we now look at the "exporting" options you have and how they work.

- **What is the difference between a package and a module?**

How Do Packages and Libraries Work?

Part of understanding Perl libraries, whether it's packages or libraries, means understanding how they work. In this portion of the module, we look at how these libraries work, so you can be prepared to use and create them on your own. This covers the following:

- Construction and destruction of the libraries

- **A package is a namespace, while a module is a package contained in a library file of the same name.**

- How to access, or load, libraries into your scripts
- How the subroutines in the packages and modules are exported, so you can understand how to create your own

Constructor and Destructor

When a package is loaded, the first thing the Perl interpreter looks for is the **BEGIN** subroutine, or the *constructor*. As mentioned earlier in the book, everything in this routine is executed before the script continues. If you want to declare any special variables or pull in any other packages for your package, this is where you do it.

On the flipside of this is something we call the *destructor*—this is the last thing the Perl interpreter looks for before exiting the scripts. If you need to perform any last tasks in your package before the scripts stop executing, such as write out to a log file, you include this functionality in the body of an **END** subroutine. This **END** subroutine is the destructor.

Now that you know all about packages, let's move on to modules, which inherit everything we've said about packages up until this point.

8

Loading Libraries

Before you can use any subroutines or access any properties in a package, you must first tell the Perl interpreter you want to use a particular package. This can be done using the following methods.

use()

The `use()` function in Perl lets you import semantics into the current package from the named module at compile time. The syntax for this function is as follows, where *Module* is the name of the Module, *LIST* is a list of subroutines you want to import, and *VERSION* is the version of Perl you need to import and use the library successfully.

```
use Module LIST
use Module
use Module VERSION LIST
use VERSION
```

To give you an idea of what this might look like in real code, here are four examples, one from each of the syntax definitions:

```
use mymodule.pm qw(sub1 sub2 sub3);
use mymodule.pm;
use mymodule.pm 5.6.0 qw(sub1 sub2 sub3);
use 5.6.0
```

The first thing you'll ask is what is the `qw()` function? This is simply a shorthand way of specifying items you wanted quoted and separated (triggered by white space). In our example `qw(sub1 sub2 sub3)` is the same as `'sub1','sub2','sub3'`, which is the parameter list the `use()` function takes to determine what subroutines you want to import.

require()

The `require()` function, which isn't quite as powerful as `use()`, lets you demand the semantics specified by *EXPRESSION,* as shown in the syntax definition, to be included in the program for proper execution when called. Part of the reason this isn't preferred over `use()`, is because it isn't loaded when the program is started. So, for instance, if the file doesn't exist, then you don't discover this until it reaches that point in your script versus when the script is started.

The syntax for this function is as follows, where *VERSION* is the version of Perl you need to run your script successfully, which also implies to import and use the library.

```
require VERSION
require EXPRESSION
```

The *EXPRESSION* is a module name, without the .pm extension, and the path to it, using `::` as the path delimiters. To give you an idea of what this might look like in real code, here are two examples, one from each of the syntax definitions. The second assumes `MyModule.pm` is in a `MyDir` directory.

```
require 5.6.0;
require "MyDir::MyModule";
```

no()

The no() function is essentially the opposite of the use() function and is a way to specify you don't want to import certain functions. You might ask why you would need this function, but think of it this way. If you have a module that contains 100 subroutines that could be imported and you want to import all but 5 of them, then it's much easier to use() the entire module and to specify those subroutines you don't want with a following no() function, rather than to list the 95 you do want with use(). The syntax for no() is as follows, where *Module* is the name of the Module and *LIST* is a list of subroutines you don't want to import.

```
no Module LIST
```

do()

Although using the do() function in include subroutines from a library file is technically possible, it isn't recommended for beginners. We won't show you this method, but we wanted to let you know it could be done, just in case you see it in someone else's code.

Tip

For more information on the do() function, check the perlfunc manpage.

1-Minute Drill

- **Why should you consider using use() rather than require()?**

The package Statement

Now that you understand how to load libraries in your scripts, it's time to see how this is possible. Before we talk about how subroutines are exported, it's important to understand what makes a package a package.

- **Besides the fact that use() provides a bit more functionality, it also is executed by the interpreter when the script is first loaded. So, no hidden traps are in the middle of your script's execution when a library cannot be found or accessed.**

Fortunately, this is simple. All you must do is use the `package` statement, followed by the name of the package at the top of your library file.

This defines the namespace to be assigned to the subroutines in the library, so users of the subroutines can properly use them. If, for instance, you had a package named MyPackage, you would expect to use the following line at the top of your file. This, again, creates a namespace that is held constant for all the items in the file until the end is reached.

```
package MyPackage;
```

This takes care of your package and defines it to the Perl interpreter as a library.

Hint

You can actually do some other interesting stuff with this statement, so we recommend you check the Perl manpage entry in `perlfunc` for more information.

The Exporter Module

The *Exporter* module is a module shipped with Perl, which more or less organizes the process of exporting items from your module. It provides mechanisms for version control and other functionality. We only discuss some of the functionality the Exporter module provides, but if you want more information on this module, check your Perl documentation (look under the `use()` entry in the Perl manpages for a link).

The general syntax for using this module in a module is as follows, where *Module* is the name of the module. We discuss `@EXPORT`, `@EXPORT_OK`, and `%EXPORT_TAGS` in the following subsections, so don't worry about those yet.

```
package Module;
require Exporter;
@ISA = qw(Exporter);
@EXPORT = qw(...);
@EXPORT_OK = qw(...);
%EXPORT_TAGS = (tag => [...]);
```

@EXPORT

@EXPORT is an array of symbols you want to export by default, so when users load a library by calling the `use()` function, they have access to these subroutines immediately. Be careful here because you may be returning subroutine names that conflict with other names other programmers using your library may be using. For this purpose, using `@EXPORT_OK` is usually the preferred method, unless you have a reason to do otherwise.

@EXPORT_OK

The *@EXPORT_OK* array is much like `@EXPORT`, except it's a list of symbols to export on request by the user of the module. This basically means the module author is making the list of symbols available for the module user to use, but they won't be automatically available unless the user specifically asks for them.

%EXPORT_TAGS

The final array, *%EXPORT_TAGS*, defines the names for sets of symbols. In other words, you could group a set of subroutines you want to export together under a specific name, which enables a user who wants to import that set to specify a single item, rather than a complete list. This also lets you provide an anonymous method of importing your subroutines without the user having to know their names.

So, for instance, if you have a module called `MyHTTP` and you want to organize the exportable subroutines in this module into two categories (let's say `header` and `body`), then you may have something like the following `%EXPORT_TAGS` entry:

```
%EXPORT_TAGS = (header => [qw(sub1 sub2 sub3)], body => [qw(sub4 sub5 sub6)]);
```

Now, if the user only wants to import `sub1`, `sub2`, and `sub3`, which we grouped under `header`, she could have the following line in her code, which simply puts a `:` in front of the `header` item:

```
use Module qw(:DEFAULT :header);
```

8

See how easy that was? OK, OK—I know you're wondering about the `:DEFAULT` parameter. As mentioned, Exporter is a module, so if you want more information about it, be sure to check the documentation. To quench your thirst for knowledge, though, here's a quick summary about `DEFAULT` and the use of the `:` before it and `header`.

Note

You cannot also use the names you specify in the `%EXPORT_TAGS` lists in `@EXPORT` or `@EXPORT_OK`. Additionally, the tags (not the names) in `%EXPORT_TAGS` MUST also appear in `@EXPORT` or `@EXPORT_OK`. So, for instance, if you have `%EXPORT_TAGS = (header => [qw(sub1 sub2 sub3)])`, then you cannot use `header` in `@EXPORT` or `@EXPORT_OK`, but `sub1`, `sub2`, and `sub3` must also appear in `@EXPORT` or `@EXPORT_OK`.

A Quick Look at Syntax

The syntax users of Exporter use has some special functionality. It lets you control some of the items imported from the module, as well as shortcut ways to import more than one item. This control is done through the use of `:`, `/`, and `!`. Table 8-1 shows how it works. Note, ! is nothing more than an optional item that tells Perl NOT to import the item. Basically, it's Exporter's answer to the `no()` function.

`import()`

This function contains all the necessary exportable items for the library and is a method you may see used instead of the Exporter module. Here's the deal with `import()`. When the `use()` functions are called in your script, the

Syntax	Description
[!]*sub*	Import or don't import this subroutine, referenced by *sub*, only
[!]:DEFAULT	Import or don't import all subroutines in the `@EXPORT` array
[!]:*tag*	Import or don't import all names in `$EXPORT_TAGS{tag}` anonymous list, which means the actual tag names aren't passed to the script, but rather their names
[!]/*pattern*/	Import or don't import all names in `@EXPORT` and `@EXPORT_OK`, which match the *pattern* specified

Table 8-1 **Exporter Syntax for Loading Modules and Their Subroutines**

first thing the Perl interpreter does is to look for the `import()` subroutine in the library. If the Perl interpreter finds the `import()` subroutine in the library, then it performs the operations within that subroutine. If not, then the Perl interpreter won't export anything.

As you might have guessed, the syntax for this function/subroutine is simply:

```
sub import(){
  # exporting directives here
}
```

This isn't rocket science—`import()` is only a launch pad for the items you want to export. We wanted to tell you about this, but what you really want to use is the Exporter module for performing this task.

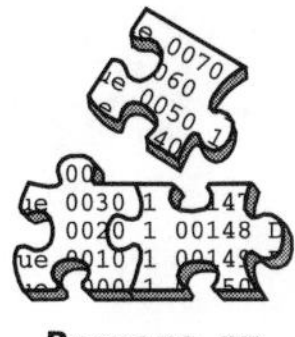

Prepare.pm

Project 8-1: Importing a Module

Now that you've had a run-through on how packages and modules work, and you have an idea about how subroutines are exported, we want to run you through a quick exercise on how to import a module. For this test, we use the `Cwd` module, which is a set of subroutines that revolves around the Current Working Directory.

Step-by-Step

1. Open a new text file for your script in your favorite editor.

2. Include the `Cwd` module using the `use()` function.

3. Using the `print()` function, print out the results of calling the `getcwd()` subroutine within the `Cwd` module.

That's it! You should be able to run the script and see the current working directory (of the script) written to your console window.

Building a Library

So far, we've covered most of what you need to know about packages and modules. Now, let's test that learning. As programmers, you want to create your own packages and modules. To accomplish this, use these few steps to make sure you create something truly useful.

Do You Really Need To?

The first thing to do before you create a module is to ask yourself an honest question: do you really need to create this module? Sure, it sounds cool and flashy, but like any other project you work on, you should first consider if a need exists. Programmers, engineers, and, yes, even authors often spend large amounts of time on unnecessary projects. If your project is a learning exercise or you're just playing at home, that's one thing, but if it's a real project, your inefficiency could dramatically affect an overall team effort.

Here are some questions to ask yourself before you start creating a Perl library.

1. Will you be able to use the subroutines you plan to put in your library in other scripts?
2. Will you share or provide access to the functionality in your library to others?
3. Will you have time to document and put comments in your library properly, so you and others can understand how your library works and how to use it?
4. Will you have time to keep up your library for others who are using it?
5. Are you prepared to make updates backward-compatible so you don't break anyone else's (or your own) codes.

A little more than you thought, huh? Making the decision to create libraries can be a serious one and you should treat it accordingly. Again, this doesn't mean you can't or shouldn't create a library. This only means you should carefully consider creating a library before you do it.

Hint

In addition to what's included here, check out the `perlmodlib` manpage on constructing new Perl modules and finding existing ones. This can help you determine if a module out there does what you want and it's also a great source of information on writing a new module.

Design Considerations

If you've made it this far, then you've decided you do, indeed, need to create a library, so let's move forward. The next thing you need to decide is how you want to design your module. Several common packages exist, such as to use the Exporter module that you need to load. You must decide to use or not to use the Exporter module for providing exportable subroutines.

Caution

When naming your packages and modules, try to avoid the use of Perl reserved words. This can lead to confusion for programmers and create a debugging nightmare. I remember having this problem back in college and it took me forever to realize I wasn't calling the Perl function—I was calling my own! Oh, the good ol' days. I'm a bit wiser now.

Hint

Do you have more questions about how to design Perl libraries correctly? Check out the end of the `perlmodlib` manpage.

Documentation

From the start of this book, we preached the concept of documenting your code. When creating Perl packages and modules this is especially true. Adding comments and instructions within your library so others can read and understand how to use it is extremely important. And, if you're designing a library to be reused by many people, such as posting it to a Web site or a newsgroup, then you should consider writing a full document on how it works and how it should be used.

Hint

You can use **h2xs -XA -n ModuleName** to create a skeleton module, which also creates a skeletal pod document.

In creating documentation for your library, consider adding the following:

- A thorough description of the library that explains what the library should be used for, what it does, and a version number.
- How to install the library, especially if you have any relative path needs.

- Copyright license, such as that defined by the GNU GPL or the Perl Artistic License.
- If your module has any other dependencies, such as other libraries, you need to list what those are and potentially where to get them.
- Changes and enhancements that have been made, as well as the dates and version numbers in which they were made.
- Planned changes you want to add at a later date, which can provide users with some insight into what you want to do with your library.

Hint

Need some help with the copyright? Try the following template, where *YEAR* should be replaced with the 4-digit year, and *Your Name* should be replaced with, of course, your name. Here's the template: "Copyright (c) *YEAR Your Name*. All rights reserved. This program is free software; you can redistribute and/or modify it under the same terms as Perl itself."

test_lib.pl

Project 8-2: Building a Library

You didn't think you could get out of this module without any code, did you? Well, we hope not! In this project, we step through building a simple package, following the steps outlined previously. This is an important step in this module because the topics covered involve more of an understanding of a concept than they require an understanding of actual coding. This project can help pull those concepts together for you and set the foundation of your exposure to packages and modules.

Step-by-Step

Because this is the first time you've written a library, we'll hold your hand through this one. We provide step-by-step instructions for both the creation of the library and the creation of the script that will use the library.

In this section of the project, we focus on defining and creating the library to hold our subroutines. By itself, the code contained here won't do anything. The code must first be loaded into another script and called before it actually interacts with your code.

1. The first thing you must do (of course you've already decided creating a library is a good idea) is to define what our library will do. For time's sake, we create a simple library that contains two subroutines. The overall focus of the library is simply to take user input from a console, prepare it, and print it back to the screen. So, we call our library `Prepare` and put it in a file named `Prepare.pm`.

2. Now that our objectives are defined, lets take our template from Module 1 and start filling in the information about and a description of our library. The following is an example of what you may want to have.

```
#!/usr/bin/perl -w
#----------------------------------------
# Script Name: Prepare.pm
# Script Version: 1.0
# Date: 12.31.2000
# Author: R. Allen Wyke
# Description: This module contains 2 subroutines. The first
#    takes a single parameter, which we assume is from a
#    console window, and removes any tailing return
#    characters. The second subroutine will print the
#    "results" to the user's screen. The library requires
#    that you have the Exporter # module accessible. To
#    install the library, simply place it # in the lib
#    subdirectory of your Perl distribution with the # other
#    modules. To load it and all the items in it use the #
#    following syntax:
#       use Prepare qw(:DEFAULT :all :version);
# Revision History:
#    1.0/12.31.2000: original version
#----------------------------------------
```

3. The first thing we need to do in our library is to define it as a package. To do this, simply include the following line:

```
package Prepare;
```

4. Next, we need to load the Exporter module and set up the list of subroutines we want to export. Because this is a short list and because we want to give our users the capability to load only the subroutines they want, we only define the `@EXPORT_OK` array. This whole section looks like the following.

```
require Exporter;
@ISA = qw(Exporter);
@EXPORT_OK = qw(clean my_print);
```

8

5. Now it's subroutine definition time. The first one we define is the subroutine that removes the trailing return character. We call this subroutine `clean()`. Because we only need to perform a simple step, we can perform the operation and specify it as the return value all in the same line. The entire subroutine itself simply looks like:

```
sub clean{
  return chomp($_[0]);
}
```

Hint

You can go back to Module 5 for more information on the `return()` function and how **$_[0]** contains the first parameter passed to a subroutine.

6. The next and final subroutine is the one that prints our results. We add the text "The Results:" before the text passed to the subroutine and, at the end, we put a newline, or return character back in. We call the subroutine `my_print()` and it looks like the following:

```
sub my_print{
  return print("The Results: $_[0]\n");
}
```

That completes the creation of our library. Now we need to create a script to use it.

The last part of our project involves the creation of a sample script that will use our new library. We'll keep this short, sweet, and to the point. Simply follow the directions here to accomplish this task.

1. First, you need to create a test script to load and implement the subroutines in your library. For this, first load the library and subroutines. This can be done using the following code:

```
use Prepare qw(my_print clean);
```

2. Next, you need to prompt the user for some input. You've done this before, but use something like the following and, remember, you needn't use the `chomp()` or `chop()` function here because that's built into our library.

```
print "Please enter a word: ";
$input = <STDIN>;
```

3. Just as a check, go ahead and write out what the user entered. Because we didn't remove the trailing return character, we needn't use the `\n` at the end of the `print()` statement. This results in the following:

```
print "You Entered: $input";
```

4. Ahhh—now comes the fun part—actually using our library. Because the first thing we need to do is remove that trailing return character, let's call our `clean()` subroutine. The following should work for that:

```
clean($input);
```

5. Now that we've "cleaned" the user's input, we want to print it using our `my_print()` function. This is another easy task:

```
my_print($input);
```

And that's it! Here's the whole program, so you can see it from start to finish.

```
#!/usr/bin/perl -w
#----------------------------------------
# Script Name: test_lib.pl
# Script Version: 1.0
# Date: 12.31.2000
# Author: R. Allen Wyke
# Description: This is just a short program to test our library.
# Revision History:
#    1.0/12.31.2000: original version
#----------------------------------------

# import our library and the two functions in it.
use Prepare qw(my_print clean);

# prompt the user for a word and store it in $input
print "Please enter a word: ";
$input = <STDIN>;

# print what the user entered
print "You Entered: $input";
```

```
# call the clean function and strip off the return character
clean($input);

# call the my_print function which adds some text, but adds back
# and prints out the return character.
my_print($input);
```

The following illustration shows the results of running our test program to verify our newly created Prepare.pm library.

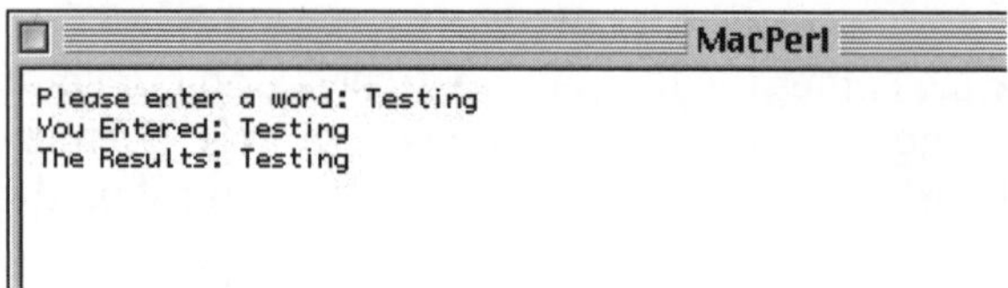

Moving On

In this module, we took you through the ins and outs of creating Perl packages and modules. We discussed what Perl packages and modules are, how they are different, how they work, and how to develop your own. Now that you have at least a basic understanding of this concept, we'll start applying that knowledge by using some real-world library files for accessing a database and for creating CGI scripts, both of which are covered in Modules 9 and 10, respectively.

Hint

Still want to know more about libraries? Besides checking out the specific functions mentioned in this module in the perlfunc manpage, you can also check out the perlmod manpage for overall information on packages and modules.

Mastery Check

1. What is the difference between a package and a module?

   A. They are the same, except a package is specially designed to have exportable subroutines

   B. They are the same, except a module is specially designed to have exportable subroutines

   C. They are the same

   D. None of the above

2. Which of the following can be used to load subroutines from a module into a program?

   A. include()

   B. import()

   C. load()

   D. use()

3. In the syntax `use CGI;` what is the name of the file imported?

   A. CGI

   B. CGI.mod

   C. CGI.pm

   D. CGI.pak

Module 9

Interacting with Databases Using the Perl DBI

The Goals of This Module

- Introduce you to some database basics
- Help you get up-and-running with the open source PostgreSQL database
- Expose you to what the DBI is and what it can do
- Make you understand connections to database
- Handle responses from your queries effectively

Working with databases is a common task in today's computing world. The old way of storing Web content, user information, or other logged information was simply in files on the file system. Today, however, this information is often stored and tracked in robust databases like Oracle, Informix, Microsoft SQL Server, or Sybase. Additionally, open source databases, such as *PostgreSQL* (pronounced *post-gres-Q-L*) and MySQL (pronounced *my-sequel*) are gaining in popularity as Linux begins to carve out a place in the market.

With this increased use of databases in the work environment, we've seen an increasing need to create applications that can tap these repositories of information. Applications that can do everything from report on the data within them to validate user logins. Applications that are independent of the database—because they may vary cross-organizationally—and platform-independent. So, are you beginning to see where Perl fits? Let's discuss a little more to clarify.

Perl is currently one of the most widely used, if not *the* most widely used, programming languages that have evolved and revolve around what the Web offers. The Web brought on the quick and broad adoption of the language. Part of this was because of its flexibility as a single language to perform a variety of tasks—tasks such as accessing databases for a multitude of reasons and objectives. Perl is a fairly easy language to understand and program in but, given all the complex things you can do with Perl, that can be misleading. So, adding database access to its repertoire was an easy decision. What better mix than taking a complex task, such as accessing databases, and an easy language to perform those tasks?

You should provide a manner in which a given Perl script could access a database for many reasons, but this doesn't make it clear how the DBI is involved. Part of the issue is accessing these databases differs from database to database, in much the same way writing applications for multiple operating systems can be. But, in the same way Perl has eased or even solved the issue of writing code for multiple systems, the DBI has done so for accessing and using many different databases. Let's stop here, though, and properly introduce some basic database concepts to get you rolling.

Hint

Are you wondering what all this SQL (pronounced *se-quel*) stuff is? *SQL* stands for *Structured Query Language* and is a language that basically lets you ask or request functions of the database. You can ask it to return certain information or you can ask it to insert, modify, or even delete items. If you want more information on SQL, the following site seems to have a good summary: http://www.jcc.com/SQLPages/jccs_sql.htm.

Understanding Databases

One of the first things we want to mention about databases is a few different methodologies exist for storing the data. Some data is stored in flat files, like *Comma Separated Value* (*CSV*) files, others are stored in some form of relational manner, while still others are stored in proprietary formats like Microsoft Excel.

Note

Is Excel really a database? The argument could go either way. Yes, Excel can store data in a specified format and order, so following those lines, it could certainly be considered one.

Relational Database Management Systems (*RDBMS*) are often considered the most robust and scalable databases around. In these systems, data is organized in specific tables, which have columns defining the information contained in the multiple rows. These tables are linked together using keys. Here's a quick example.

Hint

Recently, some growth has occurred in a concept called *Object-Oriented Database Management Systems* (*OODBMS*). Under this approach, everything in the database is an object, in much the same way that languages like Java work.

Let's say you have user information you want to store on people who purchase a product from you. In addition, you keep track of all the products people have bought. In a simple example, we could store this information in two tables: one called *users* and the other called *purchases*.

Now the *users* table would have columns like *UserID, FirstName, LastName,* and maybe *ZIP*. The *purchases* table, on the other hand, would have columns like *ItemName, ItemNumber, Cost,* and *UserID*. In the *users* table, you would define the entries in the *UserID* as unique. This means, for instance, only one user could have the ID of 1, one user with the ID of 2, and so forth. In the *purchases* table, however, this needn't be true. We want to store everything a given user buys and, because each user may buy more than one item, you can have multiple occurrences of *UserID*.

Did we completely confuse you? Don't worry, we'll draw it out to help you understand. Look at Tables 9-1 and 9-2 to see what we mean. We have populated them as an example.

Now let's try to explain what's in the tables. First, each of the users has his or her own unique ID. In addition, we have the user's first name, last name, and ZIP code stored with his or her information, and all of this is in the *users* table. In the second table, because we don't want to list first name, last name, and ZIP code again, we simply store the *UserID* for the user who made the purchases listed. So, for example, UserID 1, who is John Doe, purchased the USB Keyboard and the USB Mouse.

This is an easy example, but it illustrates a powerful point. By properly storing your data in a relational format and under a logical design, you can join items together to get a great depth of information. Just think, you could easily have another table called *accounting,* which stores past due bills or current status for the users, or maybe have a table called *services,* which stores any extra value-added services the users can sign up to use.

UserID	FirstName	LastName	ZIP
1	John	Doe	55555
2	Jane	Smith	27844
3	Fred	Johnson	48911

Table 9-1 Contents of Our *users* Table

UserID	ItemName	ItemNumber	Cost
1	USB Keyboard	28904786	19.99
1	USB Mouse	39038779	14.99
2	Corel Linux Deluxe	39988746	79.99
3	Compaq Presario	98729018	899.99
3	Microsoft Office 2000	92882766	399.99
3	Quicken Deluxe 2001	92877366	49.99

Table 9-2 **Contents of Our *purchases* Table**

Because each of these would also use the *UserID* value to identify the user, it's completely possible for you to determine who bought Quicken Deluxe 2001, lives in a certain ZIP code, and currently owes you no money. Based on this information, you could tailor your marketing effort accordingly. Pretty cool, huh?

Well, that's enough about databases for now. We simply wanted to get your feet wet in understanding what databases do and what purpose they serve. Databases can be so incredibly powerful, and knowing Perl can access and use this information means your programs and scripts can have a vast repository of information only a few lines of code away. Next, let's discuss the Perl DBI and what it brings to the table in terms of database access.

Setting Up Our Database

Before we dive into using the DBI, we need to get a database up-and-running, so we can test against it. For this, we selected the open source PostgreSQL database. This gives us a database that runs on both UNIX and Windows, and is free, which never hurts. Before we set up the database, here's a little overview.

PostgresSQL Overview

PostgreSQL is a robust relational database, first started in 1986 as the Berkley Postgres Project. The project continued to evolve and progress until 1994 when Andrew Yu and Jolly Chen added support for the Structured Query Language. This was first released to the open source community and was known as Postgres95.

In 1996, Postgres95 was completely overhauled—just as Perl 5 was—and released as PostgreSQL version 6.0, which marked one of the first major releases people began widely using. PostgreSQL version 6.0 included increased backend speed, SQL92 standard enhancements, and other important backend features, such as subselects, defaults, constraints, and triggers.

Tip

Are you a big database user? You may want to know, about the only major thing PostgreSQL doesn't have over other major databases is outer joins, but this feature is supposed to be added at a later date.

Application Details

The standard PostgreSQL installation, which we go through later, uses port 5432 to listen for TCP/IP connections. This installation—running as the *postmaster* process—listens for connections on this port. This process manages the communications between the front-end clients and the backend server.

Once running, PostgreSQL offers two operational modes. The first guarantees if an operating system or hardware crash occurs, the data has been stored and saved on the disk. This is often a slower mode than most commercially available databases because of the flushing, or *syncing,* method PostgreSQL uses. The second mode, which doesn't offer the data guarantee, often runs faster than commercial databases. As you can see, PostgreSQL offers you the choice: data security or speed. But, unfortunately, no intermediate mode offers a certain level of both.

Note

If you're concerned about this, don't worry too much. This is going to be provided in a later version of the software.

Project 9-1: Installing PostgreSQL

Because this is a beginner's book, we can't assume you have PostgreSQL running. In fact, we can't assume you even know what PostgreSQL is or even how a database works. Because we want you to have complete examples in the book, we're going to side step a bit now and have a project on installing PostgreSQL.

Because the installation of this database isn't the focus of this module or this book, for this project, we require you to install the database on your own. We give you a URL of where to start, but you're on your own from that point.

Note

Go ahead and initialize the database, as well, which creates the default database. Check the documentation on how to run the **initdb** command for help on doing this.

The Windows installation of PostgreSQL, because of its dependencies on some UNIX tools, involves the installation of other items, in addition to PostgreSQL. You can find directions at http://people.freebsd.org/~kevlo/postgres/portNT.html on how to obtain these tools and how to perform the install. In addition, if you have any trouble, please check the official PostgreSQL Web site at http://www.postgresql.org.

If you're running Linux, it's completely possible you don't even have to install PostgreSQL—it may already be running. One quick way to check is to perform a search on your system for the term "postgres." You can type **find / -name postgres –print** to do this. You can also check to see if the postmaster application is currently running by typing **ps –ef | grep postmaster**. If you need more help, check the official PostgreSQL Web site at http://www.postgresql.org for installation and configuration information.

Preparing the Database

Now that PostgreSQL is installed and running, you can start using it with the Perl DBI. This section describes the initial creation of a database you'll use throughout this module. The first thing you want to do is check your installation for the existence of a database already named "perl-begin," which the examples in this chapter will use; if it already exists, you may want to create a database with a different name.

Note

In this book, we only cover the use of PostgreSQL as the database. If you want to use another database, then you must perform the tasks in this section in a manner that reproduces the results we have here.

To check for all created databases, type **psql –l**. The psql application is the PostgreSQL client used to interact with the backend server. The `-l` option tells the program to list the available databases in the installation. When you run this command, you should see something like the following.

```
List of databases
 Database  |  Owner   | Encoding
-----------+----------+-----------
 template1 | postgres | SQL_ASCII
(1 row)
```

As you can see, a database is already called `template1`. This is the default database created when you ran the `initdb` command when setting up the database in Project 9-1. If you didn't run this, please check the PostgreSQL documentation and create it. But this isn't the database we want to use. To create our database, type **createdb perl-begin** at the command line. Once you do this, you can verify it was created by using the `-l` option with the `psql` command once again. The output this time should be similar to the following.

```
List of databases
  Database  |  Owner   | Encoding
------------+----------+-----------
 perl-begin | postgres | SQL_ASCII
 template1  | postgres | SQL_ASCII
(2 rows)
```

Creating a User

Now that our database is created, we must create a user to access the database. To do this, we have to log in to the database using the `psql` command by typing **psql perl-begin**. Before we add our user, you can check to see what users are currently entered, by typing **select * from**

pg_user; at the *perl-begin=#* command prompt. From this, we can see the *postgres* user is already entered into the system.

```
perl-begin=# select * from pg_user;
 usename  | usesysid | usecreatedb | usetrace | usesuper | usecatupd | passwd | valuntil
----------+----------+-------------+----------+----------+-----------+--------+---------
 postgres |       31 | t           | t        | t        | t         |********|
(1 row)
```

To add our user, we use the *createuser* utility included with PostgreSQL. To run this command, you can either quit out of the `psql` interface by typing **\q** at the prompt and pressing Return, or you can open another console to run the utility. Again, remember to do so as the *postgres* user.

Now, there's one thing to note about this user: it's a UNIX user name. Before you can create this user, you need to make sure it's available as a user on the system. The following shows how you can add this user. For this example, I simply add myself, *awyke,* as a user, because I already have an account on the machine running PostgreSQL. In the example, we execute the `id` command, which shows we're logged in as the *postgres* user when we create the *awyke* user.

Hint

Are you going to be accessing databases with other applications like your CGI programs? If so, make sure this user has the proper user and group permissions to perform the tasks you deem necessary. A Web server, for instance, runs as user *nobody* most often, so you want to insert *nobody* as a user in your database.

```
tuxbird:/$ id
uid=31(postgres) gid=32(postgres) groups=32(postgres)
tuxbird:/$ createuser
Enter name of user to add: awyke
Shall the new user be allowed to create databases? (y/n) y
Shall the new user be allowed to create more new users? (y/n) y
CREATE USER
```

Back in our `psql` prompt, let's check the *pg_user* table again. You should see a new entry for *awyke*.

9

Creating Our Tables

Now it's time for us to create our tables. Rather than enter everything on the psql command prompt, we store the table creation commands in two different text files. Once there, we can reference them while in the psql environment and create the tables as needed.

The first table we create is our *users* table. We store the commands, which are SQL commands, to create this table in a file called users.sql. The contents of this file are as follows:

```
create table users (
  userid      int4  DEFAULT NEXTVAL('c'),
  firstname   char (50),
  lastname    char (50),
  zip         char (10),
  primary key (userid)
);

create sequence c start 101;
grant all on users to awyke;
grant all on c to awyke;
```

These commands create a table named *users* in our *perl-begin* database. It also creates a sequence used to generate unique UserIDs, which is also the column that's our primary key. The last two lines grant permissions to the *awyke* user for the table and the sequence.

The second table we need to create is the *purchases* table. We store the commands for the creation of this table in a file called purchases.sql. Here's what to enter into this file:

```
create table purchases (
  userid        int4,
  itemname     char (50),
  itemnumber   char (50),
  cost         char (10)
);

grant all on purchases to awyke;
```

Now that our files are created, we need to run them against the database to create our tables. To do this, simply enter the following two commands. After running each command, you'll see some output that confirms the tables were created successfully.

Note

This assumes the files are in the same directory in which you started the **psql** application. If they aren't, then you also need to include the path when you reference the files.

```
perl-begin=# \i users.sql
perl-begin=# \i purchases.sql
```

We now want to double check to make sure the tables and sequence were created successfully by using the `\dt` (display tables) and `\ds` (display sequences) commands. You can also verify the permissions were set correctly by using the `\z` command. The output of running these three should resemble the following:

```
perl-begin=# \dt
      List of relations
   Name    | Type  |  Owner
-----------+-------+----------
 purchases | table | postgres
 users     | table | postgres
(2 rows)

perl-begin=# \ds
     List of relations
 Name |   Type   |  Owner
------+----------+----------
 c    | sequence | postgres
(1 row)

perl-begin-# \z
Access permissions for database "perl-begin"
 Relation  | Access permissions
-----------+--------------------
 c         | {"=","awyke=arwR"}
 purchases | {"=","awyke=arwR"}
 users     | {"=","awyke=arwR"}
(3 rows)
```

9

Everything is ready now. This is all we're going to discuss regarding PostgreSQL and specific database functionality. The rest of the concepts pertain to how the Perl DBI works with these databases. We'll write a script that inserts, retrieves, updates, and deletes data.

Tip

Do you want to know more about PostgreSQL? Visit its Web site at http://www.postgresql.org.

Introduction to the DBI

The *Perl Database Interface,* or *Perl DBI,* is an interface between the Perl programming language and a database. The DBI, whose architecture is shown in the following illustration, acts as a conduit between the Perl interpreter and the database engine. Part of this architecture, as you can see in the illustration, is a driver that must be loaded by the DBI to access the database. This is the driver (DBD) we installed after installing the DBI. For a complete list of available drivers, check http://www.symbolstone.org/technology/perl/DBI.

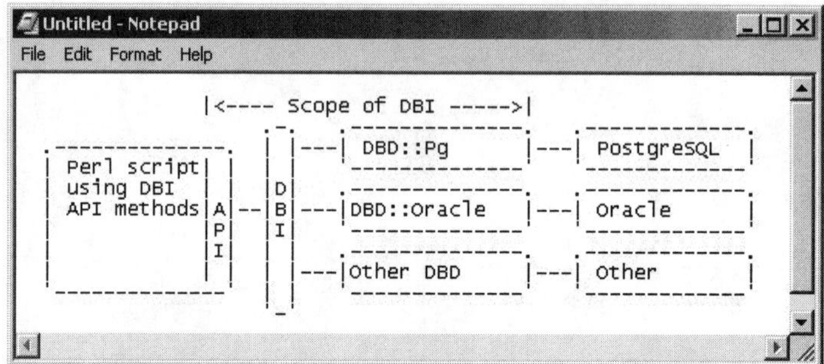

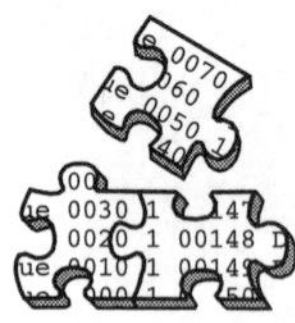

Project 9-2: Installing the DBI Module

Do you wish we'd helped you out a bit more with Project 9-1? Well, that one was a bit beyond the scope of what we're trying to do, so we had to push it back on you. This project, however, is within our scope, so we'll give you a hand.

The objective, as the title of the project dictates, is to install the DBI module on your system. Unlike some modules that are purely written in Perl, the DBI module must be *built* in much the same manner as Perl itself. Windows users do have it easy because the module is already built, but you must go through some steps to make it work.

Step-by-Step

Because we want you to get up-and-running quickly with the DBI, we broke the project into two sections. The first involves building and installing the DBI module, while the second involves building and installing the DBD::Pg module (PostgreSQL Database Driver).

Hint

Do you think the DBI module may already be installed on your machine? You can check by typing **perl -e "use DBI;"** on the command line. If the module is installed, you simply see the command prompt returned. If it isn't installed, you get an error saying the interpreter couldn't find `DBI.pm` in any of the included library paths.

1. Go to http://www.symbolstone.org/technology/perl/DBI and download the DBI module.

Note

(Windows Users) At this time, you need to open your Cygwin command prompt to enter all the following commands. Remember, the Cygwin command prompt was part of the Cygwin tools we installed in Project 9-1.

2. Because the module is distributed in a compressed format, we need to uncompress it. To do so, type **tar xvfz DBI-1.14.tar.gz**. Depending on the version of the DBI that's available when you attempt this exercise, the filename might be slightly different.
3. After you uncompress the file, change into the `DBI-1.14` directory (again, this might be slightly different, depending on the version) and read the `README` file. This gives you additional information about the installation and any last-minute pointers on getting the DBI working.

4. Once you read the `README` file, it's time to start building the DBI module into the Perl installation. Make sure you're running as the user who installed Perl back in Module 1 of this book. More than likely, this is root, but it might not be. Just be sure to be logged in as the same user who successfully installed Perl, which will avoid many potential problem areas.
5. Now type **perl Makefile.PL**. This creates the makefile you need to build the library.
6. Next, type **make**. This begins the process of building the library and making sure all package files are there.
7. Once this has completed, we recommend you test the installation process of building the library by typing **make test**. This goes through to check your system further and lets you know if any errors are building in the library.
8. Finally, you can type **make install** to build and install the DBI module. Once you complete this, type **perl -e "use DBI;"** to verify everything built and installed correctly. If you are returned to the command line with no errors, everything is fine!

Hint

Did you have trouble installing DBI? First, check the official DBI Web site (http://www.symbolstone.org/technology/perl/DBI) for answers. If you find nothing, then you can try the dbi-users@isc.org mailing.

Do you wonder why we went through the trouble of having you install PostgreSQL? Well, here's why. We can now show you how to build and install the secondary DBI module that provides access to a PostgreSQL database. The name of this module is DBD::Pg.

Hint

Do you want to run the DBI against a database other than PostgreSQL? Download the file you need from the official DBI Web site and follow the directions in the `README` file.

1. Download the DBD::Pg distribution, which, at press time, is at version 0.95. You can download this version from the official DBI Web site at http://www.symbolstone.org/technology/perl/DBI.

2. Once you download the file, you need to decompress it. We think you know how to do this by now, so we'll leave that up to you. If you do need some help, refer to the command we used in Step 2 of "Installing the DBI Module."

   Now, read the `README` file, which tells you installing this module takes four basic steps. The `README` file also tells you about two environment variables that must be set and that you should run the first three steps as a normal user (that is, as yourself and not as root). Once you read this file, you can start the installation process by typing **perl Makefile.PL**. This creates the makefile you need to build the library.

Hint

Do you want to know what shell you're using, so you can set your environment variables correctly or would you like to see all variables? Type **env** to see all variables and/or **echo $SHELL** to see only the shell. You'll probably see one of the following for your shell: sh-Bourne Shell; ksh-Korn Shell; csh-C Shell; bash-Bourne Again Shell.

1. Type **make**. This begins the process of building the library and making sure all package files are there.

2. Once this has completed, we recommend you test the installation process of building the library by typing **make test**. This goes through and further checks your system, and lets you know if any errors are building in the library.

3. Finally, you can type **make install** to build and install the PostgreSQL module and driver for the DBI. If you are returned to the command line with no errors, everything is fine!

Hint

Did you have trouble building this database driver? First, check the official DBI Web site (http://www.symbolstone.org/technology/perl/DBI) for answers. If you find nothing, then you can try the dbi-users@isc.org mailing.

Using the DBI

Now that PostgreSQL is running, the tables we need for our examples are created, and the DBI and DBD modules are installed, we can start doing some programming! In this section of the module, we introduce you to the DBI, talk about connections and queries, and discuss errors and a few other features. Some of these, as you might imagine, require a knowledge of databases, but we'll try to separate that as much as possible. If you have previous experience with databases, this can only help you.

Connections

The connection between PostgreSQL and the Perl DBI is accomplished by using the `connect()` subroutine. This subroutine accepts up to four parameters, which include the data source of the database server, the username to connect as, the password for the user, and an optional attribute list that can dictate how the connection is made and any options you want to specify. This attribute list, for instance, can be used to set the `AutoCommit` and `PrintError` values to off. We show an example of this in a second. The format for using the `connect()` subroutine is as follows, where the {*attribute_list*} is optional.

```
DBI->connect($ds, $user, $password, [{attribute_list}]);
```

Looking more at the data source parameter (`$ds`), this value can contain as little as the database name and driver name, but can also take the hostname and port of the database, or even more, depending on the driver. To illustrate this, here are some syntax examples. In these examples, you replace *<driver>* with the name of the driver being used, *<db_name>* with the name of the database, *<host>* with the machine's hostname, and *<port>* with the port number to which the database client is listening.

Note

Be sure to check the documentation of your database driver to see the exact syntax of the data source. PostgreSQL, for instance, can also take an `options` and `tty` parameter.

```
dbi:<driver>:<db_name>
dbi:<driver>:<db_name>@<host>:<port>
dbi:<driver>:database=<db_name>;host=<host>;port=<port>
```

available_drivers() and data_sources()

The Perl DBI includes two subroutines to help you verify the driver you need is installed on the system and, if the driver supports it, can help you determine the data sources (databases) to which the driver can connect. These subroutines are the `available_drivers()` and `data_sources()` routines.

The `available_drivers()` routine, when called, searches through the directories in your `@INC` environment. Basically, it looks for DBI::* modules, where * could be something like `Pg`, `Oracle`, `Informix`, and so forth. The syntax for this looks like the following.

```
@driver_array = DBI->available_drivers;
```


The second subroutine, `data_sources()`, can be used to return all the database names a given driver can access. Not all drivers support this, so you need to check to make sure the return value isn't empty or `undef`. The syntax for using this routine is the following.

```
@ds_array = DBI->data_sources($driver);
```

One of the biggest performance hits on your database by application is the initial connection. Because of this, we recommend you use persistent connections for your applications. This means you open a connection and hold it open as long as it's needed, which could be for the entire program. This is because the establishment of a connection can take upwards of 90 percent of the total time to execute a single query. If you hold the connection open for other queries, however, subsequent queries won't experience this delay.

Also important to note is connections don't only refer to connecting to a database—it also refers to disconnecting. Good programming style dictates you should close all open connections as you exit your program. This exit could be as a result of completion or an error. In either case, you should explicitly close your connection when you finish. This is accomplished in the DBI by calling the `disconnect()` subroutine. The syntax for this routine is as follows, where `$dbh` is the database handle to which you assigned your connection.

```
$dbh->disconnect
```

If we take all we learned here and apply it in a single example, called `connect.pl`, then we can use the DBI to make certain our driver is installed, make sure it can connect to our database, open a connection, and then close it. This, obviously, doesn't do much, but it does provide somewhat of a template for the other tasks we are going to run against our database.

```
#!/usr/bin/perl-w

# load in the DBI module
use DBI;

# set the username, password, and database to access
$user = "awyke";
$password = "mypass";
$dbase = "perl-begin";

# specify the driver and database to access
$driver = "dbi:Pg:" . $dbase; # generates 'dbi:Pg:perl-begin'

# make the connection to the database
$dbh = DBI->connect($driver, $user, $password) or die "\nError ($DBI::err):
$DBI::errstr\n";

# close our connection
$dbh->disconnect;
```

Transaction Management

As your database-enabled applications become more complex, you may find the need to lock tables and manage the transactions. An example might be a counter. If you have ten people connected to the database and you want to increment a counter field based on this number of connections, you need to lock and unlock the table as you increment the counter. Otherwise, it's possible two or more transactions may attempt to perform their increment at the same time, which could cause data corruption.

In the Perl DBI, the `LOCK TABLE` *`<table>`* statement, which is interpreted by the backend server, can be used to apply an explicit lock on a table, but this only works inside a transaction (that is, `AutoCommit` set equal to 0). For more information on `AutoCommit`, check the DBI manpages.

In addition to locking and unlocking the tables, you should also verify that a set of transactions completed successfully. If all don't complete successfully for any reason, then you should rollback all transactions. In other words, you don't want to have a transaction complete for the purchase, for example, for just one item, but not the second. You want the whole purchase to fail. To perform this kind of task, you can use the `rollback()` subroutine of the DBI module.

The discussion of the pros and cons of locks and rollbacks is beyond the scope of this book and is specific to database applications. Please consult the DBI manpages, your database documentation, and/or the author of your database driver to see what can be done with the driver you are using.

Queries

You perform four main types of queries routinely when you access your database. These are as follows:

1. `SELECT`
2. `INSERT`
3. `UPDATE`
4. `DELETE`

The `SELECT` query returns any information in the database matching what you requested. The `INSERT` query is used to insert new rows in the database, while the `UPDATE` query updates existing information. As you might have guessed, the `DELETE` query is used to delete items from the database.

The query process itself breaks into a four-stage process. We won't discuss these in detail, but they are evident in the underlying examples that we have in this section of the module. You can see us call and use the subroutines mentioned in this list. This process is outlined here.

- **Prepare** This process takes your query and validates it. Assuming all your syntax is OK (that is, make sure the tables you're querying exist), then a handle for the query is returned.
- **Execute** This is the process of calling the `execute()` subroutine in the DBI that executes the query on the database.
- **Fetch** This process takes place once your query has completed; the data is returned to your Perl program in the form of data structures.
- **Deallocation** This process isn't one that affects you; it's when the DBI and corresponding driver perform cleanups, such as freeing memory.

Obviously, there's more to this than we mentioned, so we'll show how each of these can be executed using the Perl DBI.

SELECT

`SELECT` statements are one of the most widely used statements in interacting with databases. These are the statements that say, "Show me these things in the database." "These things," of course, refer to the items that match the type of select you perform and the criteria you pass.

Let's take our *users* table, which we defined at the start of the module as an example. If you want to return the *lastname* of all people entered into our *users* table, you would do this by saying

```
SELECT lastname FROM users;
```

If you want to return all data from the table, you can use the * wildcard, such as

```
SELECT * FROM users;
```

If you want to return the *firstname, lastname,* and *zip* of the person with the *userid* of 2, you would say

```
SELECT firstname, lastname, zip FROM users WHERE userid = 2;
```

As you can see, SELECT statements are quite simple. After the SELECT keyword you specify what you want returned, and then you use the FROM keyword to specify the table name. You can even use an optional WHERE keyword to specify some criteria that must match.

So, what does this look like in Perl using the prepare() and execute() subroutines if we want to return all information in the *users* table? In a nutshell, it looks like this. Note, we haven't included all the code necessary to make this work, such as opening our connection, but that's because we didn't want to confuse you while we tried to show you only the SELECT parts.

```
$statement = $dbh->prepare("SELECT * FROM users");
$statement->execute;
```

Ask the Expert

Question: Using the WHERE keyword looks a lot like Boolean evaluations. Is specifying two or more sets of criteria possible?

Answer: Absolutely! You can use other keywords, like AND and OR, as well as parentheses to specify order. For instance, if you want to return only people with the last name of Smith, who live in the 27654 ZIP code, you could use the following statement:

```
SELECT * FROM users WHERE (lastname = "Smith" AND zip=27654)
```

Question: Is there any way to specify a pattern to match in my queries?

Answer: It isn't as robust as Perl's regular expression pattern matching, but you can use wildcards when you perform searches. For instance, if you want to return all users who had the last name of Smith and who lived in the 27654 ZIP code, OR whose first name started with the letter *A,* you could use the following (also notice how we did the parentheses here).

```
SELECT * FROM users WHERE ((lastname = "Smith" AND zip=27654) OR
(firstname LIKE "A%"));
```

Question: So far you have used "=" and "LIKE" in your WHERE statements. Are these the only statements that can be used?

Answer: No, there are more. You can use NOT LIKE or != (not equal), > (greater than), < (less than), >= (greater than or equal to), and <= (less than or equal to), as well.

INSERT

INSERT statements, on the other hand, are used to insert data into databases. These are the statements that say, "Please put these values into these columns in this table in the database."

Again, let's use our *users* table for an example. If you want to insert a new user into the table, you would do this by saying:

```
INSERT INTO USERS (userid, firstname, lastname, zip) VALUES ('100',
   'Allen', 'Wyke', '55555');
```

As you can see, we use the INSERT keyword, pass the columns we want to insert into, use the INTO keyword followed by the table name, and, finally, we specify the VALUES keyword to signify the values to be inserted. Now let's say you didn't want to insert the user's last name. How do you think that would be done?

```
INSERT userid, firstname, zip INTO users VALUES "100", "Allen",
"55555";
```

Like SELECT, INSERT statements are quite simple. In addition, the Perl you use to run these commands is simple, BUT it is different than with a SELECT statement. This is primarily because the INSERT command doesn't return valuable data back to your program. To execute this type of command, use the do() subroutine in the DBI package, as follows:

```
$rows = $dbh->do('INSERT userid, firstname, zip INTO users VALUES
   "100", "Allen", "55555"');
```

Note

This syntax is also true for UPDATE and DELETE commands, which we cover next.

UPDATE

Have you ever done something you needed to change later? Well, SQL has a keyword that lets you do this: UPDATE. The UPDATE keyword first takes the name of the database table you want to update, and then it "sets" the column to the values you specify. You can perform this in a conditional manner by including the use of the WHERE keyword and clause.

Using our same *users* table, if you want to change our first user, John Doe, to have a new ZIP code, the following statement would work.

```
UPDATE users SET zip="22222" WHERE ((firstname = "John") AND
   (lastname = "Doe"));
```

```
UPDATE users SET zip='22222' WHERE ((firstname = 'John') AND
   (lastname = 'Doe'));
```

Of course, if you want to change something globally (all users), you could do this by not specifying the WHERE clause.

Note

Remember, you should use the do() subroutine in the DBI module to execute the UPDATE command.

DELETE

The final type of command we discuss is the DELETE statement. This, based on the WHERE clause passed, deletes any rows that match. If you want to remove all users from our *users* table that have a ZIP code of 55555, then the following statement would work:

```
DELETE FROM users WHERE zip='55555';
```

Note

Remember, you should use the `do()` subroutine in the DBI module to execute the `DELETE` command.

1-Minute Drill

- **Write a select statement that would return everyone with the first name "Sam" in our *users* database table.**
- **Write a select statement that would return everyone with the first name "Sam" and a ZIP code starting with 5 in our *users* database table.**

Warnings and Errors

Capturing all DBI error messages in your Perl programs is always a good idea. The DBI interface to PostgreSQL includes two variables that can store this type of information for you, information you can write out to the screen or maybe a log file. These variables are as follows:

1. `DBI::err`: Contains the error code returned by the database.
2. `DBI::errstr`: Contains the error message returned by the database.

To show how this might be used, we include a simple script called `db-error.pl` that prompts the user for a data source, username, and password to connect to a database. If you run this script and enter the wrong data, then you see the error code and message written out to the screen.

- **select * where firstname = "Sam";**
- **select * where (firstname = "Sam" and ZIP like "5%");**

```
#!/usr/bin/perl -w

use DBI;

# prompt user for connection information
print "\nWhat is the data source you want to connect to: ";
chomp($ds=<STDIN>);
print "\nWhat user do you want to connect as: ";
chomp($user=<STDIN>);
print "\nWhat is the password of this user: ";
chomp($password=<STDIN>);

# try to connect
$dbh = DBI->connect($ds, $user, $password) or die "Error ($DBI::err):
   $DBI::errstr";
```

Now, although this shows how you might use the error and warning messages, it doesn't prepare you for what you might expect to see come back. For this, we include Table 9-3. In this table, we list the types of messages that can be returned, the messages themselves, and a description. This, coupled with what you know about accessing your database, should give you a good handle on how to handle problem areas.

Returned Results

We've gone over how to query the database for information, but we haven't yet discussed how that information is returned or what we can do with it, so this is our next topic. We also include a more complete example, so you can see an actual SQL query being run and processed using the DBI.

In this example, which we call `db-select.pl`, we perform several tasks. Besides the obvious tasks of loading the DBI module and setting up the connection to our *perl-begin* database, we are going to prepare and execute a `SELECT` statement that returns the values of the *firstname* and *lastname* columns in our *users* database. During all this time, of course, we are checking for errors and writing the appropriate messages as needed.

Now for the new stuff. What do we do with the results that are returned? Well, this is where the `fetchrow_array()` subroutine comes in. Each row returned from our query is stored in the DBI and we can use this routine to access them. As you soon see, we do a shortcut and read them directly into the variables `$firstname` and `$lastname` in

Message Type	Message	Description
Error	Can't call method "prepare" without a package or object reference	The $dbh handle you're using to call `prepare()` is probably undefined because the preceding connect failed. Check the return status of DBI methods or you can use the `RaiseError` attribute.
Error	Can't call method "execute" without a package or object reference	The `$sth` (statement) handle you're using to call `execute()` is probably undefined because the preceding `prepare()` failed. Check the return status of DBI methods or use the `RaiseError` attribute.
Error	DBI/DBD internal version mismatch	The DBD driver module was built with a different version of DBI than the one currently being used. Rebuild the DBD module under the current version of DBI.
Error	DBD driver has not implemented the AutoCommit attribute	The DBD driver implementation is incomplete. Contact the author of the driver or seek help at any official site that may be referenced in the `README` of that driver.
Error	Can't [sg]et %s->{%s}: unrecognised attribute	You attempted to set or get an unknown attribute of a handle. Make sure you have spelled the attribute correctly and that you have the case of the attribute correctly referenced.
Warning	Database handle destroyed without explicit disconnect	A `$dbh` (database) handle is out of scope or the program ended before the handle was disconnected from the database.
Warning	DBI Handle cleared whilst still holding %d cached kids!	Probably due to a DBI bug, but could also be a DBD driver bug. Please report it to the appropriate author of the module.
Warning	DBI Handle cleared whilst still active!	Probably due to a DBI bug, but could also be a DBD driver bug. Please report it to the appropriate author of the module.
Warning	DBI Handle has uncleared implementors data	Probably a DBD driver bug. Please report it to the appropriate author of the module.
Warning	DBI Handle has %d uncleared child handles	Probably due to a DBI bug, but could also be a DBD driver bug. Please report it to the appropriate author of the module.

Table 9-3 DBI Error and Warning Messages

the body of a `while` loop. This way, we can return each row, one item at a time. Once we have this information, we print it on the user's screen.

```
#!/usr/bin/perl -w

# load in the DBI module
use DBI;

# set the username and password to access our database
$user = "awyke";
$password = "mypass";

# specify the driver and database to access
$driver = "dbi:Pg:dbname=perl-begin";

# make the connection to the database
$dbh = DBI->connect($driver, $user, $password) or die "\nError ($DBI::err):
   $DBI::errstr\n";

# define fields we want to return
$first = "firstname";
$second = "lastname";

# prepare the SQL statement
$statement = $dbh->prepare("SELECT $first, $second FROM users") or die
   "\nError ($DBI::err): $DBI::errstr\n";

# execute the SQL statement
$statement->execute or die "\nError ($DBI::err): $DBI::errstr\n";

# print out header for returned information
print "\n\nReturning $first and $second\n";

# print out the returned values
while (($firstname, $lastname) = $statement->fetchrow_array){
  print "$firstname\t$lastname\n";
}

# Terminate the statement
$statement->finish;

# close our connection
$dbh->disconnect;
```

We know this was a fairly simple example, but it should illustrate some of the power of access databases within your Perl applications. Remember

9

this because tons of other items are in the DBI that you can use to access databases and interact with them. We didn't have time to cover many different subroutines and programming concepts here, which you should investigate. Our goal was to get your feet wet on a complex topic, so you could go out and work on your own.

Moving On

Wow! We covered a lot of topics in this module. Understanding databases is itself enough for hundreds of pages of writing but, somehow, we did it. We were able to get in enough information about databases for you AND enough information about accessing them via the Perl DBI to send you out on your own. You might not have walked away an expert and you might have many questions now, but that's exactly what we wanted to do. We wanted to get you started and push you in the right direction. And, if you want to do more reading, you can find some tutorials at http://search.dmoz.org/cgi-bin/search?search=sql+tutorial.

Now that you've been exposed to accessing databases, how about moving on to using Perl to create *Common Gateway Interface* (*CGI*) scripts? In the next module, that's exactly what we're going to do.

Mastery Check

1. What does DBI stand for?

   A. Database Interaction

   B. Database Binding Interface

   C. Database Interface

   D. Database Insertion

2. Which of the following commands can you use to tell if the DBI module is installed on your system?

   A. perl –v "DBI"

   B. perl –e "use DBI;"

   C. perl –module DBI

   D. perl –verify DBI

3. Do any additional modules need to be installed to use the DBI with Oracle?

   A. Yes

   B. No

4. Which of the following SQL statements returns all rows in a table named *customer*?

   A. select all from customer

   B. select all from table customer

   C. select * from customer

   D. select * from table customer

Module 10

Writing CGI Programs

The Goals of This Module

- Learn what CGI is and how it works
- Understand how to use Perl to write your CGI applications
- Begin practicing various formatting techniques for your output
- Create a complete project from steps *A* to *Z*

In Module 6, you got your first taste of using Perl in the real world. Then, in Module 9, you used Perl to access databases. Now it's time to look at another way to use Perl—in creating *Common Gateway Interface* (*CGI*) scripts.

CGI scripts, or programs, as they are sometimes called, are often used to create HTML pages dynamically. These pages could be anything from a Web-based shopping cart at your favorite e-commerce store or simply a result page for a user who just submitted her contact information. CGI scripts can be a powerful tool for Web developers, and using Perl as the language of choice for your CGI scripts is by no means a bad one.

Hint

A CGI script is a program that runs on the same system as the Web server and conforms to the CGI standard. For more information on the CGI standard, check out http://hoohoo.ncsa.uiuc.edu/cgi.

In this module, we look at how to use CGI and Perl. During this module, we also show you how to handle information submitted via HTML forms, which may be your most useful case of combining CGI and Perl. But, before we discuss the more complex details of CGI programming, let's look at some general concepts.

What Is CGI?

CGI is a standard for interfacing external programs, such as Perl scripts, with an HTTP server. The words "common" and "gateway" refer to the common variables and conventions (hence, the term "interface") used to pass this information to and from the HTTP server. CGI lets you use these custom programs to format and process output to browsers.

Each time a user requests a URL corresponding to a CGI script, the Web server invokes the program, passing the information sent from the browser to the script. This information includes various HTTP headers sent by the requesting browser and any information passed along with the URL, such as query string information (more on that later). The CGI script is then able to read, process, and return an appropriate response based on this information.

In a nutshell, this is what CGI is and how it works. Because it can perform complex processing, such as accessing a database, while executing, we'll look a little deeper into some of the details behind CGI and how it can be used on the Web.

Quick Introduction to CGI.pm

Most HTML is independent of the operating system running on the server. CGI, however, can be heavily reliant on the operating system and the HTTP server you are running. This could be anything from path delimiters (remember how Windows uses `\`, UNIX uses `/`, and Mac OS uses `:`) to how programs execute. For this reason, we use a common Perl module, called the CGI.pm, for our scripting. The author of this module has written it so it can be used with the following systems:

- DOS
- Mac OS
- Microsoft Windows
- OS/2
- UNIX
- VMS

10

Hint

Do you want more information on the CGI.pm module? Check the docs with your Perl distribution and you should find more information with the library (check the `lib` directory of distribution).

CGI Programming Language Options

CGI programs can be written in any number of programming languages as long as the program can be executed on the system running the Web server. Some common choices for writing CGI scripts and UNIX are the shell scripting languages, such as Bourne, C, or Korn shells, and/or various programming languages, such as C/C++, Perl, and Java. If you're using a Windows Web server, you can also use Windows-specific languages, such as Visual Basic or Delphi for these scripts.

CGI programs reside in a specific directory that the Web server uses to execute the program. For example, on most UNIX systems, these programs are typically stored in a directory named *cgi-bin* and end with a `.cgi` extension. Windows systems, on the other hand, store these programs in a scripts directory. On the Mac OS, no real default folder exists. We won't worry about this right now because we step you through checking your Web server and setting it up correctly later.

So, with all of these choices, what language should you use to create your CGI scripts? Even though this may be left up to you in the real world, the most commonly used language is Perl, which is, of course, the focus of this module and this book!

Using Perl for CGI Scripts

Using CGI scripts on your system isn't terribly complex. Because this book does address the Windows, UNIX, and Mac OS platforms, we take a quick look at how you can get it up and running on your system. To ensure the system is running correctly, use the following CGI script, which we name `test.pl` to test your setup. Don't worry about what the code means yet—we cover that later.

```
#!/usr/bin/perl -w

use CGI;
$query = new CGI;
print $query->header;
print $query->h1("It Worked!");
```

Now, look at setting it up on your system.

Hint

Because CGI.pm has built-in support for debugging from the command line, it's a good way to find any problems before you run through your Web server.

Windows

Several popular Web servers run on Windows, such as the Netscape/iPlanet line and Apache but, for this exercise, we discuss Microsoft's *Internet Information Server* (*IIS*) and Personal Web Server, which is nothing more than a stripped down version of IIS. For the book's screen shots and some of its commands, however, we demonstrate how to run Perl CGI scripts on Windows NT/2000.

First, make sure the World Wide Web Publishing Service is installed and running. You can quickly check this by opening the Services Control Panel—it should be one of the last items listed. If you don't see the service, then click the Add/Remove Programs icon in the Control Panel. From there, you can access a list of Windows components that can be installed on the machine.

If you are running Windows 2000, you can install IIS 5. If you are running Windows NT 4, this installs IIS 2. For optimal performance on your system, download the Windows NT 4.0 Resource Kit from Microsoft (http://resourcelink.mspress.microsoft.com/reslink), which provides IIS 4. Also make sure you reapply the appropriate Service Pack for your system.

Hint

Want more information on how you should install IIS? Check out http://www.microsoft.com/ntserver/nts/deployment/planguide/Install.asp.

Once IIS is installed and running, you're ready to install Perl for ISAPI, which comes with the ActivePerl 5.6 distribution. This is nothing more than what we call a CGI-engine for running CGI programs, which is a bit more efficient than running against the `perl.exe` interpreter. Perl for ISAPI is a dll version that loads into memory once and requires fewer resources.

If you already had IIS installed and running when you completed the ActivePerl 5.6 installation in Module 1, "Introduction to Perl," and you selected to install the Perl for ISAPI component, then you're ready to go. If not, start the installation process of ActivePerl 5.6 again and select to modify the installation. At that time, install the Perl for ISAPI component.

Because ActivePerl does all the configuration needed, you won't have a problem getting this to run on Windows.

Now that Perl and IIS are installed correctly, all you have to do is place the `test.pl` script (you could also use .plx as the extension) we created in the CGI directory for IIS, which will be something like `\inetpub\scripts`. While your IIS server is running, access the program by typing **http://localhost/scripts/test.pl** in the URL location. The localhost part tells your browser to access the IIS server on your local machine, rather than across the network. If this didn't work for any reason, you could always use your IP address (you can get it by typing **ipconfig** at the command line) or hostname (you can get this by typing **hostname** at the command line) in place of localhost. If you're successful, you should see something like the following illustration.

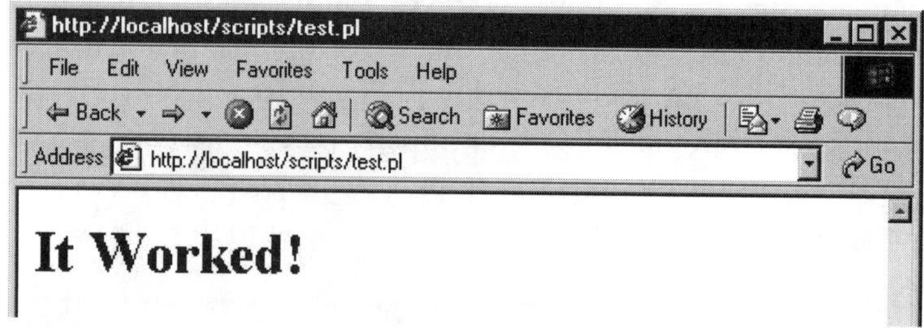

Note

Yes, you are correct. Microsoft has differed again. As you see with the UNIX instructions, CGI scripts are commonly placed in a `cgi-bin` directory. Microsoft has taken a different path by default by calling it `scripts`, which is also how it's referenced in the URL.

UNIX

Because of the large number of Web servers that can run on the various UNIX platforms, we selected the Apache Web server for this example. Apache is an open source Web server that can be built and run, like Perl, on many different operating systems. If you don't have Apache installed on your UNIX machine, although there's a good chance you do, then you can simply download it from http://www.apache.org and install it using the instructions provided. For those of you using Linux, you may be able to use your Package Manager to find and install the latest version of Apache quickly and easily.

The first thing to do after Apache is installed and running is to make sure the CGI directory is set up within the Apache configuration file. For this, we have a little project.

1-Minute Drill

- **What does CGI stand for?**

Project 10-1: Configuring Your Apache CGI Directory

Because configuring your CGI directory entry within the Apache configuration files is necessary, we want to give you a little exercise on three of the ways this can be accomplished—using Comanche, using `linuxconf`, or using a text editor. Have fun!

Once Apache is installed and ready to go, the best way to configure it to run your CGI programs is through the Comanche configuration editor. If you are running Linux and chose to have Apache installed originally, you probably can launch this application from one of your menus, which can be shown by right-clicking the desktop. If this isn't listed as Comanche, it may be listed as Apache Configuration.

Once you launch the application, double-click the icons until you see Default Web Site entry, as shown in the following illustration.

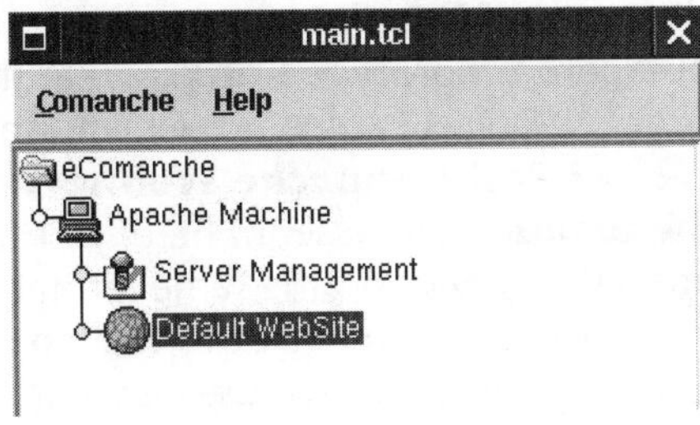

- **Common Gateway Interface**

10

From here, right-click this icon and select **Conf View** from the menu. You see a list of configuration options for the Apache Web server. Scroll down the list until you see an entry for **ScriptAlias**. If no entry appears, then add one. The format is the following, which can be seen in the following illustration.

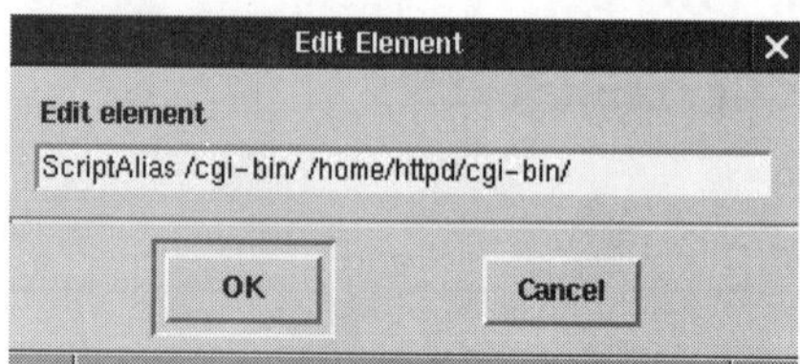

Simply replace `<path_to_cgi-bin>` with the directory path to where you plan to store your CGI scripts. Once you finish, simply select the appropriate acceptance buttons to accept any changes you have made, and then quit Comanche.

```
ScriptAlias /cgi-bin/ /<path_to_cgi-bin>/
```

Note

Be sure the proper permissions are set for the directory in which you are storing your CGI scripts. Remember, the "user" that will be accessing them is the user Apache runs as, which is possibly "nobody."

If you're using a version of Linux to run your Apache Web server and you installed Apache when you installed the operating system, you can access the proper CGI scripts configuration through the `linuxconf` application. Simply type **linuxconf** at the command line to launch this program. Once it's running, expand the **Config-> Networking->Server Tasks->Apache Web server** menu and select the **Apache defaults** entry. From here, you can scroll down and edit the Script Alias entry using the same format described previously. Figure 10-1 shows you what this will look like.

If all else fails, and you are unable to use either of these two GUI applications for editing the Apache configuration, you can always fall back on a UNIX favorite—a text editor. All you need to know is what file and what entry to edit. The entry you're looking for is, as you might have guessed, `ScriptAlias`. As for the file, it's the `httpd.conf` file. Where this file might be on your system is hard to say because Apache

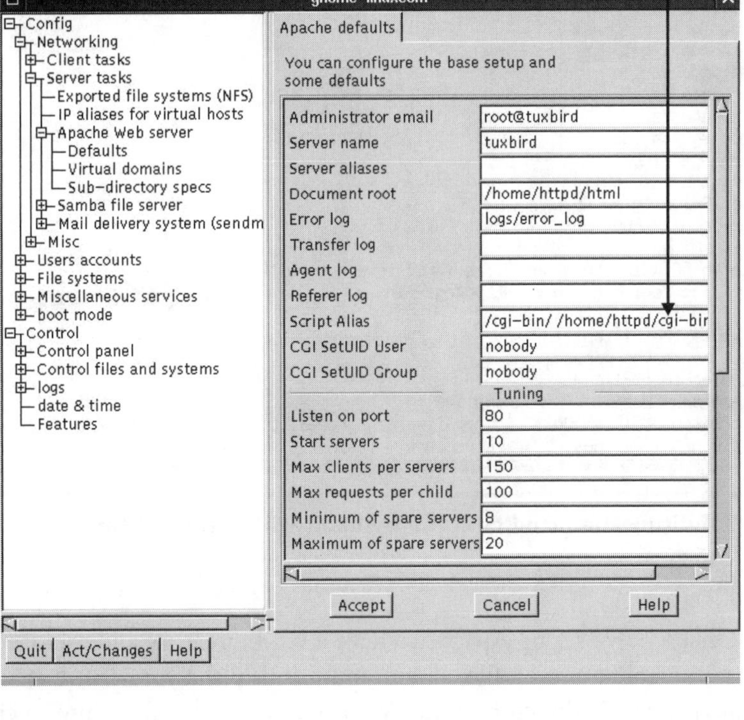

Figure 10-1 Using Linuxconf to edit your ScriptAlias setting

has changed how it distributes its software. If you aren't sure where your `httpd.conf` file is, then you can search for it using the following command. Once opened, look for the entry, as shown in Figure 10-2.

```
find / -name httpd.conf -print
```

Hint

This is usually going to be in `/etc`. On Red Hat, it's in `/etc/httpd/conf`. And on Debian, it's in `/etc/apache`.

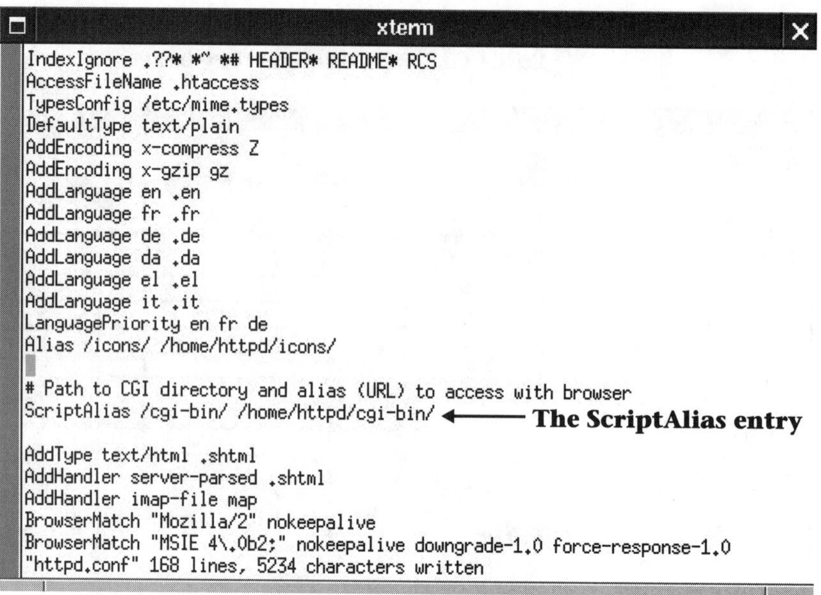

xterm
IndexIgnore .??* *~ ## HEADER* README* RCS
AccessFileName .htaccess
TypesConfig /etc/mime.types
DefaultType text/plain
AddEncoding x-compress Z
AddEncoding x-gzip gz
AddLanguage en .en
AddLanguage fr .fr
AddLanguage de .de
AddLanguage da .da
AddLanguage el .el
AddLanguage it .it
LanguagePriority en fr de
Alias /icons/ /home/httpd/icons/
Path to CGI directory and alias (URL) to access with browser
ScriptAlias /cgi-bin/ /home/httpd/cgi-bin/
The ScriptAlias entry
AddType text/html .shtml
AddHandler server-parsed .shtml
AddHandler imap-file map
BrowserMatch "Mozilla/2" nokeepalive
BrowserMatch "MSIE 4\.0b2;" nokeepalive downgrade-1.0 force-response-1.0
"httpd.conf" 168 lines, 5234 characters written

Figure 10-2 **Editing the httpd.conf file by hand with a text editor**

Once you've set up Apache to have a CGI directory and told it to reload the configuration file, all you must do is place your `test.pl` script in the CGI directory. Once your script is in there, be sure to change the permissions of the file so it's now executable. You can do this by typing **chmod 755 test.pl**.

Now, while your Apache server is running, access the program by typing **http://localhost/cgi-bin/test.pl** in the URL location. The localhost part tells your browser to access the Apache server on your local machine, rather than across the network. If this didn't work for any reason, you can always use your IP address or hostname (you can get this by typing **hostname** at the command line) in place of localhost. If you're successful, you should see something like the following illustration.

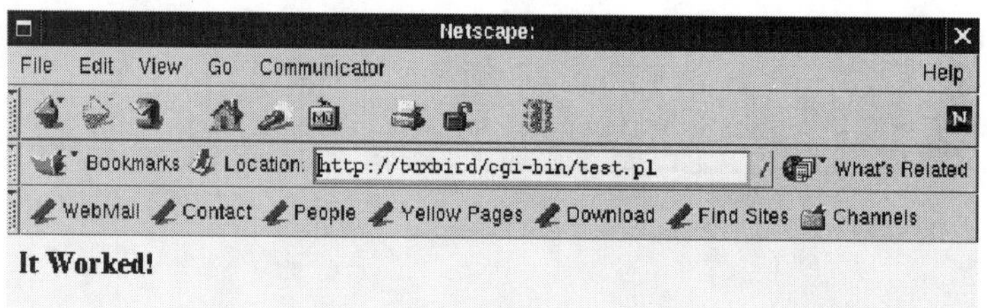

Mac OS

Unlike Windows and UNIX systems, setting up your CGI directory on the Mac OS is a bit different. The first thing you have to do, which is the same on any system, is to make sure your Web server is running. Although several Mac Web servers are floating around out there, we use the MacHTTP server that comes with the operating system.

The first thing to do is open the Web Sharing Control Panel. This panel, which is shown in the following illustration, lets you do the following.

- See your Web address, which reflects the IP address you can use to access the documents served by this server.
- Specify the folder you want to store your Web documents in, which defaults to Web Pages, which is located on the drive with Mac OS.
- Specify the default document to serve when the root of your server is requested.
- Start and stop your Web Sharing services.
- And, finally, specify the level of security you want to impose on the requests.

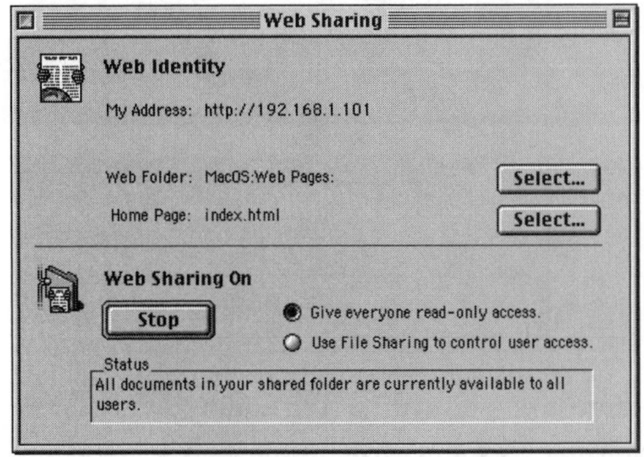

Once you've launched this Control Panel, you should verify these settings and make sure they're set to the values you want. Simply accepting the default values should be fine for anything we do in this book. Once opened, select the **Preferences** item from the **Edit** menu of this Control Panel. This displays a dialog box that has three tabs.

On the first tab, select the option that says Allow Aliases To Open Items Outside The Web Folder. Next, go to the Finder and open the `MacPerl` folder. Then, create an alias for the `MacPerl CGI` folder. Rename the folder to *cgi-bin* and move it under your Web Pages folder. By doing this, you can store all your CGI scripts within the `MacPerl CGI` folder, but still access them through the common `/cgi-bin` URL.

Go back to the Web Sharing Control Panel and click the Actions tab, which is the last tab. Under this tab is where you tell MacHTTP how to handle Perl CGI scripts. Once you do this, do the following:

- Click the **New...** button on Actions dialog.
- Use the pull-down menu and select Launch At Suffix.
- Click the **Select...** button and browse the folders on your system until you find the MacPerl application. Select the MacPerl application and click OK.
- In the Suffix text area type **`.cgi`**. Once completed, your entry should look like the following illustration.

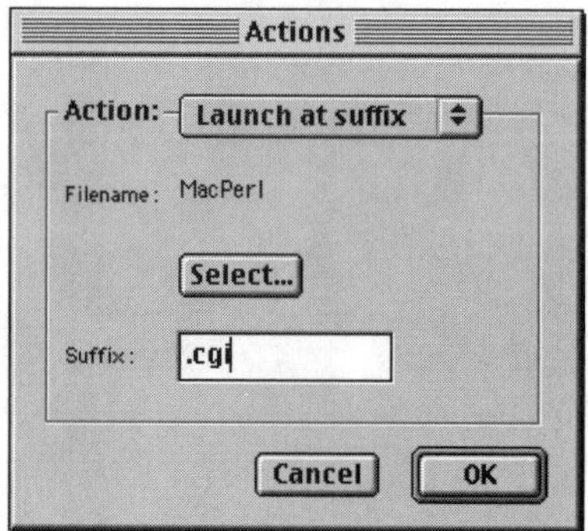

- Because there are two methods of running Perl CGI scripts on a Mac—normal CGI and asynchronous CGI—we must tell the MacHTTP about a second file type to process as a Perl CGI. Simply repeat the preceding steps, but enter **`.acgi`** as the suffix for the second type.

Once you finish entering these two Actions, you should see the same dialog entries under the Actions tab of the Preferences, as shown in the following illustration.

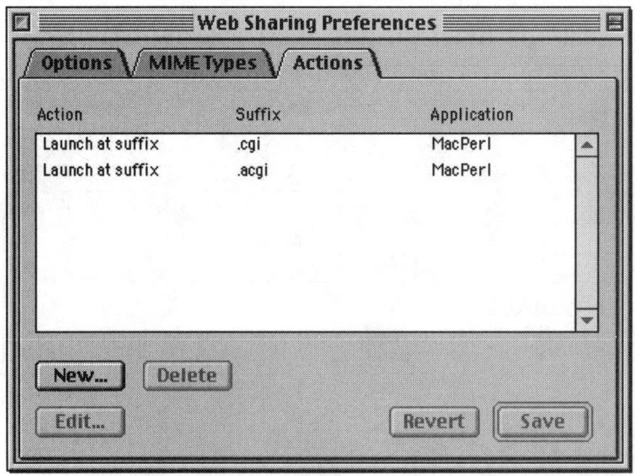

At this point, everything should be ready for your test. To make sure the proper Creator and Type are set, we recommend you open MacPerl, select to create a new program, and copy in the test code provided. When saving, however, be sure to select *CGI Script* as the type and name it `test.cgi`, not `test.pl`. Because we created the alias to our Web Pages folder, you can save this script under the `MacPerl CGI` folder. This saves the file properly. See the following illustration to see the file within the `MacPerl CGI` folder.

The last step you have to do is test your script! While your MacHTTP server is running, access the program by typing **http://localhost/cgi-bin/test.cgi** in the URL location. The localhost part tells your browser to access the MacHTTP server on your local machine, rather than across the network. If this didn't work for any reason, you can always use your

IP address (you can get this from the Web Sharing Control Panel) in place of localhost. If you're successful, you should see something like the following illustration.

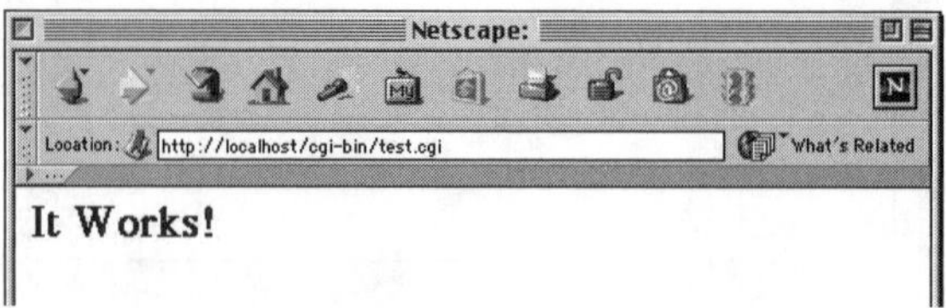

No-Parse Header Scripts

Typically, scripts produce output that's parsed by the server and sent back to the browser. However, it's possible for the script to handle this process rather than the server. This type of script is called a *NPH* (*No-Parse Header*) script.

The major advantage of a NPH script, whose name needs to begin with nph-, is it can be more efficient because the processing load is taken off your Web server. If you don't want the server to parse the header, however, you need to add the appropriate header yourself. This means your program must return a valid HTTP/1.0 or HTTP/1.1 response to the browser.

To get a better understanding of how this is used, here's a quick example. The NPH program listed communicates with the browser directly and references the `SERVER_PROTOCOL` as HTTP/1.1.

```
#!/usr/bin/perl -w

print "HTTP/1.1 200\n";
print "Content type:text/html\r\n";
print "<html>";
print "<head>";
print "<title>Test NPH Script</title>";
print "</head>";
print "<body>":
print "<h1>NPH Script</H1>";
print "<p>My sample NPH script.</p>";
print "</body>":
print "</html>";
```

Understanding Forms

Now that you have your Web server up and running Perl CGI scripts, you should step back and look at HTML forms. Forms, which supply your scripts with data to process, enable you to enter data to be sent to your CGI program. Your program takes this information and returns results to the browser in the form of a regular HTML page.

In the next few sections of this module, we introduce you to the basics of form construction. Although this isn't a necessity for programming in Perl, it does lay the foundation for understanding how browsers send data to a server and how forms interact with CGI.

Form Construction

Here, we step you through creating all the HTML form elements that could make up a Customer Information form. Figure 10-3 shows what the completed form will look like. During this exercise, our objective is to show you the various components a form can pass. This way, we can show you how to process them in your scripts later in the module.

`<form>`

An HTML form starts and ends with the `<form>` tag and can contain a variety of fields and buttons. To begin, we insert a beginning and ending `<form>` tag. Because additional attributes are needed, we add these as well. As for the attributes themselves, they are the following:

- **`action`** Provides the browser with a path to the CGI program that will handle the processing of the form. Because we are passing to a program called userinfo.cgi, this will be `/cgi-bin/userinfo.cgi`. We could have entered a complete URL with the hostname but, if you leave off the starting part of the URL, your Web browser submits the form to the host that supplied the form. This means you can actually create a form that's submitted to a host besides your own, although you get a warning in most browsers.

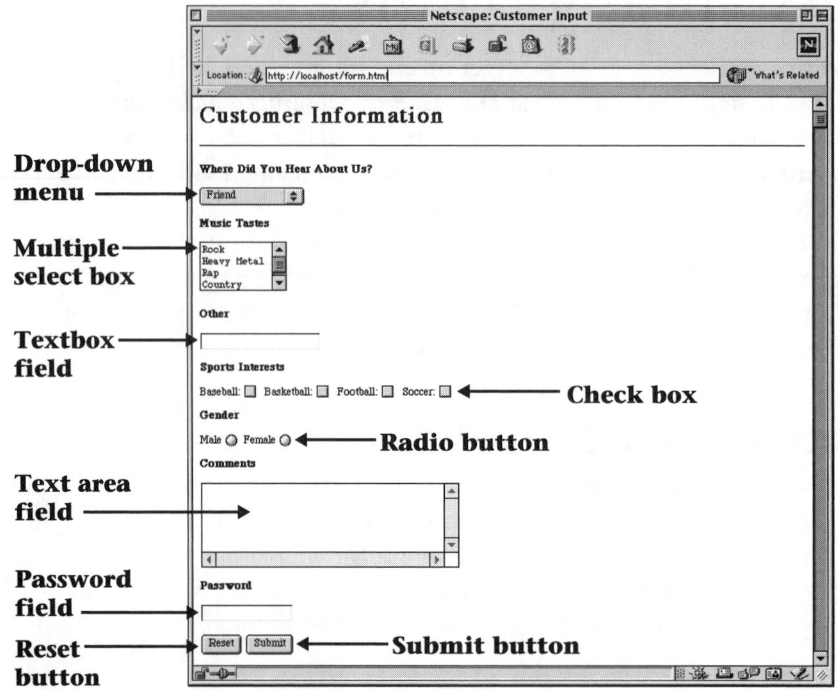

Figure 10-3 The Customer Information form

Note

Windows users should use `/scripts/userinfo.cgi`.

- **`method`** Tells the browser what method to use when submitting the form. The values you have to choose from are `GET` and `POST`. More information on these two values later, but we use `POST` for this example because this is the recommended protocol. With the `POST` method, the information from the user is put into the data stream, or body, of the HTTP request. This lets your back-end CGI script read the data via the "standard input" data stream, in much the same way command line Perl scripts can take parameters.

The GET method, however, puts the information submitted by your users at the end of the URL, after a question mark, submitted to your server. This is referred to as the *query string*. Because forms can be large, the GET method can create URLs that are huge. For this reason, this method is discouraged.

- **enctype** Provides the browser with the content type of the form submission. This is always set to application/x-www-form-urlencoded for form submissions.

Taking these attributes into consideration, we have the following full <form> tag:

```
<form action="/cgi-bin/userinfo.cgi" method="post" enctype="application/x-
  www-form-urlencoded">
```

<select> Drop-Down Menu

A <select> drop-down list box presents choices to a user in a menu-like element. This element is a box with an arrow pointing down and to the right of the menu. When the user selects the arrow, a list of choices is displayed. To include a drop-down list box in a form, you simply need to provide it with a value for its name attribute and nest <option> tags within the beginning and ending <select> tag.

Before we list the set of options in the menu, however, we want to introduce the menu by asking the user "Where Did You Hear About Us?" So the menu doesn't appear on the same line, these are specified in a heading Level 4 manner (<h4>). For our <option> elements, we give the user the choice to select one of the following:

1. Friend
2. Magazine
3. TV
4. Radio
5. Other

The complete HTML—including the heading, `<select>`, and nested `<option>` tags—looks like the following. Note, the `value` attribute of the `<option>` tag instructs a Web browser simply to use these values when it's submitted to your server, instead of the text between the opening and closing option tags.

```
<h4>Where Did You Hear About Us?</h4>
<select name="hear">
  <option value="friend">Friend</option>
  <option value="mag">Magazine</option>
  <option value="tv">TV</option>
  <option value="radio">Radio</option>
  <option value="other">Other</option>
</select>
```

`<select multiple>` Multiple Select Box

If you'd rather display a list of items a user can select from rather than a single pull-down menu, a multiple selection list box is the variant of choice. Not only does it enable you to select more than one item, but it lets the Web developer specify how many of the items will be displayed (that is, items to which you needn't scroll).

Note

The particular way a user selects elements depends on the browser. Most, however, follow some form of *control* or *option* click.

To include a multiple selection list box in our form, we must do the following:

1. Introduce the list box by saying the items reflect Music Tastes. You can do this using the code:

```
<h4>Music Tastes</h4>
```

2. As you did with the menu list box, insert a `<select>` tag after the introduction text. Within this tag, specify values for the `name` and `size` attributes. The `size` attribute tells the browser to display this number of lines in the box. Additionally, you want to include an attribute called `multiple`, which is the actual key for the browser

to display this element as a multiselect box. This should look like the following:

```
<select name="type" size="4" multiple>
```

3. Finally, use the <option> tag to enter the various items that appear within the box. In the same manner that we defined these options for the <select> menu, you simply need to place the <option> elements after the beginning and before the ending <select> tag. The <option> entries themselves would look like the following:

```
<option value="rock">Rock</option>
<option value="hm">Heavy Metal</option>
<option value="rap">Rap</option>
<option value="country">Country</option>
<option value="gospel">Gospel</option>
```

Once you finish creating this type of form element, you should have something like the following:

```
<h4>Music Tastes</h4>
<select name="type" size="4" multiple>
  <option value="rock">Rock</option>
  <option value="hm">Heavy Metal</option>
  <option value="rap">Rap</option>
  <option value="country">Country</option>
  <option value="gospel">Gospel</option>
</select>
```


<input type="text"> Text Box

The text box is the next element we discuss. A *text box* gathers a single line of text and is one of the most common fields you see used on a form. This type of element is implemented using an <input> tag and assigning its type attribute to text. In this tag, we also use the name attribute, so we can assign the value passed to a name, or key. Like the last section, we introduce the text box by saying "Other," which in our completed form, gives the user the ability to insert a new type of music—one that isn't listed in our multiselect box.

```
<h4>Other</h4>
  <input name="othermusic" type="text">
```

`<input type="checkbox">` Check Box

Check boxes are an alternative way to collect one or more choices from a list of options other than a multiselect box. When check boxes are used, the user can select any, all, or none of the choices you provide. As with text boxes, check boxes are implemented using the `<input>`. The difference in the creation of these two elements is the `type` attribute of a check box takes `checkbox` as the value.

To create a check box, do the following:

1. Introduce the element. The focus of this set of check boxes is sports, so the introduction is

```
<h4>Sports Interests</h4>
```

2. Because we want text before each check box, it's necessary to include this text before we create the check box element. A sample would be like the following, where "Baseball" is displayed just before the check box. Also notice the `value` attribute, which specifies the text that should be sent to the server when the box is checked. The `name` attribute is set to specify the key used to pass the data to the server.

```
Baseball:
<input name="sports" type="checkbox" value="base">
```

3. Now that Baseball is done, repeat Step 2 to add entries for Basketball, Football, and Soccer.

Once we're finished, the HTML for the completed list of check boxes looks like the following.

```
="checkbox" value="foot">
Soccer:
  <input name="sports" type="checkbox" value="soccer">
```

As you can see, it's quite simple to implement a check box element in an HTML form. In fact, this is one of the simplest elements you can implement. Now, let's look into another easy element to implement: the radio button.

<input type="radio"> Radio Buttons

Radio buttons are much like check boxes, except they only allow one of the choices in a group to be selected. These radio buttons, in addition to having individual values, are grouped together by using the same `name` attribute for each instance. The `value` attribute, however, is sent to the server to distinguish it from the others.

Here's how to include the set of radio buttons in your form.

1. Guess what's first? Yep—an introduction! Our user gets the chance to select his or her gender, so use the following sentence:

```
<h4>Gender</h4>
```

2. Next, add the actual HTML that creates the radio buttons. To do this, use the input tag once again. However, this time we set the `type` equal to `radio`. Because we want to have more than one option, we also group the radio buttons by specifying the `name` attribute. Finally, we give them each a value, so we can identify them on the server side.

```
Male
  <input type="radio" name="gender" value="m">
Female
  <input type="radio" name="gender" value="f">
```

The complete HTML for this is as follows:

```
<h4>Gender</h4>
Male
  <input type="radio" name="gender" value="m">
Female
  <input type="radio" name="gender" value="f">
```

Hint

You can have more than one radio button grouping within a given form by using different names for the different groups. As mentioned before, groups of radio buttons are defined by every button in the group using the same name.

<textarea> Text Areas

A text area is like a text box, except it's larger and has the capability to contain more than one row. To create a text area of the size you require, you need to specify values for its `cols` attribute, which is the number of characters, and the `rows` attribute, which is the number of rows. There is not much more to this form element, so rather than step through an example of how to implement it, we are just going to show you the code.

```
<h4>Comments</h4>
  <textarea name="comments" rows="5" cols="40"></textarea>
```

In this piece of HTML, we created a text area that contains five rows and is 40 columns, or characters, wide.

<input type="password"> Password Fields

Sometimes, when you are creating forms, you want to include the capability for the user to submit personal information, such as an ID or password. At the same time, you don't want someone who may be looking over her shoulder to see what she types. The answer for these kinds of situations is to create a text box where the characters entered aren't seen but, instead, are *masked*. On the Web browser's screen, you see asterisks appear instead of the text, which keeps wandering eyes from seeing this private information.

Creating a password field is like creating a text box, except you specify the `type` attribute with a value of `password`. Even though we didn't specify this in the text box example, we also included the use of the size and maxlength attributes that control the dimensions of the box, as well as the maximum number of characters that can be entered. For the box in our form, we use the following:

```
<h4>Password</h4>
  <input type="password" name="passwd" size="15" maxlength="15">
```

As you can see, we gave it the `name` of *passwd* and set the `size` and `maxlength` equal to 15.

<input type="hidden"> Hidden Fields

The concept of a hidden field also exists within forms. These fields are useful when you want to send information to the server, but you'd rather the user not see or modify it. For example, you might send the version number of the form. This is something the user shouldn't be able to and has no reason to modify.

The HTML code used to create this type of field simply uses the <input> element with the type attribute set to *hidden*. Then, within the tag, you use the name and value attributes to specify the extra fields and their values you want to pass.

In our form, as mentioned in the example, we use this type of field to pass the version number of the form. This looks like the following:

```
<input type="hidden" name="version" value="1.0">
```

<input type="reset"> Reset Buttons

Up to this point, we've discussed using the <input> element as a text box, check box, radio button, a password field, and as a hidden field. You can create one more type of item with this element and it has two variations. The first variation is the Reset button.

The Reset button, which isn't required to be present in all forms, has a default text of "Reset," although you can change it using the value attribute. If a form contains this element, then selecting it clears all the fields on the local form. The form isn't submitted when this action is performed, but all user entries are cleared and the default settings/selections are reapplied.

To implement an instance of this button, do the following. The value attribute was included here, but we could have left it out. By using the value attribute here, you can see where it would go.

```
<input type="reset" value="Reset">
```

Hint

Even though you can have more than one Reset button in a form, you should consider only placing a single button at the end of the form to avoid confusion.

<input type="submit"> Submit Buttons

The second variation is the Submit button. Each form you want to submit back to the server must have a Submit button of some form. True, you can get around this to some degree by using a client-side scripting language like JavaScript, but not in general.

To specify that the button is supposed to be a Submit button rather than a Reset button, you set the `type` attribute to *submit*. As with the Reset button, the Submit button can take a `value` attribute to set the text of the button. The default text for the button is "Submit Query."

To create a Submit button, you do the following:

```
<input type="submit" value="Submit">
```

Another Way to Do a Submit Button

Because we've been talking about form elements, we want to include a section on another way to implement a Submit button. This element, which includes an image, can be used in place of the Submit button we just discussed.

When you specify `image` as the `type` for an `<input>` field, you can give the URL in another attribute called `src`. This attribute, which is used in the same manner as the `src` attribute of an `<img>` tag, displays an image to the user instead of a button. Like the Submit button, when the user clicks the image, the form is submitted. When this is done, the coordinates of the mouse pointer are sent in the form *name*.x and *name*.y where *name* is the value of the `name` attribute.

Our Completed Form

At the beginning of this section, we showed you the form we planned to create in Figure 10-3. At this point, we've gone over all the fields needed. All that's left is the basic head and the ending tags of the document. These will look like the following, and will give the document a title, a heading at the top of the page, and a horizontal rule, or line, before the start of the form.

```
<!doctype html public "-//w3c//dtd html 4.0 transitional//en">
<html>
<head>
  <title>Customer Input</title>
</head>
<body>
<h1>Customer Information</h1>
```

```
<hr size="1">

<!-- our form goes here -->

</body>
</html>
```

All we must do now is plug in the form to complete the first half of our task. The completed form, including the rest of the HTML we just defined, looks like:

```
<!doctype html public "-//w3c//dtd html 4.0 transitional//en">
<html>
<head>
   <title>Customer Input</title>
</head>
<body>

<h1>Customer Information</h1>
<hr size="1">
<form action="/cgi-bin/userinfo.cgi" method="post" enctype="application/x-
   www-form-urlencoded">
  <h4>Where Did You Hear About Us?</h4>
  <select name="hear">
    <option value="friend">Friend</option>
    <option value="mag">Magazine</option>
    <option value="tv">TV</option>
    <option value="radio">Radio</option>
    <option value="other">Other</option>
  </select>
  <h4>Music Tastes</h4>
  <select name="type" size="4" multiple>
    <option value="rock">Rock</option>
    <option value="hm">Heavy Metal</option>
    <option value="rap">Rap</option>
    <option value="country">Country</option>
    <option value="gospel">Gospel</option>
  </select>
  <h4>Other</h4>
    <input name="othermusic" type="text">
  <h4>Sports Interests</h4>
    Baseball:
      <input type="checkbox" value="base">
    Basketball:
      <input type="checkbox" value="basket">
    Football:
      <input type="checkbox" value="foot">
    Soccer:
      <input type="checkbox" value="soccer">
  <h4>Gender</h4>
    Male
```

10

```
      <input type="radio" name="gender" value="m">
    Female
      <input type="radio" name="gender" value="f">
  <h4>Comments</h4>
    <textarea name="comments" rows="5" cols="40"></textarea>
  <h4>Password</h4>
    <input type="password" name="passwd" size="15" maxlength="15">
    <input type="hidden" name="version" value="1.0">
  <p>
    <input type="reset" value="Reset">
    <input type="submit" value="Submit">
  </p>
</form>
</body>
</html>
```

Hint

Want more information on HTML elements, such as the ones described here? Check out the HTML and XHTML Recommendations at http://www.w3.org/MarkUp.

Now that you've learned about forms and completed the example, let's look deeper into how forms actually work. In the following sections, we start getting into the trenches of parsing the information that users type into these forms with a Perl CGI script.

How Forms Are Submitted

Every form that's meant to pass information back to the server contains at least one element. Even if only a single text field or radio button exists, the form is submitted when the user presses the Submit button.

When a form is submitted, all the information entered in the fields is sent via HTTP to the program specified by the `action` attribute of the `<form>` tag. The information is sent in plain ASCII text in a *key=value* format, where the name of the element is sent first, followed by an equal sign, and then the value of the data. Each pair is separated with an ampersand (&). The way the information is sent, which can either be `GET` or `POST`, depends on the value defined in the method attribute of the `<form>` tag.

The server application takes this information and potentially returns a results page to the user. The page can be anything you want, ranging from a simple message to a complete query result from a database.

GET

GET is the default method for submitting forms. Although it's the default method, there is a problem with using GET. Because this method appends the information contained in the form to the URL of the action program in the form of a query string, the complete URL can be so long that it exceeds the available environment space. This can cause the server to truncate the URL, which then results in an incorrect submission.

If you decide you won't have any trouble using GET, such as with short forms with small amounts of data, then remember, the output is stored in "URL-encoded" form. When in this form, the information can be obtained from environment variable QUERY_STRING, which is available to your scripts. As mentioned before, each piece of data is sent in a *key=value* pair format. So, for example, if the reader selects a radio button with the name *gender,* the QUERY_STRING environment variable appears as *gender=on*.

POST

POST is the second, and most common, method used to submit forms. This is because it doesn't limit the amount of data that can be passed to the server program. POST can do this because the information isn't passed on the URL but, rather, in the body, or standard input (STDIN in Perl terms) of the request. You specify this method the same way you did GET, except you set the method attribute to *post*.

To read the submitted data to the server, you first need to determine its length. This can be done by using the CONTENT_LENGTH environment variable, after which you can read the exact number of bytes into another variable. The string is URL-encoded, so you need to parse it and decode the escape characters. Because the way this information comes across can be a bit confusing, here's a quick example. To see what this would look like in a browser with some values entered in, look at the following illustration.

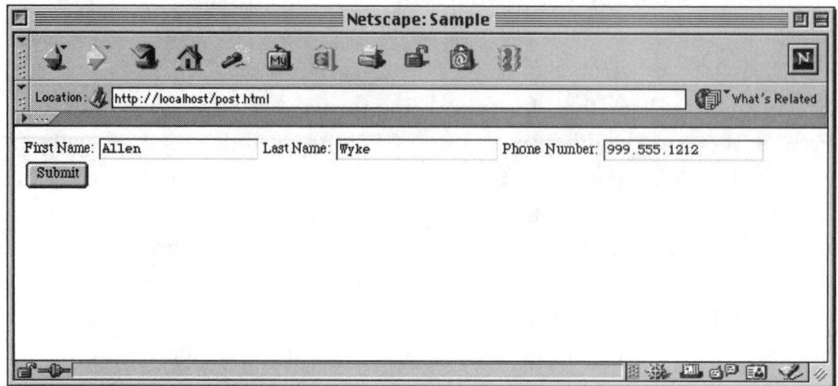

Hint

Does parsing this information by hand seem a bit intimidating to you? Because part of learning means using your resources to search other methods, check the CGI.pm documentation about using the `param()` method, which will do it for you.

```
<html>
<head>
      <title>Sample</title>
</head>
<body>
<form action="/cgi-bin/signin.cgi" method="post">
First Name:
  <input name="first">
Last Name:
  <input name="last">
Phone Number:
  <input name="phone">
  <input type="submit" value="Submit">
</form>
</body>
</html>
```

Using the values shown in the previous illustration, we find *first* would be set to ***Allen***, *last* would be ***Wyke***, and *phone* would be ***999.555.1212***. When the user clicks the Submit button, the browser puts the data in the body of the request in the same order as it was entered in the form. If you were to look at this data, it would look like the following.

```
first=Allen&last=Wyke&phone=999.555.1212
```

Note

If the person had entered a special character, such as a space, the character would be represented as the character's hexadecimal equivalent.

A Simple Perl CGI Program

By this time, you're probably ready to see a Perl program. We have a few more topics to go over before we write one, but we have included a short program for you here, along with some general comments.

As you know, Perl is made up of functions and other language elements. These elements, which you might find easier to think of as commands, let you, the programmer, perform specific functions. For example, the `print()` function sends output STDOUT, which is the user's screen when run from the command line.

When using Perl, or any other language for that matter, to create Web pages, it's necessary for your script to generate the proper HTTP headers. We won't go into great detail about how to generate these headers on your own because we're using the CGI.pm module to do this. To understand a simple Perl CGI program that generates the header using the CGI.pm module and some HTML for the user's browser, look at the following example:

```
#!/usr/bin/perl -w

use CGI;
$query = new CGI;
print $query->header;
```

```
print "<html>";
print "<head>";
print "  <title>A Sample Perl program</title>";
print "</head>";
print "<body> ";
print "  This was generated using Perl!";
print "</body>";
print "</html>";
```

Hint

Want more information on HTTP headers? Check out http://www.w3.org/Protocols and look for the link to RFC 2616.

Sending and Receiving Data

To receive information from a browser and create dynamic documents based on the information, you need to take the data passed from the browser. As we discussed in the section about forms, this is done using the GET and POST methods. No matter which method you use, the browser passes the data to the CGI program, which can then act on it.

In this section of the module, we look at how this information is sent and received.

URL Encoding

Before getting into the specifics of how data can be read, you should know that a browser encodes the data when it is passed. This encoding, which is called *URL encoding,* is the format the browser uses to represent the input from the form when it sends it to the server. During this process, the browser takes all the keys and values from the form and formats them in *key=value* pairs. No matter which method you use to pass the data, each pair is separated by the ampersand (&).

Hint

Need another look at how this will appear? It'll look something like this: *key1=value1&key2=value2&key3=value3*.

Another part of this process involves changing any special characters into their hexadecimal equivalent. These are also often called *ASCII escape sequences.* These sequences appear as %*num,* where *num* is the two-digit hexadecimal number. For example, a plus sign is %2B, and an apostrophe is %27.

Environment Variables

Once the data has been sent to the server, you can obtain that information before you process in a special way. Additionally, you may want to take other bits of information into consideration in your script. This information is stored in CGI environment variables.

When the Web server receives a request for a CGI program, it passes on a set of environment variables that contain information about the server and its environment. The Web server also adds to that set of information about the browser and the current request. After the server executes the script, it then takes the output and sends it back to the browser. Table 10-1 contains the CGI environment variables common in most servers.

Note

Different servers can have different variables. They can also have different names for variables, although this generally isn't the case.

Environment Variable	**Description**
AUTH_TYPE	Type of authentication used to validate the user.
CONTENT_LENGTH	Size of the content file returned.
CONTENT_TYPE	Content type of the `POST`ed data.
GATEWAY_INTERFACE	CGI version the server supports.
HTTP_ACCEPT	MIME type the browser accepts for this request.
HTTP_USER_AGENT	Complete name/identifier of browser.
PATH_INFO	Path information, such as `/sports/basketball`.
PATH_TRANSLATED	The translated PATH_INFO, which is also called the physical path.

Table 10-1 **Common CGI Environment Variables**

Environment Variable	Description
QUERY_STRING	Any text after the "?" in the request URL. This is where `GET` data is stored.
REMOTE_ADDR	IP address of the browser making the request.
REMOTE_HOST	Hostname of the browser making the request.
REMOTE_IDENT	Name of the remote user.
REQUEST_METHOD	Method used to request data, such as `GET` or `POST`.
SCRIPT_NAME	Path to the CGI script being executed.
SERVER_NAME	Hostname of the server.
SERVER_PORT	Port number to which the server is listening.
SERVER_PROTOCOL	Protocol name and version used in the response by the server.
SERVER_SOFTWARE	Name and version of the server software.

Table 10-1 **Common CGI Environment Variables** ***(continued)***

Do you want to see what these look like? Here are the results of running this Perl program, which displays these CGI environment variables. See Figure 10-4 to see what's returned to an Internet Explorer 5 browser from an IIS 5 Web server.

```
#!/usr/bin/perl -w

use CGI;
$query = new CGI;
print $query->header;
foreach $envvar (sort keys %ENV){
      print "$envvar:$ENV{$envvar}\n<br>";
}
```

Cookies

With all the hoopla about privacy these days, we're sure you know many sites *drop* cookies on you when you're browsing. This cookie is nothing more than a file that contains an identifier—like ID—a value—like 12345—and some other information that indicates what servers can read it and when it expires.

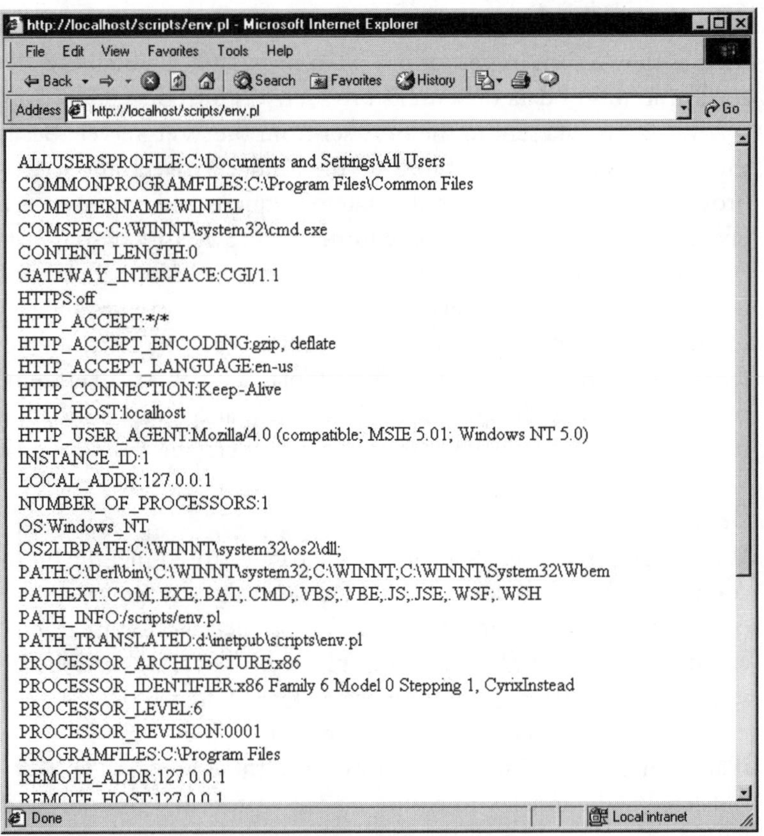

Figure 10-4 **Results of running our CGI program that outputs the environment variables**

In the next section, we look quickly at cookies because they're important in creating HTML content and tracking users. If, for instance, you want to build a shopping cart on your site, then you probably want to use cookies to identify your users as they shop, so you can keep their cart with them and up-to-date.

Why Cookies?

Because the CGI client/server connection is a stateless event, which means each request is unique and unrelated to any other, all information about a previous visit is lost when the connection is terminated (that is, the page is finished being sent back to the browser). And because identifying your users as they return to your site is often necessary, the concept of storing small amounts of data on a user's browser was introduced.

A *cookie* is data sent to the browser from the Web server. Because the cookie is sent back and forth in the header between the server and browser, it lets you preserve the state of requests and responses. This enables you to monitor, in some form, the browser requesting data.

The most common use for cookies is to store information about the user, so you can deliver new or customized information to them. For example, you may want to check to see if this person is visiting your site for the first time. If so, then you can display a different advertisement or offering each time this person visits. You can also create a shopping cart to store one or more products the person considers purchasing at a later time.

Basics

When a browser receives a cookie, the data is stored in a file on the user's computer. The name, location, and format of this storage varies, depending on the browser. Netscape browsers, for instance, store it in a single file called `cookies.txt`. Internet Explorer browser, on the other hand, store these in separate files under a "cookies" folder.

Some limits also exist to the number of cookies a browser can hold. If additional cookies are added that exceed these limits, the oldest cookie is deleted. Additionally, to ensure no site writes large amounts of data to your disk, a limitation on the size of the cookie data has been imposed, so it can be no larger than 4K.

Note

New cookies are written to the hard disk when the user exits the browser, whereas a modified cookie is written immediately. This is so any information the cookie has that has changed won't be lost in a crash.

Cookies can be created in three different ways:

- You can send a `Set-Cookie` header directive in the HTTP response, which is the method we discuss in this module.
- If the browser supports JavaScript, you can set a cookie by using the `document.cookie()` method.

- Finally, it's possible to use the `<meta>` tag within an HTML document to set a cookie.

Fields

A cookie is sent to a browser by using a `Set-Cookie` header directive. This is part of an HTTP response generated by the Web server or a CGI script. This header directive is sent in the following format:

```
Set-Cookie: key=value; expires=date; path=dirpath; domain=domain; secure
```

Not all these are required or are self-explanatory, so let's look at each of them.

- **key=value** The key and value pair contains the name of the cookie and the value you assigned to it. This is what you should look for in your CGI scripts—it contains the information you want to leave on the browser.
- **expires=date** Specifies how long the cookie persists. Once this date has passed, the browser removes the cookie. The date setting uses the following format:

```
Weekday, DD-Mon-YYYY HH:MM:SS GMT
```

These break down and mean the following:

- *Weekday* represents the day of the week, like ***Monday***.
- *DD* represents the date, such as ***23***.
- *Mon* represents the three-character abbreviation for the month, as in ***Oct***.
- *YYYY* represents the year, as with ***2001***.
- *HH* represents the hour, like ***08***.
- *MM* represents the minutes, like ***58***.
- *SS* represents the seconds, like ***43***.
- *GMT* stands for *Greenwich Mean Time*.

Note

Not all browsers require all these fields to be specified when you set a cookie. In fact, if the date isn't included, the cookie will be a session cookie and will last until the reader exits her browser.

- **path=dirpath** Specifies the path on the server for which the cookie applies. This is typically set to "/", commonly referred to as the *root,* but it's possible to specify another directory. This means only files and programs in this directory have the capability to read the cookie once it's set.

Note

If this setting isn't specified, the path defaults to the path of the document that set the cookie.

- **domain=domain** Specifies the domain for which the cookie is to be returned. This item can contain a complete machine name, such as *shop.osborne.com,* or just the domain, such as *.osborne.com.* When you use the second method, all machines within that domain have access to reading, deleting, or modifying the cookie.
- **secure** Indicates the cookie should be transmitted only if you are running a secure server. This setting keeps the cookie from being transmitted on a nonsecure port.

Note

If you're not running a secure server and you use the secure setting, the cookies won't be sent.

Setting

Setting a cookie when using the CGI.pm module is easy. It provides all the necessary methods of specifying the values for the `Set-Cookie` directive. To see how this might be done, look at the following. In this example, we set a cookie named *ID,* with a value of *12345.* It expires one year from today, it is readable by all directories starting with the root directory, can be passed back to the server located at 192.168.1.101, and isn't secure. The last line is what actually prints the cookie in the HTTP header before it's sent to the browser.

```
#!/usr/bin/perl -w
use CGI;

$query = new CGI;
$cookie = $query->cookie(-name=>'ID',
                         -value=>'12345',
                         -expires=>'+1y',
                         -path=>'/',
                         -domain=>'192.168.1.101',
                         -secure=>0);
print $query->header(-cookie=>$cookie);
```

The full header that's sent looks like the following. And, if you configured your browser to prompt you for cookies, then you see something like Figure 10-5, which shows an Internet Explorer 5 browser prompting you to accept this cookie.

```
HTTP/1.1 200 OK
Server: Microsoft-IIS/5.0
Date: Fri, 01 Sep 2000 17:40:05 GMT
Set-Cookie: ID=12345; domain=127.0.0.1; path=/;
expires=Sat, 01-Sep-2001 17:40:05 GMT
Date: Fri, 01 Sep 2000 17:40:05 GMT
Content-Type: text/html
```

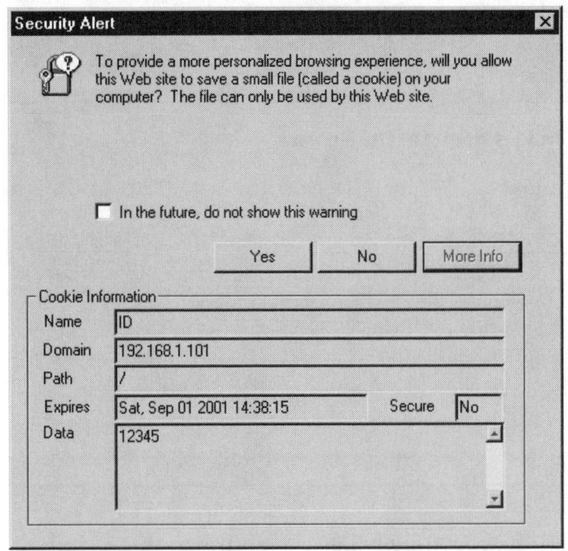

Figure 10-5 Internet Explorer 5 prompting you to accept the cookie

10

Now that you see how to set the cookie and you understand what has to happen to modify it, here's how to read a cookie.

Reading

Reading a cookie isn't complex. All you must do is access the HTTP_COOKIE environment variable to see all data. So, for instance, you might have something like the following. Look at the following illustration to see the output after we set the cookie in our last example.

```
#!/usr/bin/perl -w

use CGI;
$query = new CGI;

print $query->header;
print "<html><head>";
print $query->title('Cookies');
print '</head><body>';
print $query->h3('Cookies Sent To The Server');
print $ENV{'HTTP_COOKIE'};
print '</body></html>';
```

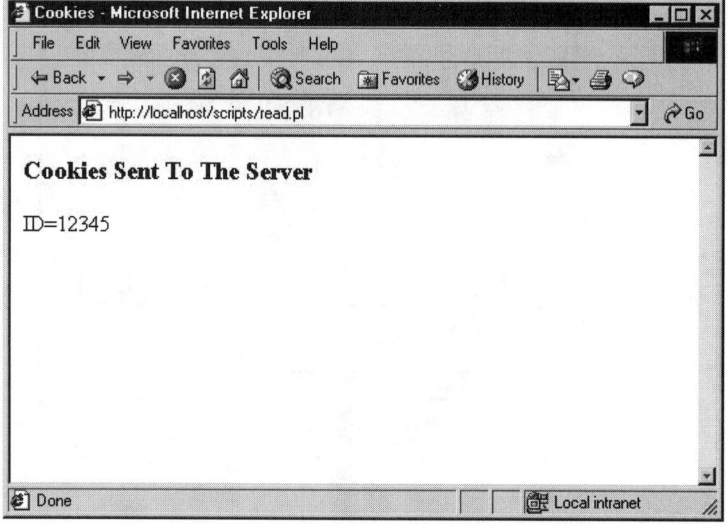

Obviously, this only prints the entire cookie string, so if you have more than one cookie the server can read, you simply see them listed in a comma-separated format. Because you may want to separate these cookies for individual reading purposes, we show you how to create an array of cookies, and then write them back to the browser.

Because we want more than one cookie, we set another cookie, called *ID2,* using the same method as before. Then we run the following script. The output can be seen in Figure 10-6.

```
#!/usr/local/bin/perl -w

use CGI;
$query = new CGI;
$i = 0;

if(defined $ENV{HTTP_COOKIE}) {
  @carray = split(/;/,$ENV{HTTP_COOKIE});
}

print $query->header;
print "<html><head>";
print $query->title('Cookies');
print '</head><body>';
print $query->h3('Cookies Sent To The Server');
print "Total Cookie String: $ENV{'HTTP_COOKIE'}<br>";
foreach $cookie (@carray) {
  print "<br>Cookie[$i]: $cookie";
  $i++;
}
print '</body></html>';
```

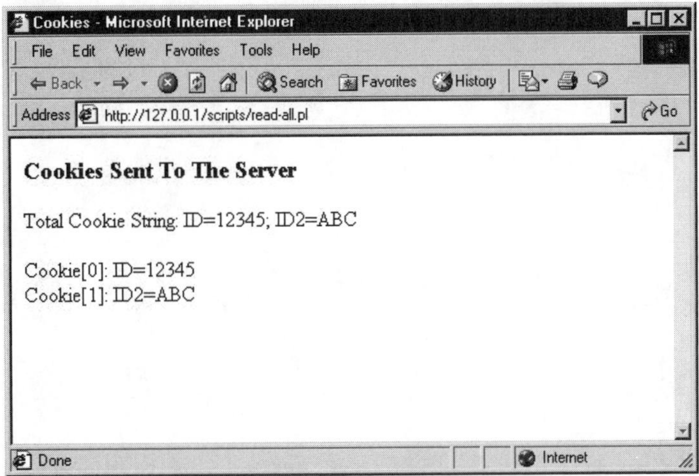

Figure 10-6 Returning the entire cookie string, and then breaking it into individual array entries

10

Once you create a cookie array, it's easy to scan for a specific cookie. All you need to do is add a function that searches the array for the name of the cookie. The following code shows you how this can be done. Notice the `&findcookie` function.

```
#!/usr/bin/perl -w

use CGI;
$query = new CGI;
$i = 0;
$j = 0;
$found = 0;

if(defined $ENV{HTTP_COOKIE}) {
  @carray = split(/;/,$ENV{HTTP_COOKIE});
}

print $query->header;
print "<html><head>";
print $query->title('Cookies');
print '</head><body>';
print $query->h3('Cookies Sent To The Server');
print "Total Cookie String: $ENV{'HTTP_COOKIE'}<br>";
foreach $cookie (@carray) {
  print "<br>Cookie[$i]: $cookie";
  $i++;
}

# call the function and look for the ID2 cookie
&findcookie('ID2');

print '</body></html>';

sub findcookie{

  # store value we are searching for in $cfind
  $cfind = $_[0];

  # print to screen what we are looking for
  print $query->h3("Looking for $cfind");

  # iterate through array
  foreach $cookie (@carray) {
```

```
    # separate keys from values and remove whitespace
    ($cname, $cvalue) = split(/=/,$cookie);
    $cname =~ s/ //;

    # see if we have a match
    if($cfind eq $cname){
      print "I found your cookie at location $j!";
      $found = 1;
    }
    $j++;
  }

  # if no match, let the user know
  if(!$found){
    print "Your cookie was not found";
  }
}
```

If you run this program on the same browser as we did our last two, then you should see the same thing as in Figure 10-7.

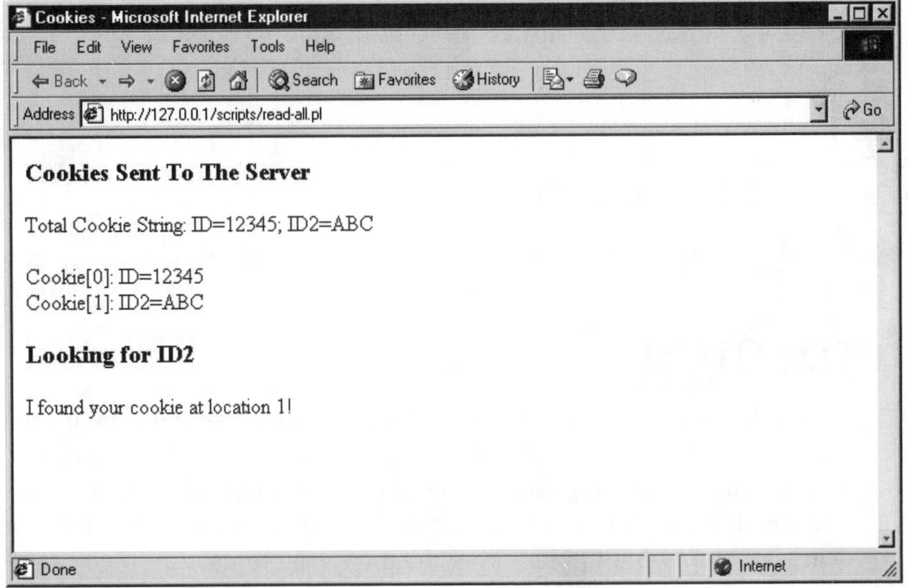

Figure 10-7 Checking to see if a specific cookie exists

Deleting

To delete a cookie quickly, simply set the expiration date to a time earlier than the current time. So, we could use the following to delete our *ID2* cookie. Notice that we passed the `cookie()` function in CGI.pm a -1 for the `expires` parameter.

```
#!/usr/bin/perl -w
use CGI;

$query = new CGI;
$cookie = $query->cookie(-name=>'ID2',
                         -value=>'ABC',
                         -expires=>'-1',
                         -path=>'/',
                         -domain=>'192.168.1.101',
                         -secure=>0);
print $query->header(-cookie=>$cookie);
```

Hint

Want more information on cookies? Check out http://www.cookiecentral.com for a wealth of information.

1-Minute Drill

- **Name one thing for which cookies are good.**

Returning Data

Now that we've built our form and have read in the information, it's time to see how the data must be returned. As mentioned earlier, most of the hard work of returning data is handled by the CGI.pm module. To return a complete, unmodified header, all you have to do is include the following in your script—but this isn't everything we want to do.

- **Some answers are shopping carts, identifying returning users, and tracking sessions**

```
# of course, you have to include the module and create an instance first
use CGI;
$query = new CGI;

# and this is the line that creates the proper header
print $query->header;
```

Processing Our Form

Now that our form is built and we've discussed how CGI scripts work and process information, let's process the form. The first thing to do is write a script that can handle the form—a script we call `userinfo.cgi`. As with most of the other scripts, we use the CGI.pm to handle our form. To do this, first include an instance of the CGI.pm object in this module and write back the header. This is done with

```
#!/usr/bin/perl -w

use CGI;
$query = new CGI;
print $query->header;
```

Now it's time to read in the keys and their values. To do this, the CGI module has a subroutine called `param`. All we must do to read in a value for a given key is to pass the key's name to the `param` subroutine. So, for instance, if we want to read in text area (comments) in our form, we use the following line of code:

```
$query->param('comments');
```


That's basically it! All we must do now is put in the code to read in each of our form elements, and then create a page on which to display them. To do this, we can use the following program. As you can see, there's nothing special here and it's quite repetitive.

```
#!/usr/bin/perl -w

use CGI;
$query = new CGI;
print $query->header;

# pulldown menu
print $query->b("Where Did You Hear About Us?<br>");
```

```
print $query->param('hear');

# multi-select box
print $query->b("<br>Music Tastes<br>");
print $query->param('type');

# textbox
print $query->b("<br>Other<br>");
print $query->param('othermusic');

# checkbox
print $query->b("<br>Sports Interest<br>");
print $query->param('sports');
print $query->param('basket');
print $query->param('foot');
print $query->param('soccer');

# radio button
print $query->b("<br>Gender<br>");
print $query->param('gender');

# textarea
print $query->b("<br>Comments<br>");
print $query->param('comments');

# password
print $query->b("<br>Password<br>");
print $query->param('passwd');

# hidden
print $query->b("<br>Hidden (Version)<br>");
print $query->param('version');
```

Now all we have to do is copy this program to our CGI directory and submit our form. Figure 10-8 shows what the form looks like after it's completed, and Figure 10-9 shows our result page.

Quick Formatting

Up until this point, we've been using the `print()` function over and over. You can actually save yourself the time of entering it by enclosing all lines within a token. For instance, you could use `print<<"_HTML_";`

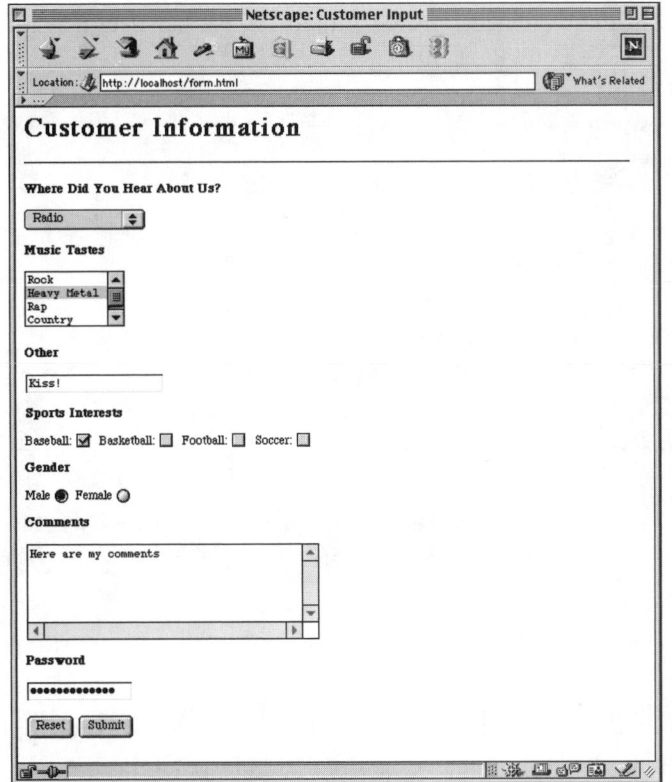

Figure 10-8 Our completed form

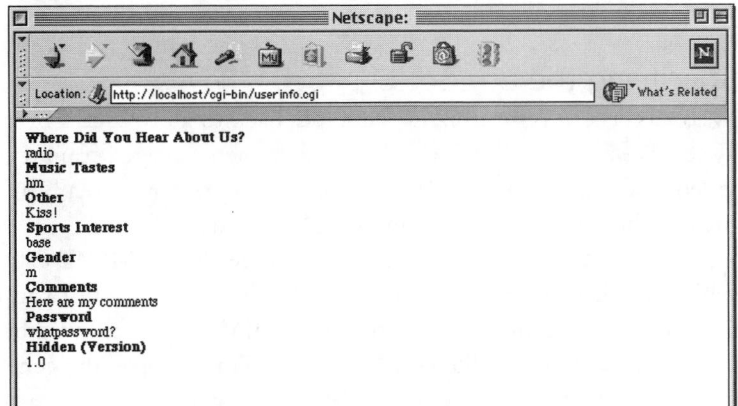

Figure 10-9 Our result page

to start the sequence, `_HTML_` to end it. Rather than trying to explain this, here's a quick example.

```
#!/usr/bin/perl -w

use CGI;

# define an instance of CGI and write out the header
$query = new CGI;
print $query->header;

# print all of the below
print<<"_HTML_";
<html>
<head>
  <title>Using Tokens</title>
</head>
<body>
<p>All of this will now be printed without having to specifically use the
print() function for each line.</p>
</body>
</html>
_HTML_
```

Extra Things You Can Do Manually

Ahhhh, the beauty of a complete Perl library. CGI.pm makes it easy, doesn't it? Well, what if you want to change some of the defaults yourself and not have it set them? Things like header directives. What then? Well, you can do this, so don't fret. Here's a quick look at a few items you may want to do yourself.

Specifying the `Content Type`

Web servers can return many data types back to a browser. For example, Web servers can send back an HTML document, images, plain text, audio, video, and many others. However, part of the response to a browser must include the type of information being returned.

The `Content-type` header lets you specify any MIME data type, which can then be properly handled by the browser. The first part of the `Content-type` header is the top-level MIME type, followed by a forward slash, and then the MIME subtype. For example, the general `Content-type` returned for HTML documents is

```
Content-type: text/html
```

When using the CGI.pm module, this header directive is set using the following format:

```
#!/usr/bin/perl -w
use CGI;

$query = new CGI;
print $query->header(-type=>'text/html');
```

Redirecting

A second popular header you may want to use is the `Location` header, which lets you redirect the browser to another location. You see this often when a page has been moved. This is one of the easiest things to implement and can be done with or without the help of the CGI.pm module.

If you want to do it without the help of the CGI.pm module, then use the following syntax. This, for example, would send a user to the `/error.html` page. Notice the `\n\r` at the end of the statement. This is necessary to tell the user agent that it ends the header portion of the response. Note, this should ONLY be used on the LAST header directive, otherwise any header directives below it is interpreted as the body and displayed in the browser.

```
#!/usr/bin/perl -w
print "Location: /error.html\n\n";
```

If you decide to use the CGI.pm module, then you can implement a redirect by simply having the following:

```
#!/usr/bin/perl -w
use CGI;

$query = new CGI;
print $query->redirect('/error.html');
```

Hint

One advantage of using CGI.pm is it also inserts the rest of the needed HTTP header directives. Browsers usually work without these HTTP header directives, but it's more complete with them.

HTTP Status Codes

When a server responds to an HTTP request, it does so with both a header and a body, as previously discussed. Part of the header, however, contains the status code of the response. This status tells the browser what kind of response is being returned. So, for instance, if an error has occurred or if the browser should be redirected to another location, this code is what tells the browser.

Generally, the Web server specifies these codes, although there may be a need in your script to do so. When using the CGI.pm module, all you need to do is set the `-status` attribute of the header property. Say, for instance, you want to send back a fictitious status of 699 to the browser. You could do this with the following code.

```
#!/usr/bin/perl -w
use CGI;

$query = new CGI;
print $query->header(-status=>'699 My Crazy Status');
```

This returns the following to the browser:

```
HTTP/1.0 699 My Crazy Status
Content-type: text/html
```

To send a real status code, you need to know what the responses are, as defined by the HTTP specification. These are grouped in the following five categories as defined by the HTTP 1.1 *Request For Comments* (*RFC*) 2616.

- **1*xx* (Informational)** Request received, continuing process.
- **2*xx* (Success)** The action was successfully received, understood, and accepted.
- **3*xx* (Redirection)** Further action must be taken to complete the request.
- **4*xx* (Client Error)** The request contains bad syntax or cannot be fulfilled.
- **5*xx* (Server Error)** The server failed to fulfill an apparently valid request.

Table 10-2 lists and describes each of the possible status codes and responses.

Code	Response	Description
100	Continue	The client should continue with its request.
101	Switching Protocols	Client has requested server switch version of HTTP protocol for its request.
200	OK	Transaction succeeded.
201	Created	Response indicates the *URI* (*Universal Resource Identifier*) by which the new document should be known.
202	Accepted	Accepted for processing, but processing hasn't completed.
203	Partial Information	Information returned isn't definitive or complete.
204	No Content	Request was received, but there's nothing to return.
205	Reset Content	The server has fulfilled the request and the user agent should reset the current document being viewed.
206	Partial Content	The server has fulfilled the partial `GET` request by the user agent.
300	Multiple Choices	Resource requested is available at multiple locations.
301	Moved Permanently	Data requested has been moved.
302	Found	Data requested has been found at the other locations.
303	See Other	Recommends the client try different URL or access method.
304	Not Modified	Client has performed a `GET`, but the document hasn't been changed.
305	Use Proxy	The request resource must be obtained from the server specified in the returned `Location:` field.

Table 10-2 HTTP Status Codes

Code	Response	Description
306	Unused	This code was used in a previous version of HTTP, but is no longer used. It is currently reserved.
307	Temporary Redirect	States the resource requested has temporarily moved.
400	Bad Request	Incorrect request, such as incorrect syntax.
401	Unauthorized	Authentication request failed.
402	Payment Required	Reserved for response with valid ChargeTo header.
403	Forbidden	Request cannot be granted.
404	Not Found	The document, query, or URL couldn't be found.
405	Method Not Allowed	The method specified in the `Request-Line` field sent by the user agent isn't allowed on the resource.
406	Not Acceptable	According to the `Accept` header sent by the user agent, the requested resource is unacceptable.
407	Proxy Authentication Required	Similar to 401, this code specifies the user agent must first authenticate itself within the proxy.
408	Request Time-out	The client didn't complete the request within the time specified by the user agent.
409	Conflict	The request couldn't be completed given the current state of the resource.
410	Gone	The resource is no longer located on the server and no forwarding address is available.
411	Length Required	Server refuses the request with the `Content-Length` being sent by the user agent.

Table 10-2 **HTTP Status Codes** ***(continued)***

Code	Response	Description
412	Precondition Failed	One or more of the Request header fields evaluated to false on the request.
413	Request Entity Too Large	The resource being requested is larger than allowed by the server.
414	Request-URI Too Large	The URI to the resource being requested is longer than allowed by the server.
415	Unsupported Media Type	The entity of the request is in a format not supported by the requested resource for the requested method.
416	Requested range not satisfiable	A request included a Range request header field, none of the range specifier values in this field overlap the current extent of the requested resource, and the request didn't include an `If-Range` request header field.
417	Expectation Failed	The expectation specified in the `Expect` request header field couldn't be met by this server or, if the server is a proxy, the server has unambiguous evidence that the request couldn't be met by the next-hop server.
500	Internal Server Error	Server experienced an internal error.
501	Not Implemented	The server doesn't support the function requested.
502	Bad Gateway	The server is temporarily unavailable. This is sometimes sent to prevent a system overload.
503	Service Unavailable	The server is temporarily overloaded or down for maintenance.

Table 10-2 **HTTP Status Codes** ***(continued)***

Code	Response	Description
504	Gateway Time-out	Gateway is overloaded; server is using another gateway or service took longer to respond than the client was configured to wait.
505	HTTP Version not supported	The server doesn't support or refuses to support the HTTP version specified in the request header.

Table 10-2 HTTP Status Codes *(continued)*

> **Hint**
>
> If you want more information on server codes, check out the complete RFC 2616 at http://www.w3.org/Protocols/rfc2616/rfc2616-sec6.html.

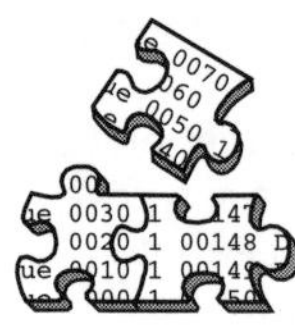

Project 10-2: Creating Your Own Form and Script

Now that we've gone through a complete example of creating a form and Perl CGI script to handle it, it's time for you to try one! Here are the step-by-step instructions to help you along.

Step-by-Step

1. Create your form and put it on your Web server.
2. Create a CGI script to handle all the necessary elements of the form.
3. Place the CGI script on your Web server in your CGI directory. If you're using UNIX, be sure to set the proper permissions (**chmod 755 <script_name>**). If you're using MacPerl, be sure to save it as a CGI script.
4. Verify the `action` attribute of your `<form>` has the correct URL to your CGI script.
5. Submit the form and see if it works!

Debugging Your Program

One of the best methods of testing and debugging a Perl program is to run it from the command line, although this may be impossible for your CGI programs. Although debugging scripts is the focus of Module 12, "Error Messages and Debugging," we give you some quick pointers here on debugging your CGI scripts.

- Make sure the file permissions are set correctly for the directories and the files your script needs to access.
- If you are running your script on a UNIX system, make sure the path to the Perl binary (found at the top of the script) is correct. To check the location, type **which perl** from a command line of a telnet session.
- Make sure you include the CGI.pm module before using it. To do so, type **use CGI;** near the top of your script.
- Because you'll be writing information back to the browser and calling subroutines, check for mismatched quote ("") or tick ('') marks in your code.
- Also check for mismatched curly braces ({}), and starting and ending HTML tags (<> and </>).
- Try compiling the code at the command line with **perl -wc scriptname.cgi**. This can uncover many common coding errors.

Moving On

In this module, we briefly touched on many issues—everything from forms, to submissions, and CGI. We discussed the general concepts of CGI and using Perl as the language of choice to create these scripts.

In the next module, we look at Perl system functions. These functions are implementations of popular system calls across the various environments in which Perl runs.

Mastery Check

1. How do you include the CGI.pm module in your code?

A. use CGI;

B. begin CGI;

C. open CGI;

2. The HTTP response is broken into two components. Which of the following two are they?

A. Beginning

B. Header

C. Body

D. Content

3. If you want to redirect a user to a different location, how can you do that?

A. Using the `redirect` subroutine from the CGI.pm module

B. Printing `Location:` and the URL in the head of your response

C. Neither A nor B

D. Both A and B

Module 11

Cross-Platform Functions and Issues

The Goals of This Module

- Learn about the `system()` function
- Understand issues that pertain to specific operating systems
- Complete a cross-platform code sample

So far, you've covered a lot of ground in the Perl programming world. You have the interpreting engine installed and running, you learned many of the semantics of the language, you've been exposed to working with directories and files, you've been taught the concepts of regular expressions and libraries, and you've applied your knowledge in working with databases and CGI scripts. That's a lot of information to cover!

But, now it's time to take another step. In previous modules, we touched on some of the issues around running Perl on different operating systems and discussed some of the differences in implementing scripts on these systems. At this point, we want to touch on some language-specific details about running Perl on Windows, UNIX, and Mac OS. In Module 1, we mentioned items like different path delimiters for each of these systems, but our focus in this module is deeper than that. In this module, we want to look at the following.

- **The `system()` function** This function lets you execute commands native to the system, including the passing of arguments.
- **Operating System Specific Issues** This section is a summary of some of the main issues you see when you write cross-platform code.

As you can see, we have our plate full for this module. Much of this information isn't easy to understand conceptually. Why does function `x()` work on one system and not on the other? Why does function `y()` work a little differently on different systems? These are questions you might have during the next few hours while you go through this module.

Don't worry, though, we do our best to present you with the information you need to know and avoid any confusing topics. Because we include hints and tips on where to get additional information, you can follow up on topics you're especially interested in after you finish this module.

Let's get started now by covering the `system()` function.

system()

Now that you're becoming more and more familiar with the Perl programming language, have you begun to think about some of the things you could automate or do on your system? Things like launching several applications at once or deleting excess files in your temporary directories? These are all tasks that usually involve invoking one or more commands each, so you could easily run into 20 or 30 commands just to accomplish a dozen or so actions you may do on a daily basis.

Well, this is where the `system()` function comes in handy. This function, which can take a single command and any arguments, or an array containing a command and arguments, executes the command that was passed with the arguments. Your script calls this function, which executes the command, and then waits until the command has finished before returning to your script.

Hint

If you want to check out another function that performs the same tasks as the `system()` function, but that *never* waits for the command to return, then check your Perl manpages for the `exec()` function.

The function itself, as previously mentioned, can take a single command with any arguments or an array with all this information. For a single command on Windows or UNIX where you want to launch the Netscape HTML editor (Composer) with a specific file, you could use

```
system("netscape", "-edit", "index.html");
```

Note

We assume the **netscape** application is in your PATH for this to work.

If you want to do this same thing using an array, you could do the following:

```
@composer_index("netscape", "-edit", "index.html");
system(@composer_index);
```

As you can see, the syntax for this function is fairly simple. You should know some things about using this function, however, in terms of error codes and what is returned.

Return Codes

The return value of the `system()` function is the exit status of the program, as returned by the `wait()` system call. If you have a -1 returned in the `$?` variable, then an error has occurred. You can obtain a description of the error by accessing the `$!` variable. The following quick example, which we name `sys_test.pl`, shows how this might work.

Note

Because of the way `wait()` works on Window's systems, you must divide the returned value by -256 to get the actual exit status. So, in the following example, you need to replace `$exit = $?` with `$exit = -$?/256`.

```
#!/usr/bin/perl -w

# store command and arguments in array
@args = ("abcdefg", "blah", "blah", "blah");

# call system() function
$result = system(@args);

# if $? contains anything, store values in appropriate variable
$exit = $?;          # contains exit status
$sig = $? & 127;     # contains signal number
$core = $? & 128;    # contains 1 if program performed core dump

# if system() call returned non-zero then problem. exit
# program and send error information to STDOUT
$result == 0 or die "\n" . "@args" . "= @args\nExit: $exit\nSignal
Number: $sig\nCore: $core\n\nMessage: $!";
```

In this example, we first stored a fictitious command, *abcdefg,* and its arguments, *blah blah blah,* in an array. We then pass them to the `system()` function and store the results of doing so in the `$result` variable. By storing the result, as you see shortly, we can check to see if an error did occur. But, before we do so, we store any values `$?` has in specific variables.

As we mentioned earlier, if `$?` contains –1, then a problem occurred. In addition, a bitwise AND comparison with 127 returns a signal number and the same type of comparison with 128 tells you if a core dump occurred. These are generated if the program performs a bad operation, whereby all the memory and state information is written to a file that can later be analyzed. In our example, we stored these values in variables, so we can output, if needed.

The final line in our program checks to see what happened when we called the `system()` function. If the result returned in our variable is equal to zero, then all went well and the program is running. If a problem occurred, however, we stop the execution of the program with the `die()` function and write the original command and argument array and our variables to STDOUT. In addition, we also write the value of `$!`, which contains a description of the error that occurred. Running this program on the Windows platform results in what is shown in Figure 11-1.

Note

As you can see in Figure 11-1, some operating systems write their own message to STDOUT if an error occurred. In our example, Windows wrote "The name specified is not recognized as an internal or external command, operable program, or batch file." This varies from system to system, but it's normal.

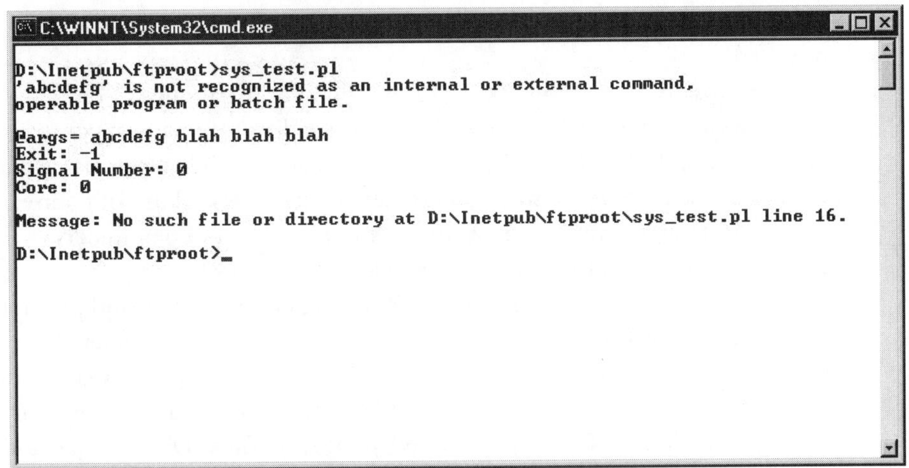

Figure 11-1 Results of running our sys_test.pl script

1-Minute Drill

- **What number do you have to divide by on a Windows system to obtain the correct exit status?**
- **What does doing a bitwise AND on `$?` and 128 give you?**

Using the Function

The real issues when using the `system()` function arise from the fact that application syntax and commands vary from operating system to operating system. For this reason, we decided to break this section into brief Windows, UNIX, and Mac OS subsections to address some of the issues. This isn't because the `system()` function responds any differently on these systems but, instead, because the systems can execute commands and call programs differently across the platforms.

Windows

In our previous example, we already exposed one Windows-specific issue—that the system may also write information to `STDOUT` if an error occurs. Another issue, however, is how Windows deals with folder and directory paths that include spaces in them. For instance, the `Program Files` directory contains a space between the word Program and the word Files. If you simply try to pass this as is, you'll find an error is returned.

For those of you who looked at how the hybrid 16- and 32-bit Windows systems—such as 95/98/Me—stores directory names, you probably found they stored them internally as an eight-character name and a three-character extension (a total of eleven characters). This, of course, isn't how they are displayed in Windows Explorer or in open folders. `Program Files`, for instance, is actually `progra~1`.

If you want to see this, go to a DOS dialog box (or command prompt, as they're often called), which uses the `command.com` environment (versus `cmd.exe` for Windows NT/2000), and type **cd progra~1** on the drive that contains your `Program Files` directory. This changes you into that directory. Now, try typing **cd program files**. Didn't work, did

---

- **256**
- **Tells if a core dump has occurred**

it? Now try this—**cd "program files"** and include the quotes. That should work. Windows NT/2000 users, if in the `cmd.exe` environment, can simply type **cd program files** because the system actually stores the longer filenames.

So, what does this mean for you? Well, if you try to launch an application where you have to specify a path that contains a space, even on Windows NT/2000, you need to put the path (not the drive letter) in quotes. Let's say, for instance, you want to open the `Program Files` folder to see the contents. This can be done using the `start` command, which is internal to the environment (that is, you won't find a `start.exe` application). Without using Perl, you could do this by typing **start c:\ "program files"**. Without the quote, Windows thinks you're passing two arguments, *program* and *files,* rather than one, so it doesn't work. In your Perl scripts, you have to do the same thing. For your argument list, then, you need to do the following:

```
@args = ("start", "c:\"program files");
```

Notice we had to use single quotes to be able to put quotes in our argument list. Let's try this in a script named `sys_win.pl`. We can use our previous program to get going—all it takes is a single change. The complete program would look like the following. See Figure 11-2 to see the result of running this program, which opens the Program Files directory in a window.

```
#!/usr/bin/perl -w

# store command and arguments in array
@args = ("start", "c:\"program files");

# call system() function
$result = system(@args);

# if $? contains anything, store values in appropriate variable
$exit = $? / 256;  # contains exit status
$sig = $? & 127;   # contains signal number
$core = $? & 128;  # contains 1 if program performed core dump

# if system() call returned non-zero then problem. exit
# program and send error information to STDOUT
$result == 0 or die "\n" . "@args" . "= @args\nExit: $exit\nSignal
Number: $sig\nCore: $core\n\nMessage: $!";
```

11

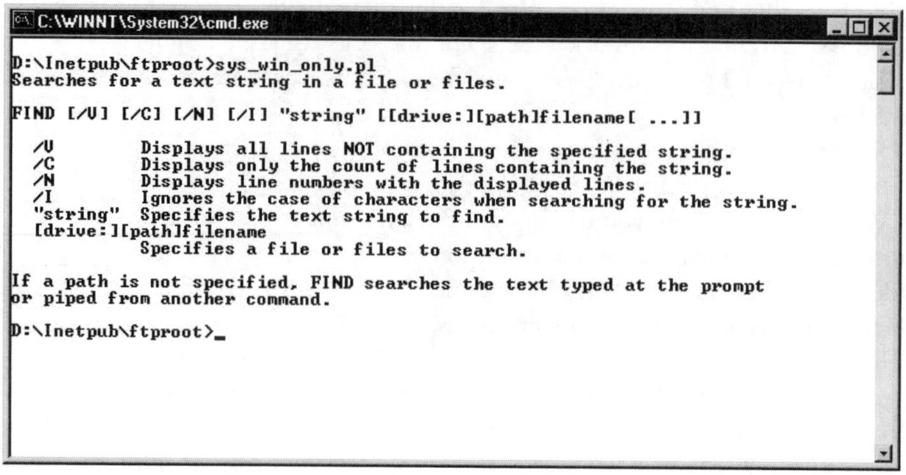

```
C:\WINNT\System32\cmd.exe

D:\Inetpub\ftproot>sys_win_only.pl
Searches for a text string in a file or files.

FIND [/V] [/C] [/N] [/I] "string" [[drive:][path]filename[ ...]]

  /V         Displays all lines NOT containing the specified string.
  /C         Displays only the count of lines containing the string.
  /N         Displays line numbers with the displayed lines.
  /I         Ignores the case of characters when searching for the string.
  "string"   Specifies the text string to find.
  [drive:][path]filename
             Specifies a file or files to search.

If a path is not specified, FIND searches the text typed at the prompt
or piped from another command.

D:\Inetpub\ftproot>_
```

Figure 11-2 **Results of running our `sys_win.pl` script to open the Program Files directory**

Another issue to watch for in the Windows environment is this: by default, nearly all Windows applications take argument options with a / in front of them. For instance, if you want to see the syntax for the find command, you type **find /?**. This means in your Perl scripts that contain argument options, you also need to include the / preceding any options you need to pass. Here's an example:

```
@args = ("find", "/?");
```

One final item that may come up in your use of the `system()` command, which is true for all systems, is you must make sure any program you attempt to launch must be internal to the system, in the `%PATH%` environment variable, or contain a complete path to the actual executable. In other words, the system must be able to find the program.

A good test is to go to a command prompt, change to the working directory of your Perl script and type the command you expect to run. If it works, great—you are fine. If not, then you need to include either the directory that contains the program you are executing in your `PATH` or to specify the entire path to the program.

Hint

Want to see what directories are in your PATH? Type **set** at a command prompt. Want to set or change your PATH? Type **set PATH=PATH;<*new_dir*>**, where <*new_dir*> is the new directory you want to add. If you have more than one, simply separate them with semicolons. PATH tells the system to keep the current PATH in the new path, as well (without it, your PATH is modified to include ONLY <*new_dir*>. Be aware this only modifies the PATH for the current session (that is, the current command prompt). If you want to make sure the entire system always has access to this change, Windows 95/98/Me users need to place the command in their autoexec.bat file. Windows NT/2000 users need to edit the PATH environment property by right-clicking My Computer, selecting Properties, and then clicking the Environment tab. Once you access this area, click the PATH entry and modify the Value text field.

UNIX

Like Windows, the UNIX PATH environment variable must contain a complete path to the actual executable. You can check your PATH setting by typing **env** at the command line to see a complete list of environment variables.

Hint

Want to see only the $PATH entry? Try typing **env | grep PATH** or **echo $PATH**.

The same test, simply typing the command you expect to run from a command prompt, also works for UNIX. If it doesn't work, then you either need to include the directory that contains the program you're executing in your PATH or to specify the entire path to the program. The method of setting this varies from shell to shell, but we include the most common methods in Table 11-1.

Like the Windows environment, UNIX has its own special syntax for passing argument options to its applications: UNIX uses a hyphen, "-", in front of them. For instance, if you want to launch Netscape Composer, mentioned previously, you would type **netscape -edit** at a command line. Here is a complete example put in a script called sys_unix.pl, which performs this on a UNIX system. This does assume, as just mentioned, the **netscape** application is on the PATH.

Shell	**Syntax**
Bourne (sh)	PATH=$PATH:<*new_dir*>; export PATH
C (csh)	set PATH =$PATH:<*new_dir*> or setenv PATH $PATH:<*new_dir*>
Korn (ksh)	PATH=$PATH:<*new_dir*>; export PATH or export PATH=$PATH:<*new_dir*>
Bourne Again Shell (bash)	PATH=$PATH:<*new_dir*>; export PATH

Table 11-1 **Ways to Set the $PATH Environment Variable in Various UNIX Shells**

```
#!/usr/bin/perl -w

# store command and arguments in array
@args = ("netscape", "-edit");

# call system() function
$result = system(@args);

# if $? contains anything, store values in appropriate variable
$exit = $?; # contains exit status
$sig = $? & 127;   # contains signal number
$core = $? & 128;  # contains 1 if program performed core dump

# if system() call returned non-zero then problem. exit
# program and send error information to STDOUT
$result == 0 or die "\n" . "@args" . "= @args\nExit: $exit\nSignal
Number: $sig\nCore: $core\n\nMessage: $!";
```

Mac OS

The most important issue with Mac OS and the system() function is it won't work on systems pre-Mac OS X without the ToolServer application installed. To obtain and install this application, you must download the application from http://developer.apple.com/tools/mpw-tools/updates.html. Once you download and extract the file, all you must do to start it running is launch it. Once running, which will display a dialog box like in the following illustration, you can use the system() function.

Note

Unlike in the Windows environment, you cannot launch or open a folder using the `system()` function on the Mac OS.

Note

Web sites often change the location of their resources, so if this link doesn't work, check the Tools section of Apple's developer site. This should be located at http://developer.apple.com/tools. From there, you can follow links to the *Macintosh Programmer's Workshop* (*MPW*).

As with the Windows 95/98/Me systems, the Mac OS has some limitations in what and how you name files. No internal mapping of filenames exists, but there is a hard limit of 31 characters for any folder or filename. Additionally, these names cannot have a null or `:` character, but they can include any other character. Also, if the files or folders have spaces in them, then you have to enclose them in single quotes.

sys_mac.pl

Project 11-1: Using the `system()` Function on the Mac OS

A good example of how this whole process works on the Mac OS is simply to launch a program that resides on the file system, but in a folder or along a path with spaces. Let's step through an example to show this.

Step-by-Step

1. Because you must have ToolServer running before you can use the `system()` function, let's go ahead and start it. To do this, all you have to do is double-click the ToolServer icon, which is available after you extract the file you downloaded from the http://developer.apple.com site.

2. Next, you need to create your script, which you can call `sys_mac.pl`. To do so, we recommend you put in the UNIX-style path to the Perl interpreter with the `-w` option, even though you are only running it on Mac OS. This tells the interpreter to write out any warnings it may encounter.

```
#!/usr/bin/perl -w
```

11

3. Next, you are going to store the path to the application in a single variable. The application you are going to launch is the Help Viewer, which is located on your system disk in the System Folder:Help:Apple Help Viewer folder. Because spaces are in this path, you need to put single quotes around some of the names. Our system disk is named *MacOS*, so we use the following line:

```
$application = "MacOS:"System Folder":Help:"Apple Help
   Viewer":"Help Viewer";
```

Note

If the application you want to launch needs to take some parameters or options, such as the name of the file you want it to load, you can store those values in an array like we did in the previous Windows example.

4. The final step is to call the `system()` function and pass it the $application variable. This completes your short program and gives you

```
#!/usr/bin/perl -w

# store command and arguments in array
$application = "MacOS:"System Folder":Help:"Apple Help
   Viewer":"Help Viewer";

# call system() function to launch application
system($application);
```

Now, if you typed anything wrong and were unable to launch the application properly, you may get a warning from ToolServer, such as the one shown in the following illustration. This is similar to how Windows works in that the system returns an error message, in addition to any messages picked up by Perl.

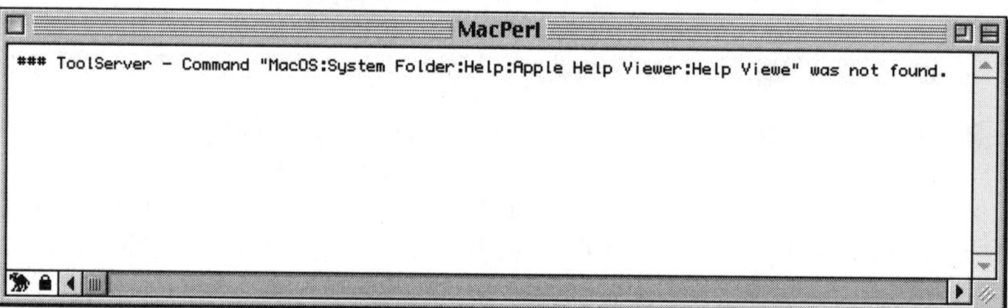

1-Minute Drill

- **What is a necessary requirement before using the `system()` function on Mac OS?**

Operating System-Specific Issues

Over the duration of this module, we've gone over using the `system()` function across the Windows, UNIX, and Mac OS systems. But we're sure you want more. You want to know of any other issues—outside what we covered so far—that exist between these environments.

In this section of the module, we give you a high-level summary of some of the overall differences between using Perl on Windows, UNIX, and Mac OS systems. Again, we've touched on some of the differences in Module 1 earlier in this module, but most of them were syntactical. These issues are more specific items to the system. Topics you should know about when you write scripts for them or scripts that need to run across multiple systems.

Windows

The first thing to watch for on Windows systems are filenames. Several, which are listed in the following bulleted list, are treated in a special way. Because of this, you should avoid using any of these as filenames in your programs.

- AUX
- COM* (where * represents an integer, as in COM1)
- CON
- LPT* (where * represents an integer, as in LPT1)
- NUL
- PRN

- **ToolServer must be installed and running**

Signal handling is one item you may find different on Windows' systems from UNIX and Mac OS systems. The `die()` and `exit()` functions from signal handlers, for example, can cause an exception because most implementations of `signal()` are limited. Because of this, signals may work only for setting flag variables in the handler and other simple tasks.

One way to handle this correctly if you're writing a script that's supposed to work on many different systems is to check the `$^O` variable. This variable returns a name for the system that you can use in the appropriate `if` statement before performing any system-specific functions. Table 11-2 shows the various strings that can be returned using this variable in Windows and DOS-based systems.

Note

The `$^O` variable wasn't added until Perl 5.002. You may want to use the `require()` function to make sure any scripts you have using it are being executed in an environment that supports it.

System	Value of $^O
Cygwin	cygwin
MS-DOS	dos
OS/2	os2
PC-DOS	dos
Windows 95	MSWin32
Windows 98	MSWin32
Windows Me	MSWin32
Windows NT	MSWin32
Windows 2000	MSWin32

Table 11-2 Possible Values of $^O on Windows and DOS-Based Systems

win_only.pl

Project 11-2: Creating a Script That Runs only on Windows

Although this is a short project, we want to step you through an example of how you could use the `$^O` variable. The idea is simple: if you're writing a script that's only supposed to run on the Windows platform, how do you do that? Here's how.

Step-by-Step

1. First, create a new Perl program file. Let's call this file `win_only.pl`. Of course we recommend you put in the UNIX-style path to the Perl interpreter with the `-w` option, even though you're only running it on Windows. This tells the interpreter to write out any warnings it may encounter. This looks like the following:

```
#!/usr/bin/perl -w
```

2. Next, use the `require()` function to make sure 5.002 is installed. Remember the previous note? This was the first version that included support for the `$^O` variable. To do this, include the following in your code:

```
require 5.002;
```

3. Now, perform a check for the Windows system. For this we check, in the condition of an `if` statement, to see if the `$^O` variable is NOT equal to *MSWin32*. If it isn't, then exit the program by calling the `die()` function.

4. Finally, add one last line. This line, if executed, simply states the user must be on a Window's system. Our completed code looks like the following:

```
#!/usr/bin/perl -w

# require Perl 5.002 for $^O support.
require 5.002;

if($^O ne "MSWin32a"){
  die "\nError: This script can not be executed on a non-Windows
```

```
system\n";
}

print "\nYou must be on a Windows system!\n";
```

If you run this script on a Windows system, you should see something like this illustration.

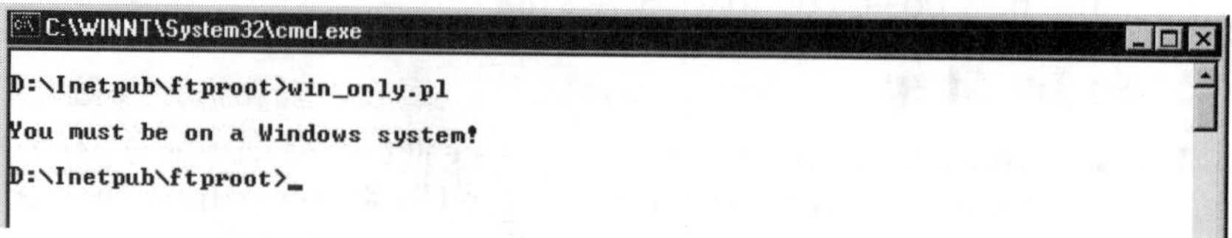

If you run it on a non-Windows system, such as a Macintosh, then you see what is shown in this illustration.

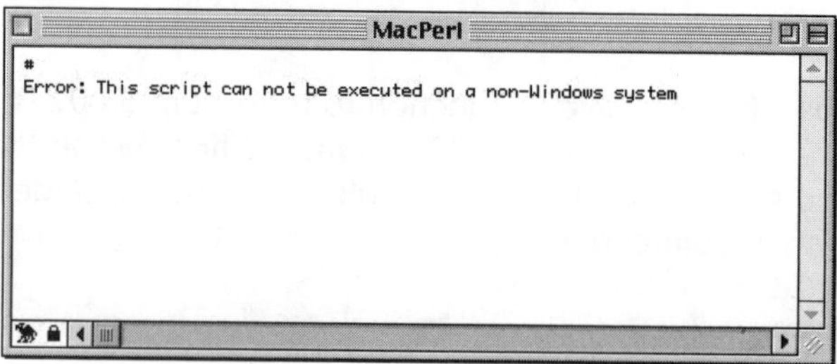

UNIX

As we mentioned with Windows, you also want to use the `$^O` variable to check the flavor of UNIX your script is running on if you're performing any system-specific tasks. Table 11-3 shows the various strings that can be returned using this variable in UNIX-based systems and their corresponding uname value.

> **Hint**
>
> Do you want more information on `uname`? Type **man uname** at a UNIX command prompt.

Return Value of uname -a	Value of $^O
AIX	aix
BSD/OS	bsdos
dgux	dgux
DYNIX/ptx	dynixptx
FreeBSD	freebsd
Linux	linux
HP-UX	hpux
IRIX	irix
Mac OS X	rhapsody
MachTen PPC	machten
NeXT 3	next
NeXT 4	next
openbsd	openbsd
OSF1	dec_osf
reliantunix-n	svr4
SCO_SV	sco_sv
SINIX-N	svr4
sn4609	unicos
sn6521	unicosmk
sn9617	unicos
SunOS	solaris
SunOS4	sunos

Table 11-3 Possible Values of $^O on UNIX-Based Systems

Note

You might have noticed Mac OS X was listed here. Remember, it too, is based on UNIX.

Now, why did we tell you this first? Mostly because there are too many variations of UNIX that Perl runs on to cover the differences in this book. Our best advice is to tell you to check the `hints` subdirectory of the source distribution for specific items. In addition, some pointers might be in the README files contained in the root directory of the distribution. If you find any issues that affect your programs, you can use the values of `$^O` in Table 11-3 to recognize the system, and then program around it.

Mac OS

One of the bigger issues with using Perl on the Mac OS is no command line interface is in versions before Mac OS X. This means you cannot pass arguments to your scripts (unless they are CGI scripts where a browser passes the arguments). A MacPerl module does exist, however, that lets you prompt the user with a dialog box for arguments to be passed in. To invoke this dialog box, you can do the following:

```
@ARGV = split /\s+/, MacPerl::Ask("Arguments: ");
```

This gives you a dialog box like the one shown in this illustration.

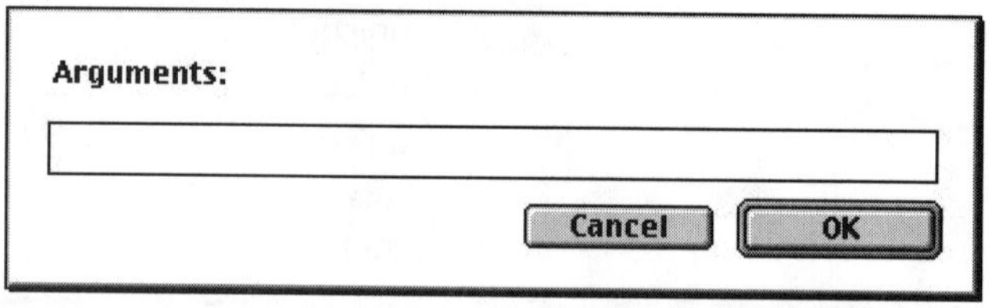

Arguments:

Cancel OK

Because we talked about it with both Windows and UNIX, we want to point out that `$^O` on Mac OS systems returns *MacOS*. But, in addition to this information, you can use the MacPerl module and obtain additional information on the MacPerl environment and architecture of the system, which is described in Table 11-4.

Tip

If you forgot how to include a module in your code, check back to Module 8.

MacPerl Command	Return Description
$MacPerl::Version =~ /App/;	Tells you if MacPerl is running as an application. If so, returns 1
$MacPerl::Version =~ /MPW/;	Tells you if MacPerl is running under the MPW environment. If so, returns 1
$MacPerl::Version =~ /^(\S+)/;	Returns the version of MacPerl you are running. Returns something like *5.2.0r4*.
$MacPerl::Architecture	Returns *MacPPC* if MacPerl is running on a PowerPC chip, and *Mac68K* if it's running on the old 68k architecture.

Table 11-4 **Additional Information You Can Obtain about the MacPerl Environment Using the MacPerl Module**

Ask the Expert

Question: **We've talked a lot about problems around specific operating systems and Perl, but are there any advantages to one operating system over another or to the discussion of the differences?**

Answer: Most major ports of Perl include additional libraries that extend Perl to take advantage of features, which only that operating system has. Here are two that might be of immediate interest.

1. **MacPerl** The MacPerl module, which is built into the MacPerl distribution, provides several Mac OS-specific features, such as the dialog boxes that can be launched and system information, both of which were touched on in this module. For more information on the MacPerl module, check out the `MacPerl.Specifics` file in your Perl distribution.

2. **Win32, Win32:OLE, and Win32API** These Windows modules, which are distributed with ActivePerl, provide features specific to the Windows environment, including such topics as accessing the registry, controlling ActiveX controls, and writing information to the Event Log. For more information, check under Module Docs in your ActivePerl documentation.

Question: **I still don't have enough information to satisfy my need to know more about Perl on specific systems. Where can I get additional information?**

Answer: First, check the perlport manpage for more information on Windows, UNIX, and Mac OS, as well as several other systems. You can also find information on modules specific to your platform, if this is the type of information you want, at http://www.perl.com and http://www.perldoc.com.

netscape.pl

Project 11-3: Creating a Cross-Platform Script

In this module, we talked a lot about how the operating environment can limit your Perl programs. Differences in implementations can sometimes cause problems for us programmers, so we need to be prepared to address and handle them. But, we must admit, the best way to approach a problem, at least at first, is to avoid it completely. So, because we know we're going to create a cross-platform script, we'll go ahead and put the Perl 5.002 requirement on the script and use the appropriate checks before we perform any system-specific tasks.

Step-by-Step

Before we start this program, here's what we want to accomplish. This program, although it could be added to at your whim, won't be a complicated one. We want to ease you into understanding how to determine the system you are on and how to deal with it, not how to build complex programs. So, we simply launch Netscape with our script on Windows, UNIX, and Mac OS systems.

Because distinct sections are in this script, we plan to break it up during this project. The first section, which we cover next, is nothing more than performing some necessary tasks, so the rest of our application can work flawlessly.

1. Create a script named `netscape.pl` and open it for editing. Go ahead and add the UNIX-style path to the Perl interpreter with the

-w option and the appropriate require() call. Together, these two should look like the following:

```
#!/usr/bin/perl
require 5.002;
```

2. Next, create some variables that show what operating system the script is running on. In the declaration of the variables, we use the $^O variable to set the variable to 1 if it's true. Otherwise, it simply contains a null value. This lets us do quick calculations later in the script on the system type.

Note, when checking for UNIX, you only need to look for Solaris, SunOS, and Linux but, if you have another flavor, you can edit what is included here, using the appropriate value from Table 11-3.

Once these variables are set, you can use if statements to perform the tasks you need. These tasks involve properly setting the path to the Netscape application so you can launch it. This means we will have sections for Windows, Mac OS, and UNIX. You also include a default section, in case the system running this script isn't one of the types for which you have written.

```
$is_win32 = $^O eq "MSWin32";
$is_unix = ($^O eq "solaris") or ($^O eq "sunos") or ($^O eq "linux");
$is_macos = $^O eq "MacOS";
```

The first system we address is the Windows system. To make sure we're only performing these tasks on a Windows system, we check our $is_win32 variable as the condition of an if statement.

1. Once we determine it is, in fact, a Windows machine, we first print out a disclaimer that for this script to work, we assume the user is using Netscape Communicator 4 and it is installed in the default location. Once the disclaimer has been written out, we store this default path in the $default_path variable. Up to this point, we have the following:

```
print "\nNOTE: This example assumes Netscape Communicator 4.x\n";
print "and the default installation location\n\n";
$default_path = "Program Files"\Netscape\Communicator\Program\\";
```

11

2. Next, we prompt the user for the drive on which they installed Netscape Communicator. If you remember from Module 1, we can read this in using `STDIN`, and then we can remove the trailing carriage return using the `chomp()` function. This yields

```
print "Drive Installed On (i.e., c, d, e, etc.): ";
chomp($drive = <STDIN>);
```

3. Next, we take the drive they entered, which we stored in the `$drive` variable, the `$default_path` variable, and the string `netscape.exe`, and we concatenate them to obtain the path to the Netscape executable. This new value is stored in a variable called `$netscape`, which is used by the `system()` function later. This completed code for this section of our script looks like:

```
if($is_win32){

  # print warning and set $default_path
  print "\nNOTE: This example assumes Netscape Communicator 4.x\n";
  print "and the default installation location\n\n";
  $default_path = "Program Files""\Netscape\Communicator\Program\\";

  # prompt the user for the drive that Netscape is installed on
  print "Drive Installed On (i.e., c, d, e, etc.): ";
  chomp($drive = <STDIN>);

  # build path to executable and store in $netscape variable
  $netscape = $drive . ":\\" . $default_path . "netscape.exe";
}
```

The next system we tackle is UNIX. As you see, UNIX is actually the easiest one to perform because most of the issues around launching the Netscape application are path-based, and the entire UNIX system is set up in a path-style environment. By this, I mean nearly all applications you need as a user of one of these systems are in your `PATH`, so you needn't specify any directory information.

1. As with the Windows system, the first thing we do is to write a disclaimer. Although, as we mentioned, the Netscape executable is nearly always in your `PATH`, it must be for this to work.

Hint

The Netscape executable isn't in your `PATH`, but you know it's on the system? Try typing **find / -name netscape -print** at the command line. Once you find the directory, you can add that path to your path. See Table 11-1 for a reminder on how to do this.

2. The second and last (we told you this was short!) item you have to do is simply set our `$netscape` variable to the string `netscape`. This finishes our UNIX section, which looks like the following when it's complete

Tip

Wondering why the `elsif` statement is there? Remember, our program needs to check for several systems, so if the first Windows `if` statement doesn't match, we need to continue evaluating, which is why we used the `elsif` statement. We don't want more than one section to execute on a given system. We also do the same for the Mac OS section.

```
elsif($is_unix){

  # print warning and set $netscape
  print "\nNOTE: This example assumes Netscape Navigator 4.x\n";
  print "is in your PATH\n\n";
  $netscape = "netscape";
}
```

The final system section, but not the final program section, in our script handles the Mac OS instance. Follow these steps to implement it:

1. First write out a disclaimer about our assumptions of Netscape Communicator being in the default location. In the same section, store the default path in our `$default_path` variable. Because this is the same conceptually as in Windows, we won't explain it again here.

2. Because Mac OS doesn't have a command line (at least not before Mac OS X or if you don't have the MPW installed), we take a different approach to asking the user for the disk on which Netscape Communicator is installed. We prompt them using the Ask dialog box we saw earlier in the module. This line is simply:

```
$drive = MacPerl::Ask("Disk Netscape Communicator Installed On: ");
```

3. Next, we build our path to the Netscape Communicator application. Once we finish this, we should have the following for our Mac OS section. We also put the default section in here because it doesn't warrant its own section in this book. This section is only executed if the system running the application is not Windows, UNIX, or Mac OS.

```
elsif($is_macos){

  # print warning and set $default_path
```

```
  print "\nNOTE: This example assumes Netscape Communicator 4.x\n";
  print "and the default installation location\n\n";
  $default_path = "Applications:\"Netscape Communicator™ Folder\":";

  # prompt the user for the name of their disk that Netscape is installed
on
  $drive = MacPerl::Ask("Disk Netscape Communicator Installed On: ");

  # build path to executable and store in $netscape variable
  $netscape = " . $drive . ":" . $default_path . "Netscape Communicator™";
} else {
  die "\nError: This script can not be executed on this system\n";
}
```

Tip

Watch out for the ™ character in both the folder and the name of the Netscape Communicator application. This needs to be present to work on this system. You may need to use a symbol table, such as within Microsoft Word, to place this in your script.

The Finished Product

At this point, all the dirty work is done. All we have to do now is use the `system()` function to launch the application stored in `$netscape` and watch for any errors. Because we have to change a few things for Windows users, we must do a check before assigning a value to our `$exit` variable. The following is the completed code you should be able to run on your own system. Feel free to modify it to accommodate your specific paths or, better yet, use what you learned in Modules 6 and 7 to search for the application.

```
#!/usr/bin/perl

# require Perl 5.002 for this script to work
require 5.002;

# initialize some variables
$is_win32 = $^O eq "MSWin32";
$is_unix = ($^O eq "solaris") or ($^O eq "sunos") or ($^O eq "linux");
$is_macos = $^O eq "MacOS";

# in these if statements, check to see what OS is running the
# script and perform any OS-specific tasks here
if($is_win32){
```

Declaring our variables

Windows support

```
  # print warning and set $default_path
  print "\nNOTE: This example assumes Netscape Communicator 4.x\n";
  print "and the default installation location\n\n";
  $default_path = "Program Files"\Netscape\Communicator\Program\\";

  # prompt the user for the drive that Netscape is installed on
  print "Drive Installed On (i.e., c, d, e, etc.): ";
  chomp($drive = <STDIN>);

  # build path to executable and store in $netscape variable
  $netscape = $drive . ":\\" . $default_path . "netscape.exe";

}elsif($is_unix){ ◄──── UNIX support

  # print warning and set $netscape
  print "\nNOTE: This example assumes Netscape Navigator 4.x\n";
  print "is in your PATH\n\n";
  $netscape = "netscape";

}elsif($is_macos){ ◄──── Mac OS support

  # print warning and set $default_path
  print "\nNOTE: This example assumes Netscape Communicator 4.x\n";
  print "and the default installation location\n\n";
  $default_path = "Applications:\"Netscape Communicator™ Folder\":";

  # prompt the user for the name of their disk that Netscape is installed on
  $drive = MacPerl::Ask("Disk Netscape Communicator Installed On: ");

  # build path to executable and store in $netscape variable
  $netscape = " . $drive . ":" . $default_path . "Netscape Communicator™";

} else { ◄──── Unsupported
  die "\nError: This script can not be executed on this system\n";
}

# call system() function and store result
$result = system($netscape); ◄──── Launching our program

# if $? contains anything, store values in appropriate variable
# contains exit status
if($is_win32){
  $exit = -$?/256;
}else{
  $exit = $?; # contains exit status
}
$sig = $? & 127;   # contains signal number
$core = $? & 128;  # contains 1 if program performed core dump

# if system() call returned non-zero then problem. exit
# program and send error information to STDOUT
$result == 0 or die "\n$netscape\n\nExit: $exit\nSignal Number: $sig\nCore:
  $core\n\nMessage: $!";
```

11

Moving On

One of Perl's major advantages is being able to use it across multiple platforms. Other languages like Java and JavaScript also boast this platform independence as part of their benefits. But Perl does have some hang-ups on certain systems and you need to watch out for them. In this module, we introduced many of these hang-ups and showed you ways around them or pointed out their limitations.

So, remember, just because your program doesn't work on a system, that doesn't mean something is wrong with your code. You could be trying to do something the Perl interpreter doesn't support in that environment.

1. Which of the following line should be in all scripts that use the `$^O` variable?

   A. `use $^O;`

   B. `require $^O;`

   C. `demand 5.002;`

   D. `require 5.002;`

2. Which of the following is the path delimiter for the Mac OS system?

   A. \

   B. /

   C. ::

   D. :

Mastery Check

3. What string should you check for in the `$^O` variable if you want something to run only on an AIX system?

   A. linux

   B. unix

   C. aix

   D. aixunix

4. What is the MacPerl subroutine that launches a prompt dialog box?

   A. MacPerl::Ask

   B. MacPerl::Prompt

   C. MacPerl::Dialog

   D. MacPerl::Dialog::Ask

Mastery Check

Module 12

Error Messages and Debugging

The Goals of This Module

- Understand error messages
- Learn how to use the Perl debugger

The world of a programmer would be perfect if it weren't for one little pesky problem: errors. In this module, we discuss the most common errors, and how to find and fix them.

Several different kinds of errors can occur but, for a new programmer, the most common are syntax errors. The first section of this module focuses mainly on how to find these errors and correct them as easily as possible.

Once a program is freed of all syntax errors, it can be executed. Any program that can be executed can be run in conjunction with the Perl debugger. The last section of this module focuses on using the Perl debugger. We also discuss the –w command line option before we finish this module.

Understanding Error Messages

Most of the error messages you see in Perl are syntactically related. Until you rid a program of all its syntax errors, it cannot be executed and, therefore, is useless. The Perl interpreter is what finds these errors when it's trying to interpret the code you have written so it can be executed. Because of this, if you have syntax errors, you see them when you try to execute a program.

Seeing Errors

As previously stated, if you have syntax errors, they appear when you try to execute your program. The Perl interpreter does its best to discover what you really meant, so it can determine what is wrong or missing. Most of the time, the error messages generated by the interpreter are good enough to help you find the errors quickly. To show you what some of the common error messages look like, let's use a simple example program from one of our earlier modules. First, we show it in working condition. The working program is as follows.

```
#!/usr/bin/perl
$a = 15;
while ($a < 25){
   $a++;
   last if ($a == 20);
   print "$a is still less than 25 \n";
}
print "exiting";
```

This program contains a while loop and a "last" condition that exits the loop prematurely if $a equals 20. Now, to demonstrate an error message, we leave the semicolon off line four in this program. The new test program is as follows.

```
#!/usr/bin/perl
$a = 15;
while ($a < 25){
   $a++
   last if ($a == 20);
   print "$a is still less than 25 \n";
}
print "exiting";
```

We know the statement, $a++, requires a semicolon at the end to be syntactically correct. Let's try executing this program to see the error message that generated.

The output of the previous programming example can be seen in Figure 12-1.

As you can see from the screenshot, the Perl interpreter told us a syntax error is on line five, somewhere near "last." The error was actually on line four in the program and this is precisely why we're going into this

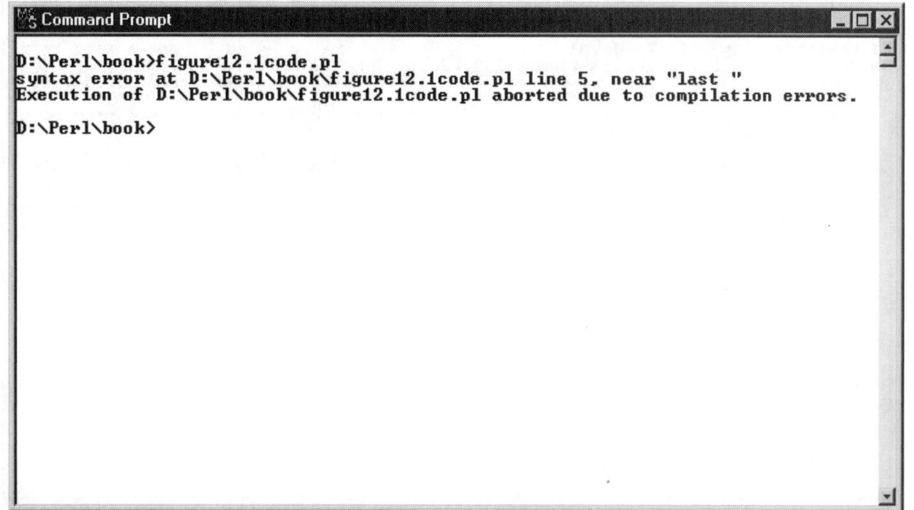

Figure 12-1 **Error messages from the Perl interpreter**

much detail about such a simple error. The interpreter doesn't pinpoint errors for you because it shows you where the error first causes a problem. It often comes close enough to help you find and fix the problem but, sometimes, it can lead you in the wrong direction.

Let's take the same program, add a few additional errors, and try executing it again. The following is the program with the new errors, which we'll attempt to execute.

```
#!/usr/bin/perl
$a = 15
while ($a < 25){
   $a++
   last if ($a == 20);
   print "$a is still less than 25 \n;
}
print "exiting";
```

The output of the previous programming example can be seen in Figure 12-2.

Before we discuss the output from the debugger, let's look at the errors present in the previous program. The first error is on line two, where a semicolon is missing at the end of the statement. The next error

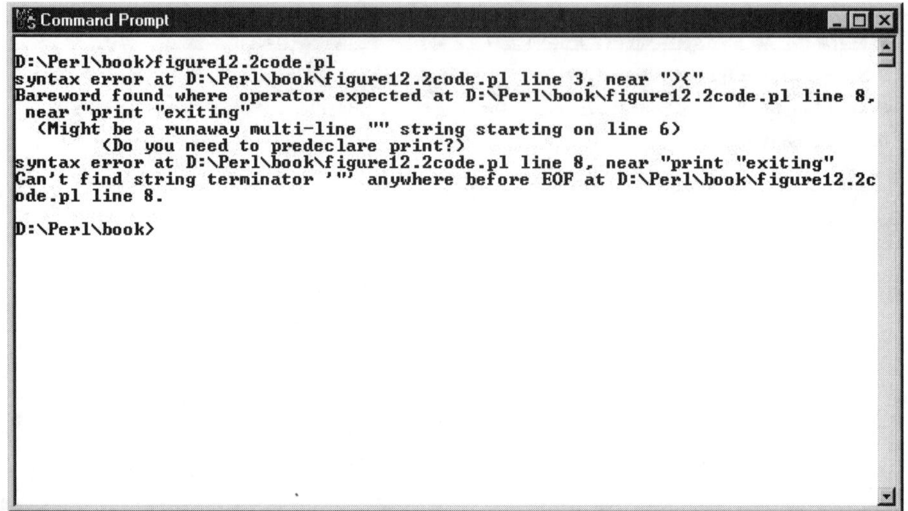

Figure 12-2 Multiple error messages from the Perl interpreter

is the same one we had before on line four of the program. The last error we added is a missing double quote on line six. Now let's talk about the information in Figure 12-2.

The first error it finds is on line three of the program near "){". Because we know where the errors are ahead of time, we know an error isn't on line three, but we know it's probably close. Normally, after a few seconds of inspection, you would find the missing semicolon on the previous line.

Note

We recommend you only try to fix one error at a time when you correct compile errors because the Perl interpreter gets confused easily and any additional errors listed may actually not be errors. Correcting one error at a time is the most efficient way to get your program up and running.

The next error in Figure 12-2 appears to be on line eight but, once again, we know no errors are on line eight. In fact, the interpreter didn't even find one of the errors we made in the file. This is a good place to follow our recommendation by fixing the first error and executing the program again. After correcting the error on line two, the following is what we got from the interpreter.

Now, in Figure 12-3, you can see we're past the first error and back to our original error on line four, even though the interpreter says the error is on line five. Correcting this error should lead us to the last error. Let's take a look.

Notice in Figure 12-4, the interpreter tells us the error is on line eight and it also gives us a bit of insight as to what it thinks the problem may be. The interpreter says the error might be a runaway multiline string and it is. The missing double quote causes a major problem because the interpreter cannot find the end of the string. Once this problem is corrected, the program can execute properly.

Common Practices

As we mentioned earlier, a common practice is trying to fix only one error at a time because errors have a way of cascading when several are present. You can spend too much time trying to determine what the interpreter really means if you focus on more than one error at a time.

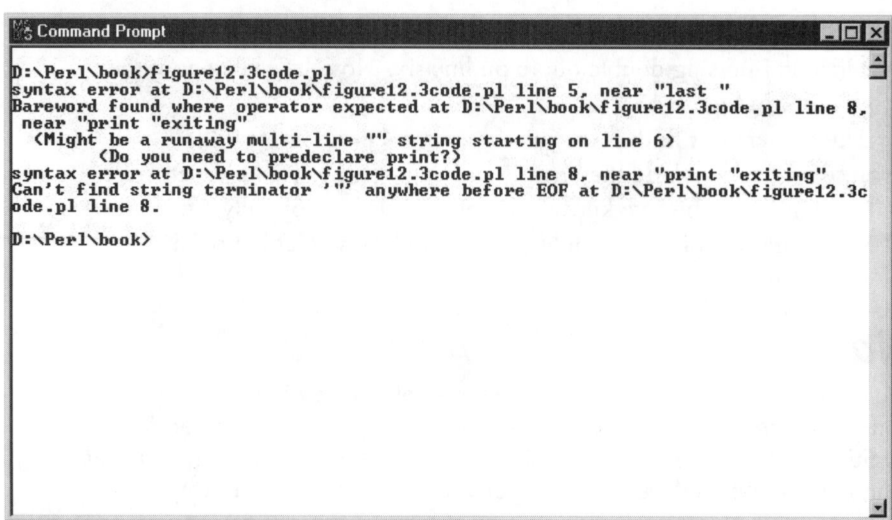

Figure 12-3 Error messages for the remaining two errors

Once you find and correct all the syntax errors so the program can execute, you usually won't see any additional warnings or errors.

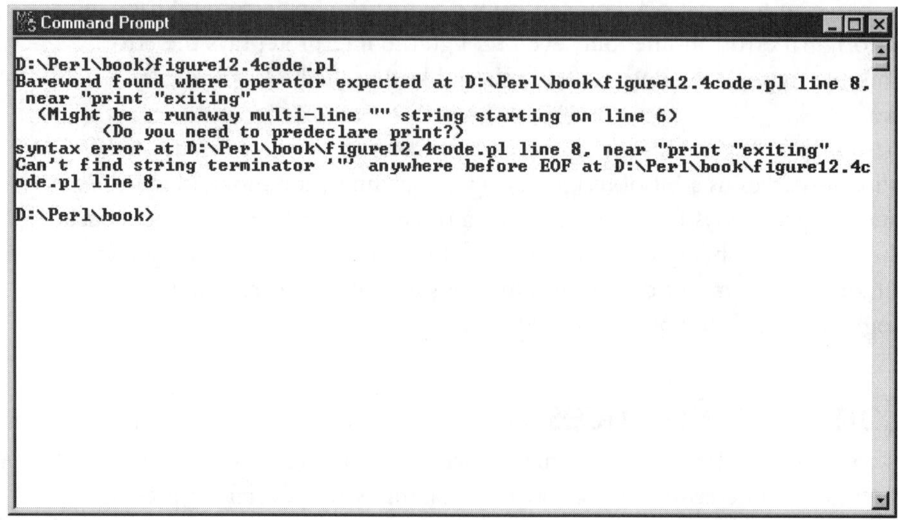

Figure 12-4 Error message for the last error in the program

Note

You can use the –w option to turn on additional warnings. This is a command line option we cover in the next section of this module.

Another common practice we recommend is the use of defined warnings. In Module 6, we discussed using the die and warn functions to print warnings that occur because of a problem during a program's execution. Using these functions is a good idea wherever a potential problem could occur during execution. You should make your warning messages clear enough so the program user can quickly determine what he has done wrong.

The last common practice we recommend is to attempt executing your programs while you are writing them. Waiting until you have a thousand lines of code before you try to execute the program is never a good idea. The complete functionality of the program needn't be present to check what you've written for syntactical errors. Debugging a program as you write can save you headaches when the final debugging must be performed.

We discussed syntax errors and some of the common practices we recommend, so now let's move on to the next section of this module and talk about debugging problems.

1-Minute Drill

- **How many syntax errors should you attempt to correct at one time?**
- **What functions can be used to create your own warning messages?**

Debugging Your Problems

12

The problems that can occur with Perl programs can be separated into two different categories: syntax errors and programming errors. *Syntax* errors are the ones that keep your program from running at all.

- **One**
- **warn and die**

Programming errors are errors the programmer made in her logic that can cause the outcome of the program to be incorrect.

Syntax errors are typically the easier of the two to fix. The Perl interpreter even helps out on the syntax errors, as you saw in the previous section of this module. Programming errors are usually the ones that are hard to debug because they aren't syntax-related, which means the program executes without errors. Two examples of programming errors are making the wrong calculations or iterating a loop too many times.

Command Line Options

If you're past all the syntax errors in a program, but you still aren't getting the right results from its execution, we recommend you start your search for the problem by issuing the –w command. This command turns on all warnings and these warnings are generated when you execute a program from the command line. To turn on this option, simply execute your program as follows:

```
perl -w program.pl
```

A good idea is always to use this option when executing programs. Some of the examples in this book generate warnings when this option is enabled because of the way we had to write them to explain different topics. When this option is enabled, it finds things such as identifiers mentioned only one time, scalar variables used before they are set equal to anything, references to undefined file handles, file handles opened in the wrong mode, using an array as a scalar, as well as numerous other warnings that can affect the behavior of your program.

If, after using the –w option, you cannot find the error or errors in your program, hope still exists for you. You can use the Perl debugger to step through your program to try and determine what is causing the problem. Let's talk about the debugger and its options.

The Perl Debugger

The Perl debugger is a useful tool that can be used to step through a program a number of different ways.

Note

The debugger cannot be used with a program that won't execute because of compile errors.

This section is dedicated to helping you become familiar with using the debugger. First, you need to know how to activate it. The following is an example of how to turn on the debugger:

```
perl -d program.pl
```

We activate the debugger on an example program and show you what happens when it's initialized. Consider the following program for our next set of examples.

```
#!/usr/bin/perl
$a = 15;
while ($a < 25){
    $a++;
    last if ($a == 20);
    print "$a is still less than 25 \n";
}
print "exiting";
```

Figure 12-5 shows what is printed to the screen when the debugger is initialized.

Let's talk about what you see in Figure 12-5. The first four lines aren't important. They tell you the debugger has been initialized. The fifth line says you can type **h** or **'h h'** for help at any time. Typing **'h h'** prints all the options on one screen, so it's easy for you to reference. The sixth line is the most important output from the debugger. Looking at it from the left, the sixth line first tells you what package you are in currently. In our case, we aren't in any package, so the default value is "main." The next part of the line tells you what program you are executing with the debugger. In our case, it's "figure12.5code.pl." Continuing on the same line, a number immediately follows the first colon. This number tells you what line of the program you are executing. The last part of that line tells you what statement is next for execution. On the last line of text in

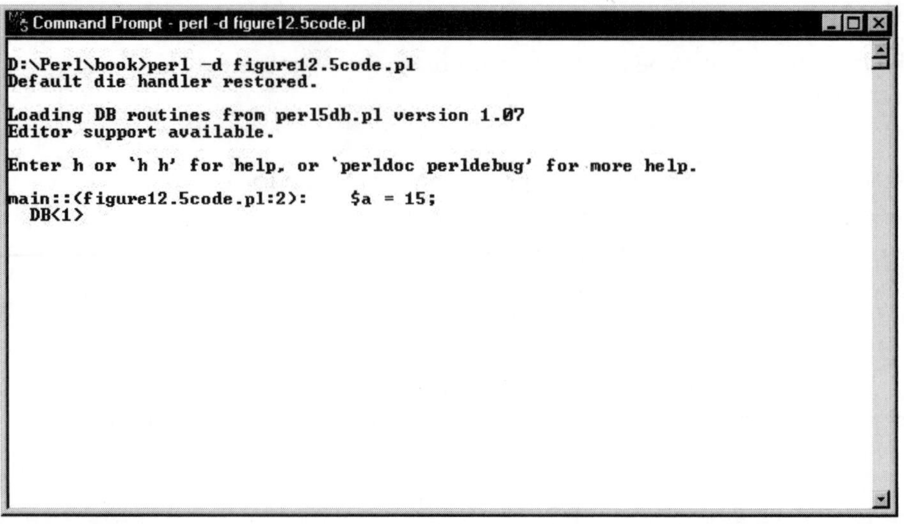

Figure 12-5 The initial debugger screen

Figure 12-5, it says "DB(1)". The *DB* stands for *debug* and the number enclosed in parentheses represents the number of commands you entered into the debugger. This is also the line where you will be prompted to enter your next command. Now that you know how to initialize the debugger, let's cover some commands.

First things first. Any valid Perl statement entered as a command is executed against the current program. You can use this to alter the behavior of your program. This option will make more sense to you as you read through this module.

The first thing to do after initializing the debugger on a program is to list the program you are going to step through. You can list a program in several different ways. We begin with the simple commands and work up to the more specialized ones.

If you simply want to list the entire program in the debugger, you can use the *l* command. Using this command prints ten lines of a program out to the screen at a time, including line numbers and the current place holder. To display the entire program, you must keep issuing the *l* command until the end of the program is reached. Figure 12-6 shows the *l* command being issued.

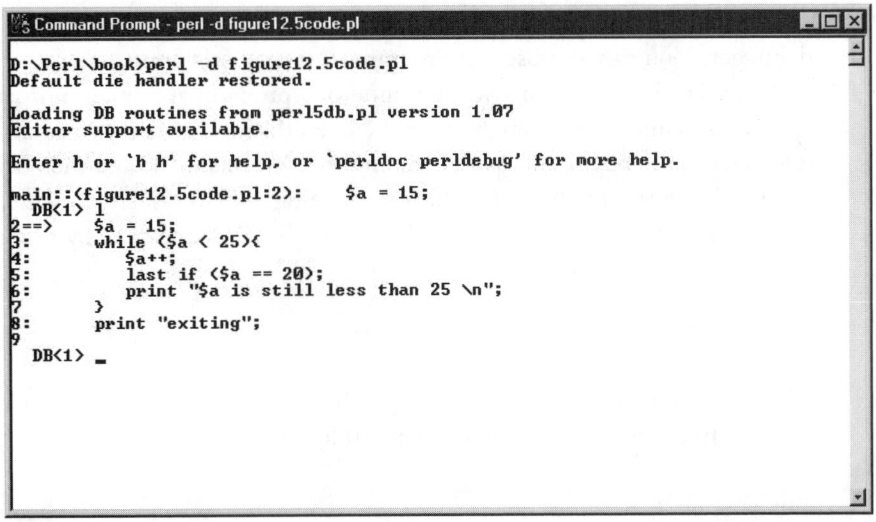

```
Command Prompt - perl -d figure12.5code.pl

D:\Perl\book>perl -d figure12.5code.pl
Default die handler restored.

Loading DB routines from perl5db.pl version 1.07
Editor support available.

Enter h or `h h' for help, or `perldoc perldebug' for more help.

main::(figure12.5code.pl:2):    $a = 15;
  DB<1> l
2==>    $a = 15;
3:      while ($a < 25){
4:         $a++;
5:         last if ($a == 20);
6:         print "$a is still less than 25 \n";
7       }
8:      print "exiting";
9
  DB<1> _
```

Figure 12-6 **Using the *l* command**

As you can see in Figure 12-6, the entire program was listed and, because we hadn't stepped any further in the program than the first line, the place holder => shows us on line two of the program. Remember, this line has yet to be executed. The list option seems like the only one you would ever need to list a program, but what happens when you want to list a program that contains thousands of lines of code? This is where some of the special options come into play that can be used in conjunction with the list command.

If you know the exact line number you want to display, you can enter it in the following manner:

```
DB(1) l 5
```


Note

We are going to show several options in the same manner as the previous one to avoid having too many screenshots in this section. We recommend you open the debugger on a program and issue these commands as we cover them.

This option lists line five of the program currently being used in the debugger. You can also use this program to reset the *l* command. Remember, the *l* command lists ten lines of a program at a time in order. If you listed lines one through ten and eleven through twenty, you can start over at the beginning by first issuing the command *l* 1, and then using *l* to list the rest of the lines. In addition to being able to display one line, you can specify a range of line numbers to be listed at one time by using the following command:

```
DB(2) l 5-8
```

This command lists lines five through eight of your program. You can also list lines five through eight by using the following command:

```
DB(3) l 5+3
```

This command tells the debugger to start with line five and display it and the next three lines.

If your program has subroutines in it, you can use the *l* command and the name of the subroutine to jump to and display it. If you want to display the previous line or lines that have already been displayed, you can use the following command:

```
DB(4) -
```

Figure 12-7 shows the - command being used.

As you can see from Figure 12-7, the - command doesn't show the exact number of lines previously displayed, but the lines will be part of the ten that are displayed.

The *w* command can be used to display ten lines of a program, one of which is a specified line number. You can also do this with the *l* command, but using *w* can make it easier for you. The following is an example of how the *w* command is issued:

```
DB(5) w 5
```

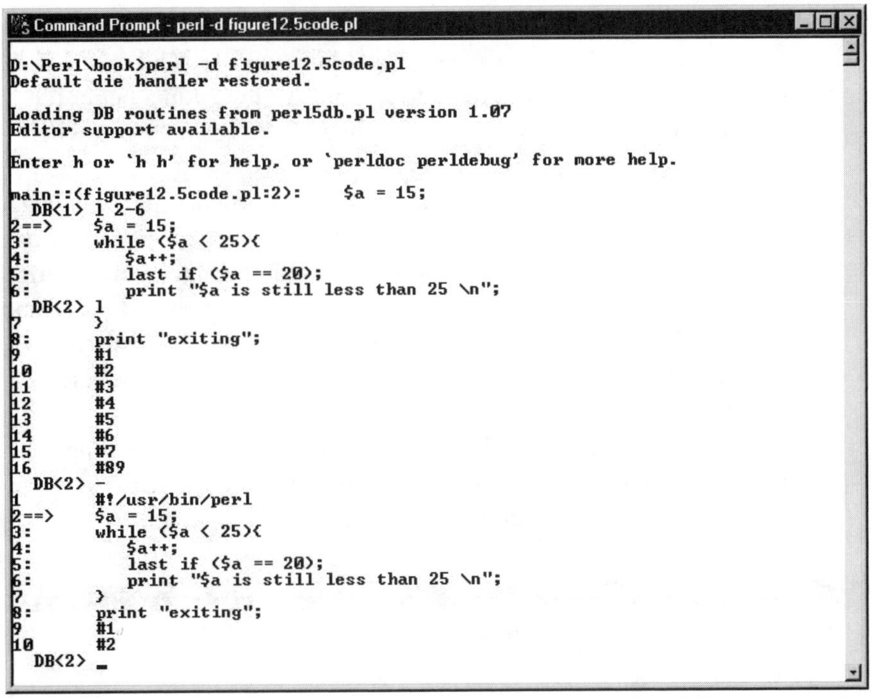

```
Command Prompt - perl -d figure12.5code.pl

D:\Perl\book>perl -d figure12.5code.pl
Default die handler restored.

Loading DB routines from perl5db.pl version 1.07
Editor support available.

Enter h or `h h' for help, or `perldoc perldebug' for more help.

main::(figure12.5code.pl:2):    $a = 15;
  DB<1> l 2-6
2==>    $a = 15;
3:      while ($a < 25){
4:         $a++;
5:         last if ($a == 20);
6:         print "$a is still less than 25 \n";
  DB<2> l
7       }
8:      print "exiting";
9       #1
10      #2
11      #3
12      #4
13      #5
14      #6
15      #7
16      #89
  DB<2> -
1       #!/usr/bin/perl
2==>    $a = 15;
3:      while ($a < 25){
4:         $a++;
5:         last if ($a == 20);
6:         print "$a is still less than 25 \n";
7       }
8:      print "exiting";
9       #1
10      #2
  DB<2> _
```

Figure 12-7 Using the - command

Let's look at the output for this command on a longer test program. The following is the program we use for the next few examples:

```
#!/usr/bin/perl
%hash1 = (a, 1, b, 2, c, 3, d, 4);
$value = $hash1{a};
print "The value stored under the a key is $value \n\n";
$value1 = $hash1{c};
print "The value stored under the c key is $value1 \n\n";
$hash1{e} = 5;
$value2 = $hash1{e};
print "The value stored under the newly created e key is $value2 \n\n";
$hash2{f} = 6;
$value3 = $hash2{f};
print "The value stored in the new hash under the f key is $value3 \n\n";
@array = %hash1;
print "the contents of %hash1 are @array \n";
```

From Figure 12-8, you can see the *w* command lists the three lines before and the six lines after the specified line number. The reason it displays the three prior lines of code is simply to give you a better idea of what has been done up to the specified line. This is to help you when you're trying to debug a statement.

So far, we've shown you several ways to list a program in the debugger, but we haven't told you how to exit it. This can be done simply by using the *q* command. Issuing the *q* command halts the debugger and returns you to the command line in the same directory where the –d command was issued. If you halt the debugger on a program and immediately reenter the debugger on the same program, everything will be reset to the initial state.

A few more options need to be covered before we step through the program. These options are helpful in debugging big programs. The first option to discuss is the search option.

```
Command Prompt - perl -d figure4.20code.pl

D:\Perl\book>perl -d figure4.20code.pl
Default die handler restored.

Loading DB routines from perl5db.pl version 1.07
Editor support available.

Enter h or `h h' for help, or `perldoc perldebug' for more help.

main::(figure4.20code.pl:2):    %hash1 = ( a, 1, b, 2, c, 3, d, 4);
  DB<1> w 6
3:      $value = $hash1{a};
4:      print "The value stored under the a key is $value \n\n";
5:      $value1 = $hash1{c};
6:      print "The value stored under the c key is $value1 \n\n";
7:      $hash1{e} = 5;
8:      $value2 = $hash1{e};
9:      print "The value stored under the newly created e key is $value2 \n\n";
10:     $hash2{f} = 6;
11:     $value3 = $hash2{f};
12:     print "The value stored in the new hash under the f key is $value3 \n\n"
;
  DB<2>
```

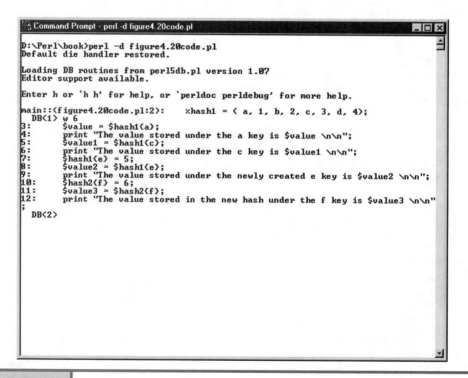

Figure 12-8 Using the *w* command

The *search* option can be used to search through a program for a certain string. You don't have to specify line numbers to use this option; you only need to supply the string you want to search for in the program. Searching for a string sounds familiar, doesn't it? Searching for a string is similar to a regular expression search, in fact, you should have implemented a program as your final project in Module 7 that does something similar to a specified file. The string you want to search for must be enclosed with forward slash characters // if you want your search to start from the beginning of the program. The following is an example of how to issue this command, and Figure 12-9 shows the screen output from the command:

```
DB(6) /key/
```

In Figure 12-9, we're searching for the string "key." The program contains this string more than one time so, to display additional occurrences, you can reenter the search command. If you enter the search command more times than the specific string occurs in the program, it starts searching from the beginning once more and shows you all the same listings again. If you want to search for a specified string starting at the end of the program, all you have to do is enclose the string with question mark characters "??" instead of forward slashes. This command also starts over at

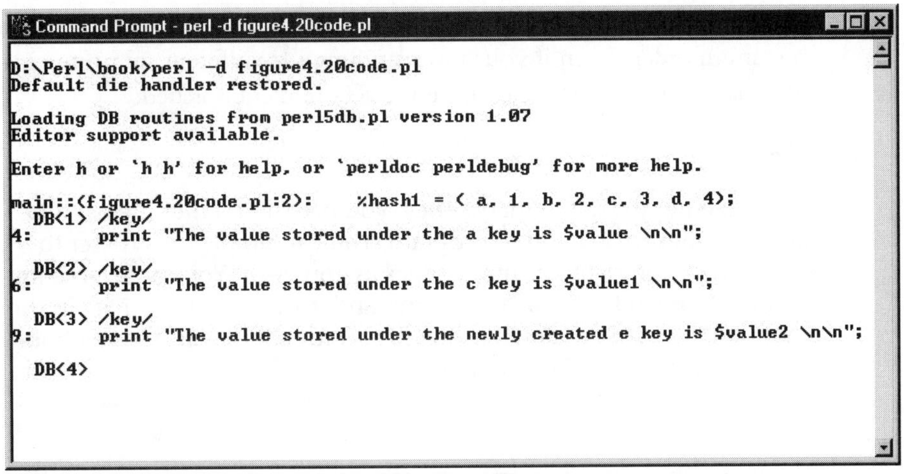

```
Command Prompt - perl -d figure4.20code.pl

D:\Perl\book>perl -d figure4.20code.pl
Default die handler restored.

Loading DB routines from perl5db.pl version 1.07
Editor support available.

Enter h or `h h' for help, or `perldoc perldebug' for more help.

main::(figure4.20code.pl:2):    %hash1 = ( a, 1, b, 2, c, 3, d, 4);
  DB<1> /key/
4:      print "The value stored under the a key is $value \n\n";

  DB<2> /key/
6:      print "The value stored under the c key is $value1 \n\n";

  DB<3> /key/
9:      print "The value stored under the newly created e key is $value2 \n\n";

  DB<4>
```

Figure 12-9 Using the search // command

the end of the program once all occurrences of the specified string have been located.

Another useful command is the '*S*' command, which prints all the subroutines in a program and specifies the package where the subroutine lives.

1-Minute Drill

- **How many lines does the *l* command list at one time?**
- **What command can be used to display a window of lines containing one specified line?**
- **If you want to search for a string in a program from the end, in what do you enclose the string?**

Now that we've covered how to initialize the debugger, list programs, and exit, we need to discuss how to step through a program.

The easiest way to step through a program is to use the *s* option. This option executes the current displayed line. Figure 12-10 shows the screen output from a few statement executions on our example program.

You can see in Figure 12-10, we executed six statements in the example program. Each time the *S* command is issued, the current line, which is listed on the previous line of output on the right-hand side of the screen, is executed. The *S* command is designed to execute each line of a program in order. Even if your program jumps to different subroutines, only one line is executed each time the *S* command is issued.

Note

After you enter the *S* command once, you needn't reenter it each time you want to execute another program. You can simply press Enter to reenter the *S* command as many times as you need. You can even enter another command, such as the *l* command, to see where you are in the program, and then continue to press Enter for additional steps without having to reenter the *S* command.

- **Ten**
- **The *w* command**
- **Question marks**

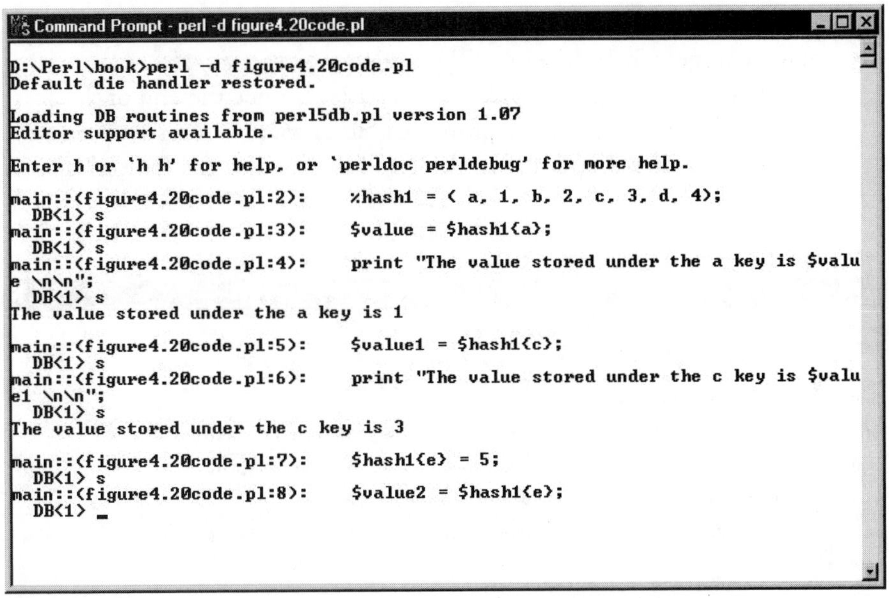

```
D:\Perl\book>perl -d figure4.20code.pl
Default die handler restored.

Loading DB routines from perl5db.pl version 1.07
Editor support available.

Enter h or `h h' for help, or `perldoc perldebug' for more help.

main::(figure4.20code.pl:2):    %hash1 = ( a, 1, b, 2, c, 3, d, 4);
  DB<1> s
main::(figure4.20code.pl:3):    $value = $hash1{a};
  DB<1> s
main::(figure4.20code.pl:4):    print "The value stored under the a key is $valu
e \n\n";
  DB<1> s
The value stored under the a key is 1

main::(figure4.20code.pl:5):    $value1 = $hash1{c};
  DB<1> s
main::(figure4.20code.pl:6):    print "The value stored under the c key is $valu
e1 \n\n";
  DB<1> s
The value stored under the c key is 3

main::(figure4.20code.pl:7):    $hash1{e} = 5;
  DB<1> s
main::(figure4.20code.pl:8):    $value2 = $hash1{e};
  DB<1> _
```

Figure 12-10 **Stepping through using the *S* command**

If you are using the *S* command to step through a program and you enter a subroutine you don't want to execute one line at a time, you can enter the *r* option, which executes the remainder of the subroutine you are currently in and returns you to the next line of code to be executed after it. The *r* command is entered just like the *S* command.

You may run into situations when you don't want to iterate through every subroutine in a program when debugging. The debugger does have an option you can use to execute subroutines automatically in their entirety. This command is the *n* command, which is issued the same as the *S* command. When a call to a subroutine is encountered, the debugger jumps to the subroutine, executes it completely, and returns you to the next statement to be executed after it.

Note

A good time to use the *n* option is when you are using library-type subroutines that should be error-free. This option enables you to attempt to debug only your own code and not waste time looking at error-free subroutines.

Now that you know how to step through a program, let's look at what you get when the end of the program is reached.

As you can see at the end of Figure 12-11, once the end of the program is reached, you are prompted either to quit or restart your session. Additional options are also listed that you might want to use.

```
Command Prompt - perl -d figure4.20code.pl

D:\Perl\book>perl -d figure4.20code.pl
Default die handler restored.

Loading DB routines from perl5db.pl version 1.07
Editor support available.

Enter h or `h h' for help, or `perldoc perldebug' for more help.

main::(figure4.20code.pl:2):    %hash1 = ( a, 1, b, 2, c, 3, d, 4);
  DB<1> s
main::(figure4.20code.pl:3):    $value = $hash1{a};
  DB<1>
main::(figure4.20code.pl:4):    print "The value stored under the a key is $valu
e \n\n";
  DB<1>
The value stored under the a key is 1

main::(figure4.20code.pl:5):    $value1 = $hash1{c};
  DB<1>
main::(figure4.20code.pl:6):    print "The value stored under the c key is $valu
e1 \n\n";
  DB<1>
The value stored under the c key is 3

main::(figure4.20code.pl:7):    $hash1{e} = 5;
  DB<1>
main::(figure4.20code.pl:8):    $value2 = $hash1{e};
  DB<1>
main::(figure4.20code.pl:9):    print "The value stored under the newly created
e key is $value2 \n\n";
  DB<1>
The value stored under the newly created e key is 5

main::(figure4.20code.pl:10):   $hash2{f} = 6;
  DB<1>
main::(figure4.20code.pl:11):   $value3 = $hash2{f};
  DB<1>
main::(figure4.20code.pl:12):   print "The value stored in the new hash under th
e f key is $value3 \n\n";
  DB<1>
The value stored in the new hash under the f key is 6

main::(figure4.20code.pl:13):   @array = %hash1;
  DB<1>
main::(figure4.20code.pl:14):   print "the contents of %hash1 are @array \n";
  DB<1>
the contents of %hash1 are e 5 a 1 b 2 c 3 d 4
Debugged program terminated.  Use q to quit or R to restart,
  use O inhibit_exit to avoid stopping after program termination,
  h q, h R or h O to get additional info.
  DB<1> _
```

Figure 12-11 Stepping through to the end of a program

Another useful option you have when stepping through a program is the capability to set breakpoints. A *breakpoint* is something you can set at a specific line that tells the debugger to execute everything up to the specified line. A breakpoint can be set using the *b* command. When you set a breakpoint, you have several options.

First, you can set a breakpoint at any line in a program.

Note

If you want to set a breakpoint on a multiline statement, you should always select the first line to do so.

Setting a breakpoint on a line is simple. The following command sets a breakpoint on line five of a program:

```
DB(1) b 5
```

Breakpoints can also be set on a line along with a conditional expression that must be evaluated. For example, you can specify that a variable must be equal to a certain value before the breakpoint is valid. You can do this using the following command.

```
DB(2) b 5 ($value = 5)
```

Another way to set a breakpoint is to specify a subroutine name. You can do this using the following command.

```
DB(3) b subroutine
```

When you specify a subroutine as a breakpoint, the actual breakpoint is set at the first line of code in the subroutine, not the call to it. You can use the *l* command to list all the breakpoints you have set in a program. Let's look at our example program with a breakpoint set on line five.

You can see in Figure 12-12 that we first set a breakpoint on line five of the program. Then we used the *l* command to list all of the breakpoints currently set. We also used the *l* command to list the first ten lines of the program.

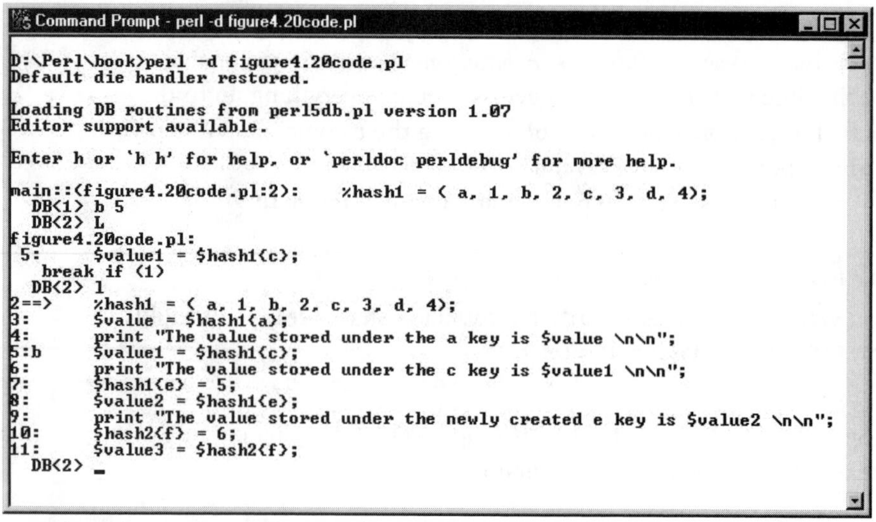

```
Command Prompt - perl -d figure4.20code.pl

D:\Perl\book>perl -d figure4.20code.pl
Default die handler restored.

Loading DB routines from perl5db.pl version 1.07
Editor support available.

Enter h or `h h' for help, or `perldoc perldebug' for more help.

main::(figure4.20code.pl:2):    %hash1 = ( a, 1, b, 2, c, 3, d, 4);
  DB<1> b 5
  DB<2> L
figure4.20code.pl:
 5:     $value1 = $hash1{c};
   break if (1)
  DB<2> l
2==>    %hash1 = ( a, 1, b, 2, c, 3, d, 4);
3:      $value = $hash1{a};
4:      print "The value stored under the a key is $value \n\n";
5:b     $value1 = $hash1{c};
6:      print "The value stored under the c key is $value1 \n\n";
7:      $hash1{e} = 5;
8:      $value2 = $hash1{e};
9:      print "The value stored under the newly created e key is $value2 \n\n";
10:     $hash2{f} = 6;
11:     $value3 = $hash2{f};
  DB<2> _
```

Figure 12-12 **Listing your breakpoints**

Note

Notice that when we used the *l* command to list the program, the breakpoint that we set on line five was signified by a *b* on the left-hand side of the line listing.

The next command we will discuss goes hand in hand with the *b* breakpoint command. It is the *c* command and it is used to execute all of the statements up until the breakpoint or the end of the program is reached. Let's take a look at our example program again with a breakpoint set at line five. This time, we execute statements using the *c* command.

You can see in Figure 12-13 that issuing the *c* command one time executed all of the statements up until the breakpoint at line five was reached. The first few lines that were executed were not displayed to the screen using the *c* command. If you want to see all of the lines that are executed, you can turn on the trace mode by using the *t* command. Trace mode tells the debugger you want to trace everything happening on the screen.

```
Command Prompt - perl -d figure4.20code.pl

D:\Perl\book>perl -d figure4.20code.pl
Default die handler restored.

Loading DB routines from perl5db.pl version 1.07
Editor support available.

Enter h or `h h' for help, or `perldoc perldebug' for more help.

main::(figure4.20code.pl:2):    %hash1 = ( a, 1, b, 2, c, 3, d, 4);
  DB<1> b 5
  DB<2> c
The value stored under the a key is 1

main::(figure4.20code.pl:5):    $value1 = $hash1{c};
  DB<2> _
```

Figure 12-13 **Executing all lines until the breakpoint is reached**

Let's look at Figure 12-14, which has the same setup as that in Figure 12-13 except, this time, we turn on the trace mode.

Notice in Figure 12-14 that all the lines leading up to the breakpoint were shown as being executed. If we had issued the *c* command once

```
Command Prompt - perl -d figure4.20code.pl

D:\Perl\book>perl -d figure4.20code.pl
Default die handler restored.

Loading DB routines from perl5db.pl version 1.07
Editor support available.

Enter h or `h h' for help, or `perldoc perldebug' for more help.

main::(figure4.20code.pl:2):    %hash1 = ( a, 1, b, 2, c, 3, d, 4);
  DB<1> b 5
  DB<2> t
Trace = on
  DB<2> c
main::(figure4.20code.pl:3):    $value = $hash1{a};
main::(figure4.20code.pl:4):    print "The value stored under the a key is $valu
e \n\n";
The value stored under the a key is 1

main::(figure4.20code.pl:5):    $value1 = $hash1{c};
  DB<2>
```


Figure 12-14 **Using the trace mode to see all lines that are executed**

more in the previous example, the rest of the program would have been traced and executed. This is because this command looks for breakpoints, as well as the end of a program.

Another option you have with the *c* command is to issue temporary breakpoints. To do this, all you must do is specify the line number where you want the breakpoint to be located after the *c*. Once the breakpoint is reached and you continue to step through the program, the breakpoint is automatically deleted.

Once you finish with the breakpoints you set using the *b* command, you can remove them one at a time by using the *d* command, along with the line number that contains the breakpoint. If you have multiple breakpoints set, and you want to delete them all at one time, you can use the *d* command by itself.

The next set of options we discuss enable you to view the contents of variables at any time during the process of stepping through a program. These are powerful tools because they enable you to watch variables as their contents are changing. This feature can come in handy when you're debugging a program that isn't functioning properly.

The first option that lets you do this is the *X* option. It displays the contents of any specified variables in the current package (which defaults to main). This option can be issued by itself, but we don't recommend doing so because it then displays all the variables in your program, along with the system defined and debugger variables Perl uses. The most efficient way to use this command is to specify the variable name you want to see. The following command displays the contents of a variable called $values.

```
DB(1) X values
```

You needn't include the dollar sign (or the at @ sign if you're looking at an array), in front of the variable name to view its contents. If the line of code that assigns the selected variable its contents hasn't been stepped through, this command won't output anything to the screen because the variable hasn't yet been defined. Figure 12-15 shows an example of using the *X* command to print all the contents of an array.

```
Command Prompt - perl -d figure4.20code.pl

D:\Perl\book>perl -d figure4.20code.pl
Default die handler restored.

Loading DB routines from perl5db.pl version 1.07
Editor support available.

Enter h or `h h' for help, or `perldoc perldebug' for more help.

main::(figure4.20code.pl:2):     %hash1 = ( a, 1, b, 2, c, 3, d, 4);
  DB<1> c
The value stored under the a key is 1

The value stored under the c key is 3

The value stored under the newly created e key is 5

The value stored in the new hash under the f key is 6

the contents of %hash1 are e 5 a 1 b 2 c 3 d 4
Debugged program terminated.  Use q to quit or R to restart,
  use O inhibit_exit to avoid stopping after program termination,
  h q, h R or h O to get additional info.
  DB<1> X array
@array = (
   0  'e'
   1  5
   2  'a'
   3  1
   4  'b'
   5  2
   6  'c'
   7  3
   8  'd'
   9  4
)
  DB<2> _
```

Figure 12-15 Using the *X* command

If you're dealing with a program that has multiple packages, you can use the *V* command to list the contents of variables, no matter in what package they're located. You need to specify the package in the following manner:

```
DB(1) V package variable
```

Other than being able to specify a different package to work with, the *V* command is identical to the *X* command.

The next set of options we discuss in this section enable you to specify additional statements to be executed, in addition to the statements in the program. These options are helpful to you when you're debugging because you can print important information that may lead you to the problem.

The first command we cover is the > command. It lets you tell the debugger to execute the supplied line of code before executing each statement in the program. The following is an example of how you might use this command:

```
DB(1) > print "The variable contains $variable\n";
```

Once this command is set, the supplied statement is executed before each line of code is executed from the program. Figure 12-16 is an example that uses this command.

Another similar command is the < command. It executes a supplied statement after each line of code from the program is executed.

```
Command Prompt - perl -d figure4.20code.pl

D:\Perl\book>perl -d figure4.20code.pl
Default die handler restored.

Loading DB routines from perl5db.pl version 1.07
Editor support available.

Enter h or `h h' for help, or `perldoc perldebug' for more help.

main::(figure4.20code.pl:2):    %hash1 = ( a, 1, b, 2, c, 3, d, 4);
  DB<1> > print "Value1 contains $value1 \n";
  DB<2> s
Value1 contains
main::(figure4.20code.pl:3):    $value = $hash1{a};
  DB<2> s
Value1 contains
main::(figure4.20code.pl:4):    print "The value stored under the a key is $valu
e \n\n";
  DB<2> s
Value1 contains
The value stored under the a key is 1

main::(figure4.20code.pl:5):    $value1 = $hash1{c};
  DB<2> s
Value1 contains
main::(figure4.20code.pl:6):    print "The value stored under the c key is $valu
e1 \n\n";
  DB<2> s
Value1 contains 3
The value stored under the c key is 3

main::(figure4.20code.pl:7):    $hash1{e} = 5;
  DB<2> s
Value1 contains 3
main::(figure4.20code.pl:8):    $value2 = $hash1{e};
  DB<2> _
```

Figure 12-16 Using the > command

Both of these commands, > and <, can be used at the same time on one program to give you a before and after picture of what's happening after each line of code is executed.

Another command similar to > and < is the *a* command. It enables you to execute a specified statement before a selected line of code is executed. The following is an example of how to use the *a* option:

```
DB(1) a 10 print "Value1 contains $value1 \n";
```

This command prints the value of $value1 before line ten of the program is executed in the debugger. You can use the *L* or *l* commands to list where you've set action statements using the *A* command. With the *l* option, any action line you select is signified by an *a* on the left-hand side of the screen beside the line number.

Any line action you specify using the *A* command can be deleted by using the *A* command. It deletes all your line actions at one time and prints the following message to the debugger screen.

```
Deleting all actions...
```

While the last few commands we cover aren't good for debugging a program, they are good for saving time when you use the debugger. The first of these commands is the *H* command. This command prints all your previous commands to the screen. If you've entered many commands, you'll probably have to scroll up to see the last commands you entered. The *H* command prints your commands, starting with the most recent and ending with the oldest used.

Printing all the commands is useful because you can use the ! command, along with the command number to reissue it without typing it all over again. This command can also be used alone to reissue the most recently used command.

This covers everything you need to know about the Perl debugger. We didn't cover a few commands and options and if you happen to need one of these, issue the debugger help option, which should give you what you need to know to use any of the supplied commands.

Project 12-1: Becoming Familiar with the Perl Debugger

For this project, all we want you to do is open a program with the debugger and go through the commands we discussed one at a time to familiarize yourself with how they function. You need to use a program with a few subroutines to test some of the commands we covered. Being familiar with the debugger can save you time and effort when you start debugging programs regularly.

1-Minute Drill

- **Which command should you use to step through a program while skipping its subroutines?**
- **What command can be used to list breakpoints and action statements?**

More Common Practices

Before we reach the end of this module, here are a few more common practices you should know.

One of these common practices is to use print statements regularly when you're debugging a program. This can help you keep track of how different values are changing while your program executes.

Another fairly common practice is trying to pinpoint the problem line or lines of code by commenting them out and restarting the program. This is useful because it should help you pinpoint problem areas in your code. Once you find a problem area, you can concentrate your efforts on fixing that one section, instead of wasting your time looking through the entire program.

That about does it for this module. We hope you feel comfortable using the Perl debugger. You should also have a head start on figuring out syntax errors in a timely manner. Try to use some of the common practices we mentioned when you debug your programs. These practices should save you both time and effort in getting everything up and running smoothly.

- **The *n* command**
- **The *l* command**

Mastery Check

1. Which of the following lines of code contains a syntax error?

   A. $name = "Harvey";

   B. print "This message will be displayed on the screen \n"

   C. if ($result = $string1 =~ /\beat/) {

   D. None of the above

2. Which of the following commands can be used to generate warnings?

   A. Perl –d program.pl

   B. Perl –w program.pl

   C. Both A and B

   D. None of the above

3. Which debugger command can be used to execute an entire program that contains no breakpoints?

   A. s

   B. r

   C. c

   D. None of the above

4. Which debugger command can be used to set temporary breakpoints?

   A. b

   B. B

   C. c

   D. None of the above

Mastery Check

5. If you want to search for an occurrence of a string from the beginning of a file, in what do you enclose the string?

   A. //

   B. ??

   C. \\

   D. None of the above

6. What debugger command can be used to list all the subroutines in a program?

   A. s

   B. sub

   C. S

   D. None of the above

7. Which debug command can be used to print the contents of a variable?

   A. X

   B. V

   C. Both A and B

   D. None of the above

8. Which of the following statements executes the supplied command before a line of the program is executed?

   A. a 10 print "Value1 contains $value1 \n";

   B. > print "The variable contains $variable\n";

   C. < print "The variable contains $variable\n";

   D. Both A and B

Module 13

Advanced Features and Concepts

The Goals of This Module

- Learn about object-oriented programming, including the concepts of encapsulation, inheritance, and polymorphism
- Understand how you can use PerlScript within Internet Explorer browsers and Active Server Pages (ASP)
- Use PerlScript with the Windows Script Host
- Acquaint yourself with the Perl/Tk to be used with Graphical User Interface (GUI) programming

You've made it to the last module in this book—and we've saved some of the more advanced topics until now. This is the module in which we chose to cover these advanced topics because you're already familiar with basic topics such as regular expressions, interacting with databases, modules, and system functions. We won't go into complete detail on the topics covered in this module, but we do give you a good head start in becoming an experienced Perl programmer.

This module first covers object-oriented programming. We discuss related topics such as encapsulation, inheritance, and polymorphism. The next section of this module covers PerlScript and its various uses, including client-side usage, server-side processing, and how to use PerlScript to perform everyday tasks. Finally, we introduce you to the Perl/Tk toolkit. We cover what the Perl/Tk toolkit is, give you an overview of the toolkit, and, finally, discuss the steps involved in designing a simple GUI application.

Objected-Oriented Programming

If you've had any experience with programming at all, you've probably heard the phrase "object-oriented programming" being tossed around a lot. If you haven't heard it, chances are you will as you become a more experienced programmer.

Before we can go any further in this section, we need to discuss what *object-oriented programming* (*OOP*) is. The basis of any object-oriented program is objects. An *object* lives in a class, which means it belongs to a certain class in which its behaviors are defined. A *class* is a group of functions and data that are related, in that everything in a class is tailored to a specific problem. A class can be thought of as a special user-defined data type.

Now that you're all confused, let's try to explain this a different way. A class defines attributes for a special data type. This new data type you created through a class can perform special tasks. These tasks are defined by the methods or subroutines you include in the class. The data type you create can be compared to the scalar data type. You know what the scalar data type is capable of and, when you need to create a scalar variable, you simply follow the special naming conventions to do so. By the same token, when you need to create a new object, you must follow the guidelines provided to you in the class. This new object's behavior is defined by the rules laid out in the class.

We hope you now have a better understanding of all this OOP jargon, so let's talk a little more about a class and how it's created in Perl.

A class, in Perl, is simply a module. You learned in the chapter on modules that to create one, you use the package mechanism. For the example we use throughout this section of the module, we call our class `Record.pm`. This file is in the current working directory for the program we use to exercise the functionality of the class. Let's look at the class and we'll explain what you are seeing immediately after the code.

This is the constructor for the class

This is the name of the package and, in this case, the class

This line is included, so that when we try to "use" the class, it will work properly

The rest of the subroutines in this class are all methods that can be called to perform a certain action

```
package Record;
1;

    sub new {
        my $person  = {};
        $person->{NAME}    = undef;
        $person->{AGE}     = undef;
        $person->{POSITION}  = undef;
        bless($person);
        return $person;
    }

    sub name {
        my $person = shift;
        if (@_) {
            $person->{NAME} = shift;
        }
        return $person->{NAME};
    }

    sub age {
        my $person = shift;
        if (@_) {
            $person->{AGE} = shift;
        }
        return $person->{AGE};
    }

    sub position {
        my $person = shift;
        if (@_) {
            $person->{POSITION} = shift;
        }
        return $person->{POSITION};
    }
```

13

The previous code listing is the package file that contains the example class we use in the section.

The first thing you see in the package is its name. The name we're giving our class is Record. The name for a class is used in a program to incorporate the functionality of it into that program. We look at exactly how this is done when we go over the example program that actually uses the class.

The second line in the file contains `1;`. This is included so that when the class is called on to be used in a program, the process will succeed, because the module containing the class returns a true value (in this case, 1). You'll get a better idea of what we mean here when we get to the program itself.

The next part of this class, beginning on line three, is a subroutine called new. This is what is called the constructor for the class. This method, or subroutine, creates a new object when it's called. This new object has all the attributes assigned to it by the constructor. This method is a constructor, not because of the name it is given, but because of the functionality it includes. The function `my` has a special meaning in Perl and we discuss it more when we get to the encapsulation section. This constructor creates a reference to a hash when it's called, which contains three keys: NAME, AGE, and POSITION. Another function you see here that's probably new to you is `bless()`. This function is covered after we look at the example program that uses this class. The last line of this method returns the newly created object.

Each of the last three methods in this class are designed to perform a special function on the object that has been created. Because of this, we can refer to them as *object methods*.

Looking at the first of the object methods—name—you can see its purpose is to set the name field of the hash for the object and return the new name for it. It also simply returns the object's name if no name is specified to set.

Note

Remember, @_ is the automatic variable assigned to a subroutine. Saying if (@_) effectively means if anything was passed in to this method, then do something. Also the `shift()` function works on the current default array as well, so if no new name to be set is passed in, the last name in the array is shifted out and returned as the name.

The last two methods in this class are similar to the one we just discussed, so we won't go into great detail on them.

Now that you've seen an example class, let's look at a program that uses this class:

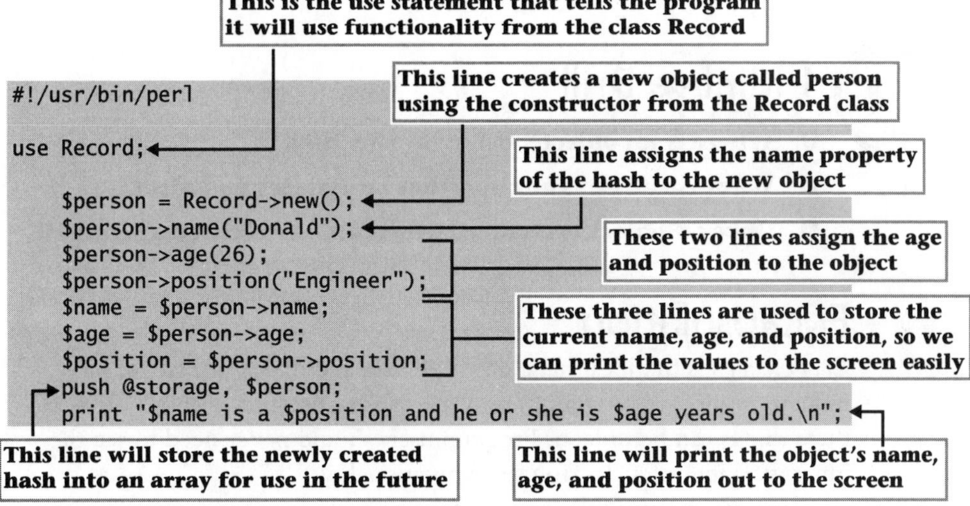
This is the use statement that tells the program it will use functionality from the class Record
This line creates a new object called person using the constructor from the Record class
This line assigns the name property of the hash to the new object
These two lines assign the age and position to the object
These three lines are used to store the current name, age, and position, so we can print the values to the screen easily
This line will store the newly created hash into an array for use in the future
This line will print the object's name, age, and position out to the screen

```
#!/usr/bin/perl

use Record;

    $person = Record->new();
    $person->name("Donald");
    $person->age(26);
    $person->position("Engineer");
    $name = $person->name;
    $age = $person->age;
    $position = $person->position;
    push @storage, $person;
    print "$name is a $position and he or she is $age years old.\n";
```

The output of the previous programming example, using a class to create an object, can be seen in the illustration.

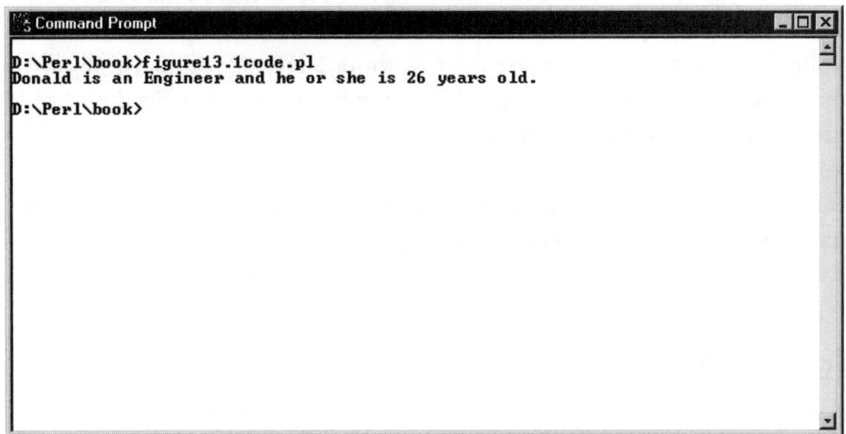
Command Prompt
D:\Perl\book>figure13.1code.pl
Donald is an Engineer and he or she is 26 years old.
D:\Perl\book>

The previous program was used to create an object, but how? Well, the key lies in the `bless()` function. This function tells the interpreter that what it just constructed can be used as an object. The expression "can be used as an object" simply means the methods created to perform some task can now be called against it.

From the previous programming example, you can see the newly created object—employee1—had each of the three methods in the class, name, age, and position called against it.

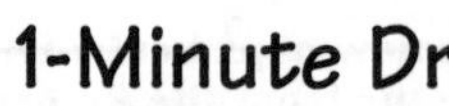

1-Minute Drill

- **Where is an object's behavior specified?**
- **What is the key function that designates an object?**
- **Once an object is created, what can be executed against it?**

Encapsulation

Encapsulation is the idea that a group of data and functionality can be hidden from other programmers. One of the great things about OOP is these things can be hidden. Program users should never need to see the inner workings of a class to use its functionality.

Let's say, for example, you are writing code for a big software company and the code you write must be used by your customers. You wouldn't want your customers to get to all your data or even be able to see what's going on behind the scenes. OOP can help you take care of these issues. One golden rule of OOP is this: you should document all your classes so any user can use them without a lot of trouble. Ideally, you want the user of your class to be able to use it without ever needing to know what is actually happening in the class.

The best way to ensure that all data is hidden is to use the `my` function. This function ensures the selected variables in a subroutine only have a scope in that subroutine. The `my()` function can be seen in use in the class example, which we discussed earlier in this module.

Inheritance

Another important concept OOP brings to the table is inheritance. No, you won't be receiving any large unexpected amounts of money from this

---

- **In a class or package**
- `bless()`
- **Methods from the class in which the object's behavior was specified**

concept, but you will find it can save you time and effort when you work with objects often.

Inheritance is the idea that a class can inherit traits from another class that already exists. It can be thought of as creating a specialized class, which has some new functionality, in addition to the functionality contained in the existing class. An inherited class is created much like a normal class because it's a package file. The one main difference is, inside the package file of an inherited class, you find one or more use and `@ISA` statements being used to select the existing class from which to inherit. The `@ISA` statement is followed by the class name that should be checked if a certain method can't be found in the current class. Here's a programming example to demonstrate the use of an inherited class. The `Record` class is modified so it inherits methods from the workweek class. The following is the code listing for the updated `Record` class.

```
package Record;

use workweek;
@ISA = ("workweek");
1;

    sub new {
        my $person  = {};
        $person->{NAME}    = undef;
        $person->{AGE}     = undef;
        $person->{POSITION}  = undef;
        bless($person);
        return $person;
    }

    sub name {
        my $person = shift;
        if (@_) {
            $person->{NAME} = shift;
        }
        return $person->{NAME};
    }

    sub age {
        my $person = shift;
        if (@_) {
```

This is the name of the package and, in this case, the class

This line tells the class to inherit from the workweek class

This line tells the interpreter that if it cannot find a certain method in the Record class, to look in the workweek class

```
            $person->{AGE} = shift;
        }
        return $person->{AGE};
    }

    sub position {
        my $person = shift;
        if (@_) {
            $person->{POSITION} = shift;
        }
        return $person->{POSITION};
    }
```

As you can see, the only things added to this class were the use and @ISA statements.

Now let's look at the new workweek class, which contains the new functionality the Record class will inherit.

```
package workweek;

1;

    sub hours {
        my $person = shift;
        if (@_) {
            $person->{HOURS} = shift;
        }
        return $person->{HOURS};
    }

    sub overtime {
        my $person = shift;
        if (@_) {
            $person->{OVERTIME} = shift;
        }
        return $person->{OVERTIME};
    }
```

This is the name of the package and, in this case, the class

This package contains two new functions the Record class can use

Now let's look at the program that uses these new functions. Notice the only class included by using the use statement is the Record class.

```
#!/usr/bin/perl

use Record;

$employee1 = Record->new();
$employee1->name("Donald");
$employee1->age(26);
$employee1->position("Engineer");
$employee1->hours(40);
$employee1->overtime(12);
$name = $employee1->name;
$age = $employee1->age;
$position = $employee1->position;
$hours = $employee1->hours;
$overtime = $employee1->overtime;
push @storage, $employee1;
print "$name is a $position and he or she is $age years old.\n";
print "He or she worked $hours regular hours and $overtime ;
print "hours of overtime this week \n";
```

This is the use statement that tells the program it will be using functionality from the class Record

These are the two new functions inherited from the workweek class

The output of the previous programming example, using an inherited class to create an object, can be seen in this illustration.

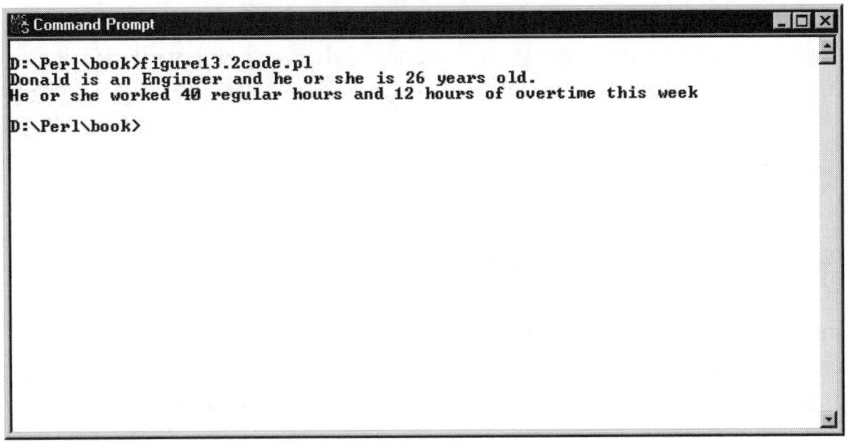

```
Command Prompt
D:\Perl\book>figure13.2code.pl
Donald is an Engineer and he or she is 26 years old.
He or she worked 40 regular hours and 12 hours of overtime this week

D:\Perl\book>
```

This covers inheritance and, now, we move on to discuss polymorphism.

Polymorphism

Polymorphism is the idea that a method can have different actions depending on what type of object called it. This idea is used often by C++ programmers who need methods to react differently to different objects. A good example would be if you have a method called shift, which exists in two different classes—one for manual and the other for automatic transmissions—designed to change gears on anything from cars and trucks to lawnmowers. This method would need to react differently depending on whether the vehicle was an automatic or a manual transmission. Polymorphism is the idea that the language can choose either method at run time without generating any problems because of type difference.

1-Minute Drill

- **What functions are used to create inheritance?**
- **What function is used to keep data specific to an enclosing block?**

Now let's move on to the next section, where we discuss PerlScript and its many uses.

PerlScript

PerlScript is a technology developed by our friends at ActiveState and is part of the ActivePerl distribution. At its core, PerlScript is an interpretation engine for interpreting and executing Perl scripts and programs. But it's different than the Perl interpreter because it contains extensions that allow these Perl scripts to be executed native to the Windows environment.

- **Use() and @ISA**
- **my()**

This is just like Microsoft's VBScript and JScript, which means PerlScript can be executed in the following, all of which are Microsoft technologies:

1. The Internet Explorer 4+ browser
2. The body of ASP documents served by the Internet Information Server (IIS) version 3+ or Peer Web Services 3+
3. The Windows Script Host environment

Tip

For PerlScript to work, both ActivePerl and PerlScript must be installed on the machines running the scripts. So, for instance, if you develop some client-side PerlScript, all machines that will load that page must have ActivePerl and PerlScript installed.

Our objective at this point is to introduce you to the concepts of each of these technologies, to show you some simple examples, and to point you to additional resources to use as you decide to pursue more information on these topics. We don't want to overload you, but we do want to get you started in the right direction.

Note

Currently, PerlScript is only available for use on the Windows operating system. So, although UNIX and Mac OS programmers should read and understand this section of the book, you won't be able to execute any of the examples here on your system.

Using on the Client Side

Using PerlScript on the client side is a concept with which you may be somewhat familiar. If you've ever written any JavaScript/JScript or VBScript, then you are ahead of the game. The concept is simple: using the Perl language, you want to write scripts that can be interpreted in a browser and used to perform tasks within that browser (for example, on the client side).

Note

This is a reminder that PerlScript and ActivePerl must be installed on all machines that might be running your scripts. For this reason alone, client-side PerlScript may not be a good solution for you and you should consider using it on the server side.

In this section of the module, we discuss this capability within the Windows environment and how it can be used to generate content dynamically.

But I Have Never Programmed in JavaScript/JScript or VBScript!

If you haven't written scripts in either of these languages before, it's beyond the scope of this book to discuss them. Just know they are all scripting languages that can have their code embedded in an HTML document between beginning and ending `<script>` tags, and can be interpreted by a scripting engine built into the browser. So, for instance, you can easily write the current date and/or time to the HTML page or create image rollovers, invoked when a user rolls her mouse pointer over a given image.

For more information on these languages, see the following sites:

- **http://developer.netscape.com** This is where you can find official documentation on JavaScript, which is Netscape's implementation of ECMAScript and the language that started client-side scripting.
- **http://www.mozilla.org/js** If you want to find out what our friends at Netscape are doing for the next generations of JavaScript, check out Mozilla.org, its open source effort for creating various Web technologies, including the Gecko rendering engine, which will be the foundation of Netscape 6.

- **http://msdn.microsoft.com/scripting** If you like JScript or VBScript, check out Microsoft's scripting site for developers. You can find documentation, scripting engine downloads, and additional information on the various locations in their products where these languages can be used.
- **http://www.ecma.ch** This site is the home of ECMA, where the ECMAScript (ECMA-262) language specification is maintained. This language, which is based on early generations of JavaScript and JScript, represents the core standardized portions of the language from which JavaScript and JScript now draw.

In a nutshell, the best way to compare using PerlScript on the client side is with JavaScript. A fair number of the objects, such as `Window` or `Document`, are the same, as are many of the methods (or subroutines in Perl terms), such as `write()` or `alert()`. The one big syntactical difference is PerlScript uses `->` as the separator between objects and subobjects, properties, or methods instead of a period (`.`). Here's an example to help clarify this.

Let's say you want to write the "Hello, World!" to the page being loaded by Internet Explorer 5. In JavaScript (or JScript, remember, they are basically the same), you would use the following lines of code:

```
<script langauage="JavaScript" type="text/javascript">
  document.write('Hello, World!');
</script>
```

Now, for PerlScript, you would use this:

```
<script langauage="PerlScript" type="text/perlscript">
  $window->document->write('Hello, World!');
</script>
```

As you can see, they are quite similar. When programming in PerlScript, you must make sure the `language` and `type` attributes of the `<script>` tag are correct, and you have to change the periods to `->`. PerlScript also requires the complete object hierarchy, which is why the `$window` portion is in our example. In JavaScript, you could include the top-level `window` object reference, but it isn't required.

Hint

For more information about PerlScript and what you can do with it, check your ActivePerl documentation that came with your installation on a Windows machine. In addition, you can check the ActiveState Web site at http://www.activestate.com.

Server-Side Processing

Because of the requirements of having both ActivePerl and PerlScript on all machines interpreting your Perl scripts, one option you might want to explore is using it on the server side in conjunction with ASP. Because all interpretations occur on this machine, it's the only machine required to have ActivePerl and PerlScript installed.

Note

If you have a farm of Web servers, you need to put ActivePerl and PerlScript on all machines that will be running your PerlScript ASP pages.

In a sense, server-side PerlScript is a lot like client side. The idea is basically that you have embedded Perl code in the body of your HTML documents. The real difference, other than a few syntactical ones, is these scripts are executed and completed on the server side before the page is returned to the requesting browser. For instance, let's say you want to use ASP's default language, VBScript, to do the same thing we did in our client-side example—write "Hello, World!" to the HTML document. To do this, you would have the following lines of code. Let's put it in a file called `hello-vb.asp`.

```
<html>
<head>
  <title>VBScript</title>
</head>
<body>
  <%
    Response.Write('Hello, World!');
  %>
</body>
</html>
```

Now, if you want to do the same thing using PerlScript as your programming language, you would use the following. Let's put it in a file called `hello-ps.asp`.

```
<%@Language="PerlScript"%>
<html>
<head>
  <title>PerlScript</title>
</head>
<body>
  <%
    $Response->Write('Hello, World!');
  %>
</body>
</html>
```

When you use PerlScript—and this is also true for any other language, such as JScript—the first thing you must do is define the language you are using as the first line in your document. This is the `<%@ Language = PerlScript %>` line. This basically tells the ASP engine it should use the PerlScript programming engine to interpret the code on the page.

Additional ways exist to tell the engine which language to use, but they are beyond the scope of this book. If you're interested, however, we recommend you check both the ActiveState Web site and the Microsoft Developer's Network site (http://msdn.microsoft.com/scripting) for more information on both PerlScript within ASP and ASP in general.

Windows Script Host

Have you ever played with batch files on DOS or Windows machines, shell scripting on UNIX, or AppleScript on the Mac OS? Well, if you have, you know batch files have the least amount of functionality and flexibility of them all. Enter *Windows Script Host* (*WSH*).

Note

For these examples to work on your Windows system, you must have the Windows Script Host installed. If you are using Windows 98+ or Windows 2000+, there's a good chance you already have it. If you don't, you can download it from http://msdn.microsoft.com/scripting.

Even though it isn't always pitched as such, WSH is a successor to the old batch file days. But WSH is much more powerful and can accomplish many more tasks: controlling ActiveX controls, popping up dialog boxes, moving files, changing permissions, writing information to the Event Log, and much more. Let's look at an example.

If you want to write a script in JScript that would pop up a dialog box simply saying "Hello, World!", you would put the following code in a file that ended with a .js extension (such as `hello.js`). In the code, we create an instance of the `WScript.Shell` object and store the reference to it in the `WSHShell` variable. Next, we call the `Popup()` method of this object and pass it the text to display, the number of seconds to wait until it pops up, and the title of the dialog box. The following illustration shows what will be displayed if you execute this script:

```
var WSHShell = WScript.CreateObject("WScript.Shell");
WSHShell.Popup("Hello, World!", 0, "JScript Sample");
```

Now, if you want to do the same thing in PerlScript, you first need to put this in a file named `hello.wsf`. The .wsf files, unlike the .js files, can contain multiple languages within a single file. On the other hand, .js files can only contain JScript and .vbs files can only contain VBScript.

Within our `hello.wsf` file, we first give the code a job ID. This is a requirement of the WSH. Next, we define the language our code is written in using the `<script>` tag and setting the `language` attribute to PerlScript. Next, we use the `Echo()` subroutine of the `WScript` object to generate a pop-up box that contains our text. To end the script, in much the same manner that HTML works, we simply put in our ending `<script>` and `<job>` tags. The next illustration shows what is displayed.

```
<job id="HelloWorldwithPerlScript">
  <script language="PerlScript">
    $WScript->Echo("Hello, World!");
  </script>
</job>
```

The WSH can be a powerful tool in performing everyday administrative tasks on your machines. Although we only touched on it here, we highly recommend you go to its Web site to learn more information about it.

GUI Components with the Perl/Tk

Perl/Tk was originally based on Tk 4.0p3, which is a widget toolkit originally associated with the *Tool command language* (*Tcl*) scripting language. You might have seen the term Tcl/Tk or heard someone mention they wrote code in "tickel." This is what they were talking about. But the Perl/Tk implementation doesn't require Tcl/Tk at all to run. Every widget in this module is written and accessed in Perl language semantics, syntax, and grammar.

Note

Perl/Tk is currently only available on UNIX and Windows systems. It isn't available for the Mac OS. If you want to find out if it's already on your system, type **perl -e "use Tk"** at a command line that has the Perl interpreter in its PATH and see if the module is found. If it isn't found, you need to download and compile it in from http://www.perl.com/CPAN/modules/by-module/Tk.

What Is Perl/Tk?

Have you ever wanted to build a native UNIX or Windows application that contained windows, dialog boxes, menus, and all the other components you see in everyday applications? More than likely, your answer here will be "Yes," or at least you'll admit you'd like to know how to do this.

Even though languages like Java have done a lot to bridge the gap, writing these GUI applications is a hard task. Each language, be it Visual Basic, C, or Java has its own perks and quirks. But, if you want to continue and learn how to write these applications, consider doing it in Perl/Tk.

Perl/Tk is a module you can use in your scripts that provide access to windowing components. This is somewhat similar to the windowing components we accessed and used in our previous WSH examples, but they're a little different. The components don't simply pop up dialog boxes or put in buttons. They are windows and buttons you must place in the appropriate locations to create your interface.

Overview of the Toolkit

The Perl/Tk comes with a wide variety of widgets you can use in your application. These include, but aren't limited to, the items listed in Table 13-1. As you can see, all these items are used to make up a graphical user interface. They're common items we see in applications everyday, so you should be familiar with what they are and how they work.

Note

You may notice many of these are similar to the items available in an HTML form. If you're familiar with HTML forms and the various elements you can use in them, then these items will be easy for you to understand.

GUI widgets alone don't make up everything, however. Once you have these widgets in place, you have to enable them to do something. For instance, when someone clicks a button or selects a check box, what happens? These items don't know what to do unless you write the appropriate code to handle these events.

To give you an idea of what can cause an interaction, we've included some common events in Table 13-2. When these events occur, then you can write code to perform a task. Think of them as the initiator of your code.

Widget Object	Description
Button	These are normal, everyday buttons that can be used for a large number of things. You can have buttons with text or bitmaps (icons) displayed.
Check button	Check buttons, or check boxes as they are normally called, are usually used in situations where you want to provide the user with the capability to select more than one item on a given dialog box.
Frame	Frames are nothing more than a way to organize the content on a given dialog box. You see this today in many applications where one section, on a preferences dialog box, for instance, may be for offline settings and another is for online settings. This is usually represented by a thin-lined border around each section or frame.
List box	List boxes let you have multiple items in the same list.
Radio button	Radio buttons are like check boxes, except you can only select one item in a given group of radio buttons.
Menu	Menus! This is something with which we're all familiar. These widgets let you easily create menus for your applications.
Scrollbar	Told you this might be harder than you thought. When creating GUIs, you even have to put the logic of displaying scrollbars in yourself. They don't just magically appear.

Table 13-1 Sample of Some of the Widgets You Can Use in Perl/Tk

Event	Description
ButtonPress	Occurs when the mouse button is pressed.
ButtonRelease	Occurs when the mouse button is released.
Destroy	Occurs when a widget is destroyed (that is, closed, exited, and so forth).
FocusIn	Occurs when a widget is active or is receiving the focus of a mouse or keyboard.
FocusOut	Occurs when a widget is no longer active or is no longer receiving the focus of a mouse or keyboard.
KeyPress	Occurs when a key on the keyboard is pressed.
KeyRelease	Occurs when a key on the keyboard is released.
Visibility	Occurs when a widget becomes visible.

Table 13-2 Events That Perl/Tk Can Intercept and Use to Perform Tasks

hello-tk.pl

Project 13-1: Hello, World! Dialog Box

The Perl/Tk is an interesting and exciting module that can be used in your programs. Covering it in enough detail to do it justice, however, is far beyond the scope of this book. Many of the terms, concepts, and programming techniques take a while to learn, but we didn't want to leave the last section of the final module without an example. And, yes, you are correct, it's another "Hello, World" example.

In this quick example, which we put in a file called `hello-tk.pl`, we create a dialog box, simply titled "Hello, World!", which has an

> **Hint**
>
> *perldoc Tk::UserGuide* is an excellent starting point for more information on the Perl/Tk.

OK button. When you click the button, the dialog box closes. The following steps perform this task.

Step-by-Step

1. Create a new file called `hello-tk.pl` that contains the necessary path to the Perl interpreter. You should know how to do this now, so we won't list the necessary code.
2. Next, load in the Tk module, which can be done using the following line:

```
use Tk;
```

3. In using the Tk module, first create an instance of the `MainWindow` object. This is done using the following:

```
$my_dialog = MainWindow->new;
```

4. Next, specify the title of the dialog box. To do this, set the `title` property of the `MainWindow` instance we created:

```
$my_dialog->title("Hello, World!");
```

5. Because we want to include an *OK* button that will close the dialog box, we must create an instance of the `Button` object, referenced through the `MainWindow` instance. This ensures the button is created on the right dialog box. In doing this, we pass arguments to assign the text of the button and the command that should occur if the button is pressed.

   On the command, we actually define the subroutine to be called within the body of the button creation. We perform the destruction of the dialog box by calling the Perl `exit()` function. This code looks like the following:

```
$my_dialog->Button(-text => "Ok", -command => sub{exit})->pack;
```

6. The final line of code in our script is a call to a subroutine in the Tk module. This subroutine starts the event handler in motion, so we can capture the button click when it occurs. Our completed code looks like the following:

```
#!/usr/bin/perl -w

# load the Tk module
use Tk;

# create a new window/dialog instance
$my_dialog = MainWindow->new;

# set the title of the dialog
$my_dialog->title("Hello, World!");

# put a button on the dialog that will close it when clicked
$my_dialog->Button(-text => "Ok", -command => sub{exit})->pack;

# start the event handlers "listening" for events
MainLoop;
```

Conclusion

Well, that does it! You've fought your way through step one of learning the Perl language and how to program in it. We want to say "Congratulations!" We know this wasn't easy at times, but you did it. You learned about the Perl language and the community of programmers who use it. You learned many of its semantics and were introduced to everything from regular expressions to CGI and database access programming. You were even exposed to several advanced topics to tease you with future exploration into the world of Perl. So, what's next?

Perl covers a vast range of topics, to which you were partially exposed in this book. Our intent was to introduce you to these topics and to make you aware of other topics. Now that you're ready to move from a beginner to an intermediate Perl programmer, we hope you continue with your educational effort. You can do so much with Perl. All it takes is a little effort and the understanding of some basic concepts—concepts which you now know.

So, go out into the world with a new look and motivation. Check the http://www.perl.com Web site often and see what's next on the list of dominating the programming world. See how you can get involved and how you can learn new tricks and tips on using Perl in places you never dreamed. Make yourself—and us—proud to be a Perl programmer!

Mastery Check

1. Which of the following describes polymorphism?
   - **A.** Being able to inherit different classes
   - **B.** Having data protected from other users
   - **C.** Being able to react to different objects
   - **D.** None of the above
2. What is PerlScript?
   - **A.** A programming language that can be used with Microsoft's ASP technology
   - **B.** A programming language that can be interpreted in Microsoft's Internet Explorer browser like VBScript and JScript
   - **C.** A programming language that can be used to copy and move files, and perform administration tasks on a Windows machine
   - **D.** All of the above
3. What does Tk stand for?
   - **A.** Too kool
   - **B.** Toolkit
   - **C.** Tickle
   - **D.** None of the above
4. What must you have installed to program using the Perl/Tk?
   - **A.** Tcl/Tk
   - **B.** Tk
   - **C.** Perl/TK
   - **D.** UNIX

Appendix

Answers to Mastery Checks

Module 1: Introduction to Perl

1. What should the first line of your Perl script include?

   D. All of the above

2. Which of the following is a valid Perl comment?

   C. #comment

3. If you need to find information about Perl, where would you go?

   D. All of the above

4. What does CPAN stand for? (You need to do a little research online here.)

   B. Comprehensive Perl Archive Network

Module 2: Scalar Data

1. What do hexadecimal numbers begin with?

   D. 0x

2. Which of the following is an octal number?

   C. 0563

3. How long can a string be?

   C. As many characters as memory will allow

4. What kind of string supports variable interpolation?

   B. Double-quoted string

5. Which of the following is a valid scalar variable name?

   B. $time1

6. Given $x = 3 * 4 + 6 / 12 – 2, select the order in which these operators execute.

   D. *, /, +, -

Module 3: Control Structures

1. Which conditional statement executes a statement block as long as the specified expression is true?

   D. Both A and B

2. How many expressions is a for statement required to have?

   A. 1

3. What makes do while and while statements unique?

   B. Do while statements always execute the statement block once

4. How many levels of control statements can be nested in Perl?

   C. An unlimited amount

5. Which of the following is a valid use of a control statement?

   D. All of the above

6. Which of the following groups of conditional statements can be used with a single line conditional statement?

   A. If, while, until, and unless

Module 4: Lists, Arrays, and Hashes

1. Which of the following is a valid list?

   D. All of the above

2. What forms of data can be used with the list range operator?

   D. Both A and B

3. Which of the following is a valid array assignment?

   B. $array[1] = 12;

4. What array function can be used to remove the last character from all the elements of an array?

   A. chop

5. What array functions mimic the behavior of a stack?

   A. Push and pop

6. What does an array slice use to determine the elements it will contain?

   B. The array index numbers

7. Which of the following are valid hash key names?

   D. All of the above

8. What hash function can be used to access all the elements of a hash?

   D. All of the above

Module 5: Program Flow and Subroutines

1. What is the statement that signifies you are creating a subroutine?

   D. sub

2. Where should you organize your programming efforts?

   D. Both A and B

3. The local() and my() functions are used to prevent the exposure of certain variables to the rest of your script. What, where *what* is a common programming term, does this define?

   A. scope

Module 6: Working with Files and Directories

1. What does the open function return if a file was opened successfully?

   D. Both B and C

2. What function can be used to halt the program if a function fails to execute properly?

   B. Die

3. What is the default mode in which a file is always opened?

   A. read

4. What function can be used to move a file?

   C. rename

5. What function is used to delete a file from the current file system?

   C. unlink

6. What function is used to select a new current working directory?

   A. chdir

Module 7: Regular Expressions

1. What character or characters are used to indicate a regular expression?

   D. forward slash

2. Which of the following strings match this regular expression /AV+/?

   C. Both A and B

3. What special character is used to make sure a pattern matches at the very beginning of a string?

   B. ^

4. Which character class abbreviation is used to represent all digits?

   B. \d

5. What special character can be used to give an optional pattern to match in a regular expression?

   D. |

6. What option should you use if you are attempting to search and replace a certain string?

   C. Both A and B

Module 8: Packages and Modules

1. What is the difference between a package and a module?

   B. They are the same, except a module is specially designed to have exportable subroutines

2. Which of the following can be used to load subroutines from a module into a program?

   D. use()

3. In the syntax `use CGI;` what is the name of the file imported?

   C. CGI.pm

Module 9: Interacting with Databases Using the Perl DBI

1. What does DBI stand for?

   C. Database Interface

2. Which of the following commands can you use to tell if the DBI module is installed on your system?

   B. perl –e "use DBI;"

3. Do any additional modules need to be installed to use the DBI with Oracle?

   A. Yes

4. Which of the following SQL statements returns all rows in a table named *customer*?

   C. select * from customer

Module 10: Writing CGI Programs

1. How do you include the CGI.pm module in your code?

   A. use CGI;

2. The HTTP response is broken into two components. Which of the following two are they?

   B and **C.** Header and Body

3. If you want to redirect a user to a different location, how can you do that?

   D. Both A and B

Module 11: Cross-Platform Functions and Issues

1. Which of the following lines should be in all scripts that use the `$^O` variable?

   D. require 5.002;

2. Which of the following is the path delimiter for the Mac OS system?

   D. :

3. What string should you check for in the $^O variable if you want something to run only on an AIX system?

   C. aix

4. What is the MacPerl subroutine that launches a prompt dialog box?

   A. MacPerl::Ask

Module 12: Error Messages and Debugging

1. Which of the following lines of code contains a syntax error?

   B. print "This message will be displayed on the screen \n"

2. Which of the following commands can be used to generate warnings?

   B. Perl –w program.pl

3. Which debugger command can be used to execute an entire program that contains no breakpoints?

   C. c

4. Which debugger command can be used to set temporary breakpoints?

   C. c

5. If you want to search for an occurrence of string from the beginning of a file, in what do you enclose the string?

   A. //

6. What debugger command can be used to list all the subroutines in a program?

   C. S

7. Which debug command can be used to print the contents of a variable?

   C. Both A and B

8 Which of the following statements execute the supplied command before a line of the program is executed?

   A. a 10 print "Value1 contains $value1 \n";

Module 13: Advanced Features and Concepts

1. Which of the following describes polymorphism?

   C. Being able to react to different objects

2. What is PerlScript?

   D. All of the above

3. What does Tk stand for?

   C. Toolkit

4. What must you have installed to program using the Perl/Tk?

   B. Tk

Index

Symbols and Numbers

A

B

C

D

E

F

G

J

K

L

M

N

O

P

Q

R

T

U

V

W